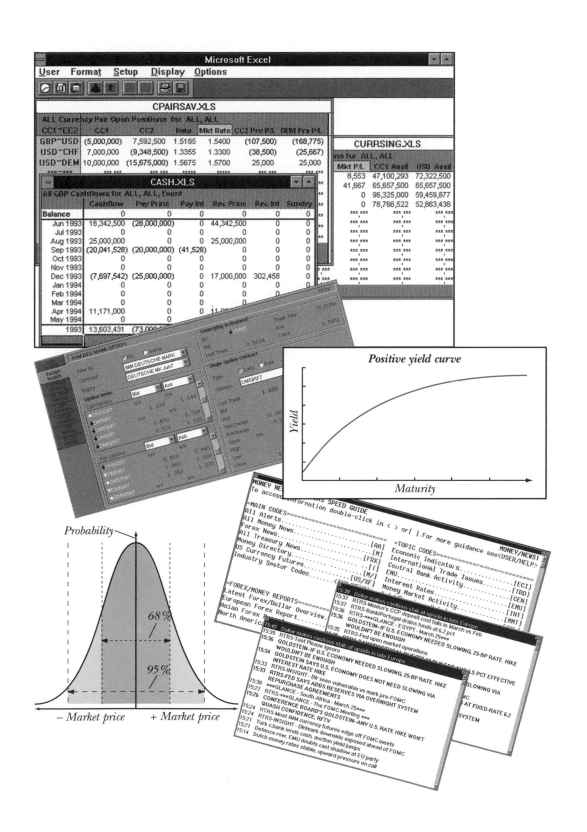

An Introduction to

Foreign Exchange & Money Markets

WILEY

John Wiley & Sons (Asia) Pte Ltd
Singapore   New York   Chichester
Brisbane   Toronto   Weinheim

Other titles in the series

You can get more information about the other titles in the series from the Reuters Financial Training series companion web site at *http://www.wiley-rft.reuters.com.*

Acknowledgments

The publishers and Reuters Limited would like to thank the following people for their invaluable assistance in this book:

Denis Nolan of Arbitrain Ltd and Nick Reed of RVC Limited for their feedback.

Keith Rogers who wrote and produced the original version of the book.

Ann McGoff of ACI – The Financial Markets Association for her involvement in this project.

Terry Lee and Ronny Tan of ACI Singapore for their contribution to the book.

Charles Kaplan, President of Equity Analytics Ltd. for use of his Glossary of Foreign Banking Terms at the back of this book.

Numa Financial Systems Ltd for use of their Directory of Futures & Options Exchanges at the back of this book.

Copyright © 1999 by REUTERS Limited
Published in 1999 by John Wiley & Sons (Asia) Pte Ltd
2 Clementi Loop, #02-01, Singapore 129809, Singapore.

This publication is designed to provide accurate and authoritative information in regard to the subject matter covered. It is sold with the understanding that the publisher is not engaged in rendering professional services. If professional advice or other expert assistance is required, the services of a competent professional person should be sought.

Other Wiley Editorial Offices
John Wiley & Sons, Inc., 605 Third Avenue, New York, NY 10158-0012, USA
John Wiley & Sons Ltd, Baffins Lane, Chichester, West Sussex PO19 1UD, England
John Wiley & Sons (Canada) Ltd, 22 Worcester Road, Rexdale, Ontario M9W 1L1, Canada
Jacaranda Wiley Ltd, 33 Park Road (PO Box 1226), Milton, Queensland 4064, Australia
Wiley-VCH, Pappelallee 3, 69469 Weinheim, Germany

Library of Congress Cataloging-in-Publication Data

An introduction to foreign exchange & money markets.
      p. cm. – (The Reuters financial training series)
    Includes bibliographical references (p.).
    ISBN 0-471-83128-X.
    1. Foreign exchange. 2. Foreign exchange futures.
    3. Money market. I. Reuters ltd.
    II. Title: An Introduction to foreign exchange and money markets.
    III. Series.
HG3821.154 1999
332.4'5 – dc21   99-17730
                                     CIP

ISBN 0-471-83128-X

Typeset in 10/12 point New Baskerville
Printed in Singapore by Craft Print Pte Ltd
10 9 8 7 6 5 4 3 2 1

An Introduction to

Foreign Exchange & Money Markets

Contents

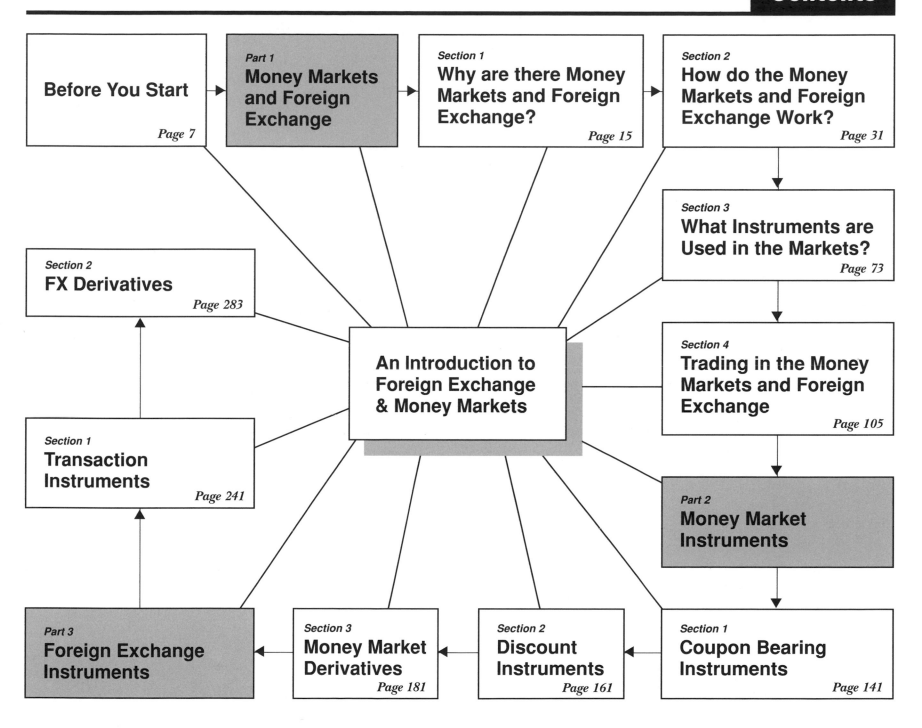

Before You Start
Page 7

Part 1
Money Markets and Foreign Exchange

Section 1
Why are there Money Markets and Foreign Exchange?
Page 15

Section 2
How do the Money Markets and Foreign Exchange Work?
Page 31

Section 3
What Instruments are Used in the Markets?
Page 73

Section 2
FX Derivatives
Page 283

An Introduction to Foreign Exchange & Money Markets

Section 4
Trading in the Money Markets and Foreign Exchange
Page 105

Section 1
Transaction Instruments
Page 241

Part 2
Money Market Instruments

Part 3
Foreign Exchange Instruments

Section 3
Money Market Derivatives
Page 181

Section 2
Discount Instruments
Page 161

Section 1
Coupon Bearing Instruments
Page 141

Contents

Contents

Contents

Part 3 – Foreign Exchange Instruments

Contents

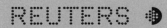

Who Should Use This Book?

This book is designed to provide an overview of the foreign exchange and money markets for a variety of readers: salespeople, support and operations staff, trainers, managers or the average investor who wants to learn how the markets work. Also, anyone about to begin an in-depth study of foreign exchange and money markets would find this book to be a useful primer.

The first part of this book gives an overview of how money markets and foreign exchange work, explaining why the markets exist, how the markets operate, what instruments are traded and who the market participants are. The second part deals with money market instruments in more detail, namely, Coupon Bearing Instruments, Discount Instruments and Money Market Derivatives. The final part takes a more detailed look at foreign exchange instruments, namely, Transaction and Foreign Exchange Derivatives.

By the time you have completed this book, you will have a better understanding of foreign exchange and money markets, and their instruments. You may find the Further Resources sections and the RFT web site helpful if you are planning to study this topic further.

This book covers the use of derivatives in four market areas:
• Money markets and foreign exchange
• Debt
• Equities
• Commodities, energy and shipping

What Will You Find in This Book?

This book provides a new approach to gaining some basic familiarity with the essential concepts of foreign exchange and money markets. The book is written in a very accessible style with jargon kept to a minimum.

Most importantly, the book includes a range of materials to help you reinforce what you are learning. Each section offers a solid explanation of basic concepts, followed by actual examples for the reader to work through. Additional exercises and quick quizzes further enhance learning. Finally, each chapter includes a graphic overview — a visual outline — of what has been covered for quick yet thorough review and ends with a listing of additional reference materials.

In addition, the **RFT Web Site** has been created as this series of books' companion web site where additional quiz questions, updated screens and other information may be found. You can find this web site at **http://www.wiley-rft.reuters.com**.

How is This Book Organised?

This book is divided into three parts with the following sections:

Before You Start

This section!

Part 1 – Money Markets and Foreign Exchange

Why are there Money Markets and Foreign Exchange?

This covers the importance of interest rates and cash markets, the definition of money markets and where they operate, the definition of foreign exchange, where the markets operate, the origins of FX and the factors influencing FX rates, and, the relationship between the money markets and foreign exchange.

How do the Money Markets and Foreign Exchange Work?

This deals with the operation or 'mechanics' of the market and includes any underlying jargon and market conventions.

What Instruments are Used in the Markets?

This is a brief review of all the instruments used in the market. Each instrument is defined and is usually accompanied by a screen giving information on the instrument selected.

Trading in the Money Markets and Foreign Exchange

This describes the market players and their trading techniques. There are also various conversations or diaries of these market players so that you can get some idea of their jobs.

Part 2 – Money Market Instruments

Coupon Bearing Instruments

This section deals with instruments that pay out interest to the holder (or lender) on a regular basis throughout the tenor of the instrument e.g., Money Market Deposits, Certificates of Deposit (CDs) and Repurchase Agreements. Each instrument is defined and accompanied by various formulas, calculations and examples.

Discount Instruments

Discount instruments are those that are issued and trade at a discount to their par value, which reflects the prevailing short-term, interest rate e.g., Treasury Bill (T-Bill), Bill of Exchange/Banker's Acceptance (BA) and Commercial Paper (CP). Various formulas, calculations and examples accompany the definition of each instrument.

Money Market Derivatives

This section looks at instruments whose value changes with changes in one or more underlying market variables, such as interest rates or foreign exchange rates. Instruments under this section are: Forward Rate Agreement (FRA), Interest Rate Futures, Interest Rate Swap (IRS), Options on Interest Rate Futures, Options on FRAs – Interest Rate Guarantee (IRGs) and Options on IRSs – Swaptions.

Part 3 – Foreign Exchange Instruments

Transaction Instruments

The instruments described in this section include Spot Transactions – Currencies versus USD, Spot Transactions – Cross Rates, Forward Outright Transactions and FX Swaps. Each instrument is defined at the beginning together with a description of what it is used for, as well as any formulas, calculations and examples of the way the instrument is used in the markets.

Foreign Exchange Derivatives

This section covers the following instruments: Synthetic Agreements for Foreign Exchange (SAFEs), Currency Futures, Currency Swap, Currency Options – on Cash and on Futures. The definition of each instrument is given followed by a description of the players in the market and the way the instrument is used. Screens, calculations and examples accompany the descriptions, as with all other sections.

Throughout the book you will find that important terms or concepts are shown in bold, for example, **interbank market**. You will also find that activities included to enhance your learning are indicated by the following icons:

This indicates the definition of a term that you must know and understand to master the material.

This means stop and think about the point being made. You may want to jot a few words in the box provided.

This indicates an activity for you to do. It is usually something written – for example, a calculation.

This indicates the main points of the section.

This indicates questions for you to answer to help you to review the material. The answers are also provided.

This indicates the one-page summary that provides a quick overview of the entire section. This page serves as an excellent study tool.

How to Use This Book

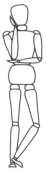

Before you start using this book, decide what you want from the material. If you are using this book as part of your work, discuss with your manager how he/she will help by giving time for study and giving you feedback and support. Although your learning style is unique to you, you will find that your learning is much more effective if you allocate reasonable sized periods of time for study. The most effective learning period is about 30 minutes – so use this as a basis. If you try to fit your learning into odd moments in a busy schedule you will not get the best from the materials or yourself. You might like to schedule learning periods into your day just as you would business meetings.

Remember that the most effective learning is an interactive process and requires more than just reading the text. The exercises in this book make you think through the material you have just read and then apply your understanding through basic activities. Take time to do the exercises. This old Chinese saying sums up this concept:

> **I hear and I forget**
> **I see and I remember**
> **I do and I understand**

The various types of activities and their icons have already been mentioned – even thinking is an activity.

Try to make sure your study is uninterrupted. This probably means that your workplace is not a good environment! You will need to find both the time and place where you can study – you may have access to a quiet room at work, you may have a room at home, you may need to use a library.

It's important to remember that learning is not a race – everyone learns at their own rate. Some people find things easy, some not quite so easy. So don't rush your learning – make sure you get the most from the book. You should now have enough information to plan the use of your book and the Web materials – remember it's your learning.

Introduction

In this Part, we will take an overview of the money markets and foreign exchange market. We will examine the relationships between them, why the markets exist, how they operate, the instruments used and the players who use them.

We will examine the money market instruments in more detail in Part 2 and in Part 3, we will take a closer look at the foreign exchange instruments.

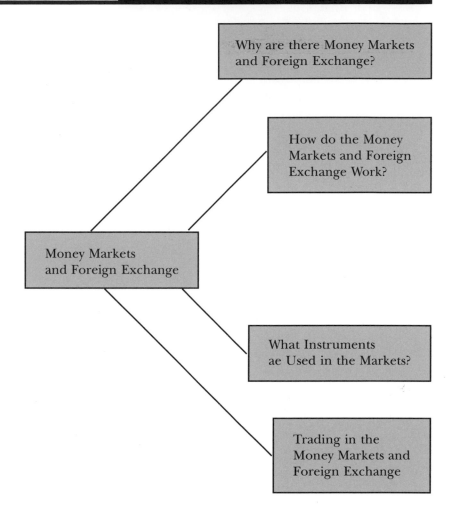

Why are there Money Markets and Foreign Exchange?

How do the Money Markets and Foreign Exchange Work?

Money Markets and Foreign Exchange

What Instruments ae Used in the Markets?

Trading in the Money Markets and Foreign Exchange

This section should take about 1 hour of study time. You may not take as long as this or it may take a little longer – remember your learning is individual to you.

There are few ways in which a man can be more innocently employed than in getting money.

Samuel Johnson 1775

Introduction

The **money markets** and **foreign exchange** markets are quite simply the largest markets in the world today. According to the Bank for International Settlements, which monitors activity in the world's money markets and foreign exchange markets, over US$1.4 trillion (US$1.400,000,000,000) is traded on average every single day.

Like any market, they exist to allow buyers and sellers of goods — in this case money — to execute transactions and exchange their assets.

The importance of these markets should not be underestimated. The price at which money is bought and sold can dictate whether a national government's economic policy is viable, and can affect the lives of billions of people.

Unfortunately, there is a lot of jargon surrounding the financial markets. This book sets out to give a clear understanding of how and why these markets function, and to explain the associated terminology.

This section is concerned with:
- **Cash markets** in the context of money markets and foreign exchange
- An overview of the money markets
- An overview of the foreign exchange markets
- The relationship between money markets and foreign exchange

Before moving on, check your current understanding of the terms mentioned above by filling in the activity opposite. Do not worry if you do not know the answers, as these topics will be covered in the rest of this chapter (although specific answers to the questions opposite will not be given).

What do you think the following terms mean?

- Rate of inflation
- Interest rates
- Exchange rates

Use the space here to write down your thoughts.

The Cash Markets

In today's global market, money flows freely between investors and borrowers, and buyers and sellers, across international borders.

Market participants use the **money markets** for their short-term borrowing or lending requirements (short-term means up to one year in maturity).

As different countries use different currencies, there is obviously a need for money in one currency to be converted to another currency for cross-border deals.

Market participants use the **foreign exchange market**, or **FX market** as it is commonly known, when they need to convert one currency into another. This conversion is achieved by selling one currency in exchange for another. The relative amounts of each currency are governed by the **foreign exchange rate**, or **FX rate**, between the two currencies.

The connection between FX rates and money market instruments is **interest rates**. The interest rate of a particular currency is essentially the price of money in that currency (ie, the cost of borrowing that particular currency). The interest rate is determined by the money market by simple supply and demand — the more people who want to borrow money, the higher the interest rate, the more people who want to lend money, the lower the interest rate.

National governments can influence the interest rates in the money markets by limiting the amount of money in circulation. This is achieved by the country's central bank, for example the US Federal Reserve, the Bank of England or the Hong Kong Monetary Authority, which controls the amount of money in circulation. The less money in circulation, the greater competition among borrowers to borrow it, and hence the higher the interest rate. The level of interest rates influences the amount of economic activity in that country. If interest rates rise, making it more expensive to borrow money, projects funded by borrowing become less attractive because they must generate higher returns to cover the cost of funding. Hence rising interest rates cause a slowdown in economic activity as increasing numbers of projects become unfeasible. Similarly, lower interest rates

tend to encourage greater economic activity, as projects funded by borrowing become more attractive, because they only need to generate lower returns to cover their costs.

The long-term value of money is also affected by the prevailing **rate of inflation** in that currency. The rate of inflation is the speed with which prices are rising in the economy. The faster prices rise, the less one can buy with a given amount of money at a future date. Inflation is said to "erode" the value of money.

Typically, interest rates are higher than the rate of inflation. This is because if the inflation rate is higher than the interest rate, the value of the money is being eroded faster than the interest is being charged on a loan. In this situation, the lender is actually paying the borrower to borrow money!

In summary, there are three main factors affecting interest rates:

1. **Supply and demand for money**
The greater demand for money, the higher the interest rate. Higher interest rates put off borrowers, and hence slow down economic activity. Lower interest rates encourage borrowers and hence stimulate economic activity.

2. **Government intervention**
Governments can influence interest rates through the actions of the central bank. Reducing the amount of money in circulation leads to higher interest rates, and therefore lower economic activity. Increasing the amount of money in circulation reduces interest rates and promotes economic activity.

3. **Inflation**
Lenders want compensation for lending their money. This compensation is in the form of the interest rate charged on the money they lend. This interest rate must be higher than the rate of inflation, otherwise the lender's money is losing value faster than it is generating interest.

Money Markets

Money markets allow market participants to borrow and lend money.

One counterparty — the borrower — borrows money from the other counterparty — the lender — at a specified interest rate for a specified period of time (the maturity or tenor of the transaction).

The interest rate is effectively the 'price' at which the deal is executed. A higher interest rate is better for the lender. A lower interest rate is better for the borrower.

The maturity of a money market loan can vary between one day and one year. A one-day loan is known as an 'overnight' loan.

When an investor places money on deposit with a bank, he/she is actually lending that money to the bank. The interest rate the investor receives on the deposit is the 'price/quote' at which the investor is lending to the bank.

At the same time, the bank pools the deposits made by investors and uses the money to make loans to other, larger borrowers in the money market. The money market borrowers pay the bank interest on the money they are borrowing. Banks make their profits by paying a lower rate of interest to depositors and receiving a higher rate of interest in the money market.

Bank also make loans to retail customers, for which they receive interest. Banks can then borrow money in the money market at a lower rate of interest. Hence banks also make profits by lending to retail customers at a higher rate of interest than the rate they pay to lenders in the money market.

The money markets are **wholesale markets in money**, whereas banks are **effectively retail markets for money**.

Money markets are typically used by financial organisations, such as banks, building societies, governmental organisations and large companies who deal with large amounts of money.

A lending transaction with a maturity of more than one year is generally referred to as a **debt market** transaction rather than a money market transaction. This is because the interest on a money market loan is usually paid at the end of the loan (also known as the maturity of the loan), whereas the interest on a debt market loan is usually paid at regular intervals throughout the tenor of the loan.

There are exceptions to this rule, but in general market practice conforms to the above description.

Why are there Money Markets and Foreign Exchange?

Where are the Money Markets?

Many money market instruments can be actively traded. That is, when a lender lends money to a borrower, it can then sell the rights to the money and interest it is owed to another market participant. Money market instruments that can be freely traded are called **negotiable instruments**.

Most transactions in the money markets take place directly between two counterparties (ie, there is no exchange on which they are traded) via a telephone or electronic data link. Such transactions are called **over-the-counter (OTC) transactions**. These counterparties can be located anywhere in the world. Hence the money markets do not exist in one particular place — they are simply wherever the counterparties happen to be.

Some money market related instruments such as T-bill futures are traded on financial exchanges, such as the Chicago Board of Trade (CBOT), the London International Financial Futures and Options Exchange (LIFFE) or the Deustche Terminborse (DTB). These transactions are known as **exchange-traded transactions**.

Exchanges typically trade only during certain 'opening hours' while OTC transactions take place 24-hours a day worldwide. This allows lenders to always seek out the highest rate of interest for their money, anywhere in the world, and also allows borrowers to search for the cheapest funds, at any time.

It is precisely this constant availability of money, irrespective of geographical boundaries, that makes the money markets an attractive place to borrow and lend money. This is why large numbers of participants are attracted to the market. The larger the number of participants and the greater the competition between lenders (or borrowers), the better the rates at which participants can borrow (or lend). This is known as the level of **market liquidity**.

Foreign Exchange

Foreign Exchange markets allow market participants to exchange one currency for another.

One counterparty buys a specified currency from the other counterparty in exchange for another currency. The relative amounts of the two currencies is determined by the foreign exchange rate between those two currencies.

The date on which the two currencies are exchanged is known as the **settlement date** or **value date**.

Foreign exchange is the single largest market in the world. More than USD 1.4 trillion is traded in the FX market each day, according to the Bank for International Settlements, which monitors FX market activity.

To put this figure in perspective, the sum total of global trade in physical goods in one year accounts for the same amount of trade as a few days in the foreign exchange market. Hence the FX market is much, much bigger than all the other markets put together.

In the FX market, trades can be executed in variable amounts, dates and denominations. There are no standardised contract sizes or dates.

REUTERS

Why Does FX Exist?

Foreign exchange exists as a result of:

- Trade and investment

Companies who import or export goods are buying them in one currency and selling them in another. This means they pay out money in one currency and receive money in another. They therefore need to convert some of the money they receive into the currency in which they pay for goods. Similarly, a company that buys an asset in a foreign country has to pay for it in the local currency, and so will need to convert its home currency into the local foreign currency.

- Speculation

The FX rate between two currencies varies in line with the relative supply and demand for the two currencies. Traders can make profits buying a currency at one rate and selling it at a more favourable rate. Speculation makes up by far the largest proportion of trading in the FX market.

- Hedging

Companies who have assets, such as factories, in foreign countries are exposed to the risk of those assets varying in value in their home currency due to fluctuations in the FX rate between the two relevant currencies. While the foreign assets may retain the same value over time in the foreign currency, they produce a profit or loss in the company's domestic currency if the FX rate changes. Companies can eliminate these potential profits or losses by hedging. This involves executing an FX transaction which will exactly offset the profit or loss of the foreign asset caused by changes in the FX rate.

Where are the FX Markets?

Foreign Exchange is traded over-the-counter (OTC), operating worldwide, 24 hours a day.

A number of foreign exchange instruments, called derivatives are traded on exchanges.

London is the world's largest FX trading centre, followed by New York and then Singapore. Trading tends to occur in a centre during its normal working hours. As a result, trading starts in Asia, then moves to London at the end of the Asian working day and continues in New York at the end of the working day in London.

The time zone chart below gives some idea of the 24-hour trading potential between the world-wide financial centres.

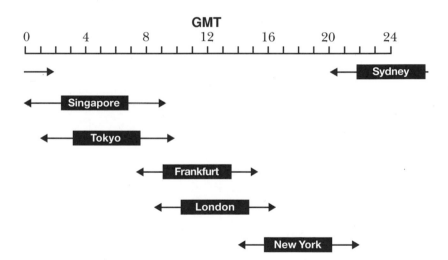

How Did It all Start?

From 1880 to the beginning of the First World War, and again briefly in the inter-war period, the **International Gold Standard** was used as the basis for foreign exchange. This meant that a country defined its monetary unit in terms of a specified amount of gold. The result of this was that gold had to be exported and imported on an unrestricted basis so that governments could exchange gold for paper currency and vice-versa.

During the 1920s and 1930s there was worldwide currency chaos and economic depression. In order to avoid any repeat of pre-war economic conditions the allied governments met at the latter end of the Second World War at the United Nations Monetary and Financial Conference. This conference was held at **Bretton Woods**, New Hampshire, USA in July 1944. At the conference two organisations were established:

- The **International Monetary Fund (IMF)**

- The **International Bank for Reconstruction and Development** – the 'World Bank'

The objectives of the IMF were to create monetary stability and to remove exchange restrictions that hampered international trade. The value of each currency was expressed in fixed amounts of gold; but it was the US dollar's convertibility into gold at a fixed rate of $35 an ounce which underpinned the system. In effect the **Bretton Woods Agreement** made the US dollar the standard international currency. All other currencies were fixed against the US dollar which was itself convertible or redeemable into gold.

Exchange rates were kept within a narrow band around an officially declared parity. For example, from 1949 to 1967 the £ was pegged at a parity of £1 = US$2.80.

By the mid-1960s West Germany and Japan were challenging the US as the foremost industrial nation. In 1971 the US suspended its policy of converting dollars into gold under the strain of capital outflows and widening trade deficits. In 1972 the UK allowed the pound to 'float' against other currencies.

By 1973 the Bretton Woods Agreement had broken down and since then exchange rates have been allowed to float. Some rates float freely, while others are constrained within certain bands.

Recently the Asian crisis has been an example of currencies which were trading within bands which were deemed by the market to be unsustainable. Under the pressure of market forces, the governments of Asia eventually had to let their currencies float freely.

On January 1, 1999, the European Union will implement European Monetary Union (EMU), which involves the exchange rates between European currencies being fixed against each other. The European currencies will be phased out in favour of the Euro, which will become the national currency for all countries participating in EMU.

The Euro, however, will still be allowed to float freely against non-European currencies.

Factors Influencing FX Rates

As you have seen, interest rates are used by a government to control its monetary policy and foreign exchange rates.

The three key factors affecting interest rates you should already know something about are:

- The supply and demand for money

- The rate of inflation

- Government intervention

There are a number of other factors which have both long- and short-term influences on exchange rates which also need to be considered for a more complete picture. These influences can be grouped broadly as shown in the following diagram:

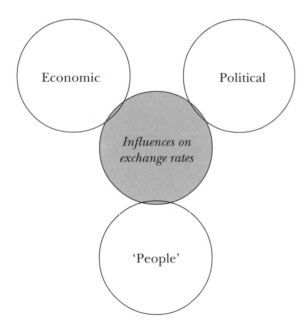

Economic Factors

In this category there are four factors to be considered:

- relative interest rates

- purchasing power parity (PPP)

- economic conditions

- supply and demand for capital

Relative Interest Rates
Large investors can easily switch investments between different currencies so it is important for them to compare the returns from investments in different currencies to make sure they obtain the best investment performances.

If an investor can receive a higher interest rate by lending money in a foreign currency than he/she can by lending money in his/her domestic currency, it makes sense for that investor to lend in the foreign currency.

This is done by exchanging the domestic currency for foreign currency (at the prevailing FX rate), lending the foreign currency at its prevailing interest rate and then converting the money plus interest back into the domestic currency at the maturity of the loan.

Comparing interest rates in different currencies in this way is called **comparing relative interest rates**.

However, as the FX rate may vary over the tenor of the loan, the investor is exposed to the risk that the foreign currency may depreciate against the domestic currency by more than the difference between the two interest rates. In this case, the investor will make a loss by lending in foreign currency.

In fact, currencies with high interest rates tend to appreciate against other currencies because more investors buy the high-interest currency in order to chase the higher returns.

Why are there Money Markets and Foreign Exchange?

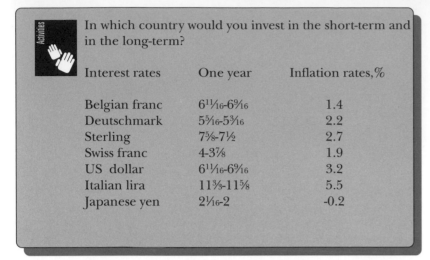

In which country would you invest in the short-term and in the long-term?

Interest rates	One year	Inflation rates,%
Belgian franc	6¹¹⁄₁₆-6⁹⁄₁₆	1.4
Deutschmark	5⁵⁄₁₆-5³⁄₁₆	2.2
Sterling	7⅝-7½	2.7
Swiss franc	4-3⅞	1.9
US dollar	6¹¹⁄₁₆-6⁹⁄₁₆	3.2
Italian lira	11⅜-11⅝	5.5
Japanese yen	2¹⁄₁₆-2	-0.2

Economic Conditions

FX exchange rates are affected in the long-term by a country's economic conditions and trends such as:

- Balance of payments

- Economic growth

- Rate of inflation

- Money supply

- Unemployment figures

- Rates of taxation

Purchasing Power Parity (PPP)

Purchasing power parity is a measure of the relative purchasing power of different currencies. It is measured by the price of the same goods in different countries, translated by the FX rate of that country's currency against a 'base currency', usually the US dollar. The concept behind purchasing power parity is that if goods are cheap in one country it pays to export them to another country where they are more expensive.

For example, the same car may cost US$20,000 in the USA and ¥2,400,000 in Japan. If the USD/Yen FX rate is 100, the car in Japan costs US$24,000 to a buyer in the USA (=2,400,000/100). This is more expensive than the car being sold in the USA, so the buyer is better off buying in his domestic market.

If the USD/Yen FX rate is 140, however, the car being sold in Japan only costs US$17,143 to a buyer in the USA (=2,400,000/140). Thus the American buyer is better off importing a car from Japan if the exchange rate is 140.

If the equivalent amount of currency purchases exactly the same amount of goods in every country then international trade is no longer profitable. That is, every currency is in purchasing power parity.

Supply and Demand for Capital

Capital flows to a country where investors see opportunities. Some countries need capital and offer appropriate interest rates — others have a surplus of money and so have lower interest rates.

However, investors do not always invest purely for high interest rate returns. For example, Japanese car and electronic manufacturers have invested in manufacturing operations in the USA and Europe to overcome tariff and quota problems.

In the short-term normal business activities affect the supply and demand for capital. The interbank market, dealing in large amounts of capital, involves small trading spreads whereas the retail market involves smaller amounts of capital with larger trading spreads.

Any sudden demand in the retail market impacts on the interbank rates which in turn affects the exchange rates.

Political Factors

Foreign exchange rates can be affected in the long- and short-term by political factors such as:

- The type of economic policies pursued by the government

- The amount of uncertainty in the political situation

- The regulatory policies followed by central banks and/or other regulatory bodies

- Central bank intervention in the FX market to strengthen or weaken its currency

Market Sentiment

Short-term changes in FX rates are often the result of what market participants call **market sentiment**. This is the perception traders have of the short-term prospects for the movement in a currency.

Market sentiment is usually said to be 'positive' or 'negative'. A currency will normally strengthen relative to other currencies on positive sentiment and weaken relative to other currencies on negative sentiment.

Traders act on news about a given economy. Often, traders will anticipate a news report or significant government announcement by buying or selling the currency before the news is actually reported. Sentiment affects how the currency moves when the news finally breaks.

For example, if market sentiment is positive ahead of the government's announcement of GDP figures, the currency will probably rise in anticipation of the figures being announced. If the government's GDP figure is less than the market was expecting, the currency will fall, even if the GDP figure is still good news for the economy.

News affects markets *relative* to the existing market sentiment.

Technical Analysis

Many market participants trade on the basis of past price movements. This is because they believe past market moves, rather than economic fundamentals or news, predict future market moves.

This practice is called **technical analysis**. Technical analysis highlights the trends in the market based on the assumption that market participants will react in the same way today as they did in the past.

This can be summarised best in the phrase:

The trend is your friend

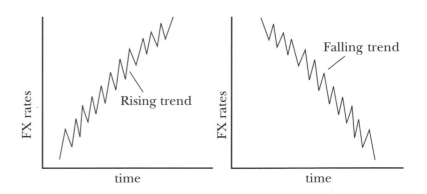

What Drives FX Markets?

FX markets are driven by a number of factors, such as economic fundamentals, the current demand for particular currencies, news events and market sentiment. Many short-term changes in exchange rates are a result of what the market expects to happen to economies or as a result of market sentiment. Dealers will be interested in economic indicators or figures that are published on a regular basis. Before a figure is actually released, the market prices itself on the forecast expectation. When the figure is released, the market reacts to the figure in comparison with the expectation. Dealers may believe that a currency will move in one particular direction based on factors such as:

- What the charts are showing — what has the recent trend been?

- What dealers in the market are saying

- Whether or not the market is long or short — how the market is feeling

- What the central banks are doing

- Whether the dealer has made or lost money recently

Dealers act in anticipation of or on actual news of the markets. News includes matters such as the release of unemployment figures or quite unexpected events such as natural disasters or political turmoils. Rumours too have a powerful effect on the market. It is often the case that the market reacts to a rumour as if it is an established fact — once the rumour is confirmed or denied the market settles down. The way the markets react to rumours is summarised by the phrase:

Buy the rumour, sell the fact

Your notes

Summary

You have now finished the first section and you should have a clear understanding of the following:

- The importance of interest rates and cash markets

- The definition of money markets and where they operate

- The definition of foreign exchange, where the markets operate, the origins of FX and the factors influencing FX rates

- The relationship between the money markets and foreign exchange

A definition of cash markets:

Wholesale markets in debt instruments with maturities of 12 months or less.

A money markets trade:

One counterparty — the borrower — borrows money from the other counterparty — the lender — at a specified interest rate for a specified period of time (the maturity or tenor of the transaction).

An FX trade:

One counterparty buys a specified currency from the other counterparty in exchange for another currency. The relative amounts of the two currencies are determined by the foreign exchange rate between those two currencies.

As a check on your understanding you should try the Quick Quiz questions on the next page. You may also find the section Overview useful as a revision aid.

Why are there Money Markets and Foreign Exchange?

Quick Quiz Questions

1. Which of the following statements is/are true?

   - ❏ a) Foreign exchange is traded on exchanges in most financial centres
   - ❏ b) The foreign exchange market is decentralised
   - ❏ c) The foreign exchange market is OTC
   - ❏ d) Foreign exchange can only be traded in London, New York and Tokyo

2. Which of the following affect interest rates directly?

   - ❏ a) Rate of inflation
   - ❏ b) Exchange rates
   - ❏ c) Supply and demand for money

3. Which of the following factors affect FX rates directly?

   - ❏ a) Economic conditions
   - ❏ b) Political factors
   - ❏ c) Market expectations

4. In which of the following maturity ranges are money market instruments usually found?

   - ❏ a) One week – one year
   - ❏ b) Overnight – one year
   - ❏ c) One year – 10 years
   - ❏ d) One year – 30 years

5. If US dollar interest rates are raised, what will be the most likely effect on the currency?

   - ❏ a) Its value will increase against other currencies
   - ❏ b) Its value will decrease against other currencies
   - ❏ c) There will be no impact

6. Name three reasons why an FX market exists:

7. When will debt instruments have an impact on money market instruments?

You can check your answers on page 28.

Overview

Cash Markets

Money markets
Foreign exchange

Factors affecting interest rates
- Supply and demand for money
- Rate of inflation
- Government intervention

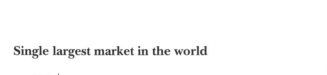

Money Markets

Interest rates

Foreign Exchange

Money Markets

Wholesale, OTC markets in money
- Money market maturities are **up to and including** 12 months
- Debt market maturities are **over** 12 months and can extend to 30 years

Why are there Money Markets and Foreign Exchange?

Foreign Exchange

Single largest market in the world

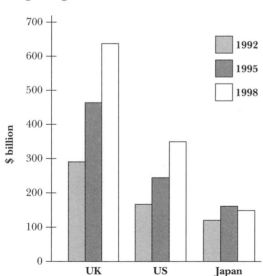

- 1992
- 1995
- 1998

$ billion

UK   US   Japan

Daily global turnover in 1998 = $1,490 billion for spot and forward transactions

Why does FX exist?
- Trade and investment
- Hedging
- Speculation

Where are the FX markets?

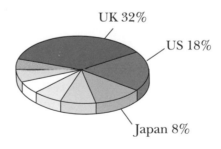

UK 32%

US 18%

Japan 8%

How did it all start?
- 1880 – International Gold Standard
- 1944 – Bretton Woods Agreement
- 1973 – Floating rates

Factors influencing FX rates
- Economic
- Political
- 'People'

The trend is your friend

Buy the rumour, sell the fact

Quick Quiz Answers

	✔ or ✘
1. b and c	❑
	❑
2. a and c	❑
	❑
3. a, b and c	❑
	❑
	❑
4. b	❑
5. a	❑
6. Trade and investment by organisations for import/export financing	❑
Hedging by market players to minimise currency risk	❑
Speculation for profit	❑
7. During the last year of a debt instrument's maturity it is comparable with a money market instrument.	❑

How well did you score? You should have scored at least 9. If you didn't you may need to revise some of the materials.

Further Resources

Books

International Money and Foreign Exchange Market: An Introduction
Julian Walmsley, John Wiley & Sons, Inc, 1996
ISBN   0 471 95320 2

How the City of London works: An introduction to its financial markets
William M. Clarke, Waterlow Publishers, 3rd Edition 1991
ISBN   0 08 040867 2

Reuters Glossary of International Economic & Financial Terms (3rd edition)
Longman, 1994
ISBN   0 582 24871-X

Publications

Swiss Bank Corporation
• Foreign Exchange and Money Market operations

Credit Suisse
• A Guide to Foreign Exchange and the Money Markets

Internet

RFT Website
• **http://www.wiley-rft.reuters.com**
This is the series' companion website where additional quiz questions, updated screens and other information may be found.

ACI – the Financial Markets Association
• **http://www.aciforex.com**
This is one of the largest fx associations with over 24,000 members in 79 countries of which 59 have affiliated national associations.

This section should take about 2 to 3 hours of study time. You may not take as long as this or it may take a little longer – remember your learning is individual to you.

'Unexpected events may move markets for a matter of a few hours or a day at the most. It is people's perceptions of fundamentals that move markets.'

Stuart Frost, Technical Analyst, NatWest Markets, May/June 1994

Introduction

This section is concerned with:

- An overview of how the money markets operate, the institutions and the market participants involved

- An overview of how FX operates, the institutions and the market participants involved

- Risk and credit in the markets — their relationship and how they are used

- An overview of regulation in the markets

You can find out more about specific financial institutions and organisations concerned with regulation by referring to the **Bank for International Settlements (BIS)** web site at *http://www.bis.org* or other similar institutions' web sites.

Before moving on it may be useful for you to try the activity opposite.

 Who do you think the market players are in the money markets and foreign exchange markets? Write down any ideas you may have here.

How do the Money Markets and Foreign Exchange Work?

Money Markets

Money markets are traded OTC, via the telephone or using electronic trading systems. Many market participants operate internationally and trading takes place 24 hours a day.

Large financial institutions can switch funds between financial centres almost instantaneously using modern computing and telecommunications systems. Growth of the internet means that retail investors can also increasingly invest internationally and switch their investments quickly.

In essence money markets are concerned with short-term loans involving financial institutions and corporations who borrow and lend money for periods of from one day to one year.

The money markets are essentially no different from any other markets. That is, markets are used to establish the price for goods, and money markets are used to establish the 'price of money'. The price of money is the interest rate payable for borrowing money (or the interest receivable for lending money).

When there is a high demand for money — ie, a lot of people want to borrow money — the 'price of money' goes up. That is, the more people who want to borrow money, the higher the interest rate.

Conversely, when there is a high supply of money — ie, a lot of people want to lend money — the 'price of money' goes down. That is, the more people who want to lend money, the lower the interest rate.

The amount of interest payable/receivable on any loan is governed by:

– the amount of money being borrowed/lent - the **principal**
– the prevailing **interest rate**
– the **maturity** or **tenor** of the loan

Central Banks

Every economy has a central bank, for example:

- The UK **Bank of England**
- The **US Federal Reserve** (the Fed)
- The German **Deutsche Bundesbank** (Buba)
- The French **Banque de France**
- The Japanese **Bank of Japan**

All these central banks use the money markets to implement the government's monetary policy. In general each country's central bank has the following responsibilities:

- Supervising the banking and money transmission system

- Controlling the money supply and domestic interest rates

- Maintaining the stability of the exchange rate

In order to balance the supply and demand of money and safeguard its currency a central bank has several financial tools available. The bank can change interest rates by using the money markets and it can buy and sell currencies in the FX markets. The central banks are able to fulfil their roles because they act as:

- Banker to their government

- Banker to other **clearing** or **settlement banks**. In this role they determine the amount of reserves which each bank must have.

How do banks such as the Fed and the Bank of England influence interest rates? Because the central banks hold accounts both for the government and the settlement banks they are in the unique position of monitoring the flow of money between both accounts on a daily basis.

Central Banks use a **discount rate** to control the supply of money to the economy in the short-term, known as the **short-term money supply**.

As the supply of money influences interest rates, this technique of money supply is used to set interest rates for the economy as a whole.

If a central bank lends money, it is increasing the supply of money to the banking system and therefore interest rates **decrease**. If a central bank borrows money, it is decreasing the supply of money to the banking system and therefore interest rates **increase**.

As the central banks are the lender of last resort, they determine, ultimately, the rate of interest in the economy.

Central banks borrow money in the market by issuing Treasury Bills, which are effectively an IOU signed by the government.

If a central bank	**then** the banking system's liquidity	**and** interest rates
Buys instruments	Increases	Decrease
Sells instruments	Decreases	Increase

Discount Markets

UK

Within the UK money markets there are a small number of **discount houses** who buy and sell short-term instruments created by commercial banks and the government.

Discount houses have been in existence for about 150 years and have their origins in **bill brokers** who bought and sold **Bills of Exchange** which had been issued to finance domestic and foreign trade. In principle the discount house paid a company wishing to sell a Bill of Exchange the face value **less** an amount for interest, that is, the bill had been **discounted**.

Originally merchant banks accepted Bills of Exchange from international merchants and effectively guaranteed payment to the holder. This was an important role for some merchant banks and they became known as **accepting houses**. A bill which was accepted and stamped was then sold on to other investors as the accepting houses did not necessarily wish to carry large stocks of bills. The investors received a lower rate of interest than the accepting house had charged originally because the bill was a secure investment and the accepting house had to make a profit! For example, an accepting house might charge 8% interest to accept a bill but sell it to an investor with an interest rate of 7%.

Discount houses are specialist banks which act as intermediaries between the Bank of England and financial institutions, corporations etc. Discount houses earn revenue by borrowing surplus short-term money from the banks, corporations etc and use it to buy financial instruments such as Treasury Bills, and **eligible** bills – bills which have been accepted by a Bank of England eligible bank. The banks loan their money to the discount houses at **call**. This means that the banks can demand their money back whenever they need it.

When the discount houses need to raise cash they have the right to sell these financial instruments to the Bank of England – any Treasury bills sold are in effect rediscounted. The effect of the Bank of England buying financial instruments from the discount houses drains cash from the banks which in turn forces them to call in their loans or raise lending rates.

The structure of the UK money markets is shown in the diagram below.

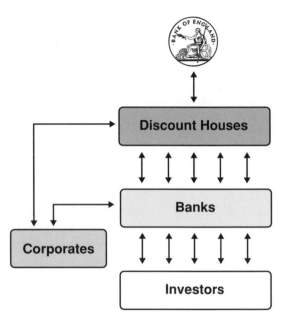

Every day the Bank of England determines the size of the surplus or shortage it expects in the money markets and publishes its daily forecast at about 9.45am. The assistance that can be provided by the Bank of England covers:

- Outright sale or purchase of eligible financial instruments

- Sale and repurchase agreements

- Lending to the discount houses overnight or for 7 days

Have a look at the Bank of England's index page shown here.

```
20:52 15JAN97 LN          BANK OF ENGLAND          UK00181        BOE/INDEX

                              GILTS
Gilt-edged market announcements          Seven pages from   <BOE/GILTS1>
Shop Window - General information                           <BOE/GILTS8>
Shop Window 1 - Stock available for outright sales and switches <BOE/GILTS9>
Shop Window 2 - Stock available for switches               <BOE/GILTS10>
Further Gilt-edged market announcements                    <BOE/GILTS11>
Prices for Gilt-edged stock near maturity                  <BOE/GILTS12>
GEMMA closing Gilt-edged prices          Eight pages from  <GEMMAGP1>
                     MONEY MARKET OPERATIONS
Open money market operations             Four pages from   <BOE/MONEYOPS1>
Sterling Treasury Bill tender result                       <BOE/MONEYOPS5>
Details of forthcoming Sterling Treasury Bill tender       <BOE/MONEYOPS6>
                       FOREIGN EXCHANGE
Sterling Exchange Rate Index                               <BOE/ERI>
BOE/BBA Spot Rates                                         <BOE/SAF>
BOE IMF SDR Rates                                          <BOE/NOONSDR>
                   FOREIGN CURRENCY BORROWING
Foreign currency debt issues                               <BOE/FCDEBT1>
                       MONEY STATISTICS
Money supply data                                          <BOE/STATS1>
                      PRESS ANNOUNCEMENTS
Euro Commercial Paper Rates                                <BOE/ECP>
The Bank's weekly balance sheet                            <BOE/NOTES>
```

At around midday the Bank publishes any revisions to its earlier forecast and assuming there is a shortage of money, which is usually the case, offers to purchase securities from the money markets. The details of all open market transactions are published some 15 – 20 minutes later, showing the type of security, its maturity date and rate of discount for each deal.

If the Bank of England is not happy with the structure of the market interest rates then it may not buy instruments to cover the shortage – in whole or in part. This means that the discount houses are left with the shortage and therefore have to raise the price at which they are prepared to bid in the market. This eventually impacts on the rates of interest in the markets.

In the **primary market**, the market place where instruments are first issued, the Treasury issues **3-month bills** via the Bank of England which invites tenders for the bills. The discount houses guarantee to take the full amount on offer after the bids are received. In the **secondary market**, the market place where instruments are freely bought and sold, the discount houses dominate the marketplace. Have a look at Bank of England tenders for Treasury Bills on the screen shown below.

In summary discount houses operate by:

- Acting as **principals** not as brokers. This means that they trade for themselves and not on behalf of clients.

- Trading in short-term instruments such as:
  - Treasury Bills
  - Certificates of Deposit (CDs). These are negotiable, interest bearing deposits of fixed maturity at a commercial bank.
  - Bank acceptances. These are, for example, Bills of Exchange that have been accepted by a bank.

- Using their stock of instruments as collateral to secure further borrowing thereby providing the liquidity – the money – the market needs.

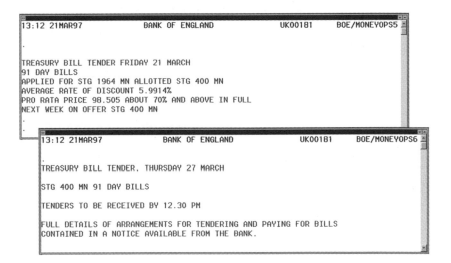

```
09:45 25MAR97 LN        BANK OF ENGLAND        UK00181    BOE/MONEYOPS1

9.45 an, Tuesday 25 March
Initial liquidity forecast, Stg 1450 nn shortage
A round of fixed rate operations is invited
The Bank's repo rate is 6%.
The operations will conprise repos to 7 & 8 April and
outright offers of bills naturing on or before 8 April
Principal factors in forecast -
Treasury bills & naturing outright purchases -271
Maturing bill/gilt repo -1012
Exchequer transactions -30     Rise in note circulation -40
```

```
13:12 21MAR97           BANK OF ENGLAND        UK00181    BOE/MONEYOPS5
.
.
TREASURY BILL TENDER FRIDAY 21 MARCH
91 DAY BILLS
APPLIED FOR STG 1964 MN ALLOTTED STG 400 MN
AVERAGE RATE OF DISCOUNT 5.9914%
PRO RATA PRICE 98.505 ABOUT 70% AND ABOVE IN FULL
NEXT WEEK ON OFFER STG 400 MN
.
.
```

```
13:12 21MAR97           BANK OF ENGLAND        UK00181    BOE/MONEYOPS6
.
.
TREASURY BILL TENDER, THURSDAY 27 MARCH

STG 400 MN 91 DAY BILLS

TENDERS TO BE RECEIVED BY 12.30 PM

FULL DETAILS OF ARRANGEMENTS FOR TENDERING AND PAYING FOR BILLS
CONTAINED IN A NOTICE AVAILABLE FROM THE BANK.
```

How do the Money Markets and Foreign Exchange Work?

US

The US Treasury raises funds in the money markets by selling **Treasury Bills** (T-bills). The US T-bills market is the largest and most important government short-term debt market in the world. This is because the US dollar remains the main currency for international trade and for FX. It is also because the US Government's ability to meet these debts is seen as a very low risk.

In the US the primary market issuing system does not use Discount houses. Instead the US Treasury offers T-bills for auction each week. Professional investors bid competitively on a discount basis based on the percentage return on an investment – its **yield** – in the secondary market. For example, $98.36 for $100 face value bills. Non-professional investors can make non-competitive bids with no price on them which are accepted in full. The remaining bills are then allocated to the professional pinvestors on the basis of lowest yield first until the lowest accepted price is reached. Competitive bidders pay their bid price; non-competitive bidders pay the weighted average price of the competitive bids.

The market in US government securities is important as it is:

- Highly liquid
- A safe haven for cash, given the guarantees of the US Treasury
- The best place to 'park' dollars
- Backed by an active futures market giving investors the opportunity to hedge and reduce market risk. Futures are discussed later in this section.
- Exempt from state, but not federal, interest taxes and a wide range of securities are available

Within the secondary market there are some 40 primary dealers and 300 traders linked by 6 Inter-dealer Brokers (IDBs). Five of the IDBs and the primary dealers set up an organisation – **Government Securities Pricing System Inc, (GOVPX)** – which contains details of all US Treasury issues traded in the IDB market.

Before moving on have a look at GOVPX on the screen shown below.

```
GovPX INDEX                                              GPXINDEX
GovPX is a specialist data service which offers the best bid and offer prices
fron 4 of the 5 interdealer brokers in the U.S. Government Bond narket.
                    U.S. TREASURY AND MONEY MARKETS
  CONTENT            PAGES       LOGICAL QUOTE    SECTOR CHAIN      VOLUME
3 Month Bill       <GVSQ>-S     <US3MT=PX>     <O#US3MT=PX>   <.TVTB=PX>
6 Month Bill       <GVSQ>-S     <US6MT=PX>     <O#US6MT=PX>   <.TVTB=PX>
1 Year Bill        <GVSQ>-S     <US1YT=PX>     <O#US1YT=PX>   <.TVTB=PX>
2 Year Note        <GVST>-X     <US2YT=PX>     <O#US2YT=PX>   <.TV2Y=PX>
3 Year Note        <GVSY>-Z     <US3YT=PX>     <O#US3YT=PX>   <.TV3Y=PX>
5 Year Note        <GVTA>-C     <US5YT=PX>     <O#US5YT=PX>   <.TV5Y=PX>
7 Year Note        <GVTD>-E     <------->      <O#US7YT=PX>   <.TV7Y=PX>
10 Year Note       <GVTF>-G     <US10YT=PX>    <O#US10YT=PX>  <.TV10Y=PX>
30 Year Bond       <GVTH>-K     <US30YT=PX>    <O#US30YT=PX>  <.TV30Y=PX>
Active Issues      <GVTL>       ---------      <O#USBMK=PX>   <.TV=PX>
Active Issues + MM <GVTM>       ---------      ----------     ---------
Trader Conpsite    <GVTN>       ---------      ----------     ---------
All Issues         ----         ---------      <O#USTSY=PX>   ---------

    ZERO COUPON, AGENCY & BASIS TRADING INDEX...<GPXINDEY>
    SwapPX...................................<GVPX260>-7
    The REPO Index...........................<GPXINDEZ>
For information on creating Reuter Instrument Codes (RICs) - see page <GVQD>-E
To receive nore information or "FREE TRIALS" of GovPX please call your Reuters
sale
```

```
GovPX               TREASURY BILLS              PG   10   GVSQ
MATURITY COUPON   BID /OFFER SIZE   YIELD    IL TRADE  VOL  YIELD  A-VOL
   03×27        5.-- /19     x5            IT 5.11    5         03×24
   04×03        5.17 /15    5x5  5.248/228 IH 5.155  20  5.233  592
   04×10        5.13 /11    5x5  5.212/192 IH 5.125   5  5.207   20
CM 04×17        5.28 /27    5x5  5.371/360 IH 5.28   29  5.371  203
   04×24        5.20 /19    5x5  5.294/284 IT 5.205   5  5.300   85
   05×01        5.21 /20    5x5  5.310/300 IT 5.21   53  5.310  110
   05×08        5.-- /215    x5  5.-- /321 IH 5.225   5  5.331   38
   05×15        5.245 /23   5x10 5.357/341 IH 5.235   5  5.347   55
   05×22        5.-- /23     x10 5.-- /347 IH 5.215  12  5.331   64
   05×29        5.235 /23   5x5  5.358/352 IT 5.23    5  5.352  288
   06×05        5.23 /225   5x5  5.358/353 IH 5.225   5  5.353   20
   06×12        5.24 /225  10x5  5.374/358 IT 5.235  20  5.369 03×24
   06×19        5.245 /24   5x55 5.385/379 IH 5.245   5  5.385  452
3M 06×26        5.25 /245  20x15 5.395/389 IT 5.25    5  5.395  470
3MW 07×03                    x            I              00/00
3M     5.25 /245  2Y  99.102/102  3Y  98.18+/186   TB VOL  9,419
5Y  98.206/20+ 10Y  96.22+/23  30Y  96.-- /09   03/25 10:18 EST
03/25 08:40 EST High Overnight Volume; See GovPX Page 3.
```

Interbank Markets

In most major banking systems all banks have to maintain reserve balances at a central bank. At the end of each trading day there has to be a minimum reserve in this account – typically 8% of the total deposits taken by the bank. Any money deposited in excess of the minimum reserve can be lent in the **interbank market**. The loan duration ranges from overnight to 2 years; most loans are usually overnight with delivery at 15.00 the following day.

Before 1963 lending in the discount money markets was always on a short-term **secured** basis backed by financial assets such as Treasury Bills. By 1963, in parallel with the emerging Eurodollar markets, merchant banks and discount houses started dealing with each other on an **unsecured** basis. By 1971 the clearing banks had entered the interbank market.

The clearing banks have to balance their books each day and maintain a cash liquidity margin to meet any emergency withdrawals. If a bank's cash desk finds its funds falling below its minimum reserve then it borrows overnight funds. A bank with excess cash lends money overnight in the interbank market and receives interest on these loans. In the US these funds are traded between banks at the Federal Funds rate.

With a highly liquid interbank market, banks can cut their liquidity margins finely to divert funds into profitable lending whilst using the interbank market to cover shortages. In this unsecured market place well known banks may borrow on their name and on-lend to less well known banks at a higher rate of interest.

The interbank rate is often used by the commercial banks over time to establish their **base lending or prime rates**.

The interbank market is also used by banks to effectively convert short-term loans into long-term loans. Banks borrow from financial institutions such as pension funds and corporations for fixed periods of a day to 2 years. They then on-loan the money to customers for up to 5 years and keep borrowing from the interbank market, for example, every 6 months to finance the loan.

Over 500 banks in London daily use the interbank markets. The fixed terms for the loans allow both counterparties to plan their operations and manage cash flows.

Since the 1980s multinational organisations who had previously placed their excess funds with banks, local authorities etc started using the interbank market for their own borrowing requirements. Corporations can either issue their own Sterling denominated financial instruments or use brokers to act on their behalf.

Within the interbank market money brokers act solely as **intermediaries** between the borrower and lender. The brokers are paid commission on the deals they complete. There is a strict code of practice governing brokers and the confidentiality of their clients.

Broking houses have grown extensively since 1963 and they now offer an extensive range of services which include interbank transactions, loans to local authorities and other government instruments.

Interbank rates are published in financial newspapers such as the *Financial Times* where you will find information like this:

LONDON MONEY RATES

Sterling Interbank	Over-night	7 days notice	One month	Three months	Six months	One year
	6¼-5¾	6¹⁄₁₆-5⅞	6¹⁄₁₆-5²⁹⁄₃₂	6¼-6⅛	6⁷⁄₁₆-5⁵⁄₁₆	6¹¹⁄₁₆-5⁹⁄₁₆

This is the interest rate at which the bank will lend money.

This is the interest rate at which the bank will pay to borrow money.

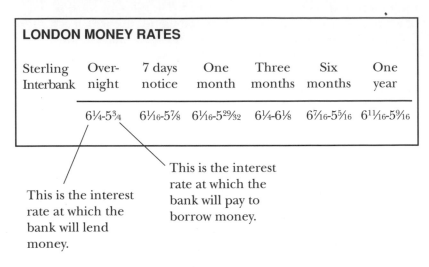

Period	GBP HBAA Bid	GBP HBEL Bid	GBP TTKL Bid	GBP TRDL Bid
ON	n/v	5.75	n/v	n/v
TN	6.3125	6.3125	6.3125	n/v
SN	6.3125	6.3125	n/v	n/v
SW	n/v	6.25	6.2813	6.34375
1M	6.58	6.40625	6.4688	6.4375

The above screen shows the latest bid prices from different contributors for GBP deposits for various dates.

The interbank market is not a single market — it consists of two distinct, yet similar markets:

- The domestic markets

- The Euro markets

The Domestic Markets

In general each country has a domestic market dedicated to trading its own money markets instruments in its own currency locally. The participants in these markets are those institutions, both foreign and domestic, that are located geographically in the currency's home country, for example, the Federal (Fed) Funds market in the US.

It is in the domestic markets that local banks conduct their day to day business, which includes the borrowing and lending of deposits to balance their books, or to take views on the market. Domestic markets range in size from huge, for example, the Fed Funds market in the US and the domestic Yen market in Tokyo, to small, for example, the Czech Koruna market in Prague.

For practical purposes, trading revolves around the chief financial centre in each country where the markets fall under the supervision of local regulatory agencies. These are usually the **central banks** of the countries which have already been considered.

The Euro Markets

So why are there Euro markets? At one time the money market deposit markets consisted solely of a series of domestic markets, loosely linked by the global FX market. Eventually, due to political events and considerations, the Euro market was created in London during the 1960s as a safe haven for US dollar holdings. Cold War antagonists of the US needed a safe haven for their US dollar holdings. These countries did not trust the US Government in terms of its regulatory influence on the US banking industry. They gravitated towards an arrangement in which London banks acted as a repository for their US dollar holdings.

Since London banks do not come under the jurisdiction of the US authorities, these depositors felt that their US dollar holdings would be insulated from any political events involving the US. Unwittingly, this arrangement broke new ground in the financial markets. No longer could a central bank have complete control over its currency abroad. Eventually Euro markets were created for all the major currencies.

One of the very first participants in the new external market in borrowing and lending dollars was a Paris-based Russian bank called the Banque Commerciale pour L'Europe du Nord who, even in the fifties, had the telegraphic address 'Eurobank'. As they were one of the most active banks, some referred to the transactions as Eurobank's dollars or, as it became known, 'Eurodollars'.

Subsequently, the term 'Euro' applied to any borrowing/lending of currency that took place outside the country or jurisdiction of that currency's central bank. If a London-based bank lends french Francs to a bank in Amsterdam, that deal is called a Euro-French franc transaction. The term was particularly significant during the strict capital and exchange controls of the 60s and 70s, where the interest rate for the Euro or external entity could be several percentage points higher (for weak currencies) or lower (for strong currencies) than corresponding domestic transactions, depending on the pressures.

As the new EC currency has already been christened 'the Euro', the use of the term to refer to external transactions may well become less frequent.

An important fact to remember is that Euro markets are free from most central bank regulations concerning **reserve requirements**.

Tax consideration also became a reason for a bank to open a branch office in a low tax environment country. This was responsible for the formation of a host of **offshore** banking centres. Even US banks eventually opened branches in the Bahamas and the Netherlands Antilles to escape the long arm of the taxman.

The Euro markets have grown and become a ready source of relatively cheap, reserve-free funding for the rapidly expanding field of international lending. This growing pool of international lending has become the primary source of funding for the institutions of the interbank market. The size of the Euro markets is tremendous – currently the Eurodollar market is the largest deposit market in the world.

To summarise, the interbank market is characterised by the following:

- Short-term money is borrowed and lent

- Loans are unsecured – no financial assets are required to back the loan

- The provision of liquidity for the market

- The basis of the Eurocurrency market

Interbank Offered Rates

The only official benchmark that exists for interest rates is that provided by a central bank for overnight funding. The rates for the other maturities are generated by the market. However, nearly every institution has a slightly different opinion of what the rate is for a given tenor. To cope with this situation the market needs a mechanism that provides an official benchmark rate for the fixed date maturities.

The banks in London use a system called **LIBOR – London Interbank Offered Rate.** This system has been imitated by other financial centres. Each day, at around 11:00 am London time, a survey is undertaken of several London banks for their fixed-date maturity lending (offer) rates to each other for the major Euro currencies. A single rate is established per currency and maturity which is known as a LIBOR **fixing**.

LIBOR rates are used for setting rates on loans, floating rate notes and interest rate derivatives. The **British Bankers Association, BBA**, publishes daily official LIBOR used for calculating settlement rates on interest rate derivatives (defined later in this chapter). It is important to note the following about LIBOR rates:

- The term LIBOR is always qualified with a currency and a maturity, for example, 3 month Deutschmark LIBOR.

- LIBOR is a reference rate, and at best can be used to fix rates for negotiated deals.

- LIBOR pertains to the Euro Market, and not the Domestic Markets.

Other countries have a similar rate fixing procedure to LIBOR, for example:

- PIBOR – The Paris Interbank Offered Rate

- FIBOR – The Frankfurt Interbank Offered Rate

- HIBOR – The Hong Kong Interbank Offered Rate

- SIBOR – The Singapore Interbank Offered Rate

London LIBOR is used for most transactions even when they are executed in other financial centres.

```
1225        INTNL SWAP & DERIVATIVES ASSOCIATION          ISDA
                      INTERBANK RATES FROM LONDON
           USD       GBP       JPY       CHF       DEM       XEU
           LONDON    LONDON    LONDON    LONDON    LONDON    LONDON
1M         5.71094   6.13542   0.80208   2.14844   3.37492   4.31250
2M         5.74219   6.25000   0.71875   2.06250   3.36971   4.32292
3M         5.78125   6.38021   0.71875   2.02344   3.36971   4.32292
6M         5.92188   6.62500   0.75000   2.00781   3.37492   4.37500
1Y         6.23438   6.97917   0.84375   2.00781   3.46346   4.43750

           LIBO      LIBP      JNBO      CHFO      DMBO      ECUO
           25/03/97  25/03/97  25/03/97  25/03/97  25/03/97  25/03/97

                  *AMENDED
```

You should note that the ISDA rates are quoted as decimals whereas the LIBOR rates are quoted as fractions

Interest Rates – Their Global Market Effects

A high proportion of business around the world is funded with loans of some description. As we have seen, the "cost" of these loans is determined by the respective interest rate on the loan. The higher the interest rate, the higher the rate of return required from the business to cover the interest on the loan.

Essentially, interest rates are the cost of doing business. As such, they affect everyone. The interest rates that consumers and home owners pay on their credit cards and mortgages, respectively, are derived from the money markets.

Interest rates determine how much it costs a business or individual to *use someone else's money* for a specified period of time. The phrase "time is money" means something – for as long as a borrower owes money, interest will be charged on the principal amount of the loan.

How Are Interest Rates Determined?

As we have seen, interest rates are determined by the supply and demand for money and the actions of the central bank. However, there is a precise mechanism that central banks use to fix the interest rate, usually the overnight loan market. They use this to establish an official **benchmark**, against which all other loans are priced.

Different countries have different names for their benchmarks, for example:

- Discount rate in US, Germany, Japan and Switzerland

- Intervention rate in France

- Bank rate in Canada

- Money market dealing rate in the UK

How Do Central Banks Manage Interest Rates?
The central banks can:

1. Release an official announcement to raise or lower the benchmark rate.

2. Create liquidity conditions that support their rate intentions.

For example, if the Federal Reserve Bank decides that economic conditions in the US warrant lower rates it will:

- Officially announce a lowering of the discount rate. This effectively reduces the Fed Funds rate which is the overnight rate traded interbank.

- These purchases are effectively loans to the banking system — ie, the central bank is increasing the supply of money to the banking system, which drives down the interest rate.

You should note that while the announcement of a rate change is a highly visible occurrence, the open market operations are often much more subtle in nature. Additionally, not all open market operations are policy related. A central bank may add or withdraw reserves from the banking system as part of its daily maintenance.

How do the Money Markets and Foreign Exchange Work?

You have now seen how the central banks function. The market generates rates for fixed maturities by taking the following into account:

- Current economic conditions in the country of the currency

- The prevailing inflation rate in that country

- The number of borrowers compared with the number of lenders in the market

- Market expectations. Does the market think that the central bank is going to increase or reduce rates?

Interest rates are a tool that a central bank uses to implement its country's monetary policy.

- **Lower rates** foster economic growth, often with an increase in inflation.

- **Higher rates** tend to choke off economic growth by making it too expensive to borrow money. Consumer spending is crucial to an economy – take away this spending power and the economy hesitates, or falters.

The actions of the central bank have a large influence on the performance of the economy as a whole, and therefore the political implications of central bank actions are significant. If a central bank is perceived by the market to be acting in the short-term interests of the government, rather than the long-term interests of the economy, it may undermine confidence in that country. Such a loss of confidence may result in an outflow of capital from that country, causing higher interest rates.

In recent years, governments have increasingly made explicit the role of the central bank, often declaring whether it has independent power to set interest rates, or whether this task is performed by the government.

Other Factors Affecting Interest Rates

In addition to supply and demand for money and the actions of the central bank, there are a number of other factors which affect interest rates for specific instruments. These include:

- The **creditworthiness of the borrower** — in other words how likely is it that the borrower will be unable to repay the loan and interest?

- The **maturity of the loan** — depending on the outlook for the economy and supply and demand factors, the interest rate for a loan of one maturity may differ from the interest rate for a different maturity.

- The **principal amount** — a borrower may find it harder to pay back a large loan than a small loan. However, a lender may be able to offer a more attractive interest rate for a larger principal amount, due to the economies of scale of one large transaction.

Most loans involve some margin to cover the risk of a borrower defaulting, the **credit risk** of the loan. Governments — or more specifically the central bank of a country — tend to be regarded as the most creditworthy borrowers in their own country, as they are the lenders of last resort. Credit risk will be considered in more detail later in this section.

In order to compare different money market instruments on the same basis, a consistent measure of how "expensive" they are is needed. This measure is known as the **yield**. The **yield to maturity (YTM)** is simply the rate of return an investor can expect if the instrument matures without default, expressed as an annualised (ie, yearly) percentage rate.

The relationship between the maturity of a loan and the interest rate for that particular maturity is normally expressed graphically as a curve, plotting the yield to maturity for all the available maturities. This curve is known as the **yield curve**. The yield curve is an extremely powerful investment tool, used by investors and borrowers to display the state of the market and the market's expectation for future movements in interest rates.

An upward (downward)-sloping yield curve, known as a positive (negative) yield curve, shows that interest rates for longer maturities are higher (lower) than interest rates for shorter maturities.

Positive and negative yield curves are shown in the diagrams below:

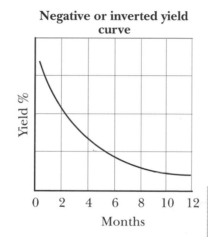

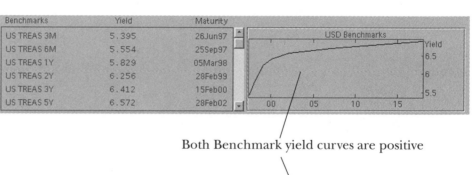

Both Benchmark yield curves are positive

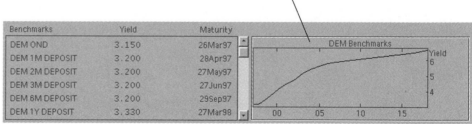

Although YTM is the rate of return if an instrument is held to maturity, short-term investors often liquidate their position before maturity. These investors are therefore concerned with the **horizon return** on the instrument which has two components:

Horizon return = Accrued interest + Capital gains

This means the **horizon return** is the rate of return achieved on an investment, from purchase to sale, expressed as a percentage per annum taking into account both components.

i *If an investment is held to maturity, then its **horizon return** equals the YTM.*

Below is a typical screen illustrations the use of **Horizon analysis**.

Select DOMESTIC BAs from the drop down menu

Select a BA instrument of your choice from the drop down menu

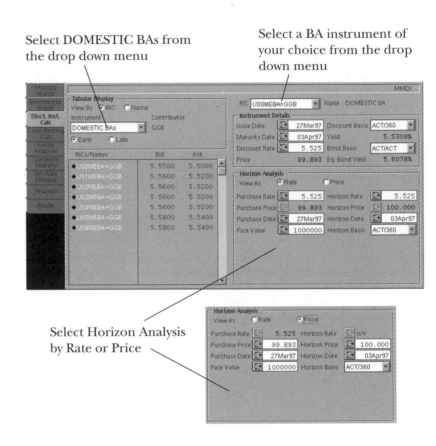

Select Horizon Analysis by Rate or Price

The Money Markets at Work

There is no market floor on which transactions are completed. The money markets are another example of an OTC market – in this case trading is done using telephones and computer quote screens from the dealing rooms of banks and brokers.

Most borrowers and lenders in the money markets conduct their transactions through dealers, who buy and sell money market instruments, even though they themselves do not need to borrow or lend money. These dealers are known as **market-makers**. They quote a buy and a sell price for each instrument they deal in, known as a **two-way price**. The borrowing price is known as the **bid**, and the lending price is known as the **offer**. The difference between these two prices is known as the **bid-offer spread**, and it is this spread which generates profits for market-makers, as they are always buying slightly more cheaply than they are selling.

In the money markets, bids and offers are expressed as interest rates, eg, $6^{12}/_{16}\%$**, or 6.75%. Where a rate is quoted as a decimal percentage, the rate is expressed in basis points**, where a basis point is one hundredth of a percentage point.

In New York

There are two ways in which you will see prices quoted – prices from traders in New York and London may appear to be different at first glance but they both mean the same. Confused? ... as you will see it all depends on your point of view:

$6^{1}/_{2}\%-6^{5}/_{8}\%$
Bid – Offer

Bid price – this is the price at which the market-maker borrows money. It is the price an investor will receive for placing a deposit.

Offer price – this is the price at which the market-maker lends money. It is the price a taker has to pay for funds. You always have to pay more for borrowing money than you receive for lending it!

In London

$6^{5}/_{8}\%-6^{1}/_{2}\%$
Offer – Bid

The convention in London is to quote Offer/Bid whereas most other parts of the world quote Bid/Offer. It is important to recognise that either way the bid is $6^{1}/_{2}\%$ and the offer is $6^{5}/_{8}\%$.

Market-makers also quote two-way prices on other financial instruments in the money markets, for example, certificates of deposit.

| Period | DEM | DEM | USD | USD |
| | Latest | Latest | Latest | Latest |
	Bid	Ask	Bid	Ask
1M	3.2	3.3	5.59	5.65
2M	3.2	3.3	5.61	5.67
3M	3.2	3.3	5.61	5.71
6M	3.23	3.33	5.74	5.84
9M	3.12	3.37	5.86	5.96

Who Uses the Money Markets?

Borrowers include corporations, banks, governments and supra-national organisations such as the World Bank who require short-term finance. Traditionally each type of borrower uses a different instrument and these are described in the next section. All the organisations mentioned use FX to hedge or take currency positions.

As investments, most money markets instruments are **liquid** which means that they can be bought and sold rapidly. The instruments are also **low risk** which means that the return on the investment is lower than for other financial instruments. Many corporate treasurers use the money markets to 'park' spare cash as a temporary measure before making a financial decision. The following users are described in a little more detail:

- Central banks

- Commercial banks

- Discount houses

- Investment banks

- Local authorities

- UK building societies

- Finance houses

- Corporations

- Brokers

Central Banks
Central banks use the money markets to control short-term money supply by buying and selling instruments such as Treasury Bills.

Commercial Banks
The traditional business of commercial banks involves customer deposit taking and lending. The balance between these two activities is funded using the interbank market. Banks with surplus cash deposit funds with other banks whilst banks requiring cash borrow funds.

Transactions cover maturity periods from overnight to trading periods for fixed dates – 1, 2, 3, 6, 9 and 12 month periods.

Commercial banks also provide integrated FX and payment facilities for customers and make an active market in currencies between themselves.

Banks acting as market-makers continuously show two-way prices. The difference between these prices – the spread – is their **turn** or profit.

The banks not only use the money markets to cover funding and FX exposures but they use them also to act on their own accounts and take speculative positions for profit.

Discount Houses
Within the UK banking system the Bank of England uses a small number of discount houses to act as intermediaries for its dealings in the money markets. Banks and their dealers, brokers and corporations then trade with the discount houses.

Investment Banks

Investment banks or securities houses specialise in promoting new issues to the market and also making a secondary market in these issues. Investment banks thus operate as intermediaries acting as client brokers for commission. The investment bank dealers also take positions in instruments for their own account looking to take profits from market price movements.

UK Local Authorities

Since 1981 Local Authorities have come to the money markets for short term funds – up to 364 days – but their long-term funding is met by the **Public Watch Loans Board**.

UK Building Societies

With permission from the Registrar of Friendly Societies, building societies have been allowed to both lend and borrow funds in the money markets since 1982. This has had the effect of making the building societies more like high street banks.

Finance Houses

These operate in relatively high risk lending, through hire purchase or secondary mortgage arrangements directly with the public. These financial houses fund themselves independently from the money markets.

Corporations

Large international corporations such as General Motors, IBM, Ford etc use the money markets for their own direct borrowing requirements. These corporations either use brokers to get the best deal or issue their own **Commercial Paper**. A Commercial Paper is an unsecured instrument issued for short-term credit. It normally has a maturity of up to 270 days and is usually sold at a discount from face value.

Brokers

Brokers play an important role in the money markets in preserving the anonymity of the counterparties in a transaction until a deal has been made. Brokers do not take positions in the market but act as agents for different market-makers in order to match transactions. For providing this service brokers charge a fee. But how does the system work?

Dealers have direct lines to specialist brokers through which they feed their bid and offered prices. The brokers take the highest bid and the lowest offered prices from the market and broadcast these back to their clients through a **squawk box** or, increasingly, onscreen.

The prices broadcast are live rates at which the quoting banks must be prepared to deal – usually for accepted market amounts. Within seconds of a dealer providing prices to the broker they are broadcast and a subscriber wishing to trade can call the broker using a dedicated telephone line.

Brokers do not disclose the names of counterparties to each other until the deal has been made thus preserving anonymity on both sides of the trade. In some cases, for complete anonymity, brokers work on a no-name basis acting as principal to both sides of the deal. Once the deal is made the counterparties are revealed for settlement purposes. By using a broker even smaller banks can trade at prices they might not be quoted if they went directly to a market-maker.

In markets such as Treasury Bills where the credit risk is established, dealers save a lot of time 'shopping around' with other market-makers by dealing through brokers. In other markets, such as CDs, where the credit rating of the borrower is important, the broadcast of market prices by a broker is less useful. In such markets dealers prefer to trade directly.

Foreign Exchange

Banks will generally lend their customers money in any currency they demand. Thus banks regularly have to participate in the foreign exchange market to buy and sell the currencies they are lending or receiving.

In order that banks may deal quickly and efficiently in the FX market, there is an interbank market, in which banks may buy and sell currencies in wholesale amounts.

 A correspondent bank is a bank in one country that acts as an agent for a bank in another country.

However, as has already been mentioned, the bulk of FX trading is not directly related to international trade or investment. Most FX trading is carried out interbank and is for profit.

 Before moving on you should be clear on what the term OTC means. Could you explain OTC to a colleague if they didn't know what it meant?

The FX markets are OTC where currency amounts and settlement dates for transactions are both negotiable. Although there are no fixed contract conditions, market-makers use a system of **fixed dates** for settlement similar to those used in the money markets and conventional **market amounts** for trading.

The main methods of trading FX are via:

- Direct interbank using systems such as Reuters Dealing 2000-1

- Voice brokers

- Electronic broking systems such as Reuters Dealing 2000-2

Most FX dealers specialise in one or a small group of closely related currencies. The three most important currency pairs in 1998 were as follows:

Currency pair	Transactions world-wide
USD/DEM	30%
USD/JPY	21%
GBP/USD	11%

Liquidity in the major currencies is good but some of the more 'exotic' currencies can be thinly traded. The US dollar remains the major currency in FX terms with over 90% of world trade being settled in USD. In 1995 the USD was involved in 86% of FX transactions world-wide.

The creation of Economic and Monetary Union in Europe in 1999, and in particular the launch of the Euro, promises to challenge this existing world order in the foreign exchange market. Many analysts predict that the Euro may become as important to the world economy and FX market as the US dollar.

We have seen that foreign exchange rates and interest rates are closely linked and affect one another, and in turn both can make an impact an a country's domestic economy.

The FX rate also affects a country's balance of payments — the net amount of inflows and outflows of money from a country in relation to trade payments. A strong domestic currency makes imports cheaper and tends to stimulate demand for imports, resulting in a balance of payments deficit. Conversely, a weak currency makes imports expensive and dampens demand for imports, resulting in a balance of payments surplus. Similarly, a strong (weak) currency makes exports more expensive (cheap) in other countries, dampening (stimulating) demand for exports and resulting in a balance of payments deficit (surplus).

While we have discussed the nature of FX markets, we have yet to examine the details of a foreign exchange transaction.

The FX Deal

A foreign exchange deal can be defined as:

 A contract to exchange one currency for another at an agreed rate on a specified delivery date.

Foreign Exchange markets are **OTC** operating worldwide, with trading hours overlapping to make a 24 hour global market.

The principal components of a deal are:

- Trade date

- Counterparty

- Currencies

- Exchange rate

- Amounts

- Value date

- Payment instructions

How do the Money Markets and Foreign Exchange Work?

Currencies

The names of the currencies must be identified, usually by the three letters which are used in the **SWIFT** payments system. Based in Belgium, the **Society for Worldwide Interbank Financial Telecommunications (SWIFT)** is a multinational facility jointly owned by over 1000 banks dedicated to interbank funds transfer. Payment instructions are transmitted over the SWIFT network using specially formatted, password controlled messages. Examples of SWIFT codes are shown below:

SWIFT Code	Currency
USD	US Dollar
GBP	UK Sterling
JPY	Japanese Yen
DEM	German Deutschmark
CHF	Swiss Franc
FRF	French Franc
CAD	Canadian Dollar

Exchange rate

An exchange rate is the price of one currency in terms of another. Currency quotations consist of a **base** and a **counter** currency – the convention when writing a currency pair exchange rate quotation is to put the base currency first and the counter currency second. For example:

Base currency → USD / DEM → Counter
GBP / USD → currency

The quotations may be described in **European** or **American** terms or as **Direct** or **Indirect** quotations respectively.

American terms or Indirect quotation

This is when a **fixed** amount of **domestic currency** is quoted against a **variable** amount of **foreign currency** – it is also known as an **inverse** quotation. Traditionally GBP was quoted this way because in pre-decimal times this was the easiest method. Even though GBP now uses a decimal system the indirect quotation remains. Other countries using American terms include the New Zealand dollar (NZD), Australian dollar (AUD), Irish Punt (IEP) and European Currency Unit (XEU).

Example
A GBP/USD rate of 1.6870 means the following:

1. £1 can be exchanged for 1.6870 US dollars
2. The GBP is the **base** currency and the USD is the **counter** currency.
3. If you **buy** GBP then you **sell** USD and vice versa

European terms or Direct quotation

This is when a **fixed** amount of **foreign currency** is quoted against a **variable** amount of **domestic currency**.

Example
A USD/DEM rate of 1.4085 means the following:

1. $1 can be exchanged for 1.4085 Deutschmarks
2. The USD is the **base** currency and the DEM is the **counter** currency.
3. If you **buy** USD then you **sell** DEM and vice versa

To summarise, most currency pairs are direct quotations in the international FX market.

Direct quotation European terms	**1 unit of foreign currency** can be exchanged for a **variable amount of domestic currency**
Indirect quotation American terms	**1 unit of domestic currency** can be exchanged for a **variable amount of foreign currency**

Amounts

Unless specified, spot trades are quoted for amounts of base currency.

Example

If a trader asks for a quote in *'dollar mark in ten'*, then it is understood the request is for 10 million of the base currency, USD, unless the trader asks for *'dollar mark in ten marks'*. The quotation is still European regardless of whether you trade in dollar or mark amounts.

Likewise for a quote in *'Sterling mark in twenty'* it is understood that the request is for 20 million of the base currency, GBP.

Value Date

The date on which the exchange of currencies takes place. It is important to consider a number of variables when computing value dates. These variables include:

- Bank holidays in the countries of the currencies dealt

- Weekends – in the western world the weekend is Saturday and Sunday but in Islamic countries it is Friday and Sunday

Payment Instructions

Whenever a deal is executed, instructions must be given to the counterparty detailing where the currency to be received should be paid.

Example

A bank executes a deal with a counterparty to buy USD and sell DEM. It must specify to which bank the USD should be paid, and the location of that bank.

Suppose Citibank NYC sells DEM against USD in a trade to Société Générale Paris. Citibank NYC has one **correspondent bank** per currency it is active in. For example,
- its USD are held at Citibank NYC
- its DEM are held at Citibank Frankfurt, a/c Citibank NYC
- its FRF are held at BNP Paris, a/c Citibank NYC

Société Générale Paris similarly has correspondent banks. For example,
- its USD are held at Chase NYC, a/c Soc Gen Paris
- its DEM are held at Deutsche Frankfurt, a/c Soc Gen Paris
- its FRF are held at Société Générale Paris

So for the above trade to settle:

- Citibank NYC will instruct Société Générale Paris to pay the USD it bought to its own account at Citibank NYC. Société Générale Paris will pay the USD from its account at Chase NYC. All Citibank says is *'my dollars to my NY'*.

- Société Générale Paris will instruct Citibank NYC to pay the DEM it bought to its account at Deutsche Frankfurt. Citibank NYC will pay the DEM from its account at Citibank Frankfurt. Société Générale Paris will say *'my marks to Deutsche, FFT'*.

These accounts are known as **nostro** accounts which comes from the Latin for 'ours'.

Forward FX and the Money Markets

The Importance of Interest Rates

Market participants are always seeking ways of maximising their profits. A key factor in recognising investment opportunities is the **real rate of return** on an investment. For the currency involved this is calculated as follows:

Real rate of return = Interest rate − Perceived rate of inflation

Money tends to flow to countries with high real rates of return. If a central bank wishes to attract capital into its country, it will often raise interest rates. Higher rates attract capital, which results, hopefully, in a greater demand for the domestic currency which leads to a higher exchange value. If market participants want to take advantage of the high returns they need to invest in the country and buy the domestic currency.

When a central bank raises interest rates it makes the real rates of return in its domestic economy higher, and therefore attracts an inflow of capital; a lowering of interest rates conversely produces an outflow of capital. These inflows and out flows of capital tend to produce a strengthening and weakening of the currency, respectively. In order to influence the foreign exchange rate, the central bank needs to change interest rates, which it does by means of its operations in the domestic money markets.

An interest rate differential is the difference in the rates of two currencies over similar maturities.

If 3 month Eurodollars are yielding 5% and 3 month Euro marks are yielding 4%, the interest rate differential is 1%, or 100 basis points.

In fact, there is a market that trades purely on changes in interest rate differentials – this is the **FX Forward Market**.

The Forward FX Markets

The currencies traded in a spot FX transaction are usually actually delivered two business days after the trade is executed. But what if the currency is not required until a future date but you want to agree the price today? Forward FX transactions cater for such needs and are derived from spot FX and money market interest rates.

There are two types of forward FX transactions used extensively in the markets:

- Forward outright transactions

- FX Swaps

The importance of these instruments is reflected in the latest survey – **Bank for International Settlements (BIS):** *Central Bank Survey of Foreign Exchange and Derivatives Market Activity in 1995*. This survey details a number of important statistics which are highlighted here:

- Of the $1,490 billion daily turnover in FX some $900 billion is traded in Forward outright transactions and FX Swaps – this represents 60% of the market. In 1995 the market share was 56%.

Market turnover	1995	1998
Spot	44%	40%
Forward	56%	60%

Forward FX quotations are expressed in **forward points**. The prices quoted are not exchange rates but **interest rate differentials**. It is also useful to remember:

> **The forward rate is not a prediction of what the future spot rate will be.**

A forward outright FX transaction is a non-negotiable, OTC deal which is defined as follows:

> An FX deal which is executed today to buy one currency for another currency at a rate which is agreed today, for delivery at an agreed future date.

There is no exchange of funds until the future delivery date.

Most Forward FX transactions are FX Swaps which can be defined as follows:

> An FX deal which involves the simultaneous purchase and sale, or sale and purchase, of a specified amount of one currency against another for two different value dates.

Although an FX Swap is a single transaction with a single counterparty, the transaction has **two value dates**, or **legs**, when the exchanges of funds occur.

Forward FX transactions also share common methods for calculating:

- Forward value dates

- Forward points

The FX Markets at Work

The Dealing Arena
The range of products available in the FX market has increased dramatically over the last 30 years. Dealers at banks provide these products for their clients to allow them to invest, speculate or hedge.

The complex nature of many of these products, combined with the huge volumes of money that are being traded, mean banks must have three important functions set up in order to record and monitor effectively their trades.

Front Office/Dealing Room
This is where the OTC trading in the financial markets takes place. As you have probably seen from media coverage it is a hectic environment with dealers surrounded by screens and telephones.

Middle Office
This provides the dealers with specialist facilities, support, advice and guidance from risk managers, economists, technical analysts, legal advisers etc.

Back Office
This is where the processing, confirmation, settlement, query handling and cash management functions are carried out. It is important to remember that dealers cannot trade without the back office.

The Mechanics of a Deal

Once a deal has been made the dealer will produce a **deal ticket** which is passed to the **back office**. The **deal ticket** summarises the following information:

- Trade date
- Type of deal (spot, forward, etc.)
- Counterparty
- Currencies
- Exchange rate
- Amounts
- Payment instructions
- Value date
- Via (broker, direct)
- Deal direction – bought or sold

Depending on the system used the deal ticket is either handwritten or generated automatically as part of a computerised system.

In addition to the deal ticket, dealers keep their own personal logs called **blotters, deal sheets or position sheets** to record their positions. The information may be passed electronically to the bank's computer using a product such as Dealing 2000.

The screen dump below shows a deal ticket for an FX Swap transaction.

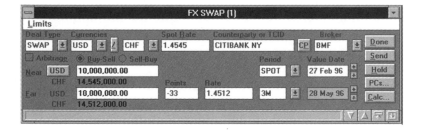

You may have seen pictures of busy dealing rooms and lots of desks, computer terminals etc. What kind of dealers do you think work in the dealing room of a bank? How do you think the dealing room operations are structured – the types of desks? Have you any idea which desks need to interrelate their activities?

The Dealing Room

How does a dealing room operate? How is it structured? Who is involved? To illustrate the strong interrelationships between FX and the money markets, the following description of a dealing room structure and personalities involved is taken as typical. However, in practice every bank does it slightly differently. The type of dealing room described here allows the dealers flexibility and encourages cross-fertilisation of ideas and cross market deals. For example money market positions may be covered by forward FX trades and vice versa.

A bank's dealing room will be divided into various sections but everyone will be able to communicate with each other via computers, intercomms etc ensuring that everyone is kept up to date. The room is usually grouped under a **Treasury Manager**.

The room is normally divided into **desks** which deal with the various aspects of the money markets and foreign exchange. Each desk will have a **Chief Dealer**. The different desks are as follows:

- **Spot desk**. This breaks down into the various currencies, for example, parts of the desk will deal with USD/DEM, USD/JPY, GBP/USD etc on a spot basis.

- **Forwards desk**. This handles forward FX contracts to supply currencies at dates in the future.

- **Money Markets desk**. This trades money market instruments in various currencies. The changing interest rates in the money markets will impact on the Forwards desk.

- **Derivatives desk**. This handles derivatives whose prices are derived from spot and forward FX rates and interest rates in various currencies.

- **Corporate desk**. This liaises with the bank's corporate customers.

All the desks are supported by the middle and back offices. While the back office records all the trades and makes sure settlement instructions are carried out, the middle office monitors the overall activity of the trading desks on an aggregate basis. The function of the middle office is to ensure that all trades are recorded and that the 'front office' traders are not taking excessive risks. Usually, the middle office will also monitor the profit or loss that each trader is making, and ensure their methods of calculating prices for their deals are correct.

The structure and important interfaces in the dealing room are summarised in the diagram below.

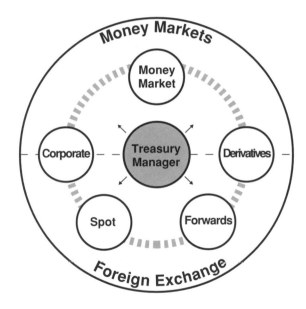

How do the Money Markets and Foreign Exchange Work?

Treasury Manager

The treasury manager has overall responsibility for the dealing room and the activities of the dealing teams. He/she decides on the

strategy of the dealing room and on the markets and products the teams will operate in. Just as important, the treasury manager allocates the financial limits and controls which apply to the teams.

The treasury manager has to make a profit for the bank so dealing limits need to be established for the dealing room. The treasury manager is also constantly in touch with individual team members, covering market activities, positions held, profit and loss etc.

Chief Dealers

Chief dealers have ultimate control over their teams with the responsibility for co-ordinating and controlling individual dealers' day-to-day activities. They have to monitor all aspects of FX so as to maximise profit and minimise loss.

Spot FX Dealers

Spot FX dealers trade in one or more chosen currencies, for example USD/JPY or USD/DEM, buying and selling for profit. Profits can be

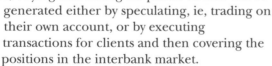

generated either by speculating, ie, trading on their own account, or by executing transactions for clients and then covering the positions in the interbank market.

These are the currency dealers usually featured by the media. They work on a second-by-second basis and are allowed to run positions as determined by the chief dealer. Most positions are created and unwound during the length of that working day – **intra day**. Some banks allow dealers to run positions into the next day – **overnight**. The spot dealer's function is to purchase or sell a currency in the belief that it will appreciate or depreciate in value. They do not actually need the currency – they use it for profit.

Forward FX Dealers

Although these dealers operate in forward contracts they also work closely with the spot dealers and money market dealers. The forward dealers' view is long-term and they are interested in the **interest rates** of the currencies in which they deal. In particular it is the difference between the two currency interest rates – the **interest rate differential** – in which they are interested.

Money Market Dealers

The dealers have much the same responsibilities as their counterparts in FX but with reference to the money markets.

The currency traded by the bank may be domestic, for example, a UK bank trading in Sterling, or it may be a **Eurocurrency**. In the latter case, for example, DEM or USD are traded by the UK bank. The money market dealers quote clients a two-way price and attempt to run their positions such that they 'lend high, borrow low' in order to maximise their profits.

Money market dealers work with forward FX dealers in the **arbitrage** market. This is where one currency is borrowed, switched to another currency through the forward swap market, and then the second currency is lent at a profit.

Derivative Dealers

Derivatives dealers trade and quote prices on a range of FX and money market instruments, all of whose prices are derived from the interest rates in the money markets and the FX rates in the FX markets. As derivatives involve prices derived from all the other desks, the derivatives desk usually executes most of the arbitrage deals. The derivatives desk can also create **structured products**, which combine instruments from the other desks, and which are packaged up into one single transaction.

REUTERS

Corporate Dealers

The role of the corporate dealer is different from the interbank dealers. In many respects they are the bank's front-line representatives with corporate customers. Depending on the client's needs corporate dealers may need money market rates, FX rates and/or derivative quotes. They obtain prices from the other dealers and liaise between the corporate customer and the bank's dealers. They also supply market information and advice to their corporate customers on a daily basis. A good corporate base of customers is an essential part of the dealing room's strategy and its maintenance is therefore very important.

Large corporate clients such as Sony, ICI, BT etc often need large amounts of foreign currency. If a bank has a large corporate client base it is likely to be given large orders, for example, $50 million to sell against Deutschmarks.

The events of typical FX transactions are summarised in the diagram below:

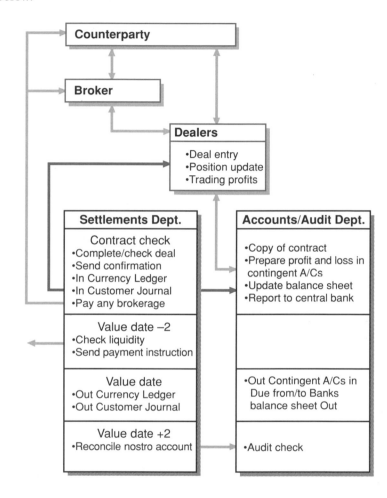

Who Uses FX Markets?

Traders: Market-makers/Market-takers

The FX trader who is quoting is a **market-maker** – he is 'making a market'. The FX trader who is dealing on a price quoted is a **market-taker**.

Traders can be both market-makers and market-takers if they make prices to the market as well as deal on prices quoted to them.

Commercial and Investment Bank Traders

The majority of FX trading is conducted by these banks whose traders 'make' the market through continuous interbank trading. Most of the trading is for speculation or hedging but these banks also provide foreign exchange services for their corporate customers.

Central Banks

These are banks such as the Bank of England and the US Federal Reserve who use FX to manage reserves and intervene to maintain an orderly marketplace.

Corporate Customers

Many organisations who import/export goods and services require FX for trade and investment. They also need to minimise their currency risk.

Brokers

These act as intermediaries between counterparties, matching buying and selling orders – the counterparties remain anonymous to each other until the deal is struck. Brokers know which dealer has the highest bid (buying) rate and which has the lowest offer (selling) rate. Brokers do not hold a position but earn their income from the commission they charge on deals.

Electronic broking systems such as Reuters Dealing 2000-2 and its competitor EBS/Minex account for a growing percentage of the total market turnover.

The major participants in the FX market are banks. Although the FX market is traded OTC and is therefore a decentralised, 24-hour market, some instruments are traded on exchanges. For example, currency futures are actively traded at the Chicago Mercantile Exchange (CME) and currency options are traded at the Philadelphia Stock Exchange (PHLX).

Apart from these exchange traded products, there is no central register of FX deals, although the Bank for International Settlements estimates the level of overall market activity every three years. To do this, it surveys the central banks from each of its member countries, which have the best estimate of the amount of their domestic currency traded.

Risk and Credit

Understanding and managing risk is the key to successful money market and FX trading. For every potential reward, there is a corresponding risk.

Risk in financial markets can take several forms, each of which will be addressed in the following sections. In recent years, large amounts of time and money have been dedicated by banks and central banks to better understand the nature of financial risk.

The history of financial markets is littered with examples of companies — or even whole sectors of economies — that have gone out of business due to their inability to effectively manage risk. Some of the more famous examples include Barings Bank, which failed in 1995, the US Savings and Loan sector, which was devastated in the 1980s, and Bank Herstatt, which failed in 1974, nearly causing global financial markets to grind to a halt.

Financial institutions that trade in financial markets must have a set of risk policies drawn up by the board of directors. In addition, institutions must have risk control systems which can measure and aggregate the risks incurred by traders in all the bank's trading operations. Banks which do not have these measures in place are liable to have their licences revoked by the central bank, which monitors banks' risk management guidelines and systems.

The main types of risk include market risk, credit risk and settlement risk.

Market Risk

Market risk is the risk that the positions taken by the bank in its trading operations may generate losses from changes in interest rates or foreign exchange rates. Put more simply, market risk is the risk of currencies moving adversely, creating a loss from the trading position.

For example, let us say ABC Bank is a US bank which trades FX. ABC's base currency is USD, and all accounts are measured and reported in USD. If ABC Bank sells USD 10 million to XYZ Bank for DEM at a rate of 1.5000, ABC Bank receives DEM 15 million from XYZ Bank on the settlement date.

If the USD/DEM rate changes from 1.5000 to 1.5012, ABC Bank can only buy USD 9,992,006 with the DEM 15 million. This represents a loss of USD 7,994.

Banks value their transactions frequently, usually on a daily basis. This activity of valuing deals and calculating the corresponding profit or loss is called **marking to market**.

Almost all financial transactions involve market risk. It is an integral part of financial trading. It is almost always necessary to take market risk in order to generate profits from trading.

Generating trading profits without taking market risk is called **arbitrage trading**. As the creation of profits without market risk is a very desirable activity for traders, opportunities for arbitrage trading tend to be taken very quickly by traders who constantly monitor numerous markets for these opportunities.

Settlement Risk

Settlement risk is the risk that arises from a non-simultaneous exchange of payments. In a spot FX transaction, this is the risk that a counterparty may not deliver on its leg of the deal when the first leg of the deal has already been paid out.

This arises as a result of the timing differences in the payments due on an FX trade. On the settlement day of the FX deal between ABC Bank and XYZ Bank, XYZ Bank due to pay ABC Bank DEM 15 million, while receiving USD 10 million. The problem for XYZ Bank is that it must make the payment to ABC Bank's correspondent in Frankfurt several hours before it receives the USD 10 million in New York.

The dangers of this gap in time were clearly demonstrated by the Bank Herstatt case. The closure of the private German bank in June 1974 took place late in the afternoon, after payments of Deutschmarks had been received by Herstatt, but before the corresponding US dollar payments in New York were due to be made. Settlement risk is therefore often referred to as 'Herstatt risk'.

Banks manage settlement risk by establishing a **settlement limit**, which restricts the total US dollar volume of deals that are to settle on any given day. While this would not stop a bank from being exposed to a Herstatt disaster, it at least puts a cap on potential losses.

When a spot FX trade is done, the full value of the deal is applied against the settlement limit for the value date of the trade. Credit is usually replenished at the close of business of the settlement or maturity date.

Credit Risk

Credit risk is the risk that the counterparties the bank trades with may not be able to repay their debts (or, for example, deliver currency in a forward transaction).

Credit risk is by far the largest source of risk in the banking system, accounting for over 80% of the total risk to which banks are exposed. Primarily, this is because the vast majority of banking business is lending money, where the only risk is that the customer will not repay the debt. This risk is credit risk.

However, credit risk also arises in FX markets. In an FX deal, credit risk is the risk that a counterparty will be unable to meet its obligations at some future date. Whereas settlement risk is a very short-term risk, credit risk is longer term risk, covering the whole life of a financial transaction. For example, if a bank executes a six month FX swap, it faces the risk that at any point during the six month tenor of the deal, the counterparty may go out of business and be unable to repay the currency at maturity.

Banks manage credit risk by reviewing the **creditworthiness** (ie, the likelihood of default) of each of its counterparties on a regular basis. Counterparties of high credit quality are allowed to borrow more than counterparties who are more likely to default. This is called the **credit review process**.

The Credit Review Process

Credit limits are usually administered by the head office of a banking institution. A Credit Committee, whose function is the evaluation of the creditworthiness of potential counterparties, reviews the financial status of these counterparties, on at least a yearly basis.

There is a constant tug-of-war over trading limits in nearly every institution between the trading room and the Credit Committee. The traders argue that large limits should be extended to every potential trading partner, while the Credit Committee tries to limit the size and number of credit limits in order to control risk.

Traders also argue that without sufficient limits, their ability to make money is impeded – they can miss trading opportunities. The Credit Committee operate a policy that credit limits given to the wrong names or in the wrong amounts can result in the demise of their institution. This makes credit a precious commodity in its own right – without credit limits a bank cannot trade.

Credit Committees, in addition to their own investigations, rely on agencies who provide **credit rating** opinions on the creditworthiness of institutions. This rating, along with the Credit Committee's opinion, determines the size of a limit granted to a potential counterparty. Since the credit agencies, and the banks themselves, use similar criteria to judge creditworthiness, it is not surprising that many banks have the same opinion of their dealing colleagues.

Each month, a Credit Committee reviews several countries and analyses banks that have their head office in those countries. However, credit modifications can happen at any time when conditions warrant. For example, if the Swedish Central Bank announces that Swedish banks have suffered large real estate-related losses, the conclusion could easily be reached that Swedish banks' creditworthiness is not as high as it was. The credit limits that an institution had set for these banks were calculated before the bad news hit, and will need to be modified depending on the severity of the news.

The trading room often has the discretion to restrict trading to counterparties while awaiting the assessment of the Credit Committee. At the most, the dealing room can reduce or suspend a limit. In almost all cases, the dealing room can never create or increase a limit.

How Is the Size of a Credit Limit Determined?
The size of the limit that Bank A has for Bank B depends primarily on two things:

1. Bank A's opinion of the creditworthiness of Bank B

2. The relative size of Bank A

For example, MegaBank, which is a large institution, may have a USD 500 million limit for the ABC Bank which is a highly regarded institution, while having only a USD 25 million limit for XYZ Bank which is not nearly as well rated as ABC.

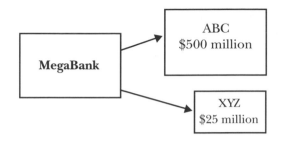

OkiBank, a much smaller institution than MegaBank, may have a limit of only USD 25 million for ABC, and USD 5 million for XYZ.

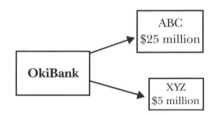

Why the disparity? MegaBank, because of its size, would be able to withstand a much bigger 'hit' than OkiBank in the event that one of its counterparties defaulted – it has a much larger capital base to offset any losses. Therefore, MegaBank's limits are larger than the smaller institution's.

After a bank establishes an overall counterparty limit, it must decide how to allocate that limit to the counterparty's branches with whom it wants to trade, and among its own trading branches.

Allocating Credit: Group and Global Limits

Credit is a scarce and valuable resource. Depending on their technological sophistication, banks have made greater or lesser efforts to optimise credit limits, and so to use their limited credit resources more efficiently. Credit use is optimised by pooling, and not by dividing it up. In order to see how a credit limit can flow from the Credit Committee to the dealer at the trading desk have a look at the following example.

Example

ABC Bank is an institution with a head office in London, and branches in Paris, Zurich, Tokyo and New York. When ABC Bank issues a limit for the XYZ Bank organisation as a whole, trades done with any of the branches of XYZ Bank worldwide would affect the XYZ counterparty limit. The Credit Committee has determined that XYZ Bank is worthy of a USD 200 million line of credit. This limit may be made available to the head office and branches in one of two ways:

- Group credit allocation

- Global credit allocation

Group Credit Allocation

The head office and each branch receive a defined percentage of the overall limit for their own individual use. Perhaps ABC Bank London receives USD 100 million of the limit, and the four other branches USD 25 million each. Each office can only use the allocated amount for their trading with XYZ Bank.

This method is used by institutions that are not linked electronically for credit purposes, and is an inefficient use of credit. As an example, the Paris branch could use up all of its allocation – USD 25 million – and see a promising trading opportunity which will not be available due to a credit restriction, while at the same time there may be a substantial limit still available at one of its sister trading floors.

Global Credit Allocation

This method, which is really not an allocation, requires an on-line credit system with all branches linked electronically to the head office, and each other. There is no dividing up of XYZ Bank's credit line between the branches of ABC Bank. The USD 200 million credit limit is used as a pool that any branch can access on a first come, first served basis. This is recognized as more efficient due to the fact that there are no wasted trading opportunities, except when the overall counterparty limit is reached.

Up to now, it may have appeared as though a single, universal, credit limit has governed counterparty exposure. In fact, there is an extensive matrix of limits that aim to manage the various types of risks arising from FX trading.

Credit Rating

The two best known credit rating agencies are those of Standard & Poor (S&P) and Moody's Investors Service (Moody's). Although both organisations use different rating systems they are directly comparable. The ratings for short and long-term instruments are shown in the tables below.

S&P	Moody's
A1+	P1
A1	
A2	P2
A3	P3

Short-term ratings

Grade	S&P	Moody's
Best quality	AAA AA+	Aaa Aa1
Highest quality	AA AA- A+	Aa2 Aa3 A1
Upper medium	A A- BBB+	A2 A3 Baa1
Medium	BBB BBB-	Baa2 Baa3

Long-term ratings

> *i* *Most top banks are rated AA+ to AA- (S&P) or Aa1 to Aa3 (Moody's). Very few institutions manage the top ratings of AAA or Aaa.*

Although the long-term table shows both rating systems ending in the B range, ratings are made down to a single C. Such low ratings are not considered suitable for institutional investment and are termed 'below investment grade'. Most **junk bonds**, otherwise known as **high-yield bonds,** in the debt market have these kind of ratings.

Borrowers pay the agencies to carry out investigations in order to rate specific issues of their **long-term** instruments as they need to attract a wide range of international investors. The agencies do not rate the issuer itself for these long-term issues. However, to retain their credibility the agencies remain fully independent.

While the rating systems are comparable, S&P and Moody's carry out their risk evaluations independently. It is quite common to see a long-term instrument with different ratings from the agencies, although it is unusual to see a difference in more than one level.

Short-term ratings usually apply to all short-term instruments from a particular issuer. This time the ratings reflect an assessment of the asset backing and liquidity of the issued instruments.

Moody's P1 is intended to cover S&P's A1+ and A1, although in practice the division between P1 and P2 is a little higher than between A1 and A2. Thus it is common to see ratings of A1/P2 and A2/P3 but not A2/P1 or A3/P2. There are no ratings below A3 or P3 as instruments rated below these are not regarded as worthy of investment.

Before rating agencies change either short- or long-term ratings they normally put the issue or issuer on **credit watch with positive/negative implications**. Events such as a takeover bid can alter gradings but some regrades are not tied to specific events.

An issuer's credit rating affects the rate of interest which has to be paid to investors on borrowings and issued instruments. The difference in the cost of money between A1/P1 and A2/P2 issuers can be as high as 2% per annum.

To distinguish between credit risk associated with particular instruments, the pricing of instruments from corporate issuers is made in terms of a margin or spread over the current yield on government instruments for the same maturity. This spread is usually expressed in basis points. For example, a 3-month US commercial paper typically trades between 25 bp and 150 bp above the 3-month Treasury Bill. The instruments are identical in every respect except in the credit rating of the issuers.

An alternative benchmark in the money markets is to price corporate debt as a spread over LIBOR, which is the banks' key reference rate for the cost of Eurocurrency funding.

For certain instruments such as commercial papers, Reuters Money 3000 allows you to select the credit rating for the relevant bid and ask prices.

Regulation

The failure of Bank Herstatt caused a major incident in the foreign exchange market, and prompted not only market participants but also regulators such as central banks to reappraise the credit risks involved in foreign exchange trading.

Bank Herstatt failed on June 25th 1974 after market risk-related foreign exchange losses later estimated at USD 400 million. It did not bring the markets to a halt but sparked a dramatic worldwide reappraisal of the credit risk element of FX deals which slowed down and reduced FX dealing for several months.

Many banks were unaware of the 100% delivery risk which applied to FX deals as the Bundesbank halted payments from Bank Herstatt in the early afternoon European time, leaving Deutschmark deals to be delivered to Herstatt that day unaffected but leaving the US dollar deliverables to counterparties in the US unpaid as the US Federal reserve froze the balances.

The short-term effect was that FX market participants decided only to deal with very high quality counterparties, whose risk of default was extremely low. Thus most banks found that the market would no longer deal with them, resulting in a dramatic fall in FX market traded volume.

In order to make it clearer to the market which banks represented an acceptable credit risk, most central banks now require FX trading banks to report their positions to the central bank on a daily basis and to satisfy the central bank that they have the necessary internal controls to accurately record and process their volume of business.

Also, the Bank for International Settlements has issued guidelines for banks for the effective management of their capital reserves. The aim of the guidelines is to ensure banks have sufficient resources to cover the risk to which they are exposed in the FX and money markets.

Summary

You have now finished the second chapter and you should have a clear understanding of the following:

- An overview of how the money markets operate, the institutions and the market players involved

- An overview of how FX operates, the institutions and the market players involved

- Risk and credit in the markets – their relationship and how they are used

- An overview of regulation in the markets

As a check on your understanding you should try the Quick Quiz questions on the next page. You may also find the section Overview useful as a revision aid.

Your notes

Quick Quiz Questions

1. Four banks are quoting these prices. From which bank/s would you borrow and to which would you lend?

   ❑ a) $6^5/_8 - 6^9/_{16}\%$
   ❑ b) $6^{11}/_{16} - 6^5/_8\%$
   ❑ c) $6^9/_{16} - 6^5/_8\%$
   ❑ d) $6^9/_{16} - 6^1/_2\%$

   Borrow from:

   Lend to:

2. Is the following statement true or false?
   Eurodollar deposits must be made in banks outside the UK.

   ❑ a) True
   ❑ b) False

3. Which of the following are accurate statements about the Bretton Woods Agreement? The agreement attempted to establish:

   ❑ a) The elimination of exchange controls
   ❑ b) Making all currencies convertible
   ❑ c) Stable exchange rates

4. Which of the following can be directly controlled by the Federal Reserve Bank?

   ❑ a) The discount rate
   ❑ b) The liquidity within the banking system
   ❑ c) The level of exchange rates against the US dollar
   ❑ d) The Fed Funds rates

5. Which type of risk is Herstatt risk?

   ❑ a) Market
   ❑ b) Settlement
   ❑ c) Replacement

6. Name five desks into which a typical dealing room may be divided.

7. By what means do financial institutions try to control risk with counterparties?

You can check your answers on page 69.

Overview

> **How do the Money Markets and Foreign Exchange work?**

Money Markets

Discount Markets
Central banks
- UK discount houses – Treasury Bills, Gilts
- US GOVPX – Treasury Bills, T-bills

Interbank markets
- **Domestic markets**
- **Euro markets**

Interbank offered rates
LIBOR

Interest rates – their global market effects
- Role of the central banks
- Other factors
  - ⇨ Credit rating
  - ⇨ Maturity period – Yield curves
  - ⇨ Amount involved

Market-makers two way prices

Bid	The price at which the market-maker **borrows** money
Offer (Ask)	The price at which the market-maker **lends** money

Users
- Central banks
- Commercial banks
- Discount houses
- Investment banks
- Local authorities
- UK building societies
- Finance houses
- Corporations
- Brokers

Foreign Exchange

FX deal
Components
- Trade date
- Counterparty
- Currencies
- Exchange rate
- Amounts
- Value date
- Payment instructions

Forward FX and the Money Markets
- **Forward outright transactions**
- **FX swaps**

> **The forward rate is not a prediction of what the future spot rate will be.**

The dealing arena
- Front office/dealing room
- Middle office
- Back office

- Spot desk
- Forwards desk
- Money markets desk
- Corporate desk

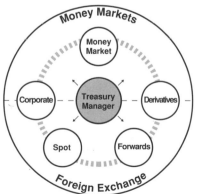

Overview

> **How do the Money Markets and Foreign Exchange work?**

Foreign Exchange

Events involved with a FX transaction

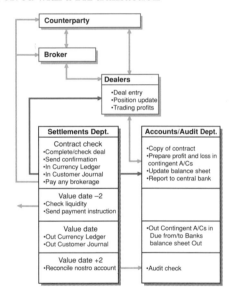

Users

- Traders: market-makers/market-takers
- Commercial and investment bank traders
- Central banks
- Corporate customers
- Brokers

Risk and Credit

Types of risk
- **Market risk**
- **Credit risk**
- **Settlement risk**

Credit rating

Short-term ratings

S&P	Moody's
A1+	P1
A1	
A2	P2
A3	P3

Long-term ratings

Grade	S&P	Moody's
Best quality	AAA AA+	Aaa Aa1
Highest quality	AA AA- A+	Aa2 Aa3 A1
Upper medium	A A- BBB+	A2 A3 Baa1
Medium	BBB BBB-	Baa2 Baa3

Regulation

Banks have to:
- Report their positions to the central bank on a daily basis
- Satisfy the central bank that they have the internal systems necessary to process their volume of business and monitor the risks involved

Quick Quiz Answers

	✔ or ✘
1. Borrow from d) – 6⁹/₁₆%	❑
Lend to b) – 6⁵/₈%	❑
2. b – False	❑
3. a, b and c	❑
	❑
	❑
4. a – This is the only thing the Fed controls directly. The others are influenced by Fed policy	❑
5. b	❑
6. Spot desk	❑
Money markets desk	❑
Forwards desk	❑
Corporate desk	❑
Derivatives	❑
7. Using exposure limits for counterparties based on credit ratings and other factors.	❑

How well did you score? You should have scored at least 10. If you didn't you may need to revise some of the materials.

Further Resources

Books

The Times Guide to International Finance
Margaret Allan, Times Books, 1991
ISBN   0 723 00408 0

The Money Machine: How the City Works
P Coggan, Penguin, 2nd Edition, 1992
ISBN   0 140 09147 5

How to Read the Financial Pages
Michael Brett, Century Business, 3rd Edition, 1991
ISBN   0 091 74889 5

The Foreign Exchange and Money Markets Guide
Julian Walmsley, John Wiley & Sons, 1992
ISBN   0 471 53104 9

How the Foreign Exchange Market Works
Rudi Weisweiller, NYIF, 1990
ISBN   0 134 00862 6

Getting Started in Futures
Todd Cofton, John Wiley & Sons, Inc.,
3rd Edition, 1997
ISBN   0 471 17759 8

Getting Started in Stocks
Alvin D. Hall, John Wiley & Sons, Inc., 3rd Edition, 1997
ISBN   0 471 17753 9

Publications
Bank of England
• Fact Sheet – The Foreign Exchange Market

Internet
RFT Website
• **http://www.wiley-rft.reuters.com**
This is the series' companion website where additional quiz questions, updated screens and other information may be found.

Your notes

What Instruments are Used in the Markets?

This section should take one and a half to two hours of study time. You may not take as long as this or it may take a little longer – remember your learning is individual to you.

Advice to Young Tradesman

Remember that Time is Money. He that can earn Ten Shillings a Day .. and .. sits idle one half of that Day .. has .. already thrown away Five shillings.

Benjamin Franklin 1748

Introduction

There is a wide variety of instruments, or products, traded in the money markets and foreign exchange market. Some are traded on exchanges, although the vast majority are traded over-the-counter (OTC).

In order to gain a full understanding of these products – and the important relationships between the various products – it is necessary to look at some of the most important instruments in more detail. We will consider money market instruments and foreign exchange instruments separately, although it is important to bear in mind that no such distinction exists in the typical dealing room.

This section is concerned with:
– An overview of instruments used in the money markets
– An overview of instruments used in the foreign exchange market.

These instruments will be covered in greater detail in later chapters.

How many money market and FX instruments do you know about already? Do you need to know about any instrument in particular? Write down any ideas you have here.

Money Market Instruments

There are two basic ways of considering the different types of instrument or paper used in the money markets. One method differentiates according to whether or not the instrument is negotiable and uses the categories:

- Money market deposits
- Negotiable paper

The second method differentiates between how the instruments generate income and uses the categories:

- Coupon bearing instruments
- Discount instruments

In addition both methods of categorisation include derivatives and are illustrated in the diagram below.

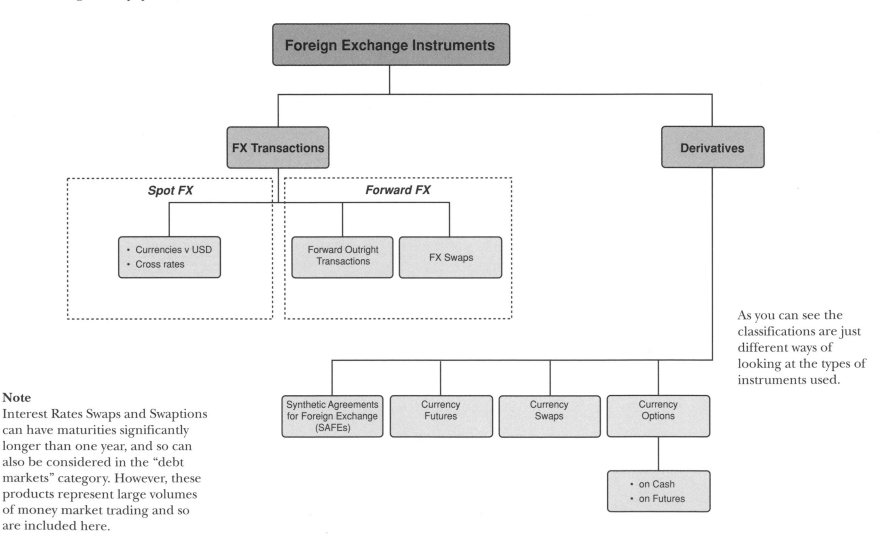

As you can see the classifications are just different ways of looking at the types of instruments used.

Note
Interest Rates Swaps and Swaptions can have maturities significantly longer than one year, and so can also be considered in the "debt markets" category. However, these products represent large volumes of money market trading and so are included here.

For convenience the second method of classification indicated in the table below will be used in this book.

Coupon Bearing
• Money Market Deposits
• Certificate of Deposit (CD)
• Repurchase Agreement (Repo)
Discount
• Treasury Bill (T-bill)
• Bill of Exchange/Banker's Acceptance (BA)
• Commercial Paper (CP)
Derivatives
• Forward Rate Agreement (FRA)
• Interest Rate Future
• Interest Rate Swap (IRS)
• Interest Rate Option

• Option on - Interest Rate Future
             - Forward Rate Agreement
             - Interest Rate Swap (Swaption)

Before moving on to consider the three categories of instruments outlined here it is necessary to consider briefly the features and characteristics of **negotiable** instruments.

Negotiable Instruments

Negotiable money market instruments can be bought and sold in the secondary market and have a number of common features:

- They are issued with a fixed 'face value' or redemption amount, also known as 'par value'

- They mature at a specified future date at which time the face value or redemption amount is repaid to the holder of the paper

- They usually pay fixed amounts of interest either during their life or at maturity; the interest rate is fixed at the time of the paper's issue

This means that income from negotiable instruments can be precisely calculated in advance because the terms of the contract are fixed. The important characteristics of these instruments can be summarised as follows:

1. Any financial instrument which gives its holder a known future income amount – a **future value** – no matter how irregular, can be priced by discounting all the future cash flows back to a **present value**.

2. Since future income amounts are fixed, the **higher** the discount rate applied to an instrument, the **lower** its present value and therefore the **lower** its market price.

> ℹ️ When **interest rates rise** the market value of money market negotiable instruments will **fall** and vice versa.

When calculating the interest due for an instrument it is important to know the **day count** convention being used. For example, most instruments issued in the US use **Actual/360 (A/360)**, whereas many UK instruments use **Actual/365 (A/365)**. You may need to confirm the day count convention being used for any particular instrument.

What Instruments are Used in the Markets?

Coupon Bearing Instruments

Coupon bearing instruments are also termed **interest bearing** because interest payments are associated with them. Originally a coupon was part of an instrument which could be detached and presented by the bearer to the issuer to collect interest payments. There are three types of coupon bearing instruments used in the Money Markets which are:

- **Money Market Deposits** – non-negotiable instruments

- **Certificate of Deposit (CD)** - negotiable instruments

- **Repurchase Agreement (Repo)** - negotiable instruments

Money Market Deposits

Interbank Deposits
There are two basic types of deposits made in the Interbank markets which are defined as follows:

A **fixed deposit** is one where the rate of interest and the maturity date are agreed at the time of the transaction.

A **notice** or **call deposit** is one where the rate of interest may be changed or the termination of the deposit requested with effect from a specified number of working days. A working day means that the Money Market financial centre involved with the trade must be open for business.

Money market dealers quote two-way rates which are quoted on a percentage per annum basis.

As London rates are very important in the deposits markets you will often see **LIBOR** and **LIBID** rates quoted by banks:

- **London Interbank Offered Rate, LIBOR** – the rate a bank **offers** funds, that is, the rate it charges for **lending** money

- **London Interbank Bid Rate, LIBID** – the rate a bank **bids** or **buys** funds, that is, the rate it pays for **taking** a deposit

Look at the LIBOR shown on the screens below.

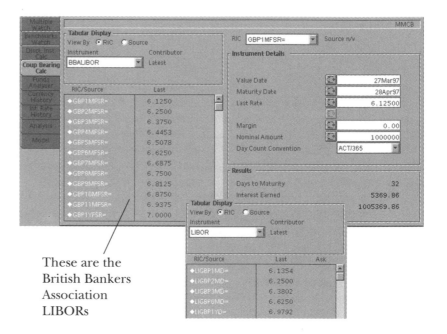

These are the British Bankers Association LIBORs

Certificates of Deposit (CDs)

A CD can be defined as follows:

> A negotiable receipt for funds deposited at a bank or other financial institution for a specified time period and at a specified interest rate.

In other words it is an IOU with a fixed coupon. Most CDs issued by banks are **negotiable instruments** and are **bearer certificates,** which means that ownership belongs to whoever possesses the certificate.

The difference between a deposit and a CD is as follows:

- A deposit has a fixed maturity and is non-negotiable

- A CD has a fixed maturity but is negotiable – it can be bought and sold

Have a look at the screens below which show prices for **USD Domestic CDs** and **GBP Clearing Bank CDs**..

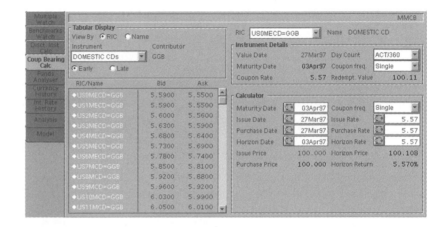

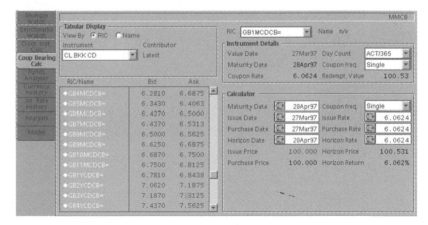

---

1 Year Certificate of Deposit USD 10,000,000 under a monthly issue of certificates of deposit programme	
Issuer	ABC Bank
Issue on a monthly basis	Certificate of Deposit
Use of proceeds	Financing consumer loans
Aggregate principal amount	USD 10,000,000
Issue price	100
Issue date	June 30, 1997
Maturity date	June 30, 1998
Interest rate	7.0% on a 365 days basis
Subscription period	From June 1, 1997 to June 30, 1997
Denomination	USD 100,000
Payments	June 30, 1998 Capital + Interest
Delivery	Physical

These details of a CD issue have been taken from a bank's Internet site.

Repos

A Repo is an instrument used by central banks to control monetary policy and used by traders as a form of financing. It can be defined as:

A Repo, or Repurchase Agreement, is an agreement between two counterparties under which one counterparty agrees to sell an instrument to the other on an agreed date for an agreed price, and simultaneously agrees to buy back the instrument from the counterparty at a later date for an agreed price

A **Reverse Repurchase Agreement – Reverse Repo –** is an agreement for the **purchase** of an instrument with the simultaneous agreement to **resell** the instrument at an agreed future date and agreed price.

The largest repo market is in the US with trading in overnight T-Bills. In this case a **repo** is where the Fed is initially buying the instruments to temporarily add more money to the banking system, while a **reverse repo** will temporarily drain cash from the system.

Look at **Treasury Repo** prices on the screen below.

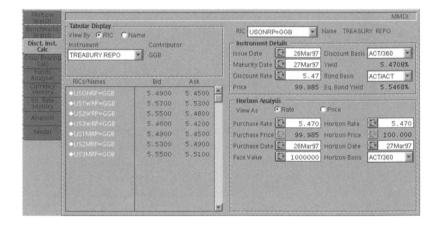

Discount Instruments

These are money markets instruments which do not explicitly pay interest. Instead the instruments are issued and traded at a discount to face value. The discount is equivalent to interest paid to the investor and the amount is the **difference** between the price of the instrument **at purchase** and that **at maturity**. There are three negotiable discount instruments commonly encountered in the money markets:

- **Treasury Bill (T-bill)**

- **Bill of Exchange/Banker's Acceptance (BA)**

- **Commercial Paper (CP)**

Discount instruments are quoted on the basis of a discount from **par** – the full value of the instrument at maturity. This is a matter of tradition dating back to when Bills of Exchange were first traded. The comparable maturities of these instruments makes them suitable for straddling positions across two or more markets. The US is the largest market for discount instruments.

Treasury Bill (T-bill)
A T-Bill can be defined as follows:

> A short-term negotiable Bill of Exchange issued by a government to help finance national borrowing requirements.

In the US the Fed typically auctions 13 and 26-week T-bills on behalf of the US Government every Monday for delivery on Thursday. The Fed also auctions 52-week T-bills every month.

In the UK, T-bills – typically 91 and 182-day bills – are also issued by auction. The main holders of these T-bills are the discount houses which act as intermediaries between the Bank of England and the commercial banks.

A UK Treasury Bill issued by the Bank of England

Look at some prices and yields for 3-month T-bills on the screens below.

```
GovPX INDEX                                                   GPXINDEX
GovPX is a specialist data service which offers the best bid and offer prices
from 4 of the 5 interdealer brokers in the U.S. Government Bond market.
                    U.S. TREASURY AND MONEY MARKETS
   CONTENT          PAGES        LOGICAL QUOTE     SECTOR CHAIN      VOLUME
3 Month Bill      <GVSQ>-S       <US3MT=PX>      <O#US3MT=PX>    <.TVTB=PX>
6 Month Bill      <GVSQ>-S       <US6MT=PX>      <O#US6MT=PX>    <.TVTB=PX>
1 Year Bill       <GVSQ>-S       <US1YT=PX>      <O#US1YT=PX>    <.TVTB=PX>
2 Year Note       <GVST>-X       <US2YT=PX>      <O#US2YT=PX>    <.TV2Y=PX>
```

```
O#US3MT=PX        USD    GovPX-UST     3M
   Issue/Issuer   Coupon Maturity       L a t e s t      Yield:  MAT   Time  Date
UST 27MAR97              27MAR97  IB   5.385  IA   5.365                23:06 26MAR
UST 03APR97              03APR97  IB   5.2475 IA   5.2275 5.323  5.302 09:11 27MAR
UST 10APR97              10APR97  IB   5.0725 IA   5.0525 5.150  5.130 09:11 27MAR
UST 22APR97              22APR97  IB   5.3925 IA   5.3725 5.483  5.463 09:12 27MAR
UST 17APR97              17APR97  IB   5.2625 IA   5.2425 5.349  5.329 09:11 27MAR
UST 24APR97              24APR97  IB   5.0975 IA   5.0775 5.186  5.166 09:11 27MAR
UST 01MAY97              01MAY97  IB   5.180  IA   5.160  5.275  5.255 09:11 27MAR
UST 08MAY97              08MAY97  IB   5.2325 IA   5.2125 5.335  5.314 09:11 27MAR
UST 15MAY97              15MAY97  IB   5.2475 IA   5.2275 5.356  5.335 08:48 26MAR
UST 22MAY97              22MAY97  IB   5.195  IA   5.175  5.307  5.286 09:11 27MAR
UST 29MAY97              29MAY97  IB   5.1925 IA   5.1725 5.310  5.289 09:46 27MAR
UST 05JUN97              05JUN97  IB   5.1875 IA   5.1675 5.310  5.289 09:11 27MAR
UST 12JUN97              12JUN97  IB   5.200  IA   5.180  5.328  5.308 09:11 27MAR
UST 19JUN97              19JUN97  IB   5.215  IA   5.195  5.349  5.329 09:11 27MAR
UST 26JUN97              26JUN97  IB   5.1875 IA   5.1675 5.326  5.306 09:11 27MAR
UST 3M WI                03JUL97  IB   5.215  IA   5.195  5.358  5.337 09:12 27MAR
```

Bill of Exchange/Banker's Acceptance (BA)

These instruments have been used in financing international trade for hundreds of years. A bill of exchange in the UK is essentially the same as a BA in the US.

A commercial **Bill of Exchange,** or **Trade Bill,** is an order to pay a specified amount of money to the holder either at a specified future date – **Time Draft** – or on presentation – **Sight Draft**. It is a short-term IOU in support of a commercial transaction.

A **Banker's Acceptance,** or **Banker's Bill,** is a Bill of Exchange drawn or accepted by a commercial bank. Once accepted the instrument becomes negotiable.

The Bank of England and Fed both buy and sell BAs which have been accepted by banks subject to reserve requirements. These banks are known as eligible banks giving rise to the BAs they issue being termed **eligible bills**.

This is an example of a Bill of Exchange from 1739 when the exchange rate was £1 for 35 schellings and one grot Flemish

This screen shows the **Benchmarks Watch** page for USD Domestic BA prices which are compared directly with the Treasury benchmark instrument prices.

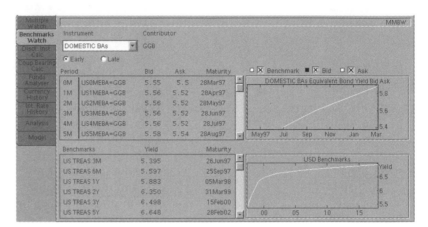

Commercial Paper (CP)

A CP can be defined as follows:

> A short-term unsecured, promissory note issued for a specified amount and maturing on a specified date. It is a negotiable instrument typically issued in bearer form.

CPs tend to have a maximum maturity of 270 days and are issued by large organisations as an alternative to bank loans and bills of exchange etc. As a CP is unsecured, no assets are pledged by the issuer in the event that the CP cannot be paid on maturity. This means an investor has only the issuer's standing on which to base an investment decision. Hence only large organisations with good credit ratings can issue and sell CPs.

XYZ Group

Press Release

XYZ Group today announces its intention to set up a multi-currency Euro-Commercial Paper programme, to be arranged by NatWest Markets. The programme size will be £500 million.

The programme is rated A-1 by Standard and Poor's and P-1 by Moody's.

Dealers for the programme will be:

- NatWest Markets
- UBS Ltd
- Citibank International plc
- Barclays de Zoete Wedd Securities Ltd

The programme will be used for general corporate purposes.

This is a Press Release for Euro-CPs for a corporation as it appeared on the Internet.

Have a look at the **CP** prices shown on the screens below.

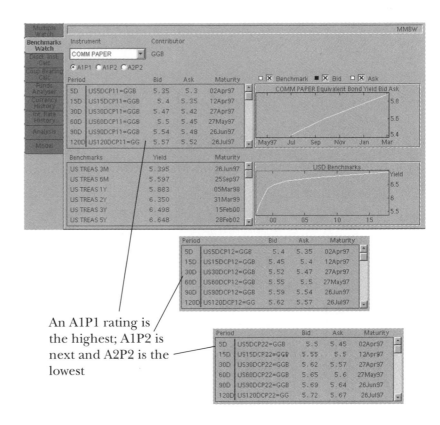

An A1P1 rating is the highest; A1P2 is next and A2P2 is the lowest

Derivatives

The following descriptions of the derivative instruments used in the money markets are brief – if you need to know more about trading conventions and techniques used for derivatives, then you may find *An Introduction to Derivatives* ISBN 0-471-83176-X useful.

Within the money markets the following derivatives are commonly encountered which are all concerned with **interest rates**:

- **Forward Rate Agreements (FRAs)**

- **Interest Rate Futures**

- **Interest Rate Swaps (IRSs)**

- **Interest Rate Options on**
    - **Interest Rate Futures**
    - **FRAs – Interest Rate Guarantees (IRGs)**
    - **IRSs – Swaptions**

Forward Rate Agreements (FRAs)

These are one of the most widely used of the OTC money market derivatives. An FRA can be defined as follows:

A contract between two parties which fixes the rate of interest that will apply to a **notional** future loan or deposit for which the following have been **agreed**:
- The amount and its currency
- A future date for the loan/deposit to be drawn/placed
- The maturity

Both parties agree a rate at which they will deal, then settle the difference between that rate and a settlement rate on the start date of the period in question. There is no exchange of principal involved nor any commitment to borrow or lend the underlying funds. FRAs are quoted using two figures as illustrated in the following examples:

1 x 4   This FRA commences 1 month forward and lasts 3 months.

3 x 6   This starts 3 months forward and lasts 3 months.

Typical FRA prices can be seen on the screen below, which shows prices for USD, DEM and GBP 3-month FRAs.

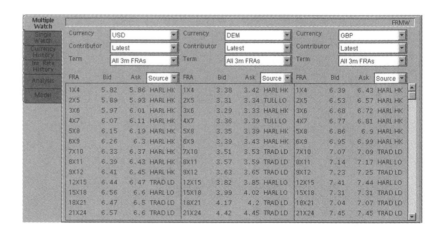

Interest Rate Futures

Interest rate futures contracts are based on financial instruments whose prices are dependent on rates such as 3-month time deposits. Interest rate futures contracts can be defined as follows:

These are forward transactions with standard contract sizes and maturity dates which are traded on a formal exchange.

Short-term interest rate futures contracts are almost exclusively based on Eurocurrency deposits and are cash settled based on an Exchange Delivery Settlement Price (EDSP) or the last price traded.

Long-term interest rate futures contracts are settled based on government bonds or notes with a coupon and maturity period specified by the exchange.

Exchanges such as LIFFE offer 3-month future contracts on Sterling deposits and the Chicago Mercantile Exchange offers interest rate futures on 3-month Eurodollar time deposits, one month LIBOR and 3-month T-bills.

The screen below shows LIFFE interest rate futures on Short Sterling and Long Gilts.

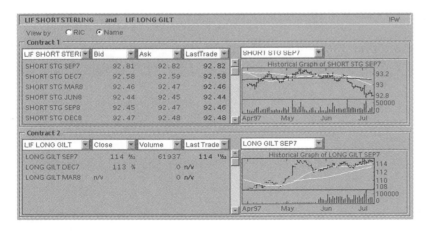

Interest Rate Swap (IRS)

An IRS is an OTC derivative in which two parties swap interest rate payments on loans for the same notional amount but with different interest bases. An IRS usually involves a long maturity and performs a similar role to a forward rate agreement but for a longer period, that is, 2 – 10 years for the major currencies. In essence an IRS is a series of FRAs.

An **Interest Rate Swap** is an agreement between counterparties in which each party agrees to make a series of payments to the other on agreed future dates until maturity of the agreement. Each party's interest payments are calculated using different formulas by applying the agreement terms to the **notional principal** amount of the swap.

A typical trade would involve one party swapping interest payments on an instrument on which interest is paid at a **fixed** rate, for example a bond with a coupon, for interest payments on a **floating** basis. A floating rate is one where the interest due varies with the market and is usually linked to a specific indicator such as LIBOR.

Swaps prices are displayed on the screen shown here.

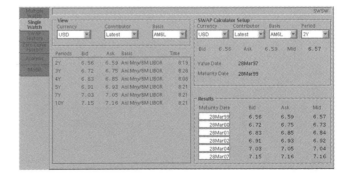

What Instruments are Used in the Markets?

Interest Rate Options

In general an options contract may be defined as follows:

> A call (put) option contract is an agreement between two counterparties giving the holder the right, but not the obligation, to buy (sell) a financial instrument at a specified price (the strike price) on or before a specified date in the future (the maturity).

There are two basic types of options contract available:

Call option	This is the right, but not obligation, to **buy** an underlying instrument in the future.
Put option	This is the right, but not obligation, to **sell** an underlying instrument in the future.

Options on Interest Rate Futures

The simplest types of options contracts are borrower's and lender's options where the underlying instrument is a **loan** or **deposit**. The strike price of the option is the interest rate on the loan or deposit. In the money markets the underlying financial instruments for most options contracts involve T-bills and short-term Eurocurrency interest rates.

Options on FRAs – Interest Rate Guarantees (IRGs)

These are also known as **caps** and **floors** and are interest rate options actively traded on the OTC markets.

Each cap and floor can be imagined as a series of calls and puts on FRAs.

Caps

Caps set a **maximum** payable interest rate and act as a series of **call options** which coincide with the roll-over dates on a loan. Another way of viewing them is as 'lids' on the rates of a series of FRA transactions.

Floors

These are the opposite of caps. They provide a holder with a guaranteed **minimum** interest rate receivable.

Options on Interest Rate Swaps — Swaptions

The buyer of a swaption has the right, but not the obligation, to enter into a swap at an agreed fixed rate of interest on or before a future date. For example, a swaption might involve an option to swap from a floating to a fixed rate at a particular swap rate – the strike rate.

As with any option the buyer pays the seller a premium. Swaptions are available in most major currencies with expiry dates up to 10 years. The most common option period is between 1 month and 2 years.

A typical screen is shown here for an option on LIFFE Short Sterling Interest Rate futures.

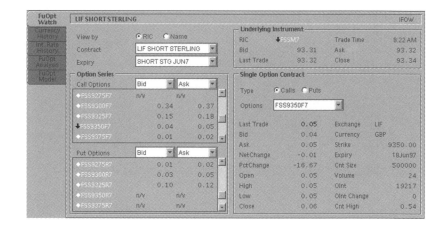

Foreign Exchange Instruments

The FX markets exist to exchange one currency for another and there are three broad categories of instruments and transactions involved. These categories are:

- FX transactions
- Derivatives

Although some of the instruments illustrated in the diagram below are not strictly 'instruments', the categories have been used to help you understand the nature and operation of the FX markets. FX transactions have also been separated to help your understanding as follows:

- Spot FX transactions
- Forward FX transactions

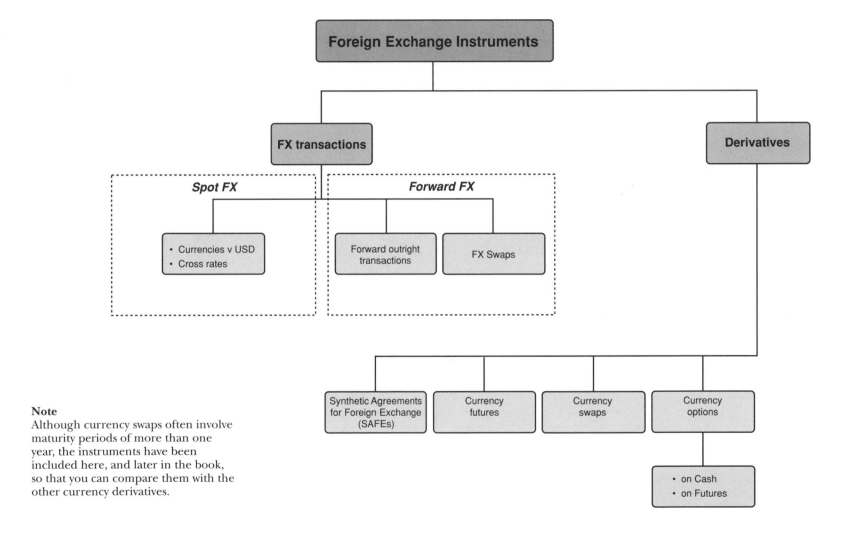

Note

Although currency swaps often involve maturity periods of more than one year, the instruments have been included here, and later in the book, so that you can compare them with the other currency derivatives.

What Instruments are Used in the Markets?

For convenience the categories indicated in the table below will be used in this workbook.

FX transactions

• Spot transactions
    • Currencies versus USD
    • Cross rates
 	
• Forward outright transactions
 	
• FX swaps

Derivatives

• Synthetic Agreements for Foreign Exchange (SAFEs)
 	
• Currency futures
 	
• Currency swaps
 	
• Currency options
    • on Cash
    • on Futures

FX Transactions

As was mentioned earlier FX is the largest market in the world today with a daily global turnover estimated at $1,490 billion in April 1998. Involved with this turnover are three basic types of transaction – spot, Forward outright and FX Swaps.

Type	Description
Spot	An exchange of currencies in which delivery or settlement usually occurs 2 business days – the **value date** – after the trade date.
Forward outright	An exchange rate is agreed to buy/sell currencies at a **future date**. By buying/selling in the forward markets, investors can protect themselves against exchange rate volatility.
FX Swaps	These are concerned with the combination of a spot deal with a simultaneous forward deal.

Both forward outright transactions and FX swaps form the **forward FX markets** as they involve future dates for the currency exchange. Up until 1995 spot transactions accounted for 43% of the daily turnover but by 1998 Forwards and FX swaps had become increasingly important and accounted for over 60% of total turnover.

Most FX deals involve the USD but what happens if you require an exchange rate for two currencies not involving the USD, for example a DEM/CHF rate? In this case a **cross rate** is calculated which involves theoretically first buying USD with DEM and then selling the USD for CHF or vice versa: DEM ⇄ USD ⇄ CHF.

The types of FX transaction which are briefly described here cover:

- **Spot transactions**
    - **Currencies versus USD**
    - **Cross rates**
- **Forward outright transactions**
- **FX Swaps**

The spot FX rates for 3 different currencies against the USD are shown on the screens below.

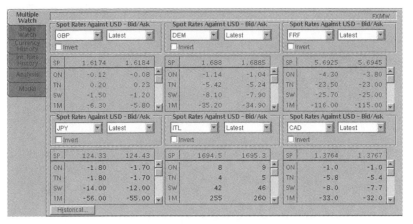

This shows snap shot prices for all the major currencies against the USD

Spot Transactions

Currencies versus USD

Spot traders usually specialise in a specific currency pair such as USD/DEM, GBP/USD etc. Originally most FX deals were done 'on the spot'. This meant that delivery would take place in **two business days** which was the quickest time that banks could 'settle' the deal giving both parties time to organise settlement details, coping with time differences etc. Although technology has improved the speed with which transactions can take place, the majority of spot deals are still for delivery two business days after the trade date which is known as the **value date**.

Example
A trade done on a Monday will show a value date on Wednesday.

Trade date	Mon	Tue	Wed	Thurs	Fri
Value date	Wed	Thurs	Fri	Mon	Tue

If a holiday falls in the country of one or both of the currencies involved in the trade, then the spot value date will move back one day – in this case to Thursday.

Spot quotations are **bid (buy)** and **offer or ask (sell)** rates at which a market-maker will **buy and sell** the base currency against another currency.

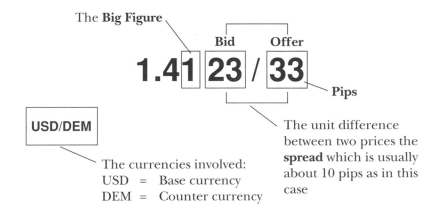

The **Big Figure**

Bid   Offer

1.41 **23** / **33**

Pips

USD/DEM

The currencies involved:
USD = Base currency
DEM = Counter currency

The unit difference between two prices the **spread** which is usually about 10 pips as in this case

What Instruments are Used in the Markets?

The table below explains these Spot FX terms used commonly in the market in a little more detail.

The Big Figure	This part of the price is not quoted by dealers. The Big Figure is only mentioned when it is necessary to confirm the trade or in extremely volatile markets. In the example on the previous page the Big Figure is 1, although traders may also say the Big Figure is 41, or 1.41. In the US this figure is also known as **The Handle**.
Pips	The smallest increment a price moves. Spot traders quote the last two digits of the price. Pips are also known as **points**.
The Spread	This is the variable unit difference between the Bid and Offer prices – in this case 10 pips.
Bid	This is the price at which the market-maker is prepared to buy the base currency. In the example on the previous page the market-maker will buy $1 for DEM 1.4123. The market-maker **buys** dollars; **sells** marks.
Offer	This is the price at which the market-maker is prepared to sell the base currency. In the example on the previous page the market-maker will sell $1 for DEM 1.4133 . The market-maker **sells** dollars; **buys** marks.

The table here summarises the Bid and Offer arrangements using an example for USD/DEM which is known as **Dollar-mark**:

Quote: USD/DEM	Market-maker intends to	Market-taker can
Bid	Buy USD Sell DEM	Sell USD Buy DEM
Offer	Sell USD Buy DEM	Buy USD Sell DEM

The market-maker intends buying low and selling high.

Direct and indirect currency rates are quoted using the usual letter combinations but some of the currency pairs have their own terms –

GBP/USD is known as a **Cable**
USD/CHF is known as a **Dollar-Swissy**
USD/DEM is known as **Dollar-mark**
USD/FRF is known as **Dollar-Paris**

REUTERS

Cross Rates

In practice a cross rate is the exchange rate between two currencies not involving the US dollar. Although many cross rates are quoted in the financial press such as the *Financial Times*, it is still useful to know how a cross rate is calculated.

Although the dollar rates do not appear in the final cross rate they are usually used in the calculation and so must be known.

Suppose you are in France on your way to Canada and need to convert French francs into Canadian dollars. You need to use the exchange rate for CAD/FRF. In theory you would need to do two things:

1. **Buy** USD with your FRF at the market-maker's **offer** price – the price the bank sells you dollars for francs.

2. **Buy** CAD with your USD at the market-maker's **bid** price – the price the bank buys dollars for Canadian dollars.

The result is:

	You buy	You sell
1.	~~USD~~	FRF
2.	CAD	~~USD~~
=	CAD	FRF

This screen section shows cross rates for DEM against FRF, GBP and CHF.

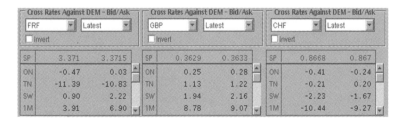

For **direct** or **dollar rates**, bid and ask cross rates for currency pairs may be calculated using the chart below, where for currencies 1 and 2 the bid and ask rates are B1 and A1, B2 and A2 respectively.

Currency pairs	Bid	Ask
USD/Currency 1	B1	A1
USD/Currency 2	B2	A2

Cross rates	Bid	Ask
Currency 1/Currency 2	$\dfrac{B2}{A1}$	$\dfrac{A2}{B1}$
Currency 2/Currency 1	$\dfrac{B1}{A2}$	$\dfrac{A1}{B2}$

If an **indirect** and a direct exchange rate are involved in the calculation of a cross rate then the bid and ask rates are simply **multiplied** to obtain the appropriate rates.

Currency pairs	Bid	Ask
Currency 1/USD	B1	A1
USD/Currency 2	B2	A2

Cross rates	Bid	Ask
Currency 1/Currency 2	B1 x B2	A1 x A2

Forward Outright Transactions

A forward outright foreign exchange transaction is a non-negotiable, OTC deal which can be defined as follows:

 A forward outright FX transaction is an FX deal between two counterparties in which one currency is bought in exchange for another at a rate which is agreed today, for delivery at an agreed future date.

Forward outright transactions usually take place between a bank and a corporate customer and no funds are exchanged until the delivery date.

The forward rate is usually different from the spot rate and is determined by the **interest rate differentials** between the two currencies. Forward prices are **not a prediction of what the future spot rate will be**.

Prices are quoted in **forward points** for maturities of 1, 2, 3, 6 and 12 months. If customers want a different maturity then a bank will quote for any maturity date – this is called a **broken date** rate.

In order to obtain the forward rate from the actual exchange rate you must **add or subtract** the forward points from the spot quote. But how do you know whether to add or subtract?

Whether to add or subtract the forward points is indicated in the table and diagram below.

Forward points	Base currency trading	Forward rate =
Greater value first **High/Low**	at a **discount**	Spot **minus** forward points
Smaller value first **Low/High**	at a **premium**	Spot **plus** forward points

The following may help to remember what to do:

points **D**escend – **D**educt points

points **A**scend – **A**dd points

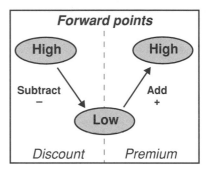

To summarise, forward outrights are transactions involving:

- **Non-negotiable, OTC trades**

- **A rate agreed today for exchange of funds in the future**

- **No exchange of funds at the spot value date**

- **Quotations in forward points**

- **Forward rates which are calculated from spot and forward points**

- **Forward points are calculated from the interest rate differential between the currencies — they are not a prediction of where the spot rate will be**

FX Swaps

Most forward FX transactions are of this type and they are traded mostly interbank, OTC. An FX swap can be defined as follows:

> An FX deal which involves the simultaneous purchase and sale of a specified amount of one currency in exchange for another for two different value dates.

The dealer arranges the swap as a **single** transaction with a **single** counterparty. The FX swap has two value dates, or **legs**, when exchange of funds occur.

Three types of swap are commonly used.

- **Spot against forward**
  In this case the first exchange – **first leg** – takes place on the spot date, two business days following the transaction, and the reverse of that exchange – **second leg** – takes place on the forward date, for example, 3 months from the spot date.

- **Forward against forward**
  In this case the first exchange – **first leg** – takes place on the forward date and the transaction is reversed – **second leg** – on a later forward date, known as the **forward forward date**. For example, a forward against forward swap may begin in 3 months time from spot – first leg – and end in 6 months time from spot – second leg. This is know as a **3 x 6 forward/forward swap**.

- **Short dates**
  These are swaps which run for less than a month. For example, the first leg could be spot, and the second leg 7 days later (1 week). Some short dates are even earlier than spot value, for example, the first leg could be today, and the second leg tomorrow.

To summarise, FX swaps are transactions involving:

- **A single OTC transaction involving two value dates**

- **Two legs to the trade – the second leg is the reverse of the first leg**

- **Two exchanges of funds – one at each leg**

- **Value dates one day to 12 months**

- **Base currency amounts usually identical on both legs**

- **Quotations in forward points**

With USD as the selected currency, the screen below shows GBP, ITL and DEM forward points.

Forward points are used for forward outright transactions and FX swaps

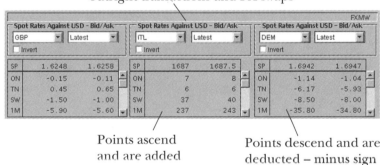

Points ascend and are added

Points descend and are deducted – minus sign

Derivatives

The following descriptions of FX derivative instruments are brief, as the principles involved are similar to those covered in the previous section. If further details are required, it is suggested that readers refer to more detailed sources as listed on page 98.

Within Foreign Exchange the following derivatives are commonly encountered which are all concerned with **forward FX**:

- **Synthetic Agreements for Foreign Exchange, SAFEs**

- **Currency futures**

- **Currency swaps**

- **Currency options**
    - **on Cash**
    - **on Futures**

Synthetic Agreements for Foreign Exchange (SAFEs)

SAFEs are the collective name for Foreign Exchange Agreements (FXAs) and Exchange Rate Agreements (ERAs) which are both used to lock-in forward FX differentials. There is no exchange of the underlying amounts.

FXA   This is where settlement is based on the difference between the forward rate on the start date of the contract and spot rate at settlement.

ERA   In this case settlement is based on two forward rates and not on a forward and spot rate.

SAFEs are in effect OTC derivatives which perform the same role for forward FX as FRAs do for short-term interest rates, that is guarantee exchange rates for a fixed period commencing in the future.

Currency Futures

Currency futures contracts are agreements on the rate of exchange between two currencies for a fixed date in the future. The contract allows market participants to manage risk by buying or selling a futures contract in the opposite direction to an existing commitment in a cash market. This means that any profit/loss in cash transactions is offset by profit/loss in the futures market. Currency futures contracts can be defined as follows:

These are forward transactions with standard contract sizes and maturity dates which are traded on a formal exchange.

The contract is a binding obligation to buy or sell one currency against another at an agreed rate of exchange for a future delivery date.

Currency futures are traded on exchanges such as the Chicago Mercantile Exchange (CME), Singapore International Monetary Exchange (SIMEX), and Marché à Terme International de France (MATIF).

The screens below show futures contracts on the JPY and USD for a variety of contracts on different exchanges.

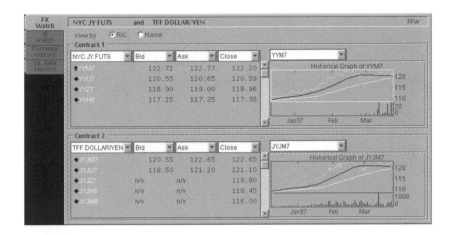

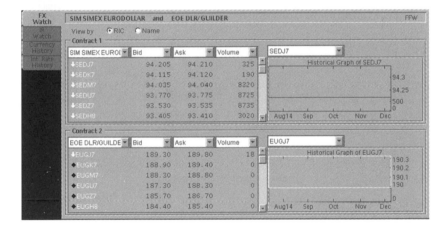

Currency Swaps

A currency swap is an OTC agreement between two parties to swap interest rate payments on foreign currency loans. The swap allows both parties to offset the effects of FX movements or changes in financing costs in the required foreign currency. A currency swap can be defined as follows:

An agreement between counterparties in which one party makes interest payments in one currency and the other party makes interest payments in a different currency on agreed future dates until maturity of the agreement.

Currency swaps are important derivatives in the capital markets. In principle they are very similar to interest rate swaps but involve two different currencies.

The screen here shows the swap interest rates for GBP, USD and DEM.

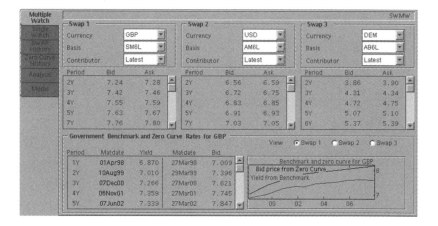

Currency Options

The principle of currency options is exactly the same as for interest rate options described previously.

 A currency options contract is an agreement giving the holder the right, but not the obligation, to buy or sell a specified amount of currency at an agreed price and at a time in the future.

The rights and obligations of options are summarised in the table below.

Who?	Call	Put
Buyer or Holder	Right to buy	Right to sell
Seller or Writer	Obligation to sell if the buyer or holder decides to buy	Obligation to buy if the buyer or holder decides to sell

There are also two further ways in which options can be defined:

American options give the buyer the right, but not the obligation, to buy or sell a fixed quantity of an underlying instrument on or before the expiry date at a fixed price.

European options confer much the same rights and obligations as the above but the option cannot be exercised before the expiry date – only on that date.

Currency options are available on cash and currency futures contracts and are traded OTC and on exchanges such as the Philadelphia Stock Exchange, CME and MATIF using an open outcry system or an automated matching system.

Currency option premiums are influenced by the FX forward prices and the volatility of the exchange rates. A currency option can be considered an insurance policy against adverse foreign exchange rate movements.

The turnover in the OTC currency options markets was some $87 billion per day in April 1998. This market is dominated by a small number of large banks and investment houses running global books who use in-house or third party computer software to manage their FX option risk positions.

Currency options prices for options on cash and options on futures contracts for DEM are shown on the screens below.

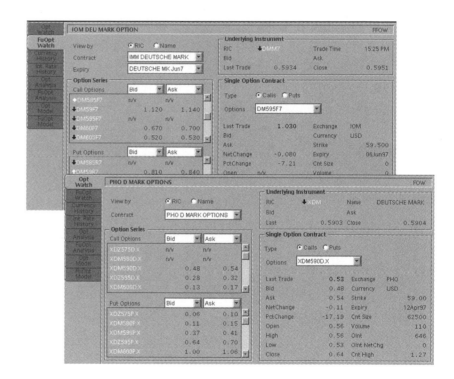

Summary

Your notes

You have now finished this chapter and you should have a clear understanding of the following:

- The instruments used in the money markets

- The instruments used in foreign exchange

If you need to know more about each instrument then you will find more details of what they are, who uses them and how they are used in the later chapters.

As a check on your understanding you should try the Quick Quiz Questions on the next page. You may also find the section Overview useful as a revision aid.

Quick Quiz Questions

1. Which of the following could be considered to be a money market instrument?

   ❑ a) A 3-year Eurobond issued by IBM
   ❑ b) A US Treasury Bill
   ❑ c) A six month Commercial Paper issued by IBM
   ❑ d) A 10-year German Government bond

2. Which of the following is the usually agreed value date for spot FX transactions?

   ❑ a) Seven business days following the trade date
   ❑ b) Five business days following the trade date
   ❑ c) Two business days following the trade date

3. XYZ Bank is quoting the following spot rates against the USD:

DEM	1.6100/10	GBP	1.5280/90
CHF	1.4020/30	JPY	104.40/50

   a) A customer wishes to buy DEM. What is the rate and is this XYZ's bid or offer rate?

   b) What is the spread on the Swiss Franc?

   c) At what rate would XYZ Bank buy GBP?

   d) What rate does XYZ Bank pay to buy Yen 5 million?

4. Which of the following statements about forward rates is/are true?

   ❑ a) Dealers use forward rates to estimate the likely future direction of exchange rates
   ❑ b) A six month forward rate can be known as an outright forward
   ❑ c) Forward rates are frequently quoted out to 10 years
   ❑ d) The USD/CHF forward rate reflects the interest rate differential between Euro Swiss Francs and the Euro USD

5. Which of the following statements match with the financial instruments?

   ❑ a) The purchase of instruments with the simultaneous agreement to sell them at a later date
   ❑ b) The sale of instruments with the simultaneous agreement to buy them back at a later date
   ❑ c) A deposit of US dollars in banks outside the US
   ❑ d) Short-term obligations of the US Government

1. Treasury bill	2. Repo
3. Reverse repo	4. Eurodollar deposit

a) =	b) =	c) =	d) =

6. How are T-bills quoted?

   ❑ a) At a discount
   ❑ b) As a coupon bearing instrument

You can check your answers on page 100.

Overview

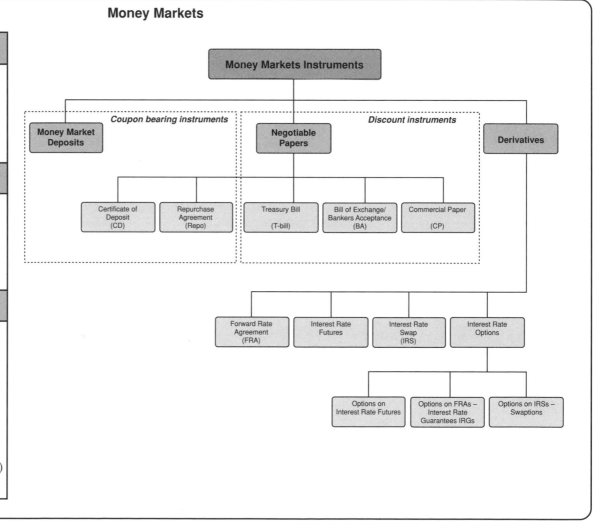

What Instruments are Used in the Markets?

Money Markets

Coupon bearing
❑ Money Market Deposits
❑ Certificate of Deposit (CD)
❑ Repurchase Agreement (Repo)

Discount
❑ Treasury Bill (T-bill)
❑ Bill of Exchange/Banker's Acceptance (BA)
❑ Commercial Paper (CP)

Derivatives
❑ Forward Rate Agreement (FRA)
❑ Interest Rate Futures
❑ Interest Rate Swap (IRS)
❑ Interest Rate Options on • Interest Rate Futures • FRAs – Interest Rate Guarantees (IRGs) • IRSs – Swaptions

Overview

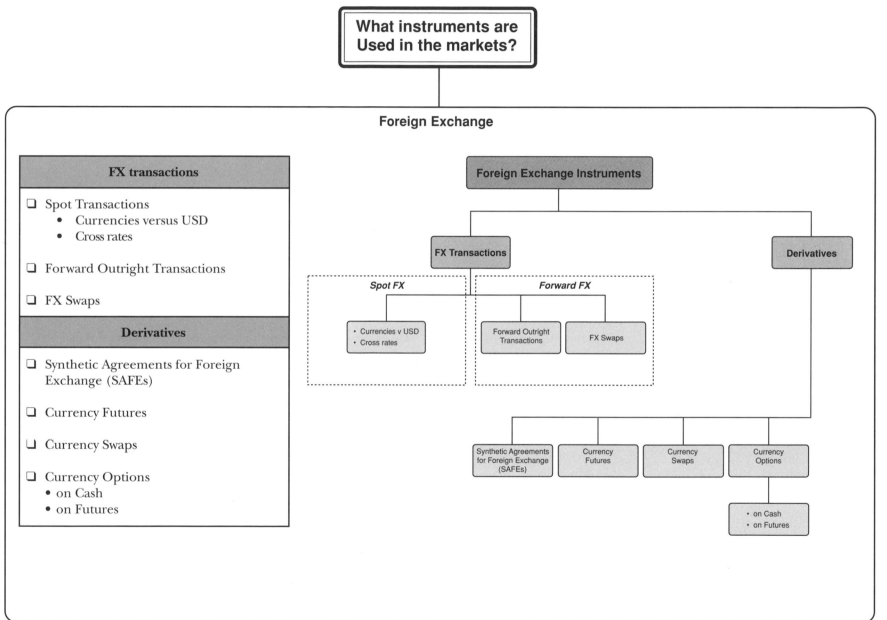

What instruments are Used in the markets?

Foreign Exchange

FX transactions

❏ Spot Transactions
  - Currencies versus USD
  - Cross rates

❏ Forward Outright Transactions

❏ FX Swaps

Derivatives

❏ Synthetic Agreements for Foreign Exchange (SAFEs)

❏ Currency Futures

❏ Currency Swaps

❏ Currency Options
  - on Cash
  - on Futures

Foreign Exchange Instruments

FX Transactions — **Derivatives**

Spot FX
- Currencies v USD
- Cross rates

Forward FX
- Forward Outright Transactions
- FX Swaps

- Synthetic Agreements for Foreign Exchange (SAFEs)
- Currency Futures
- Currency Swaps
- Currency Options
  - on Cash
  - on Futures

Quick Quiz Answers

	✔ or ✘
1. b and c	❏
	❏
2. c	❏
3. a – 1.6100. The bank's bid for buying USD against DEM	❏
b – Spread is 10 pips	❏
c – 1.5280	❏
d – JPY 104.50 – the bank is buying JPY and selling USD on the offer	❏
4. b and d	❏
	❏
5. a = 3	❏
b = 2	❏
c = 4	❏
d = 1	❏
6. a	❏

How well did you score? You should have scored at least 10. If you didn't you may need to revise some of the materials.

Further Resources

Books

Derivatives Handbook: Risk Management and Control
Robert J. Schwartz and Clifford W. Smith (ed.),
John Wiley & Sons, Inc., 1997
ISBN   0 471 15765 1

Options, Futures and Exotic Derivatives
Eric Briys, John Wiley & Sons, Inc., 1998
ISBN   0 471 96909 5

Derivatives: The Wild Beast of Finance
Alfred Steinherr and Folkerts-Landau, John Wiley & Sons, Inc., 1998
ISBN   0 471 96544 8

Credit Derivatives: Trading & Management of Credit & Default Risk
Satyajit Das (ed.), John Wiley & Sons, Inc., 1998
ISBN   0 471 24856 8

Derivatives: The Theory and Practice of Financial Engineering
Paul Wilmott, John Wiley & Sons, Inc., 1998
ISBN   0 471 98389 6

Derivatives Demystified: Using Structured Financial Products
John C. Braddock, John Wiley & Sons, Inc., 1998
ISBN   0 471 14633 1

Merton Miller on Derivatives
Merton H. Miller, John Wiley & Sons, Inc., 1998
ISBN   0 471 18340 7

The Penguin International Dictionary of Finance
Graham Bannock & William Manser, Penguin, 2nd Edition, 1995
ISBN   0 140 51279 9

Trading in Futures
Ed. TH Stewart, Woodhead-Faulkner, 5th Edition, 1989
ISBN   0 859 41548 1

All About Futures
Thomas McCafferty and Russell Wasendorf, Probus, 1992
ISBN   0 557 38296 4

Further Resources (continued)

Booklets

Chicago Mercantile Exchange
- An Introduction to Futures and Options: Interest Rates
- An Introduction to Futures and Options: Currency

Swiss Bank Corporation
- Financial Futures and Options
- Options: The fundamentals
  ISBN   0 964 11120 9
- Introduction to Foreign Exchange Options

Chicago Board of Trade
- Financial Instruments Guide
- An Introduction to Options on Financial Futures
- Trading in Futures

London International Financial Futures and Options Exchange
- An Introduction
- Options: a Guide to Trading Strategies

If you have access to the Internet, then you may find these websites useful.

Internet Websites

RFT Website
- **http://www.wiley-rft.reuters.com**

This is the series' companion website where additional quiz questions, updated screens and other information may be found.

What Instruments are Used in the Markets?

Your notes

REUTERS

This section should take about two hours of study time. You may not take as long as this or it may take a little longer – remember your learning is individual to you.

Electronic Trading

The use of automated brokerage (electronic order matching) has grown rapidly from virtually nothing in 1992. Almost half the volume of brokered spot transactions and 13% of total market volume was conducted through automated brokerage systems.

Federal Reserve Bank of New York, Central Bank Survey of FX Market Activity, April 1995

Introduction

By now you should have some understanding of why the markets exist, how the markets operate and what instruments are traded. You should also be clear on who the market participants are and in particular on the roles of dealers, traders, and brokers. **Traders** are the market players who buy and sell in the financial markets. **Brokers** act as intermediaries between traders and do not usually deal on their own account but earn commissions on the deals that they arrange. This section is concerned with how trading takes place in the markets, specifically.

- Over-the-counter (OTC)

- Using electronic trading systems

- On an exchange floor

Brokers and traders both need financial data such as market and international news, bid/offer quotes, analysis services etc which are provided by information vendors such as Reuters, Bloomberg and Bridge Information Systems. However, in many cases it is brokers who create an interest in financial instruments in order to get their clients to buy or sell.

The use of automated electronic trading systems is becoming increasingly more important in these markets in which trading takes place 24 hours per day.

The various needs of traders in the money markets and FX are summarised in the chart opposite.

Money Markets	Foreign Exchange
Money market traders work in banks and corporate treasury departments buying and selling currencies and trading short-term debt instruments of maturity O/N to 1 year. Trading is 24 hours per day and is either OTC or using automated electronic systems.	FX traders work in the same environment and use the same trading methods as money market traders.
Financial data needs • FX rates • Bank deposit rates • News • Graphical/Technical Analysis • Economic indicators	*Financial data needs* • FX rates • Bank deposit rates • News • Graphical/Technical Analysis • Economic indicators

Derivatives

Derivatives traders can operate across all the markets buying and selling futures, options, swaps etc, trading on their own account or for clients.

Financial data needs
- Information on underlying instruments
- Prices from exchanges
- Technical Analysis
- News

Dealers trade in a number of different ways – the main methods include:

- Direct trading over the phone – interbank

- Direct electronic trading, for example on Reuters Dealing 2000-1 – interbank. Reuters Dealing 2000-1 is a direct dealing service for dealers. The dealing 'conversation' is displayed on screen, the details of which are recorded and can be reviewed. The system also produces a deal ticket automatically. Reuters Dealing 2000-2 is an electronic broking system where dealers can enter bid and offer prices or take prices quoted by dealers.

- Trading using a voice broker

The different methods are summarised in the diagram opposite.

Currently, interest in the Internet — specifically the World Wide Web — as an electronic medium allowing trading to take place is growing. Some FX dealers have already created web-based services for spot FX and FX outright forwards. However, these services are currently only available for retail investors. Nevertheless, many wholesale banks are in the process of developing FX and money market trading services that use Internet protocols across secure private electronic networks.

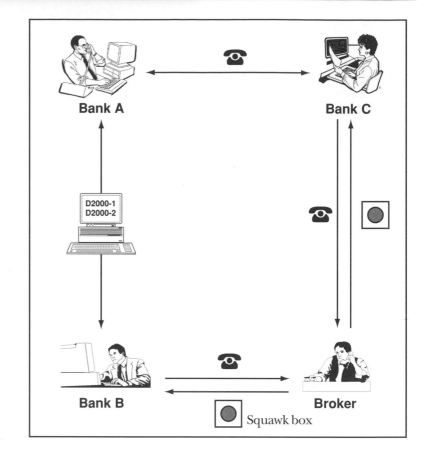

Factors Influencing Trading

Although both money markets and foreign exchange are primarily influenced by interest rates, the way in which the two markets operate are fundamentally different. FX is bought or sold whereas money market transactions involve borrowing or lending.

FX contracts involve the exchange of an amount of one currency for another. In the money markets, loans involve a much greater risk. Once the principal has been paid, it will not be repaid until maturity. If the borrower defaults then the investor can lose the principal and any interest due.

Interest and Deposit Rates

Interest and deposit rate calculations for instruments vary and depend on different year bases. For example,

For UK instruments	1 year	=	365 days
For US instruments	1 year	=	360 days
For Eurocurrency instruments	1 year	=	360 days

It is very important, therefore, that the correct number of days is used in the calculation of interest due.

Many of the money market and FX instruments involve a two-way method of quoting rates – the bid and offer/ask system. Before moving on just remind yourself what the terms mean...

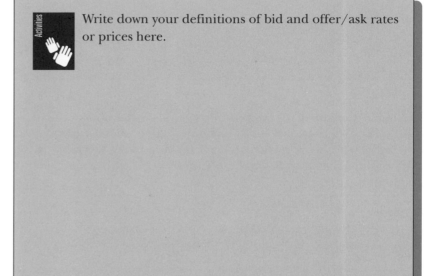

Write down your definitions of bid and offer/ask rates or prices here.

You can check your answers over the page.

You should not have had a problem with this one!

- **Bid**
  This is the rate at which the market-maker is prepared to **buy** or **borrow**.

- **Offer or ask**
  This is the rate at which the market-maker is prepared to **sell** or **lend**.

The **bid/offer spread** for interest rate can vary, depending on market conditions. When the market is calm and trading volumes are high, the spread tends to be small, say only a few basis points. When the market is more volatile, or if volumes are thin, the spread may widen to tens of basis points.

Example
In the UK rates are expressed as Offer/Bid, for example, 6¼–6⅛
In the US rates are expressed as Bid/Offer, for example, 6⅛–6¼

The meaning is the same in both cases:

> The market-maker **lends** at 6¼
>
> The market-maker **borrows** at 6⅛

Position Control

Within a busy dealing room many transactions are taking place every second. In order to control the risk of over exposure to an individual counterparty, dealing room management must be able to control and evaluate positions quickly.

For example, during a trading period the value of spot deals varies constantly and dealers need to know their average position – are they making a loss or profit on their existing position? Obviously the slower the average position is calculated the greater the risk to the dealer.

There is a wide variety of systems available to help traders monitor and manage their positions.

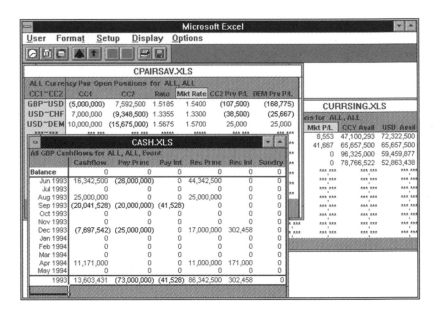

Arbitrage

Swap transactions take advantage of the interest rate differential between two currencies. The swap rate is determined by the currencies' spot rates, interest rates and the tenor of the swap.

If the swap rate goes 'out of line' with that predicted by the current spot rate and interest rates, traders can make a risk-free profit by buying the cheap instruments and selling the expensive instruments. As the prices will converge at maturity the trader knows he will make a profit when the instruments mature.

The point of arbitrage is that it takes advantage of the relationships between the prices of different instruments, for example money market deposit interest rates, spot FX rates, foreign currency deposit interest rates and forward FX rates (which are derived from the interest rate differentials).

We have seen previously how all these instruments combine to produce the forward points, and hence the forward FX rates. If the quoted forward FX rate differs from the 'implied' forward FX rate derived from the range of instruments, a trader can make a riskless profit buy transacting an FX swap and a 'mirror image' trade using money market deposits, spot FX and forward outright FX.

The Importance of News

Early access to news is essential to market players and the various news services offer a number of ways traders can access all the financial information and news they require. Different market players have different requirements.

Below are some screens from the Reuters Terminal (RT).

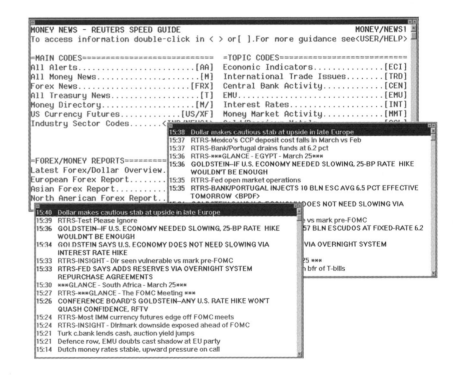

FX Dealers

How Do They Operate?

Most dealers will specialise in one of the major currency pairs or they will trade in several of the less active pairs. The USD is the predominant currency in FX dealing and appears in over 80% of all transactions.

The areas of FX activity for 1998, as indicated by the BIS Central Bank Survey, were divided as shown in the chart below.

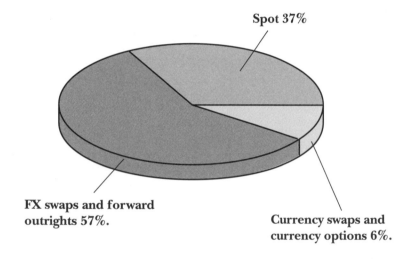

Spot 37%

FX swaps and forward outrights 57%.

Currency swaps and currency options 6%.

Source: BIS Central Bank Survey 1998

FX dealers are motivated by profit and in their fast moving environment they have to be quick thinking and able to prioritise information.

Dealers most often trade with their opposite numbers in other banks – the counterparty. The majority of transactions are performed between dealers in banks; the rest is with other financial institutions and customers. Trading is usually carried out electronically or by telephone.

In both the UK and the US about 35% of FX dealing is via brokers. Brokers do not take positions in the market but earn commission on deals they arrange between counterparties. Brokers are most active in the spot and forward FX markets.

Where Do They Work?

A dealing room is open plan and noisy. Individual dealers will be surrounded by telephones and they will be calling across the room to other dealers. There is a constant noise from dealers shouting prices and orders, and to add to the din brokers' prices are broadcast through 'squawk' boxes.

Dealers typically have 3 to 4 screens for computer systems built into their desk or work space.

Dealers perform deals with counterparties in other banks using electronic **conversations**. It is quicker to trade electronically than use a telephone.

An electronic dealing system matches buy and sell orders based on precise criteria of price, quantity available, credit and time of entry. Once a match has occurred, the system notifies the parties to the deal and provides the information each one needs to be able to settle the deal. An electronic dealing system provides banks with anonymous deal matching similar to using a broker but at a cheaper rate – dealers only pay for the service if they 'hit or take' a price. Dealers need only quote a one-way price which is advantageous if they only wish to buy or sell a particular currency.

The dealer may be linked to the back office from the system which provides a control for position keeping and a facility for updating trading profit and loss.

FX Dealing Tasks

Form an Opinion

FX dealers have an early morning start – typically 7.30 am. Their first job is to find out what has happened to the world markets overnight. For example, a dealer in London will contact his/her Hong Kong/Tokyo/Singapore opposite number as it is the end of the trading day in the Far East. Later in the day the London dealer will talk to his/her New York dealer when that market opens.

The dealers will then integrate all the news and information they have gathered, including interest and inflation rates, to help them form an opinion on the way markets will move. In order to form their opinion and set rates for currencies, dealers assess the following factors:

- **Fundamental factors**. These are the underlying economic and financial conditions of the country which include interest rates, inflation, money supply, government deficits, balance of payments etc. The release times and dates of the monthly or quarterly statistics on such information are well known in the markets and are followed avidly.

- **Technical factors**. Using technical analysis and charting techniques the trends and patterns of price movements are assessed to help determine trading strategies.

- **Institutional factors**. The government policy framework surrounding the currency, for example, exchange controls, fixed parities, international agreements etc.

Electronic systems can be used to display forecast, historic and technical analysis information. The screens overleaf show the **Forecast Economics**, **Historic Economics** and **Technical Analysis** respectively for the Deutschmark.

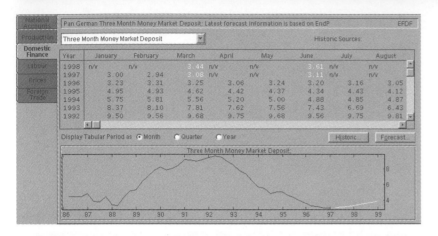

Receive Analysts' Predictions

In larger banks the dealers will next have to attend a strategy meeting to be briefed by the bank's analysts/economists on their predictions for market movements.

In smaller banks third party analysts' reports may be subscribed to and accessed via a computer service and you will see screens like those below...

```
SPECIALIST DATA - REUTERS SPEED GUIDE                              SPECIAL
Welcome to the Specialist Data Guide.  Double click in < > for more information.
Note: Specialist Data is available through your terminal for an additional fee.

=KEY MARKETS============================   =KEY SPEED GUIDE DISPLAYS================
Fixed Income .............<DEBT/SPEC1>    Fixed Income.....................<BONDS>
Money ....................<MONEY/SPEC1>   Money and Forex..................<MONEY>
Equity ..................<EQUITY/SPEC1>   Equities........................<EQUITY>
Commodity ..............<COMMOD/SPEC1>    Commodities.....................<COMMOD>
Energy .................<ENERGY/SPEC1>    Energy..........................<ENERGY>
Specialist News .........<SPEC/NEWS1>     Reuters News......................<NEWS>
Emerging Markets .........<EMG/SPEC1>     Emerging Markets.............<EMERGING>
All Markets
```

```
MONEY SPECIALIST DATA - REUTERS SPEED GUIDE                   MONEY/SPEC1
Welcome to the Money Specialist Data Guide. Double click in < > for more
information.  Note: Specialist Data is available through your terminal for an
additional fee.
=INFORMATION SOURCE=============================FREE TRIAL PAGE======OVERVIEW==
Analytics Research Corporation.....................<ANRSH/CU01>.....<ANRSHINDEX>
Capital Management - Dollar Outlook....................<CRSS>......<         >
Capital Management - Dealer Perspective................<CRSS>......<         >
Capital Management - Cross Outlook.....................<CRSS>......<         >
Elliott Wave - North American Fin. Market..............<EWAVE>......<         >
Elliott Wave - Currency Outlook........................<EWAVE>......<         >
Forexia........................................<FOREXIA>.....<FRX/SPEC1>
ID AG..............................................<GKAA>.....<IDAG/SPEC1>
IDEA - WWFX Series..............................<IDEAINDEX>.....<IDEA/SPEC1>
IDEA - FX Options Series........................<IDEAINDEX>.....<IDEA/SPEC1>
Market News Service....................................[MNSI].....<MNS/SPEC1>
MCM Currency Watch..............................<MCMINDEX>.....<MCM/SPEC1>
MCM Money Watch.................................<MCMINDEX>.....<MCM/SPEC1>
MMS Canadian...................................<MMSINDEX>.....<MMS/SPEC1>
MMS Currency...................................<MMSINDEX>.....<MMS/SPEC1>
MMS Emerging Asia..............................<MMSINDEX>.....<MMS/SPEC1>
==================================================
Money Guide <MONEY>  Specialist Data Guide <SPECIAL>  Continued on <MONEY/SPEC2>
   Lost? Selective Access?...<USER/HELP>   Reuters Phone Support...<PHONE/HELP>
```

The screen here shows a **Spot Rate Composite** page.

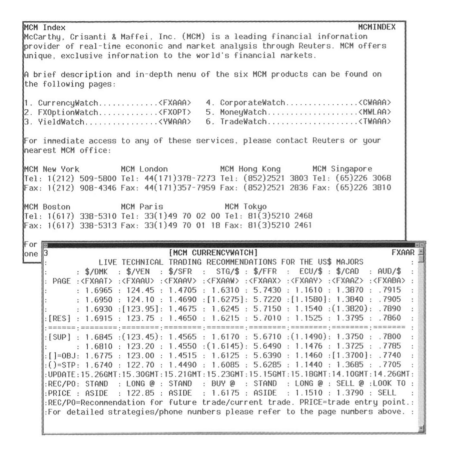

```
MCM Index                                                        MCMINDEX
McCarthy, Crisanti & Maffei, Inc. (MCM) is a leading financial information
provider of real-time econonic and market analysis through Reuters. MCM offers
unique, exclusive information to the world's financial markets.

A brief description and in-depth menu of the six MCM products can be found on
the following pages:

1. CurrencyWatch............<FXAAA>    4. CorporateWatch...............<CWAAA>
2. FXOptionWatch............<FXOPT>    5. MoneyWatch...................<MWLAA>
3. YieldWatch...............<YWAAA>    6. TradeWatch...................<TWAAA>

For immediate access to any of these services, please contact Reuters or your
nearest MCM office:

MCM New York         MCM London         MCM Hong Kong       MCM Singapore
Tel: 1(212) 509-5800 Tel: 44(171)378-7273 Tel: (852)2521 3803 Tel: (65)226 3068
Fax: 1(212) 908-4346 Fax: 44(171)357-7959 Fax: (852)2521 2836 Fax: (65)226 3810

MCM Boston           MCM Paris          MCM Tokyo
Tel: 1(617) 338-5310 Tel: 33(1)49 70 02 00 Tel: 81(3)5210 2468
Fax: 1(617) 338-5313 Fax: 33(1)49 70 01 18 Fax: 81(3)5210 2461
For
one 3                    [MCM CURRENCYWATCH]                       FXAAR
:        LIVE TECHNICAL TRADING RECOMMENDATIONS FOR THE US$ MAJORS        :
:      $/DMK  :  $/YEN  :  $/SFR  :  STG/$  :  $/FFR  :  ECU/$  :  $/CAD  :  AUD/$  :
: PAGE :<FXAAT> :<FXAAU> :<FXAAV> :<FXAAW> :<FXAAX> :<FXAAY> :<FXAAZ> :<FXABA> :
:      : 1.6965 : 124.45 : 1.4705 : 1.6310 : 5.7430 : 1.1610 : 1.3870 : .7915 :
:      : 1.6950 : 124.10 : 1.4690 :[1.6275]: 5.7220 :[1.1580]: 1.3840 : .7905 :
:      : 1.6930 :[123.95]: 1.4675 : 1.6245 : 5.7150 : 1.1540 :(1.3820): .7890 :
:[RES] : 1.6915 : 123.75 : 1.4650 : 1.6215 : 5.7010 : 1.1525 : 1.3795 : .7860 :
:======:=======:=======:=======:=======:=======:=======:=======:======= :
:[SUP] : 1.6845 :(123.45): 1.4565 : 1.6170 : 5.6710 :(1.1490): 1.3750 : .7800 :
:      : 1.6810 : 123.20 : 1.4550 :(1.6145): 5.6490 : 1.1476 : 1.3725 : .7785 :
:[]=OBJ: 1.6775 : 123.00 : 1.4515 : 1.6125 : 5.6390 : 1.1460 :[1.3700]: .7740 :
:()=STP: 1.6740 : 122.70 : 1.4490 : 1.6085 : 5.6285 : 1.1440 : 1.3685 : .7705 :
:UPDATE:15.26GMT:15.30GMT:15.21GMT:15.23GMT:15.15GMT:15.18GMT:14.10GMT:14.26GMT:
:REC/PO: STAND  : LONG @ : STAND  : BUY @  : STAND  : LONG @ : SELL @ :LOOK TO :
:PRICE : ASIDE  : 122.85 : ASIDE  : 1.6175 : ASIDE  : 1.1510 : 1.3790 : SELL   :
:REC/PO=Reconnendation for future trade/current trade. PRICE=trade entry point.:
:For detailed strategies/phone nunbers please refer to the page nunbers above. :
```

You may find it useful to look at other specialist data reports.

OTC Conversations and Traders' Days

OTC trading is obviously difficult to witness because, in most cases, the conversations take place over the telephone. However the following 'conversations' and an explanation of what is happening may help your understanding of the various markets a little better. You may also find the "24 hours in the life of a ..." scenarios useful. The conversations and scenarios described are as follows:

- A spot deal in foreign exchange

- A 3-month FX swap deal

- 24 hours in the life of an FX dealer

- 24 hours in the life of a forward FX dealer

- 24 hours in the life of a voice broker

A Spot FX Deal

Company XYZ needs to buy $2m, with Sterling, on the spot market to pay for machine parts from a company in New York.

XYZ contact the corporate desk at MegaBank to ask for a price.

The Corporate dealer asks the spot desk for a price for XYZ and acts as the intermediary.

The GBP/USD rate is about 1.5963/67.

It's the 4th April. The conversation between Alan at XYZ and Ben the corporate dealer might go like this:

Alan: 'Hi, Ben, can I have cable in 2 dollars'

Ben: '60/70'

Alan: 'At 60, I buy $2 million'

Ben: 'OK, done. I sell you $2 million at 1.5960. Value 6th April. Thanks for the deal and bye.'

A **spot deal** means that delivery will take place in 2 working days time.

XYZ are good customers with MegaBank and have existing credit arrangements.

Using Money 3000, the latest contributor or specific contributor prices for GBP/USD can be displayed.

At this stage Alan doesn't tell Ben whether or not he wants to buy or sell.

Cable is the term for the GBP/USD currency pair. Ben is obliged to quote a two-way bid/ask price which he **has** to deal at. The amount involved is $2 million dollars.

Ben quotes only the **pips** as the Big Figure is known by both Alan and Ben. Ben is quoting 1.5960 dollars per pound to **buy** pounds for dollars and 1.5970 dollars per pound to **sell** pounds for dollars.

This means Alan agrees to sell pounds to buy dollars at Ben's bid price of 1.5960. It is only at this point that Alan has revealed he wants to buy dollars. If Ben knew XYZ was a seller of pounds he might shift the price to 60/65.

Ben confirms the deal and delivery date of 2 working days ahead.

The whole deal has lasted no more than 25 seconds!

The jargon differs between dealers – some of the more common terms are explained below:

	Might say ...or	yours/mine
Sellers or lenders of base currency	**I sell at...** **I offer at...** **I give at...** **Offered at...** **Coming at...**	**Yours** + amount of base currency
Buyers or borrowers of the base currency	**I buy at...** **I bid at...** **I take at...** **I pay ...**	**Mine** + amount of base currency

Your notes

A 3-month FX Swap Deal

Bank A

Hi, Chase London here.
Can I have a 3 month dollar-mark in 50 dollars?

Today is 14th November and Bank A requests a 3 month FX swap quote for US dollars against Deutschmarks for 50 million dollars. It is important to state the currency since Bank A might wish to deal 50 million Deutschmarks. It is assumed that it is spot /3 months.

Bank B

66/65

The **market-maker**, Bank B, will check **credit limits** before quoting a two-way price in forward points.

At 66

The **market-taker**, Bank A, trades at 66.

Done. Spot is 10/15, so shall we do 12?

Bank B, the **market-maker**, agrees. It is the market-maker who proposes a spot which is usually a middle rate of the current USD/DEM spot.

Fine. I buy and sell 50 dollars. Spot 1.4112, Minus 66 points, so that's 1.4046. Spot date November 16, 3 months February 16. My dollars to Chase New York, marks to Chase Frankfurt.

The **market-taker** agrees on the spot. It is a fair spot proposal since it lies within the current bid and ask level. He now confirms the deal:
- What has been bought (spot) and sold (forward)
- The forward rate
- First and second leg value dates
- Payment instructions for his USD on spot date and DEM on the forward date.

OK. My dollars to BHF New York, marks to BHF Frankfurt.

The **market-maker** also announces his payment instructions.

Cheers.

24 hours in the Life of an FX dealer

20.00

It 's been a really busy day with a tremendous amount of turnover for which my broker will be eternally grateful and we reviewed the day's business together over a drink.

22.00

After a meal I took stock of the day's proceedings. I still have a position in USD/DEM – I am short of USD 5 mio against DEM at 1.4550. This is a relatively small position but the market's been extremely volatile and if it moves my way I will certainly make enough to put a dent in my monthly target.

As I have a position then I had to leave stop loss orders with the international branch network, so my position will be watched 24 hours a day. If I didn't leave the order I could lose a lot of money—and my job!

My stop loss position is 1.4650. If the 1.4620 resistance level is broken then the USD is going much higher. On the profit side I have left an order that if 1.4400 is reached then my branches should give me a call.

Confident that my orders are circulating the globe I make a final check of the rates on my pocket Reuters machine – 1.4480 – still in the money.

02.00

The phone rings. I think it is good news but it's not! My old friend Chan is phoning from Singapore to tell me that 1.4620 has been broken and the market looks like heading for my stop loss at 1.4650. Although the USD is looking good at the moment he believes it is a bout of short covering in anticipation of the resistance level being broken. However, he has a client who has a massive sell order (for USD/DEM at 1.4660) and suggests I raise my stop loss to 1.4675 so that I won't be cut out of my position on a false break of the 1.4620 level.

A short position means that the dealer has sold USD against DEM in anticipation of a fall in prices. The reasoning behind the position is that the dealer has heard a rumour that there will be a statement from a Fed official that US interest rates will be cut because of slowing economic activity. This will make the USD less attractive in the short term and money will flow out of USD into DEM and other currencies – all things being equal. The market met some resistance at 1.4620 and should look to test the support levels around 1.4350. If the rumour is correct then the downside could be tested very quickly at which point the dealer will take some profit.

If the dealer did not leave a stop loss position and war broke out for example, then the US dollar could rise sharply and he could incur heavy losses.

The resistance level is a line on a technical analysis chart which indicates the price action where selling is strong enough to overcome buying pressure so that the price does not rise above the line.

The dealer is in the money for DEM 35,000. This is calculated from the potential profit: $1.4550 - 1.4480 = 0.007 \times 5,000,000$
$$= 35,000$$

05.30

Alarm goes off. No more phone calls. First thing I do is check Reuters – USD/ DEM is 1.4500. Chan was right – I owe him one. I still have my position and it is still in court. I catch the 06:00 train and settle down to read the morning papers.

06.15

My pocket Reuters buzzes. A bit embarrassing until I find everyone else wants to know the latest news— and it's good: '...US interest rates have peaked...' – that was an accurate rumour! USD/DEM starts dropping rapidly and I call our Singapore office. They say that the USD is still well offered with USD/ DEM trading at 1.4370. I decide to bring my stop loss down to 1.4450 (so as to protect some profit) and leave a take profit order at 1.4320.

If the order is filled at 1.4450 the dealer will make –

$$1.4550 - 1.4450 = \quad 0.01 \times 5,000,000 = \quad \text{DEM } 50,000$$

07.00

Arrive at the office and switch everything on at my desk—which looks very like the controls of the USS Enterprise. USD/DEM has dropped to 1.4320 and Singapore has filled my order, so I start the day with a good profit.

At 1.4320 the dealer stands to make –

$$1.4550 - 1.4320 = \quad 0.023 \times 5,000,000 = \quad \text{DEM } 115,000$$

We don't start making prices to customers and other banks until 07.30 and this first half an hour in the office is extremely important. I read all the overnight news and note important events which will happen during the day. Also I speak to my contacts at other banks and swap ideas as to the likely direction of currency moves over the next few hours.

The only significant event of the day is the BUBA – Bundesbank – meeting.

The Bundesbank meets every two weeks on a Thursday to discuss monetary conditions and normally announces any changes or otherwise of domestic DEM interest rates.

The market feeling is that they will leave 'credit policies unchanged'. However I have my doubts, as US interest rates are down and the DEM is very strong. There have been many calls over the last few months from German exporters to call a halt to the strength of the DEM as their products overseas are becoming uncompetitive. If the BUBA cuts its rate, as I suspect will happen, then the DEM will weaken and the USD/DEM rate will rise. I decide to build a long USD position.

A long position means that the dealer wants to buy USD against DEM in anticipation of a rise in the USD against DEM.

07.30 – 10.00

The first calls appear on my screen and they are predominantly from the Far East. They are all asking for USD/DEM– mostly in USD 10 mio and upwards. The price of USD/DEM is being constantly shouted at me by my brokers through the speaker boxes on my desk.

USD/DEM is now 1.4330/35 and wanting to build a long position I quote a touch higher at 32/37. He gives me USD 10 mio at 32 – this suits me and I decide to sit with it.

The dealer has bought USD 10 mio at 1.4332.

It soon becomes clear that there are more sellers emerging from early European trading and the USD starts dropping. On the screen I see 1.4300 offered – this is not good! I am still 10 mio long at 1.4332 and if I had to get out of my position now I would lose DEM 32,000.

The dealer stands to lose –
$$1.4332 - 1.4300 = 0.0032 \times 10,000,000 = \text{DEM } 32,000$$

However my technical analyst has told me that there is a good support level at 1.4285 and I should hold. I see 1.4290/95 is being quoted and I decide to buy more USD at this level so I ask my colleagues to get me some prices from other banks! The prices we get are 90/95, 92/97 and 85/90 – I lift the 85/90 price for 10 mio. So now I am USD 20 mio long at an average rate of 1.4311 and well under water!

The dealer has bought USD 10 mio for 1.4332 and now adds a purchase of USD 10 mio at 1.4290 – the lowest rate offered. The average rate = 1.4311.

$mio	DEM
+10	14,332,000
+10	14,429,000
+20	28,622,000 ÷20
	1.4311

I make another price – 87/92 to a big American bank and he gives me another 10 mio. I am now USD 30 mio long at 1.4303. Although I still believe the rate will go up I don't want such a big position so I offer the last USD 10 mio at 92 and get paid. My position is now USD 20 mio at 1.4308. I am happy with this and sit back and hope that nobody else wants to sell USD.

The American bank sells the dealer USD 10 mio at his bid price of 1.4287. So the dealers average rate is now 1.4303.

$mio	DEM
+10	14,332,000
+10	14,429,000
+10	14,287,000
+30	42,909,000 ÷ 30
	1.4303

11.30

USD/DEM is still trading at below the 1.4300 level and the BUBA has not made any announcement yet. If German rates are not cut then I will lose a fortune!

$mio	DEM
+10	14,332,000
+10	14,429,000
+10	14,287,000
+30	42,909,000
–10	–14,292,000
+20	28,617,000 ÷ 20
	1.4308

12.00

Still no announcement so I send out for a sandwich.

12.30

Great news! BUBA has cut discount and Lombard rate by 0.5%. USD/DEM moves higher sharply and the screen lights up like a Christmas tree with banks wanting a USD/DEM price. My first price after the announcement is 1.4400/10 – a bit wider a spread than normal but the market is now very volatile. I lose 10 mio at 1.4410 and so now my position has been reduced but the average has improved – it's now standing at 1.4207. The market is still moving higher and while I may have sold a little cheap, a profit is a profit.

14.00

There is a rumour that the Central Banks have now decided to intervene to drive the $ higher – this sends the market into chaos! Brokers are screaming and shouting, the dealing room is like a mad house.

15.00

*USD/DEM is now trading at 1.4630 and I decide to take the profit. I lose (**sell?**) the last USD 10 mio and my profit on the position is DEM 423,000. The total days trading profit, including the overnight position is DEM 538,000 – best day of the year! Maybe I'll get that Ferrari...*

16.00

Finish trading for the day. Make sure that all my deals have been input and check that the Risk Management system agrees with my profit figure. By 16.30 they eventually agree!

17.00

Invite everyone to the pub to celebrate the good day.

00.00

Arrive home. What a great day! But in this game you're only as good as your last trade, and tomorrow is another day.

The Lombard rate is the rate charged by central banks for commercial banks to borrow overnight against collateral.

$mio	DEM
+10	14,332,000
+10	14,429,000
+10	14,287,000
+30	42,909,000
−10	−14,292,000
+20	28,617,000
−10	−14,410,000
+10	14,207,000 ÷10
	1.4207

The dealer's profit can be calculated by subtracting the difference in pips from the last sale price and previous average, from the last trading price –

$$(1.4630 - 1.4207) \ = \ 0.0423 \times 10,000,000$$
$$= \ \text{DEM } 423,000$$

24 hours in the Life of a Forward Dealer

London: 5:00 am
*The radio bursts into life. I'm driving to the station when the car phone buzzes - it's my regular 5:45 call from our **Singapore office** with their comments and views of the day. They sound tired. I arrive in the next town to get the 6:00 train.*

As the foreign exchange markets never close, dealers make use of contacts in different time zones to gain insights to how the day's trading has progressed. Often dealers will leave overnight orders or open trading positions with their overseas offices to monitor and execute if given price levels are reached. An unexecuted order may be returned to the originator after passing through the care of more than one overseas office.

London: 6:50 am – 7:00 am
*By 6:50 I'm at my desk. I take some **run throughs** from my brokers and transfer them to my **rate sheet**. Stella calls me from a well known broking house. Each*

day we are proffered rates and views from brokers and I listen but remember that they want me to deal as I pay brokerage on each trade I do through them. Stella knows the forward market well and I am happy to use her for some of my trades. The rates have not changed that much from yesterday and I have read or heard nothing overnight that will change my views.

Run throughs are what a dealer will receive from his broker each morning. They are a combination of indicative forward points of where the broker believes the forward market to be and firm quotes that they have had from other dealers. A standard run through would provide prices for all short dates and 1, 2, 3, 6 and 12 months. A complete run through would include 4, 5, 7, 8, 9, 10 and 11 months.

Rate sheets are set up each morning listing all the short date and fixed date periods together with the number of actual calendar days plus the date. Rate sheets can be paper-based but are more usually set up on PC spreadsheets. Forward dealers also use a Dayfinder calendar. The calendar is kept open on spot value and shows the whole year with fixed value dates highlighted. It is very easy for the dealer to see the forward dates and to know how many days are in that period.

*I took a **long one year DEM position** last month (**mainly covered in the 3 months at 85 points, the balance in the short dates**), as I believe DEM rates are now very stable and will be for quite a while. US Dollar rates, I believe, are heading up.*

The dealer has **bought USD spot** and **sold USD 1 year forward** against DEM. The dealer paid 340 points for this position (market was 340/335). This position has to be funded since USD were bought and DEM were sold spot. This can be done in several ways depending on the views and current cashflows of the dealer. In this example, the dealer has covered most of his position in the 3 months, that is, he has sold and bought USD against DEM spot 3 months for most of the amount. The rest of the amount is covered in the short dates, that is, he has sold and bought spot one week and will roll this over at the end of the week. This leaves the position open from 3 months to the year, ie he is still long USD on the original 3 month value date and short the original 1 year value date.

*This I expect to be confirmed with the release of **non-farm payroll figures** later today. One year rates will move much more than 3 month rates, since long term rates are more volatile than short term rates.*

Non-farm payroll figures are published on a monthly basis from the US Department of Labor. These figures are released at a fixed time of 08:30 New York and measure the number of people who are employed in all non-farm industries. The financial markets focus on the monthly change in this figure.

Our 7:00 morning meeting is lively. We debate the possibility of a rate hike (increase) and the consensus is that it is on the cards.

If USD rates do go up, this will widen the interest rate differential between USD and DEM and will move the forward points to the left. For example, prices that were shown for 12 months at 340/335 might now be shown as 380/377. So the dealer could close his open position by selling and buying USD against DEM at 377. The profit is shown by the fact that he will receive more points than he paid for his position (340). The total profit and loss on this position will also take into consideration the points received when covering some in the 3 months and some in the short dates.

7:15 am to 10:00 am
*I then square up some of the more inactive Tom/Next **balances** I have been given with my **nostro accounts**. I have one bank counterparty I call often and use regularly for various types of trade, and the relationship works well. I find that the market is moving more and more towards 'relationship banking'.*

Part of my job is to **balance the books** of the dealing room. This is a cash management operation and has to be done on a daily basis. The quicker this is done, the better. **Nostro accounts** are 'our' accounts held with correspondent banks. For example, our DEM nostro account is 'our' account in DEM held at our correspondent bank in Frankfurt. Currencies are therefore settled within the originating country. It is not good practice for any bank to go overdrawn in any of its nostro accounts and so **squaring up** relates to ensuring that the debits and credits balance on a day-to-day basis. As the dealer is squaring T/N, he is squaring his position for value tomorrow.

For the major currencies I know I'm going to be quoting prices to callers during the morning, so I calculate the levels through which I want and am likely to trade and cover some of the amounts using the brokers, leaving myself as much scope as I need to quote to other market makers and customers. I call my friends in the market to see if they have any firm views and to reiterate my own.

10:00 am

*All the T/N positions are square, and I am looking at some of the short dates periods where I have some **mis-matches**. I am also short of CHF at the moment — I have been looking at the arbitrage possibilities, but nothing works for me at the moment.*

*One of my biggest customers calls in, asking for a 6 month USD/DEM swap. Stella, my broker, quotes – 176/174. (Reuters also show the same price, contributed by RBS on DEM6M=). I am happy with my current position and **read** him up to 177.5/176. He should not deal at 177.5, and if I buy and sell the dollars at 176, I will keep this position into the figures. Sure enough he does not trade, which helps reinforce my own view that I have the right position.*

*My attention turns to my in-tray which is full of the material we receive from top economists and analysts. We are receiving some of the pamphlets on trial. I am also producing a report for my boss about the **limits** we have for other banks - they need to be increased so that I can trade more, and not miss any opportunities. I doubt if this will be a problem, but approval has to come from Head Office, which might take some time.*

Because of the figures, I won't be able to go out to lunch today. I'll make up for it tomorrow - I'm meeting a new line broker for lunch. He's young and keen to introduce himself. We use his company and he's just taken over the line from another guy. He knows he must build up his credibility and I'm happy to get to know him.

A **mis-match** shows when there is a difference in maturities of funds borrowed and funds invested. Mis-matches can be spotted when a dealer reviews the size and settlement dates of trades he already has on his books. For example, he reviews his cashflows to see if he can better manage his assets/liabilities and do a 1-week swap instead of day-to-day T/N swaps.

Dealers will fend off unwanted positions or encourage advantageous ones by the rates they offer counterparties. Good rates with tight spreads will encourage a deal. However, a certain amount of '**reading a counterparty**' will also take place. In this example, the market-maker is not interested in selling and buying (left side of price) so he makes it expensive. The market-taker is unlikely to deal at 177.5 when he can go elsewhere and pay only 176 points.

Limits ensure that the dealers operate according to their bank's risk policy. All the dealers have to observe a variety of limits such as counterparty limits, settlement limits, country limits, which are set by senior bank personnel and not by the dealers. Individual dealers are often given position limits within which they can trade.

1:15 pm

Everyone is waiting for the figures. Tempers are running short — one of our team snarls at the credit officer who has chosen a bad time to tell him of an excess limit utilisation. Any bank calling for a price now gets a wide price quoted as I don't want to carry any unwanted position over the figures.

The figures are published at 08:30 NY time which with the 5 hours' time difference, means this happens around our lunchtime. Dealers are always tense just before important figures are issued especially those that relate to inflation or the strength/weakness of the economy. These figures have an impact on interest rates. An important point to note concerns the market's expectations of a figure. If the figures come out according to forecasts (even if the announcement is bad for the economy), then this fact will already be anticipated in the current prices. Prices may move rapidly if the market is caught by figures that are outside expected ranges.

1:30 pm

*Here we go ...! YES! The figures are well outside the expected ranges and everyone is worrying about the same thing - higher US interest rates! The spot market is really moving and I 've also been tracking the bond and futures market. I decide to take profit and maybe re-establish my position if the opportunity arises. Banks are calling and brokers are asking for **support prices** for all periods. Before the figures, the 3 month and one year prices were 85.5/85 and 340/335 respectively. They are now around 95/94 and 380/ 373. I quote the one year aggressively – 377/372 – hoping to sell and buy the dollars. I get the deal done at 377. I show nothing special to other callers. Our open position is now in the 3 months with a slight mis-match in the one year.*

Support prices are dealable prices for brokers to broadcast.

The forward prices have indeed moved to the left in expectation of higher USD interest rates.

4:00 pm

*After all the excitement it's now time to **revalue my book** and get my profit and loss figures to the chief dealer. It's dull but necessary. I've been left with a slight mis-match, but nothing too drastic and I've made a very good profit on the day.*

There was something that one of my customers said about future rate movements in CHF – I alert my technical analyst to this and make a note to look at this tomorrow.

Revalue my book means applying new rates to all forward positions held to reflect them in one base currency (often USD or the currency of the head office) for profit and loss reporting purposes**.** Position-keeping systems will be updated with a live feed of up-to-date market rates. This allows the trader to monitor his positions in real-time.

24 hours in the Life of a Voice Broker

London: 7:00 am

Few of the traders are ready to start trading at this time so you can get a couple of things done.

I have already prepared my forward sheet from the previous day. I did it by calculating where the forwards should be, assuming no overnight movement, using the closing prices from the previous evening and the number of days in each period compared with the number of days in each period the previous day.

About this time I also check if the Far East or European links have any prices, but they rarely do at the start of London trading time.

I then give each of my lines a run through of where we 'think' the forwards are: the emphasis is on 'think', as we are often corrected by traders if they have already seen some price action in direct dealings with the Far East.

The priority at this time in the morning is T/N. We invite our banks in London and our links in the Far East and Europe to make firm prices or close the prices we have already obtained.

I broadcast the closest price to all my lines, with any qualifications such as particular amounts etc, in the hope that somebody will show an interest and trade. If I do trade I will immediately indicate that I am trading with either my colleague or my own bank. I inform all other lines that the price has traded and is no longer good. Then I go to the counterparty who has traded and find out his amount.

A forward sheet will have columns marked and headed with the periods, that is, T/N through to medium term periods 2–5 years. Although the medium term is not traded frequently on the forward desk, the traders will expect you to know the correct level throughout the day.

A **link** is an overseas broker. The broker speaks to other brokers overseas in order to have a better chance of seeing every price. A **line** is a bank – brokers are connected to banks via broker boxes. The broker may not have a direct line to some banks. If he trades with a bank via an overseas broker, the broker will receive brokerage on his side and the overseas broker will receive brokerage from his side.

Most traders will like to square their T/N position early – before 11:30 am (lunchtime). The reason for this is to allow the Back Office time to pay the counterparty on time. Dealers view their T/N business as a cash management exercise, rarely a source of profits and want those sorted out as early in the trading day as possible.

I pass the name of the counterparty to my colleague who passes it to his bank for checking. In the meantime I pass the name to my bank for checking. If the names have mutual credit and the amounts suit both parties, the deal is done and the spot rate is agreed.

8:30 am – 11:30 am

By 8:30 am we are quoting sets of forwards, that is, 1,2,3,6 and 12 months – sometimes for 4, 5,7 and 8 months. The brokerage increases as the periods extend out. This is due to less liquidity plus a move in the longer periods will have more of an impact on the P/L – so we try and concentrate on them.

Lunchtime: 11:30 am – 1:30 pm

I have lunch with a client. Cementing relationships over lunch or dinner is very important and could mean the difference between you or a competitor getting an order.

1:30 pm – 4:00 pm

The afternoon session is much the same as the morning, but you also have the New York market to deal with.

4:00 pm

Around 4:00 pm the market is relatively quiet and arrangements for the evening's entertainment are discussed. The idea is to thank the traders for their business and try to ensure that this situation continues. The competition between brokers is intense with each one trying to increase their market share.

If one party has no credit with the other or the amount does not suit, we will usually 'go choice' and it is courteous to ask if you may 'go choice'. However, it is considered unprofessional of the trader if he backs out. On occasion he will pull his price if he is dealing elsewhere.

Throughout the day brokers are constantly calculating broken dates for clients. Brokers exchange a lot of information during the day, for example on which way they have traded, rumours in the market of large amounts going through on a certain period, particular interest in a period from a certain centre etc. Brokers also liaise a lot with the arbitrage desk where they are trying to put packages together using FRAs, forwards, IRS, deposits etc.

Summary of voice broker trading

Typically trading via a voice broker – 'a number cruncher' takes place in the following way:

- The voice broker broadcasts prices in given periods over speaker boxes located in bank dealing rooms
- Dealers in the dealing rooms relay their buy and sell orders by phone
- Once a broker has matched a buyer with a seller this is considered a trade and all banks are informed of the price traded
- The broker returns to the counterparties to check the amounts involved and so that each counterparty can check each other's creditworthiness
- Once both counterparties agree that their credit ratings are good and the amounts acceptable, the trade is made and the spot rate agreed

Electronic Trading Systems

Because electronic systems have developed for the specific requirements of different financial markets and exchanges there is no simple description which covers all the systems currently used. For example, in the London Stock Exchange, Big Bang largely replaced the floor based trading system with an OTC market based on the telephone for communications and screens providing information. Advances in communications using computers are now making the telephone somewhat redundant and all-screen based trading systems are the logical progression.

There are three types of system in use which broadly may be described as electronic:

- Direct dealing systems

- Automated matching systems

- Support systems directly used by direct dealing or automated matching systems

Direct Dealing Systems

These are used in OTC markets. In this case the system is often described as a **transaction product** as it simply provides a means of conducting a deal conversation between two counterparties which is executed by the system on agreement. The conversations can be in a free format style and the system ensures that both parties to the conversation receive identical text. When the deal is executed the system analyses the conversation and produces a deal ticket for the back office of both parties for processing.

Automated Matching Systems

These systems are also known as electronic brokers which offer anonymous trading. This method of trading is used when traders are seeking the best prices in the market and they are not particularly bothered with whom they trade – obviously both sides of the trade satisfy themselves that each side is creditworthy etc before the deal is completed. The exchange operated automated trading systems have the same trading rules as those for pit trading regarding margin payments, settlement etc. There are three characteristics of an automated matching system:

- Users send their bids and offers to a central matching system

- The bids and offers are distributed to all other market participants

- The system identifies possible trades based on price, size, credit and any other rules relevant to the market

In the equities, spot FX and derivatives markets automated matching systems are proving to be more cost effective than using traditional brokers and hence their share of market turnover is increasing. For example, in the FX markets, the world's largest OTC markets, the average daily turnover in April 1998 was $1,490 billion.

An Overnight FX Swap Deal – D2000-1

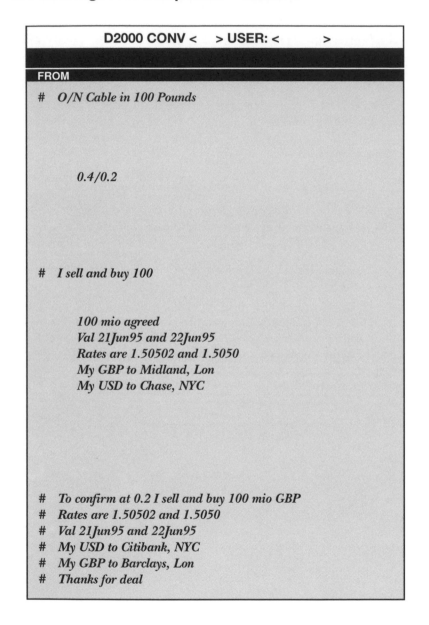

```
          D2000 CONV <    > USER: <        >


FROM

#    O/N Cable in 100 Pounds




     0.4/0.2




#    I sell and buy 100



     100 mio agreed
     Val 21Jun95 and 22Jun95
     Rates are 1.50502 and 1.5050
     My GBP to Midland, Lon
     My USD to Chase, NYC




#    To confirm at 0.2 I sell and buy 100 mio GBP
#    Rates are 1.50502 and 1.5050
#    Val 21Jun95 and 22Jun95
#    My USD to Citibank, NYC
#    My GBP to Barclays, Lon
#    Thanks for deal
```

It is 21st June and Bank A requests an FX swap quote for Sterling against US dollars for 100 million of the **base currency, Sterling**, for a short date of **overnight**. The market-taker specifies the amount is for pounds and not for dollars.

Once Bank B, the **market-maker**, has checked credit limits he quotes a **two-way price**. In doing this he is committed to selling and buying the base currency at 0.4 or buying and selling the base currency at 0.2 value today against tomorrow. The price is quoted in **forward points**.

Bank A is a seller and buyer of the base currency, Sterling 100 against US dollars.

The **market-maker** now confirms the trade, giving both dates of the swap transaction. The trade date is June 21st 1995. The first date he confirms, today 21 June 95, is the **first leg** of the swap and 22 June 95 is the **second leg** – tomorrow. He also sets the rates – 1.50502 is chosen as the spot rate to simplify the second leg calculation – deducting 0.00002 points makes the second leg 1.5050. A spot rate is used although neither date is spot. The payment instructions are then given – for the first leg he buys Sterling and for the second leg he buys US dollars. **Both legs** of the transaction are for Sterling 100 million.

Bank A confirms the details and gives his payment instructions – for the first leg he buys US dollars and for the second leg he buys Sterling.

Trading on An Exchange

Money market and FX futures and options instruments can be traded OTC using the techniques of trading already described, or on an exchange such as the **London International Financial Futures and Options Exchange (LIFFE)** or the **Chicago Mercantile Exchange (CME)**. The **open outcry** system used on exchange floors combines the use of shouting and hand signals. However, most exchanges are introducing electronic trading systems either alongside or in place of open outcry trading.

The primary role of an exchange is to provide a safe environment for trading. Exchanges have approved members and rules governing matters such as trading behaviour and the settlement of disputes. Open outcry involves traders or brokers operating on an exchange floor where they communicate their deals by shouting at each other and using hand signals. Open outcry trading is both noisy and exciting to experience. Depending on the particular exchange visited the floor may also be a very colourful place with people wearing a multitude of different coloured jackets. However chaotic the exchange proceedings may appear, they are well organised and efficiently run financial institutions.

In general, exchanges comprise members who buy or lease a **seat** or trading permit. Such a seat allows a member to trade on the exchange floor in areas known as **pits** or **rings**. Different pits or rings specialise in different futures and options contracts. Traders must be qualified by the exchange to trade on the floor and they are not allowed to deal directly with the public. The intermediaries between traders and the public are brokers.

The exchanges have standard trading hours but extend the floor hours using computer based trading systems such as **Automated Pit Trading (APT)** at LIFFE.

Some exchange floors are quite small involving a few pits only; others are large. For example, the CME covers 70,000 square feet on two floors and can have several thousand traders operating in the pits during hectic trading sessions. The following chart indicates the floor area for some of the larger exchanges world wide.

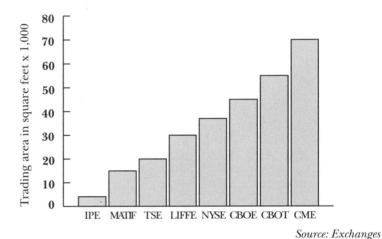

Source: Exchanges

The basic processes of trading on the larger exchanges such as the CME and LIFFE are described next; these are followed by brief descriptions of some of the smaller exchanges.

Client decides to buy/ sell a future/option instrument.

Client contacts broker who is an exchange member.

Broker contacts his booth on the exchange floor with client instructions. The order is received and time stamped.

Yellow or Gold jacket booth clerk communicates the information using hand signals or with a written order.

Pit traders wear **Red** or **Multicoloured** jackets. They then trade with a counterparty. Both parties input the deal details into the exchange matching system.

Blue jacket exchange officials act as pit observers to ensure that trading is conducted according to the rules. They also monitor the prices being traded which are relayed to the exchange computer for display on the floor and worldwide. On the CME there are also member firm clerks who wear a **green jacket** with a **black spot** on the back. These clerks resolve discrepancies in trades.

Trading on an Exchange such as LIFFE or CME

Broker informs the client that the order is filled.

Matched trades are passed to the clearing house for processing.

The trading floor on CME

The trading floor on LIFFE

Hand Signals

On many of the exchange floors hand signals are used by traders as a means of complementing their communications and trading procedures. There are many different types of signals, some of which are specific to particular contracts. However, there are four basic types of information which hand signals are used to convey:

- **Buy or Sell**

Buy – you see the back of the hand

Sell – you see the palm of the hand

- **Prices** – these are conveyed by signals **away** from the face

- **Quantity** – these use the same signals for prices but the hand is either on the **chin** or on the **forehead**

- **Month** – although traders usually trade on the next month of the delivery cycle of a futures contract – **March, June, September** and **December** – each month does have its own signal

 The delivery months are 3 months apart – if you are wondering why, have a look in *An Introduction to Derivatives* ISBN 0-471-83176-X.

Prices

The price indicated by the trader is usually the last digit or digits as displayed on the electronic boards around the exchange floor.

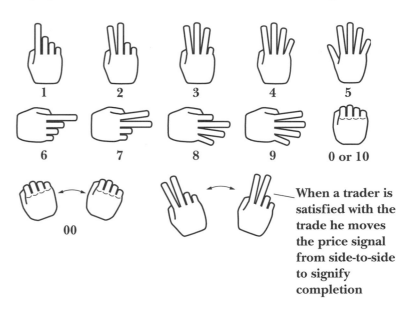

When a trader is satisfied with the trade he moves the price signal from side-to-side to signify completion

The price signals shown above are all for traders who are **buying** or in a **Bid** position – you see the back of their hand. For traders who are **selling** or in an **Offer (Ask)** position you would see the signs the other way round with the palm facing you.

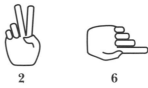

2   6

Quantity

Units are registered on the chin; tens on the forehead. Intermediate values are indicated using a combination of tens and units.

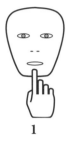

| 1 | 6 | 10 | 60 |

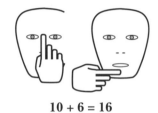

10 + 6 = 16

Months

March

 June

September

December

Your notes

Summary

You have now finished this section and you should have a clear understanding of the following methods of trading:

- Over-the-counter (OTC)

- Using electronic trading systems

- On an exchange floor

As a check on your understanding you should try the Quick Quiz questions on the next page. You may also find the section Overview useful as a revision aid.

Your notes

Quick Quiz Questions

1. Which of the following functions is/are the back office usually responsible for?

   ❑ a) Initiating and making deals
   ❑ b) Arranging for the settlement of deals
   ❑ c) Deciding which institutions the bank will do business with
   ❑ d) Maintaining the bank's overall FX position

2. Which of the following terms match with the appropriate phrases?

	a)	b)	c)	d)	e)
Bid price	☐	☐	☐	☐	☐
Offer price	☐	☐	☐	☐	☐

   ❑ a) Price at which the dealer is willing to sell
   ❑ b) Also known as the ask price
   ❑ c) Lower of the two prices
   ❑ d) Higher of the two prices
   ❑ e) Price at which the dealer is willing to buy

3. Which of the following conduct the majority of FX dealing?

   ❑ a) Central banks
   ❑ b) Investment funds
   ❑ c) International commercial banks
   ❑ d) Large corporations

4. Which of the following statements about FX Brokers is/are true?

   ❑ a) Brokers act as intermediaries to match buyers and sellers
   ❑ b) The broker brings the two participating parties together to meet before the deal is completed
   ❑ c) The rate charged by the broker is determined by the size of the transaction

5. Which of the following items of news would be expected to affect the world financial markets?

   ❑ a) UK retail sales have fallen sharply from the previous month
   ❑ b) The US President has been wounded
   ❑ c) The Japanese Minister of Finance announces his intention to prevent the Yen from appreciating further
   ❑ d) A volcano has erupted in Mexico

You can check your answers on page 136.

Overview

Methods

OTC
- Direct interbank
- Voice broker

Electronic trading systems

Exchange floor

Bank A

Bank C

D2000-1
D2000-2

Bank B

Broker

Factors Influencing Trading

Interest and deposit rates
- Different day counts for different instruments

Position control

Arbitrage

The importance of news

FX Dealers

Areas of activity

Spot 37%

FX swaps and forward outright 57%

Currency swaps and currency options 6%

Trading in the Money Markets and Foreign Exchange

FX Dealing Tasks

Form an opinion
- Fundamental factors
- Technical factors
- Institutional factors

Receive analysts' predictions

Trading on an Exchange

Open outcry

Pit or ring trading

Hand signals
- Buy or sell
- Prices
- Quantity
- Month

Electronic Trading Systems

Direct dealing systems

Automated matching systems

Support systems

Quick Quiz Answers

	✔ or ✖
1. b and d	☐
	☐
2. Bid c and e	☐
	☐
Offer a, b and d	☐
	☐
	☐
3. c	☐
4. a and c	☐
	☐
5. a, b , c and d	☐
	☐
	☐
	☐

How well did you score? You should have scored at least 10. If you didn't you may need to revise some of the materials.

Further Resources

Books
Trading for a Living: Psychology, Trading, Tactics, Money Management, SG
Alexander Elder, John Wiley & Sons, Inc., 1993
ISBN   0 471 59225 0

Cybernetic Trading Strategies: Developing a Profitable Trading System with State-of-the-Art Technologies
Murray A. Ruggiero, John Wiley & Sons, Inc., 1997
ISBN   0 471 14920 9

The Intuitive Trader: Developing Your Inner Trading Wisdom
Robert Koppel, John Wiley & Sons, Inc., 1996
ISBN   0 471 13047 8

Publications
London International Financial Futures and Options Exchange
• Hand Signals

Chicago Mercantile Exchange
• A World Marketplace

Reuters
Deal Manager: An Introduction to Dealing

Customer Profiles Version 1.0

Internet
RFT Website
• **http://www.wiley-rft.reuters.com**
This is the series' companion website where additional quiz questions, updated screens and other information may be found.

ACI – the Financial Markets Association
• **http://www.aciforex.com**
This is one of the largest fx associations with over 24,000 members in 79 countries of which 59 have affiliated national associations.

Introduction

In Part 1 we took an overview of the money markets and foreign exchange market, and examined the relationships between them. In addition, we briefly considered the instruments commonly used in the money markets and foreign exchange markets.

Part 2 will take a more detailed look at money market instruments. In particular, we will examine the parameters which must be defined in order to place a value on these instruments, together with basic valuation techniques.

This Part is split into three sections, reflecting the characteristics of groups of money market instruments. The sections are: Coupon Bearing Instruments, Discount Instruments and Money Market Derivatives.

Foreign exchange instruments will be examined in Part 3. For now we will concern ourselves purely with money market instruments.

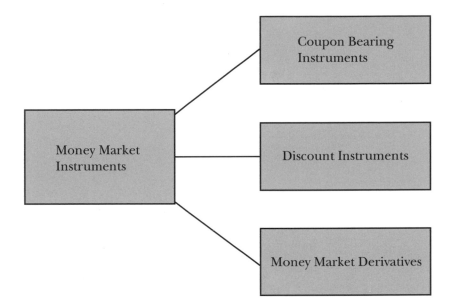

This section should take about one hour of study time. You may not take as long as this or it may take a little longer – remember your learning is individual to you.

Financial assets can bob all over the place, but they do not collapse unless there is evidence the fundamentals are eroding.
– Eric H. Sorensen of the investment firm Salomon Brothers, quoted in the *New York Times*, August 31, 1997.

Coupon Bearing Instruments

Coupon bearing money market instruments are instruments that pay out interest to the holder (or lender) on a regular basis throughout the tenor of the instrument.

This is in contrast to discount instruments, which are issued at a discount to par value and redeemed at par at maturity, and derivative instruments, which are essentially contracts to buy, sell or exchange assets on an agreed future date at an agreed price.

Money Market Deposits

Interbank Deposits

An **interbank deposit** is an unsecured, non-negotiable, fixed rate loan between financial institutions which is traded Over-the-counter (OTC).

Interbank deposits are a fundamental element of the money markets and foreign exchange market, as the interest rates paid in the interbank deposit market are used as a basis for other money market and foreign exchange instruments. These include:

- Certificates of Deposit (CDs) and Repurchase Agreements (Repos)
- Commercial Paper (CP)
- Forward Rate Agreements (FRAs), Interest Rate Futures
- Interest Rate Swaps (IRSs) and Floating Rate Notes (FRNs)
- Forward FX and FX Swaps

Interbank deposits can be found in two basic types, fixed and notice.

A **fixed deposit** is one where the rate of interest and the maturity date are agreed at the outset of the transaction.

A **notice deposit** is one where the rate of interest and the maturity date may be changed or the termination of the deposit requested with effect from a specified number of working days.

Terms and Specifications - Interbank Deposits

When an interbank deposit is transacted, the borrower pays interest based on:

- An agreed **interest rate**
- A **principal amount**, the amount of money being borrowed
- The **tenor**, the length of time money is being borrowed for
- The **maturity date**, when the principal and any interest due are paid back

The transaction takes place on the **trade date**. Interest is calculated from the **value date**, or delivery date, which is the date on which the lender delivers the principal to the borrower. The value date is normally the **spot date**, which is two working days after the trade date. At **maturity**, the borrower pays back the principal to the lender, plus any interest due.

Typical maturities include:

Overnight	O/N	Deposit today – return tomorrow
Tomorrow/next	T/N	Deposit tomorrow – return next day
Spot/next	S/N	Deposit on spot date – return next day
Spot/week	S/W	Deposit on spot date – return 7 days later
1 Month	1M	Deposit on spot date – return 1 month later
2 Months	2M	Deposit on spot date – return 2 months later
3 Months	3M	Deposit on spot date – return 3 months later
6 Months	6M	Deposit on spot date – return 6 months later
12 Months	1Yr	Deposit on spot date – return 12 months later

Components of a Trade— Interbank Deposits

When an interbank deposit is transacted, all the terms of the deal must be recorded by both the borrower and the lender. These terms are:

Trade Date	The date on which the trade takes place.
Value Date	The start date of a deposit. On this date, the lender delivers the principal of the trade to the borrower. Interest on the deposit begins to accrue on this date.
Maturity Date	The end date of the deposit. On this date, the borrower repays the lender the principal of the trade, plus all interest due. The last day for interest accrual on a deposit is the day before the maturity date.
Rate	The agreed upon interest rate expressed as a percentage on a per annum basis. This may also be called a **yield**.
Basis	The number of days in a year used to calculate interest. Most of the world uses a 360 day basis, meaning that a year is said to contain 360 days. Countries such as Canada, Ireland, Singapore, Hong Kong, Belgium and the UK use a 365 day basis.
Currency	The currency of the deposit.
Amount	The amount of the deposit.
Taking Bank	The bank that borrows the money. The deposit is recorded as a liability on this bank's books.
Placing Bank	The bank that lends the money. The deposit is recorded as an asset on this bank's books.
Payment Instructions	Precise instructions advising each bank as to the appropriate details for the delivery of principal on the value date to the **taking bank**, and subsequent repayment of principal plus interest to the **placing bank** on the maturity date.
Method/Via	The method used to transact the trade. (Direct, via a broker, etc.)
Confirmation	Printed verification of all the terms of the trade. Each counterparty sends the other a confirmation.

As in the FX markets, the deposit markets have a **bid** side – taker, and an **offered** side – placer. The table below compares some of the terminology and components of FX and deposit deals.

Term or Component	Spot FX Contract	MM Deposit Contract
No. of Currencies	2	1
Value Date	Date on which the currencies are exchanged	Date on which the **placer** delivers the principal to the **taker**. This is the start date of the deposit
Maturity Date	Not applicable	Date on which the **taker** repays the principal plus interest to the **placer**. This is the end of the deposit
Price/Rate	The agreed upon rate expressed as an amount of the quote currency per single unit of the base currency	The agreed upon rate expressed as a percentage per annum
Bid **means**	Expression of an intent to **buy** the base currency	Expression of an intent to **borrow** the specified currency
Offer **means**	Expression of an intent to **sell** the base currency	Expression of an intent to **lend** the specified currency
Hit the bid **means**	To **sell** the base currency at the **bid** price	To **lend** the specified currency at the **bid** price
Take the offer **means**	To **buy** the base currency at the **offered** price	To **borrow** the specified currency at the **offered** price

Money Market Deposits in the Market Place: Valuing Interbank Deposits

Interest (I) is calculated by taking into account the **principal** amount of the deposit (P), the agreed upon interest **rate** (R) expressed in its decimal form, the year **basis** (B) of the currency, either 360 or 365, and the **amount of days** (N) that the deposit lasts. The formula looks like this:

$$\text{Interest due (I)} = \frac{\text{Principal (P)} \ \text{x} \ \text{Rate (R)} \ \text{x} \ \text{Amount of days (N)}}{\text{Basis (B)} \ \text{x} \ 100}$$

...Equation 1

Interest on deposits maturing within 12 months is paid at maturity only. Longer date contracts usually pay interest at regular intervals — typically half-yearly.

Coupon bearing instruments have two values:

- **Present Value, PV** – the fair market value at a particular time before maturity

- **Future Value, FV** – the total repayment value, including interest, on maturity

$$\text{Future Value} = \text{Principal} + \text{Interest due} \qquad \textit{...Equation 2}$$

$$= P + \left(\frac{P \ \text{x} \ R \ \text{x} \ N}{B \ \text{x} \ 100} \right)$$

$$\text{Future Value} = P \ \text{x} \left[1 + \left(\frac{R \ \text{x} \ N}{B \ \text{x} \ 100} \right) \right] \qquad \textit{...Equation 3}$$

Depending on the calculations you need to perform concerning interest, present values and future values, a knowledge and understanding of *Equations 1 – 3* will be useful.

Coupon Bearing Instruments

Example 1

The interest due on a three month deposit of USD 10,000,000 at 6½% that has a tenor of 92 days would be calculated as follows:

$$\text{Interest due (I)} = \frac{10,000,000 \text{ (P)} \times 6.5 \text{ (R)} \times 92 \text{ (N)}}{360 \text{ (B)} \times 100}$$

$$= 166,111.11 \text{ USD}$$

The basis for USD is 360. The basis is seen as A/360 which means the actual number of days (92) over a 360-day year. Actual days include weekends and holidays.

It is important to recognise that the interest paid at the maturity of the deposit is **simple interest**. Compound interest, which is sometimes encountered in capital markets, involves adding the interest to the principal amount of the loan every time it is paid.

Suppose now that the deposit had been GBP 10,000,000. Using the same tenor and rate the interest due is now:

$$\text{Interest due (I)} = \frac{10,000,000 \text{ (P)} \times 6.5 \text{ (R)} \times 92 \text{ (N)}}{365 \text{ (B)} \times 100}$$

$$= 163,835.62 \text{ GBP}$$

The basis for GBP is 365, seen as A/365. Note the difference in interest amounts due to the different day bases.

i Year day basis conventions		Except GBP, CAD, BEF, ECU where:	
Domestic	360	Domestic	365
Euro	360	Euro	365

The difference in Basis can be important if you are comparing the **Money Market Yields, MMY** between different instruments. To compare rates between instruments you have to compare like with like. To do this you need to calculate the **true annual yield** for both deposits.

Example 2

You wish to compare a GBP deposit which uses **Actual/365 (A/365)** to calculate interest with a Eurodeposit which uses **Actual/360 (A/360)** for interest calculations. To compare like with like you need to add interest for 5 more days for the Eurodeposit. To do this simply multiply the rate by **365/360**.

For example, a Euromark deposit for DEM 100 million has a quoted rate of 10%. What is the true annual yield for this deposit on a 365 day year basis?

$$\text{True annual yield} = \frac{10 \times 365}{360}$$

$$= 10.14\%$$

Similarly if you need to compare an A/360 quoted instrument with one using A/365, the Rate will need to be multiplied by **360/365** – the interest is less because only 360 days are used to calculate the true annual yield.

This means that you must be careful when comparing the data for instruments onscreen!

Exercise. The screen below displays Bid and Ask prices for a number of currencies from different contributors simultaneously. For example you want to lend £5 million for 3 months and at the same time you need to borrow 2 million DEM. You use the screen to determine GBP Bid rates and DEM Ask rates from different contributors to select who you want to trade with. Assume 3 months is 90 days in both cases.

1) Which GBP contributor would you deposit funds with for the best rate of return and what interest would you expect to receive?

Answer:

2) Which DEM contributor would you borrow funds from and what interest would you pay?

Answer:

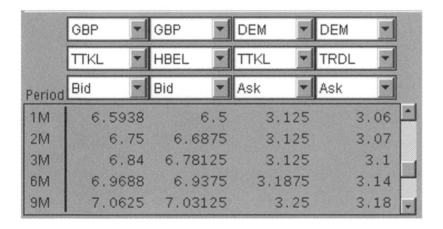

Period	GBP TTKL Bid	GBP HBEL Bid	DEM TTKL Ask	DEM TRDL Ask
1M	6.5938	6.5	3.125	3.06
2M	6.75	6.6875	3.125	3.07
3M	6.84	6.78125	3.125	3.1
6M	6.9688	6.9375	3.1875	3.14
9M	7.0625	7.03125	3.25	3.18

You can check your answers over the page.

Answers to Exercise

1) The highest Bid rate is from TTKL at 6.84 %. The interest for 90 days is £84328.70.

   Use Equation 1.
   $$\text{Interest} = 5{,}000{,}000 \ \times \ \frac{90}{365} \ \times \ \frac{6.84}{100}$$

2) The lowest Ask rate is from TRDL at 3.10%. The interest due for 90 days is 15500 DEM.

   Use Equation 1.
   $$\text{Interest} = 2{,}000{,}000 \ \times \ \frac{90}{360} \ \times \ \frac{3.10}{100}$$

Your notes

Certificates of Deposit (CDs)

 A **Certificate of Deposit (CD)** is a negotiable receipt for funds deposited at a bank or other financial institution for a specified tenor paying interest at a specified interest rate.

The rate of interest payable on a CD depends on factors including the currency of the CD, the current interbank deposit interest rate and the credit quality of the bank offering the deposit.

The holder of the CD can retain it until maturity, thus receiving all interest and principal, or he/she can sell the CD in the money market at the prevailing market price. This 'tradability' of CDs gives them an advantage over interbank deposits, and hence, in return for the right to trade them, they pay a lower rate of interest than interbank deposits.

In addition to fixed rate CDs, there are two variations commonly found in the money markets:

Discount CDs, which are issued and traded at a discount to par. On maturity, the principal is repaid, giving the lender a return on the principal amount. The interest rate received is calculated from the discount to par at which the CD is issued/traded.

Floating Rate CDs (FRCDs), which are similar to a consecutive string of fixed rate CDs. For example, a 1 year floating rate CD may pay interest every three months, based on the prevailing three month fixed rate CD interest rate for each period. FRCDs can be viewed as fixed rate CDs which are **rolled** at maturity into similar fixed rate CDs at the current fixed rate CD interest rate.

CDs in the Market Place

A short-term CD where interest is payable at maturity is termed a **bullet** security. For CDs issued with maturities of 12 months and greater, interest is typically paid semi-annually.

 A **bullet** security is one where the principal of a loan is paid in full on maturity

On maturity the bearer of a CD will receive the instrument's principal plus the agreed interest which is due. But supposing the bearer requires cash for a project and decides to sell the CD. What is a fair market value for the CD? What is its **Present Value, (PV)**?

A dollar received in the future is worth less than a dollar today because there is no opportunity to invest the dollar and earn interest. The **Future Value (FV)** – the repayment amount – is the amount of money you will receive if you invest a sum today, PV, for a period of time at a given rate of interest.

Future Value = Principal + Interest due	*...Equation 2*

The fair value, or settlement amount, of the CD should be that amount of money (PV) which, when placed on deposit today until maturity, would result in the same FV if the CD were left to mature. So the return on the CD should equal the return currently available on a deposit for the same maturity.

Example 1
Consider the following CD:

CD face value:	$1,000,000
Issue date:	1st January 1996
Maturity date:	1st January 1997
Coupon:	8.5% pa
Year basis:	360 days

Coupon Bearing Instruments

The CD has an original maturity of 366 days – a leap year! The interest due is simply calculated from the formula:

$$\text{Interest due (I)} = \frac{\text{Principal (P) x Rate (R) x Amount of days (N)}}{\text{Basis (B) x 100}}$$

...*Equation 1*

$$= \frac{1,000,000 \ \times \ 8.5 \ \times \ 366}{360 \ \times \ 100}$$

$$= \ \$86,416.67$$

So the Future Value of the CD = **$1,086,416.67**

You now decide that you must sell the CD for settlement on the 1st November 1996 when there are only 61 days left to maturity.

Suppose the current 2-month deposit rate is 9.75%. The fair value of the CD should be that amount of money, PV, which if placed on deposit today at 9.75% for 61 days would also result in a FV of $1,086,416.67.

Using Equations 2 and 3:

$$\text{Future Value} = \text{Principal} + \text{Interest due}$$

$$= P + \left(\frac{P \ x \ R \ x \ N}{B \ x \ 100} \right)$$

$$\text{Future Value} = P \ x \left[1 + \left(\frac{R \ x \ N}{B \ x \ 100} \right) \right] \qquad \text{...Equation 3}$$

In this case the Principal is the Present Value:

$$\text{Present value} = \text{Future value} - \text{Interest due}$$

$$= \frac{1086416.67}{\left[1 + \dfrac{9.75 \ x \ 61}{360 \ x \ 100} \right]}$$

$$\text{Present Value} = \ \$1,068,759.87$$

So the fair value for this CD, 2 months from maturity, discounted at 9.75% is $1,068,759.87.

The general equation for calculating the Present Value for a CD which has not reached maturity is given in Equation 4.

$$\text{Present Value} = \frac{P \ x \left[1 + \left(\dfrac{R \ x \ N}{B \ x \ 100} \right) \right] \ \text{— Future Value}}{\left[1 + \left(\dfrac{r \ x \ n}{B \ x \ 100} \right) \right] \ \text{— Interest due}}$$

...*Equation 7*

Where		
P	=	Principal or the CD face value
R	=	Quoted coupon rate for the CD
N	=	Number of days to maturity
B	=	Year basis – 365 or 360
r	=	Current market interest rate
n	=	Current number of days to maturity

You may or may not be offered a fair price if you want to sell your CD. What is required is a measure of how good or bad the price you are offered is. The important factor for the value of a CD in the secondary market is its **Yield To Maturity, YTM** which is also known as the **Money Market Yield, MMY**. The YTM is:

The **rate of return** on a fixed income instrument, such as a CD, if it is held to maturity.

In order to compare the value of a CD with interest rates on deposits and other instruments, market-makers quote a **yield basis** rather than cash values.

> ℹ️ *CDs are quoted on a **YTM (MMY) basis** rather than in cash terms.*

Example 2

Using the CD details from Example 1 you are offered $1,065,000.00 by a market-maker for its purchase with 61 days left to maturity. What YTM does this represent? Should you sell to the market-maker?

Using Equation 3 and rearranging for R, where P is taken as the PV:

$$R = \left(\frac{B \times 100}{N} \right) \times \left(\frac{FV - PV}{PV} \right) \qquad ...\textit{Equation 5}$$

$$= \frac{360 \times 100}{61} \times \frac{1086416.67 - 1065000.00}{1065000.00}$$

$$= 11.87\%$$

At the price offered the CD yields over 2% more than the comparable deposit rate of 9.75%. This represents a good purchase for the market-maker, but a poor sale for you!

Although YTM is the rate of return if an instrument is held to maturity, short-term investors often liquidate their position before maturity. These investors are therefore concerned with the **horizon return** on the instrument which has two components:

Horizon return = Accrued interest + Capital gains

This means the **horizon return** is the rate of return achieved on an investment, from purchase to sale, expressed as a percentage per annum taking into account both components.

> ℹ️ *If an investment is held to maturity, then its **horizon return equals the YTM**.*

The market-maker is unlikely to quote the price of $1,065,000.00 for the CD, which is the settlement amount. What the market-maker will quote is a two-way price, for example, 11.92/11.87.

This means that the market-maker will buy a CD from you (bid) for a cash amount that produces a yield of 11.92% for him, or that the market-maker will sell you (offer) a CD for a sum that will yield you 11.87%.

It is important to remember that the yields here are **Money Market Yields** and not true annual yields. Using this method of quotes makes the true value of CDs very transparent and easy to compare with interest rates on fixed deposits. When trading CDs the yield price is agreed and then the cash settlement is calculated for the purchase/ sale of the CD.

> ℹ️ *The **higher** the quoted yield, the **lower** the value of the asset.*
>
> *If you hold a CD you want broker quotes to go **down** – the lower the quoted yield, the **greater** the price receivable for selling before maturity.*

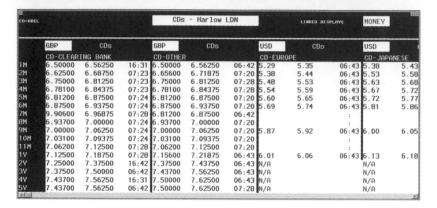

The screen above shows the GBP CD prices from the broker Harlow Butler.

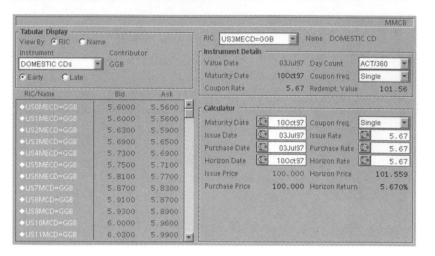

The screen above shows prices for Domestic CDs from Garvin Guy Butler.

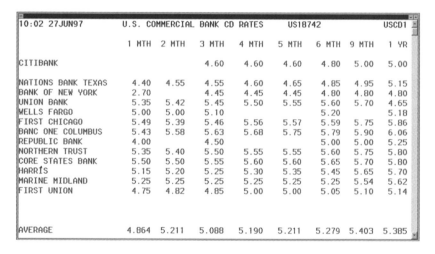

The screen above displays a variety of CD prices from different US Commercial Banks.

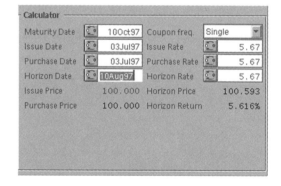

The screen above is a Calculator which is useful if you need to calculate the Horizon return for a CD for a date before maturity.

Repurchase Agreements (Repos)

 Definitions

A **Repurchase Agreement (Repo)** is an agreement for the sale of an instrument together with the simultaneous agreement by the seller to repurchase the instrument on an agreed future date at an agreed price.

A **Reverse Repurchase Agreement (Reverse Repo)** is an agreement for the purchase of an instrument together with the simultaneous agreement by the purchaser to resell the instrument on an agreed future date at an agreed price.

A Repo is a form of loan involving collateral and is executed as follows:

(i) The **seller** in the Repo sells the collateral (usually Treasury Bills) for cash and simultaneously agrees to repurchase the collateral on a future date at an agreed price.

(ii) The **seller** also receives interest, in addition to the cash, throughout the tenor of the deal at a rate known as the **repo rate**.

(iii) At maturity, the **seller** repurchases the T-bills for cash.

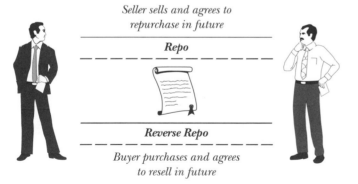

Seller sells and agrees to repurchase in future

Repo

Reverse Repo

Buyer purchases and agrees to resell in future

Conversely, in a Reverse Repo, the **buyer** buys T-bills for cash and simultaneously agrees to resell the T-bills for cash on an agreed date at an agreed price. During the tenor of the transaction, the **buyer** pays interest to the seller at the **repo rate**.

The valuation of Repos involves complex mathematics and is beyond the scope of this book.

Coupon Bearing Instruments

Summary

You have now finished this section and you should have a clear understanding of the following Coupon Bearing Instruments:

- Money Market Deposits
  - Interbank Deposits

- Certificates of Deposit (CDs)

- Repurchase Agreements (Repos)

As a check on your understanding you should try the Quick Quiz questions on the next page. You may also find the section Overview useful as a revision aid.

Your notes

Quick Quiz Questions

1. Which of the following Money Market instruments is not negotiable?

   ❑ a) Cash deposit
   ❑ b) Certificate of Deposit
   ❑ c) Eligible Bill
   ❑ d) Commercial Paper

   Answer a)

2. What is the true annual yield of a 12 month Euromark deposit quoted at 3.00%?

   ❑ a) 3.00%
   ❑ b) 3.02%
   ❑ c) 3.04%
   ❑ d) 3.05%

   Answer b)

3. You are the Treasurer of a large corporation in London and at times you need to deposit and borrow dollars. There are four banks you could deal with quoting the following Eurodollar rates for one month (31 days) on a 360-day year basis.

   Answer c)

Bank A	Bank B	Bank C	Bank D
$6^{11}\!/_{16} - 6^9\!/_{16}$	$6^3\!/_4 - 6^5\!/_8$	$6^7\!/_8 - 6^{11}\!/_{16}$	$6^{13}\!/_{16} - 6^3\!/_4$

   a) From which bank would you borrow Eurodollars and at what rate?
   b) From your answer in a), if you borrowed $5 million what is the total amount payable at maturity?
   c) With which bank would you deposit funds and at what rate?

4. What is the main advantage of a CD over other Money Market instruments? A CD:

   ❑ a) Pays a higher rate of interest
   ❑ b) Can be resold in the secondary market
   ❑ c) Is the safest form of investment

Quick Quiz Questions

---

5. You have bought a Sterling CD in the secondary market with a nominal value of £1,000,000. There are 87 days left to maturity and a yield of 6.5%. The CD was issued for 90 days with a coupon of 6.75%. How much do you receive at maturity?

    ❑ a) £1,015493.10
    ❑ b) £1,015,631.65
    ❑ c) £1,016,643.80
    ❑ d) £1,018,643.60

6. On 19th February you buy a 6-month (180 days) Euro CD at 8.40% with the following details and which has 90 days to maturity:

CD face value:	$100,000
Issue date:	20th November
Maturity date:	20th May
Coupon:	9.5% pa
Year basis:	360 days

    Calculate the following:
    a) The purchase cost of the CD
    b) The interest actually paid
    c) If the CD was sold on 29th February at 8.30% how much profit is made and what is the Horizon return?

Answer a)

Answer b)

Answer c)

You can check your answers on page 156.

Overview

Definition

Coupon bearing money market instruments are instruments that pay out interest to the holder (or lender) on a regular basis throughout the tenor of the instrument.

Main types

• Interbank Deposits

An **interbank deposit** is an unsecured, non-negotiable, fixed rate loan between financial institutions which is traded Over-the-counter (OTC).

• Certificates of Deposits (CDs)

A **Certificate of Deposit (CD)** is a negotiable receipt for funds deposited at a bank or other financial institution for a specified tenor paying interest at a specified interest rate.

• Repurchase Agreements (Repos)

A **Repurchase Agreement (Repo)** is an agreement for the sale of an instrument together with the simultaneous agreement by the seller to repurchase the instrument on an agreed future date at an agreed price.

• Reverse Repurchase Agreements

A **Reverse Repurchase Agreement (Reverse Repo)** is an agreement for the purchase of an instrument together with the simultaneous agreement by the purchaser to resell the instrument on an agreed future date at an agreed price.

A **fixed deposit** is one where the rate of interest and the maturity date are agreed at the outset of the transaction.

A **notice deposit** is one where the rate of interest and the maturity date may be changed or the termination of the deposit requested with effect from a specified number of working days.

Discount CDs, which are issued and traded at a discount to par. On maturity, the principal is repaid, giving the lender a return on the principal amount. The interest rate received is calculated from the discount to par at which the CD is issued/traded.

Floating Rate CDs (FRCDs), which are similar to a consecutive string of fixed rate CDs. For example, a 1 year floating rate CD may pay interest every three months, based on the prevailing three month fixed rate CD interest rate for each period. FRCDs can be viewed as fixed rate CDs which are **rolled** at maturity into similar fixed rate CDs at the current fixed rate CD interest rate.

Seller sells and agrees to repurchase in future

Repo

Reverse Repo

Buyer purchases and agrees to resell in future

Key Concepts:
- **Components of a Trade— Interbank Deposits**
  When an interbank deposit is transacted, all the terms of the deal must be recorded by both the borrower and the lender. These terms are:

Trade Date	The date on which the trade takes place.
Value Date	The start date of a deposit. On this date, the lender delivers the principal of the trade to the borrower. Interest on the deposit begins to accrue on this date.
Maturity Date	The end date of the deposit. On this date, the borrower repays the lender the principal of the trade, plus all interest due. The last day for interest accrual on a deposit is the day before the maturity date.
Rate	The agreed upon interest rate expressed as a percentage on a per annum basis. This may also be called a **yield**.
Basis	The number of days in a year used to calculate interest. Most of the world uses a 360 day basis, meaning that a year is said to contain 360 days. Countries such as Canada, Ireland, Singapore, Hong Kong, Belgium and the UK use a 365 day basis.
Currency	The currency of the deposit.
Amount	The amount of the deposit.
Taking Bank	The bank that borrows the money. The deposit is recorded as a liability on this bank's books.
Placing Bank	The bank that lends the money. The deposit is recorded as an asset on this bank's books.
Payment Instructions	Precise instructions advising each bank as to the appropriate details for the delivery of principal on the value date to the **taking bank**, and subsequent repayment of principal plus interest to the **placing bank** on the maturity date.
Method/Via	The method used to transact the trade. (Direct, via a broker, etc.)
Confirmation	Printed verification of all the terms of the trade. Each counterparty sends the other a confirmation.

- **Yield To Maturity (YTM)**

The **rate of return** on a fixed income instrument, such as a CD, if it is held to maturity.

Quick Quiz Answers

✔ or ✖

1. a) ☐

2. c) ☐

3. a) Bank A – This has lowest offer rate of $6^{11}\!/_{16}\%$. ☐

    b) \$5,028,793.00 ☐

    Use Equation 3.
    $$\text{Total amount} = 5,000,000 \times \left[1 + \left(\frac{6.6875 \times 31}{100 \times 360}\right)\right]$$

    $$= 5,000,000 \times (1.0057586)$$

    c) Bank D – This has the highest bid rate of $6^3\!/_4\%$. ☐

4. b) ☐

5. c) ☐

    Use Equation 3.
    $$\text{Sum at maturity} = 1,000,000 \times \left[1 + \left(\frac{6.75 \times 90}{100 \times 365}\right)\right]$$

6. a) Purchase cost = \$102,621.33 ☐

    Use Equation 4.
    $$\text{Purchase cost} = 100,000 \times \frac{\left[1 + \left(\dfrac{9.50 \times 181}{100 \times 360}\right)\right]}{\left[1 + \left(\dfrac{8.40 \times 90}{100 \times 360}\right)\right]}$$

    $$= \frac{1.0477638}{1.0210}$$

✔ or ✖

b) Actual interest = \$9631.94 ☐

   Annually $= \dfrac{9.50 \times 100,000 \times 365}{100 \times 360}$

c) Profit = \$257.51 ☐
    Horizon rate = 9.159% ☐

   $$\text{Selling cost} = 100,000 \times \frac{\left[1 + \left(\dfrac{9.50 \times 181}{100 \times 360}\right)\right]}{\left[1 + \left(\dfrac{8.30 \times 80}{100 \times 360}\right)\right]}$$

   $$= \frac{1.0477638}{1.0184444}$$

   $$= \$102,878.84$$

   Profit $=$ Selling – Purchase price
   $\quad\;\; = 102,878.84 - 102,621.33$

   Horizon return $= \dfrac{257.51}{102,621.33} \times \dfrac{360 \times 100}{10} \times \dfrac{365}{360}$

How well did you score? You should have managed to get most of these questions correct. If you didn't you may need to revise some of the materials.

Further Resources

Books

The Foreign Exchange and Money Markets Guide
Julian Walmsley, John Wiley & Sons, Inc., 1992
ISBN   0 471 53104 9

New Financial Instruments, 2nd Ed.
Julian Walmsley, John Wiley & Sons, Inc., 1998
ISBN   0 471 12136 3

Derivatives: The Wild Beast of Finance
Alfred Steinherr and Folkerts-Landau, John Wiley & Sons, Inc., 1998
ISBN   0 471 96544 8

Derivatives Handbook: Risk Management and Control
Robert J. Schwartz and Clifford W. Smith (ed.), John Wiley & Sons Inc., 1997
ISBN   0 471 15765 1

The Penguin International Dictionary of Finance
Graham Bannock & William Manser, Penguin, 2nd Edition 1995
ISBN   0 14 051279 9

Booklets

Chicago Board of Trade
• Financial Instruments Guide

Internet

RFT Website
• **http://www.wiley-rft.reuters.com**
This is the series' companion website where additional quiz questions, updated screens and other information may be found.

Your notes

Coupon Bearing Instruments

Your notes

This section should take about one and a half to two hours of study time. You may not take as long as this or it may take a little longer – remember your learning is individual to you.

Discount Instruments

Example 1 – A US T-bill
Calculate the settlement amount for the following US T-bill which has 50 days to maturity.

T-bill face value:	$100,000
Settlement date:	9th May
Maturity date:	28th June
Discount rate:	8.12%
Year basis:	360 days

Using Equation 6:

$$ S = 100,000 \times \left[1 - \left(\frac{8.12 \times 50}{360 \times 100} \right) \right] $$

Therefore the settlement value = $98,872.22. This is also written as 98.87% of face value.

If the discount rate remains constant, then as the instrument approaches maturity N becomes smaller and the settlement price for the T-bill rises to converge with its face value.

Example 2 – A UK T-Bill
Calculate the discount rate for the following UK T-bill which has 91 days to maturity.

T-bill face value:	£100,000
Settlement date:	9th May
Maturity date:	8th August
Settlement value:	£98,485
Year basis:	365 days

Using Equation 7:

$$ \text{Discount rate} = \frac{100,000 - 98,485}{100,000} \times \frac{365 \times 100}{91} $$

$$ = 6.0766\% $$

As in the case of other money market instruments, quoting a rate may not be that useful if you need to compare rates of return from different instruments. Rates of return for instruments held to maturity are compared by calculating the **Money Market Yield, MMY** for each instrument.

The MMY for an instrument can be calculated as follows:

1. Calculate the profit to maturity on the instrument. This is equal to (P – S).

2. Express 1. as a proportion of the amount invested. This is equal to (P – S) ÷ S

3. Express 2. on a percentage annual basis

Therefore:

$$ MMY = \left(\frac{P - S}{S} \right) \times \left(\frac{B \times 100}{N} \right) \qquad \text{...Equation 8} $$

Equation 8 is very similar to Equation 7 which can be used to express MMY in terms of the Discount rate as in Equation 9.

$$ MMY = \frac{R/100}{\left[1 - \left(\frac{R \times N}{B \times 100} \right) \right]} \qquad \text{...Equation 9} $$

Example 3 – A US T-bill
Using the same information from Example 1 calculate the MMY for the US T-bill which has 50 days to maturity.

T-bill face value:	$100,000
Settlement date:	9th May
Maturity date:	28th June
Discount rate:	8.12%
Year basis:	360 days

Using Equation 9:

$$MMY = \frac{8.12/100}{\left[1 - \left(\frac{8.12 \times 50}{360 \times 100}\right)\right]}$$

Therefore the MMY   =   8.21%

To convert this yield into a true annual yield you would need to multiply MMY by 365/360.

$$\text{True annual yield} = \frac{8.21 \times 365}{360}$$

$$= 8.32\%$$

Although the MMY is useful for comparing short-term money market instruments a different yield basis is used for comparisons with coupon bearing instruments which are nearing maturity.

The **Bond Equivalent Yield, BEY** allows such a comparison to be made and is particularly useful for comparing T-bills with Treasury Bonds and Notes with only a short time to maturity.

BEY takes into account compounding of interest for coupon payments and adjusts for a coupon period of 365 days. A complicated formula is used for calculations which will not be discussed here. However, a good approximation for US T-bills with a maturity of 6 months or less is given by the following equation:

$$BEY = \frac{MMY \times 365}{360} \qquad \textit{... Equation 10}$$

In the case of UK T-bills (as both bills and Gilts are priced on a 365 basis), using Equation 10 means that MMY equals BEY.

Your notes

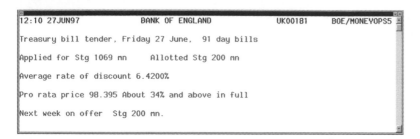

```
12:10 27JUN97              BANK OF ENGLAND           UK00181      BOE/MONEYOPS5

Treasury bill tender, Friday 27 June,  91 day bills

Applied for Stg 1069 mn     Allotted Stg 200 mn

Average rate of discount 6.4200%

Pro rata price 98.395 About 34% and above in full

Next week on offer  Stg 200 mn.
```

The screen above displays the T-Bill tender results from the Bank of England.

The screens below show the prices for Barclays Bank PLC and Clive Discount Co. Ltd. respectively.

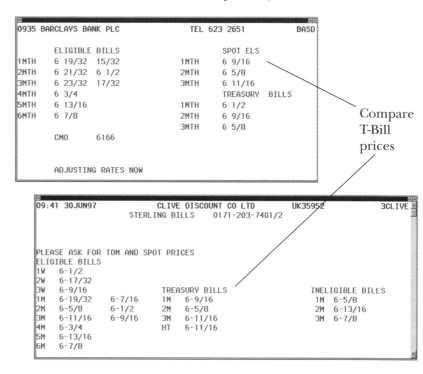

```
0935 BARCLAYS BANK PLC                  TEL 623 2651          BASD

        ELIGIBLE BILLS                      SPOT ELS
1MTH    6 19/32  15/32        1MTH         6 9/16
2MTH    6 21/32  6 1/2        2MTH         6 5/8
3MTH    6 23/32  17/32        3MTH         6 11/16
4MTH    6 3/4                              TREASURY   BILLS
5MTH    6 13/16              1MTH         6 1/2
6MTH    6 7/8                2MTH         6 9/16
                            3MTH         6 5/8

        CMO      6166


        ADJUSTING RATES NOW
```

Compare T-Bill prices

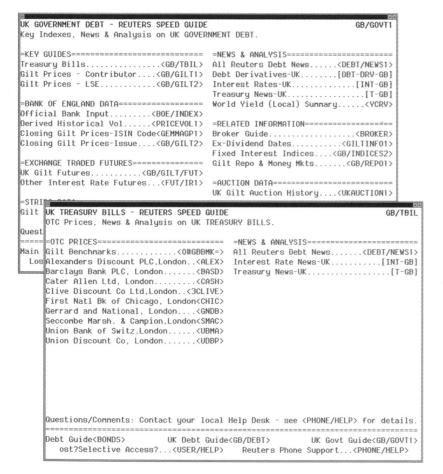

```
UK GOVERNMENT DEBT - REUTERS SPEED GUIDE                        GB/GOVT1
Key Indexes, News & Analysis on UK GOVERNMENT DEBT.

=KEY GUIDES=============================  =NEWS & ANALYSIS====================
Treasury Bills................<GB/TBIL>   All Reuters Debt News......<DEBT/NEWS1>
Gilt Prices - Contributor....<GB/GILT1>   Debt Derivatives-UK........[DBT-DRV-GB]
Gilt Prices - LSE............<GB/GILT2>   Interest Rates-UK..........[INT-GB]
                                          Treasury News-UK...........[T-GB]
=BANK OF ENGLAND DATA=================     World Yield (Local) Summary......<YCRV>
Official Bank Input.........<BOE/INDEX>
Derived Historical Vol......<PRICEVOL1>   =RELATED INFORMATION================
Closing Gilt Prices-ISIN Code<GEMMAGP1>   Broker Guide...................<BROKER>
Closing Gilt Prices-Issue....<GB/GILT2>   Ex-Dividend Dates..........<GILTINF01>
                                          Fixed Interest Indices....<GB/INDICES2>
=EXCHANGE TRADED FUTURES==============     Gilt Repo & Money Mkts.......<GB/REP01>
UK Gilt Futures...........<GB/GILT/FUT>
Other Interest Rate Futures...<FUT/IR1>   =AUCTION DATA=======================
                                          UK Gilt Auction History....<UKAUCTION1>
=STRI...
Gilt  UK TREASURY BILLS - REUTERS SPEED GUIDE                        GB/TBIL
      OTC Prices, News & Analysis on UK TREASURY BILLS.
Quest
     =OTC PRICES========================  =NEWS & ANALYSIS====================
Main Gilt Benchmarks............<O#GBBMK=>  All Reuters Debt News.......<DEBT/NEWS1>
 Los Alexanders Discount PLC,London..<ALEX>  Interest Rate News-UK..........[INT-GB]
     Barclays Bank PLC, London.......<BASD>  Treasury News-UK..............[T-GB]
     Cater Allen Ltd, London.........<CASH>
     Clive Discount Co Ltd,London..<3CLIVE>
     First Natl Bk of Chicago, London<CHIC>
     Gerrard and National, London...<GNDB>
     Secconbe Marsh. & Campion,London<SMAC>
     Union Bank of Switz,London......<UBMA>
     Union Discount Co, London.......<UDBP>




     Questions/Comments: Contact your local Help Desk - see <PHONE/HELP> for details.
     ================================================================================
     Debt Guide<BONDS>      UK Debt Guide<GB/DEBT>       UK Govt Guide<GB/GOVT1>
       ost?Selective Access?...<USER/HELP>    Reuters Phone Support...<PHONE/HELP>
```

```
09:41 30JUN97              CLIVE DISCOUNT CO LTD    UK35952       3CLIVE
                  STERLING BILLS   0171-203-7401/2


PLEASE ASK FOR TOM AND SPOT PRICES
ELIGIBLE BILLS
1W   6-1/2
2W   6-17/32
3W   6-9/16                     TREASURY BILLS              INELIGIBLE BILLS
1M   6-19/32   6-7/16     1M   6-9/16                 1M   6-5/8
2M   6-5/8     6-1/2      2M   6-5/8                  2M   6-13/16
3M   6-11/16   6-9/16     3M   6-11/16                3M   6-7/8
4M   6-3/4               HT   6-11/16
5M   6-13/16
6M   6-7/8
```

The first screen shows the UK Government Debt Speed Guide. The second screen shows OTC prices for Treasury Bills.

Bills of Exchange/Banker's Acceptance

A **Bill of Exchange** is an order to pay a specified amount of money to the holder on a specified future date (time draft) or on presentation (sight draft). It is a short-term IOU in support of a commercial transaction.

A **Banker's Acceptance (BA)**, or **Banker's Bill**, is a Bill of Exchange drawn or accepted by a commercial bank.

A Bill of Exchange issued by the government is simply a Treasury Bill.

A Bill of Exchange in the UK is essentially the same as a BA in the US. These instruments are generally used for financing trade and originated when importers would agree to pay exporters in foreign countries a specified sum of money on a specified future date for goods.

Once the importer acknowledges his obligation to honour the bill he writes ACCEPTED across the bill which now becomes a **Banker's Acceptance**.

Often, exporters will obtain a Bill of Exchange from an importer's bank as proof that they will be paid. This is known as a **Letter of Credit** and is a non-negotiable order from a bank, drafted when an exporter produces all the necessary documentation, such as a Bill of Lading, invoices, warehouse receipts etc. The importer's bank stamps the draft ACCEPTED, and the resulting Banker's Acceptance means the importer's bank will pay the full amount at the due date.

The exporter can now sell the BA to raise cash if necessary, as it is a negotiable instrument carrying the bank's obligation to pay. If sold in the secondary market, the BA trades at a discount to its face value, which reflects the interest on the money the buyer is effectively lending the exporter when he/she buys the BA. At maturity, the buyer of the BA receives the face value from the exporter's bank.

Typically, the exporter sells the BA to its own bank before maturity in order to improve its cash flow. The bank can either hold the BA to maturity or re-sell it in the secondary market.

The following diagram summarises the processes described in issuing and trading a typical BA.

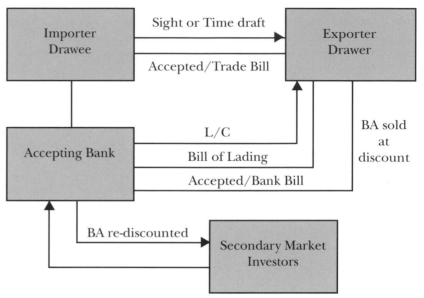

Who Uses BAs

Banks

In London Bills of Exchange and Banker's Acceptances have been issued by Merchant Banks or Accepting House for centuries. In taking on the credit risk for the original drawee, the bank charges a fee to guarantee payment of the bill's face value at maturity. The more creditworthy the accepting bank, the easier it is to sell the bills in the secondary market.

The accepting bank's fee is derived from the difference between the discount rate at which the bank buys the original bill from its customer and the lower re-discount rate at which it sells the accepted bill in the secondary market.

The majority of BAs in the US are created by international subsidiaries of money-centre banks. Originally the US market developed to finance US import and export markets – in much the same way as Bills of Exchange had developed in the UK. However, many BAs now issued in the US finance trade in which neither importer nor exporter are US organisations.

Eligible BAs

The type of BA described so far is one created for a commercial transaction involving the supply of goods or services and which is usually supported by a Letter of Credit. However, BAs are also issued on the basis of less formal contractual agreements as a means of satisfying credit demand which avoids central bank rules and penalties.

During the 1960s and 1970s central banks in both the US and the UK attempted to control the growth of money supply through bank credit rationing rather than by raising interest rates. If banks exceeded their domestic lending targets, then they were penalised by their central bank.

To overcome these difficulties banks developed the following tactics:

- Lending was channelled through the Eurocurrency markets which were not subject to the same central bank rules and regulations.

- Working Capital BAs or Finance Bills were created which were then sold in the secondary markets. Finance Bills are a major source of working capital for organisations which lack the credit rating to issue a Commercial Paper.

The result was that both the Bank of England and the Fed made these bills ineligible for re-discount at the central bank and they made the sale of such bills subject to reserve requirements.

What then is an eligible bill?

 An **eligible bill** is a BA which a central bank is prepared to buy and sell which does not incur a reserve requirement.

In broad terms an eligible bill is an acceptance which has been created to fund specific types of short-term – usually up to 6 months – commercial transactions.

Eligible BAs issued in the US tend to track T-bill rates quite closely. The distinction between eligible and ineligible BAs is therefore important and it is normal to see quotes only for eligible BAs.

Valuing Bills of Exchange

The market value of a Banker's Acceptance is the present value of the redemption amount payable at maturity.

This is given by Equation 6:

$$\text{Settlement amount} \quad = \quad P \times \left[1 - \left(\frac{R \times N}{B \times 100} \right) \right] \qquad \textit{...Equation 6}$$

Where
- P = Redemption value, FV
- R = Discount rate as a decimal
- N = Number of days to maturity
- B = Year basis – 365 or 360

Example 1

You are a corporate treasurer who needs to borrow £500,000 for the next 182 days. Your bank offers you the following BA. If you took this BA what would be the redemption value or cost of the instrument at maturity?

Settlement value:	£500,000
Issue date:	5th January
Maturity date:	5th July
Rate:	$6^{15}\!/_{16}\%$ pa
Year basis:	365 days

Using Equation 6:

$$500,000 \quad = \quad P \times \left[1 - \left(\frac{6.9375 \times 180}{365 \times 100} \right) \right]$$

Therefore the redemption or face value, P

$$P = \frac{500,000}{\left[1 - \left(\dfrac{6.9375 \times 180}{365 \times 100}\right)\right]}$$

$$= \frac{500,000}{(1 - 0.03421)}$$

$$= £517,705.52$$

The cost of using the BA is therefore £17,705.52

Example 2
What would be the settlement amount for the following
BA issued by Barclays Bank Plc.

Underlying trade:	Beet export
Face value:	£200,000
Days to maturity:	142
Quoted rate:	6.5% pa
Year basis:	365 days

Using Equation 6:

$$\text{Settlement amount} = 200,000 \times \left[1 - \left(\frac{6.5 \times 142}{365 \times 100}\right)\right]$$

$$\text{Settlement amount} = 200,000 \times (1 - .02529)$$

$$= £194,942.46$$

In this case you would expect to pay £194,942.46 if you purchased this
BA with 142 days remaining to maturity. At maturity you would
receive £200,000. The difference between the two values is the
discount – the amount you receive to lend your money.

Your notes

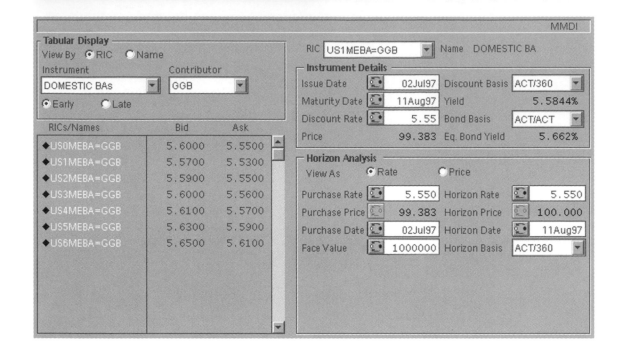

The screen on the left displays US Domestic BA rates from Garvin Guy Butler.

The screen on the right shows Reuters prices for BAs from primary dealers.

```
1242        REUTERS - BA PRIMARY DEALER SOURCED INDICATIONS      NYAS
              (U.S. BA RATES)                 (JAPANESE BA'S)
            EARLY CHG  - LATE CHG            EARLY   -   LATE
            -------------------------        ------------------

AUG         5.50  -01  - 5.51  UNC           5.60    -   5.61
SEP         5.51  -01  - 5.52  UNC           5.62    -   5.63
OCT         5.52  -01  - 5.53  UNC           5.64    -   5.65
NOV         5.53  -01  - 5.54  UNC           5.66    -   5.66
DEC         5.54  -01  - 5.54  -01           5.67    -   5.68
JAN         5.56  -01  - 5.56  -01           5.69    -   5.70
  BANK OF NEW YORK   - 07/08/97  1-90  DAYS   5.9375
  JAPANESE POSTED RATES FOR BAS 91-180 DAYS  5.9375
```

Commercial Paper (CP)

A **Commercial Paper** is a short-term unsecured promise to pay a specified amount on a specified date in the future. It is a negotiable instrument typically issued in bearer form.

A CP is a form of loan which is not backed by assets of the issuer. Therefore, lenders face the risk of not recovering their money if the issuer should default on the loan. Due to the credit risk inherent in CP, only large companies with good credit ratings typically issue commercial paper.

Euro Commercial Paper (EURO CP, ECP)

A **Euro Commercial Paper** is a commercial paper issued on a Eurocurrency basis. This means the regulatory conditions which apply to normal CPs in their country of issue do not apply to ECPs which are issued outside the country in which the issuer is located.

Euro CPs are similar in most respects to CPs. However, there are two main differences:
- CPs are quoted on a **discount to par basis**
- Euro CPs are quoted on a **discount to yield basis**. This means that the quoted rate is the same as the **Money Market Yield, MMY**.

Valuing Commercial Paper

Within the discount markets instruments have two values which you need to understand:

Present Value, PV — the fair market value at a particular time

Future Value, FV — the redemption amount payable on maturity

The settlement amount payable on a discount instrument before maturity is calculated using Equation 6:

$$\text{Settlement amount, } S = P \times \left[1 - \left(\frac{R \times N}{B \times 100} \right) \right] \qquad \textit{Equation 6}$$

Where
P = Redemption value, FV
R = Discount rate as a decimal
N = Number of days to maturity
B = Year basis — 365 or 360

By rearranging Equation 1 the Discount rate can be calculated using Equation 7.

$$R\% = \left(\frac{P - S}{P} \right) \times \left(\frac{B \times 100}{N} \right) \qquad \textit{Equation 7}$$

As in the case of other money market instruments, quoting a rate may not be that useful if you need to compare rates of return from different instruments. Rates of return for instruments held to maturity are compared by calculating the **Money Market Yield, MMY**, for each instrument.

The MMY for an instrument can be calculated as follows:

1. Calculate the profit to maturity on the instrument. This is equal to (P – S)

2. Express 1. as a proportion of the amount invested. This is equal to (P – S) ÷ S

3. Express 2. on a percentage annual basis

Discount Instruments

Therefore:

$$MMY = \left(\frac{P-S}{S}\right) \times \left(\frac{B \times 100}{N}\right) \qquad \textit{Equation 8}$$

Equation 8 is very similar to Equation 7 which can be used to express MMY in terms of the Discount rate as in Equation 9.

$$MMY = \frac{R/100}{\left[1 - \left(\frac{R \times N}{B \times 100}\right)\right]} \qquad \textit{Equation 9}$$

Example 1 – A US CP

Calculate the settlement amount and the MMY for the following US CP issued by Motorola Finance. The quoted rate is on a discount to par basis for a normal CP.

CP face value:	$100,000
Settlement date:	1st April
Maturity date:	1st May
Discount rate:	8.83%
Year basis:	360 days

Using Equation 6:

$$S = 100,000 \times \left[1 - \left(\frac{8.83 \times 30}{360 \times 100}\right)\right]$$

Therefore the settlement value = $99,264.17

Using Equation 9:

$$MMY = \frac{8.83/100}{\left[1 - \left(\frac{8.83 \times 30}{360 \times 100}\right)\right]}$$

Therefore the MMY = 8.8955%

Example 2 – A Euro CP

Calculate the settlement amount and the MMY for the following Euro CP issued by Eurotunnel. The quoted rate is on a discount to yield basis for a Euro CP. In this case the settlement value is calculated using an equation similar to that used for CDs.

CP face value:	$100,000
Settlement date:	1st December 1995
Maturity date:	1st January 1996
Discount rate:	7.12%
Year basis:	360 days

$$\text{Settlement value, } S = \frac{P \times \left[1 + \left(\frac{R \times N}{B \times 100}\right)\right]}{\left[1 + \left(\frac{r \times n}{B \times 100}\right)\right]} \qquad \textit{...Equation 11}$$

Where
- P = Redemption value
- R = Quoted coupon rate which is zero for a CP
- N = Number of days to maturity
- B = Year basis – 365 or 360
- r = Current discount rate
- n = Current number of days to maturity

So for a Euro CP where R = 0, Equation 6 reduces to:

$$\text{Settlement value, } S = \frac{P}{\left[1 + \left(\frac{r \times n}{B \times 100}\right)\right]} \qquad \textit{...Equation 12}$$

Using Equation 12:

$$\text{Settlement value, } S = \frac{100{,}000}{\left[1 + \left(\dfrac{7.12 \ \times \ 31}{360 \ \times \ 100}\right)\right]}$$

Therefore the settlement value = $99,390.63

In the case of a Euro CP the MMY is the same as the discount rate so no calculation is involved!

Exercise

You are considering buying an A1P1 US CP and you view the GGB prices on Money 3000. You are considering a CP with a 60 day maturity period and face value of $1,000,000. The prices on screen are as follows:

Tabular Display		
View By ⦿ RIC ○ Name		
Instrument	Contributor	
COMM PAPER ▼	GGB	
⦿ A1P1 ○ A1P2 ○ A2P2		

RICs/Names	Bid	Ask
◆ US5DCP11=GGB	5.6700	5.6200
◆ US15DCP11=GGB	5.6500	5.6000
◆ US30DCP11=GGB	5.6000	5.5500
◆ US60DCP11=GGB	5.6100	5.5600
◆ US90DCP11=GGB	5.6200	5.5700
◆ US120DCP11=GGB	5.6200	5.5700
◆ US150DCP11=GGB	5.6200	5.5700
◆ US180DCP11=GGB	5.6400	5.5900
◆ US270DCP11=GGB	5.6600	5.6100

a) If you bought the 60 day CP as quoted, what would the settlement rate or price be?

b) Calculate the Money Market Yield and the true annual yield for the CP.

You can check your answers over the page.

Discount Instruments

Your notes

Your notes

✔ or ✖

a) $990,650.00 or price 99.065   ❑

Use Equation 1.

$$\text{Settlement} = 100,000 \times \left[1 - \left(\frac{5.61 \times 60}{360 \times 100} \right) \right]$$

$$= 100,000 \times [(1 - (0.0093500)]$$

b) Money Market Yield   = 5.6629%   ❑
   True annual yield   = 5.7416%   ❑

Use Equation 4.

$$\text{MMY} = \frac{5.61/100}{[(1 - (0.009350)]}$$

$$\text{True annual yield} = \frac{5.6629 \times 365}{360}$$

Discount Instruments

Summary

You have now finished this section and you should have a clear understanding of the following Discount Instruments:

- Treasury Bill (T-bill)

- Bill of Exchange/Banker's Acceptance (BA)

- Commercial Paper (CP)

As a check on your understanding you should try the Quick Quiz Questions on the next page. You may also find the section Overview useful as a revision aid.

Your notes

Quick Quiz Questions

1. You want to buy a UK T-Bill with a face value of £100,000 maturing in 3-months (91 days). Barclays Bank is quoting $6\frac{5}{8}\%$ whilst Clive Discount House is quoting $6\frac{11}{16}\%$.

   a) Which Bank would you buy the T-Bill from?

   b) What is the settlement rate for the bill?

   c) What is the Money Market Yield for the bill?

2. You check on the RT and find the latest price for a US T-Bill with a face value of $100,000 with a 3-month maturity (90 days) is 5.05%.

   a) What is the settlement rate for the bill?

   b) What is the Money Market Yield for the bill?

   c) What is the true annual yield for the bill?

You can check your answers on page 176.

Discount Instruments

Overview

Discount Instruments

Definition

Discount instruments are issued and trade at a discount to their **par value** which reflects the prevailing short-term interest rate. In this way, a lender who lends money by buying a discount instrument receives interest in the form of the appreciation in price of the discount instrument.

Main Types

• Treasury Bills

A **Treasury Bill (T-bill)** is a short-term negotiable instrument, issued by the government, to pay the holder a specified amount of money on a specified future date.

At maturity, the holder of a Treasury Bill will receive the instrument's principal amount, commonly known as the **redemption amount**. This means the interest rate receivable on a T-bill, known as the **discount rate**, determines the prevailing T-bill market value.

The market value of a T-bill is the **present value of the redemption amount payable at maturity**. In other words, the price of a T-bill is the discounted value of the redemption amount, discounted at the prevailing **discount rate**.

• Bills of Exchange/Banker's Acceptance (BA)

A **Bill of Exchange** is an order to pay a specified amount of money to the holder on a specified future date (time draft) or on presentation (sight draft). It is a short-term IOU in support of a commercial transaction.

A **Banker's Acceptance (BA)**, or **Banker's Bill**, is a Bill of Exchange drawn or accepted by a commercial bank.

• Eligible Bill

An **eligible bill** is a BA which a central bank is prepared to buy and sell which does not incur a reserve requirement.

• Commercial Paper (CP)

A **Commercial Paper** is a short-term unsecured promise to pay a specified amount on a specified date in the future. It is a negotiable instrument typically issued in bearer form.

• Euro Commercial Paper (Euro CP, ECP)

A **Euro Commercial Paper** is a commercial paper issued on a Eurocurrency basis. This means the regulatory conditions which apply to normal CPs in their country of issue do not apply to ECPs which are issued outside the country in which the issuer is located.

Importer Drawee — Sight or Time draft / Accepted/Trade Bill — Exporter Drawer

Accepting Bank — L/C, Bill of Lading, Accepted/Bank Bill; BA sold at discount; BA re-discounted → Secondary Market Investors

Key Concepts:

• Money Market Yield
As in the case of other money market instruments, quoting a rate may not be that useful if you need to compare rates of return from different instruments. Rates of return for instruments held to maturity are compared by calculating the **Money Market Yield, MMY** for each instrument.

• Bond Equivalent Yield
Although the MMY is useful for comparing short-term money-market instruments a different yield basis is used for comparisons with coupon bearing instruments which are nearing maturity.

The Bond Equivalent Yield, BEY allows such a comparison to be made and is particularly useful for comparing T-bills with Treasury Bonds and Notes with only a short time to maturity.

BEY takes into account compounding of interest for coupon payments and adjusts for a coupon period of 365 days.

• Present Value
Present Value, PV — the fair market value at a particular time.

• Future Value
Future Value, FV — the redemption amount payable on maturity.

Quick Quiz Answers

✔ or ✘

1. a) Barclays Bank – the lowest discount rate ❏

   b) £98,348.29 ❏

   Use Equation 1.
   $$\text{Settlement} = 100{,}000 \times \left[1 - \left(\frac{6.625 \times 91}{100 \times 365}\right)\right]$$

   $$= 100{,}000 \times [(1 - (0.0165171)]$$

   c) 6.74% ❏

   Use Equation 4.
   $$\text{MMY} = \frac{6.625/100}{[(1 - (0.0165171)]}$$

   $$= \frac{0.06625}{0.98348}$$

✔ or ✘

2. a) $98,735.50 ❏

   Use Equation 1.
   $$\text{Settlement} = 100{,}000 \times \left[1 - \left(\frac{5.05 \times 90}{100 \times 360}\right)\right]$$

   $$= 100{,}000 \times [(1 - (0.012625)]$$

   b) 5.115% ❏

   Use Equation 4.
   $$\text{MMY} = \frac{5.05/100}{[(1 - (0.012625)]}$$

   c) 5.186% ❏

   $$\text{True annual yield} = \frac{5.115 \times 365}{360}$$

How well did you score? You should have managed to get most of these questions correct. If you didn't you may need to revise some of the materials.

Discount Instruments

Further Resources

Books

The Foreign Exchange and Money Markets Guide
Julian Walmsley, John Wiley & Sons, Inc., 1992
ISBN   0 471 53104 9

New Financial Instruments, 2nd Ed.
Julian Walmsley, John Wiley & Sons, Inc., 1998
ISBN   0 471 12136 3

Derivatives: The Wild Beast of Finance
Alfred Steinherr and Folkerts-Landau, John Wiley & Sons, Inc., 1998
ISBN   0 471 96544 8

Derivatives Handbook: Risk Management and Control
Robert J. Schwartz and Clifford W. Smith (ed.), John Wiley & Sons Inc., 1997
ISBN   0 471 15765 1

The Penguin International Dictionary of Finance
Graham Bannock & William Manser, Penguin, 2nd Edition 1995
ISBN   0 14 051279 9

Booklets
Chicago Board of Trade
• Financial Instruments Guide

Internet
RFT Website
• **http://www.wiley-rft.reuters.com**
This is the series' companion website where additional quiz questions, updated screens and other information may be found.

Your notes

This section should take about two hours of study time. You may not take as long as this or it may take a little longer – remember your learning is individual to you.

Financial risk management is not just a theoretical nicety; it is a practical necessity. Derivatives instruments don't create surprises. They help minimize them.
– David B. Weinberger, managing director of Swiss Bank Corporation and general partner of O'Connor Partners, Chicago, quoted in *Harvard Business Review*, January-February 1995.

Derivative Instruments

We have so far considered coupon-bearing instruments and discount instruments. We will now consider **Derivative Instruments**.

A **Derivative Instrument** is one whose value changes with changes in one or more underlying market variables, such as interest rates or foreign exchange rates. A Derivative Instrument is essentially an agreement between two counterparties in which they agree to transfer an asset or amount of money on or before a specified future date at a specified price.

As the price of this asset may vary over the tenor of the derivative contract, the present value of this contract can be very sensitive to the price of the underlying asset.

Basic derivatives include Forward Rate Agreements (FRAs), Interest Rate Futures, Interest Rate Swaps (IRSs), Forward FX, FX Swaps, Interest Rate Options and Options on Interest Rate Futures. Derivative instruments are also known as **contingent claims**, as their payout to the holder at maturity is contingent on the price or rate of the underlying asset.

One of the most important uses of derivatives is to allow users to offset their exposure to fluctuations in interest rates by assuming an opposite exposure to their existing exposure, on a loan for example. This activity is called **hedging**.

Hedging

Hedgers seek to transfer the risk of future price or interest rate fluctuations by selling forward contracts which guarantee them a future price for their asset.

If in the future the asset price falls, the hedger will have protected himself by having hedged — ie, made forward sales which guaranteed the price at the sale date before the price fell. However, if the future cash price rises the hedger has lost the opportunity to make a profit, as he has already committed himself to the forward price at the outset of the hedge transaction.

Thus, hedging reduces risk but also reduces the opportunity for reward. It increases the certainty of future cash flows and allows market participants to plan into the future based on the certainty of the future cash flows guaranteed by hedging. Hedging does not increase or decrease the **expected returns** for a market participant, it simply changes the **risk profile** of those expected returns.

The underlying principle of hedging is that as price movements in the cash market move one way, the move is offset by an equal and opposite move in the price of **the hedging instrument** (almost always a **derivative instrument**).

Hedging a Long Position

If an investor holds, or intends to hold, a cash market asset, such as a treasury bill, this is said to be a **long position**. To hedge this position, he needs an offsetting **short position**. This can be achieved by selling a forward rate agreement or an interest rate futures contract in the appropriate amount to create offsetting cash flows (see next 2 sections for a more detailed discussion of these instruments). The profits or losses on the cash market instrument and the derivative instrument offset each other, creating an aggregate position which is unaffected by movements in interest rates. This is known as a **market neutral position**.

Hedging a Short Position

If a borrower borrows money, or intends to borrow money, in the cash market by issuing commercial paper, this is said to be a **short position**. To hedge, he needs a **long position**. This is achieved by buying an FRA or interest rate future in the appropriate amount. The offsetting cash flows create a market neutral position.

Forward Rate Agreements (FRAs)

A **Forward Rate Agreement** is an agreement between two counterparties which fixes the rate of interest that will apply to a specified notional future loan or deposit commencing and maturing on specified future dates.

An FRA is essentially a promise to pay/receive a specified rate of interest in the future, regardless of what the prevailing rate of interest in the market is at that time. They are usually used by borrowers in the money markets to fix the short-term rates of interest they will pay on their short-term loans.

FRAs are **cash-settled**. This means the **buyer** will be paid in cash by the seller for any **rise** in the reference interest rate over and above the agreed contract rate. Borrowers who wish to hedge the risk of borrowing costs rising in the future therefore **buy** FRAs to hedge out this risk.

The **seller** of an FRA will be paid in cash by the buyer for any **fall** in the reference interest rate below the agreed contract rate. Lenders who wish to hedge the risk of falls in future interest rate therefore **sell**.

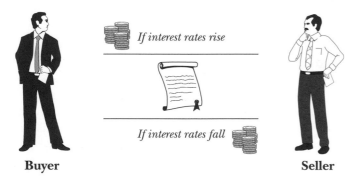

If interest rates rise

If interest rates fall

Buyer   **Seller**

Terms and Specifications: Forward Rate Agreements (FRAs)

FRAs have a number of features which market players need to assess before they decide on using the instrument. These features include the following:

- **Cash settlement**. As the loan/deposit is for notional funds there is no exchange of principal. Cash compensation is paid at the **beginning** of the notional loan/deposit period.

- **Flexibility**. As the loan/deposit is for notional funds there is no obligation by buyers/sellers in the markets to actually lend or deposit their funds. Market players can use other instruments which offer the best returns of their specific needs.

- **Lock-in rate**. Like forward FX contracts, if future interest rates fall the buyer will have to compensate the seller and forego any benefit from lower interest rates. Equally, if interest rates rise the seller has to compensate the buyer. FRAs effectively lock-in future interest rates for market players.

- **Low credit risk**. As there is no exchange of principal an FRA is an off-balance sheet instrument. The credit risk is low because the main risk is concerned with finding a replacement counterparty should the original party default. The risk involved is therefore on **differentials** rather than the notional amount.

- **Cancellation and assignment**. An FRA is a binding contract and cannot be cancelled or assigned to a third party without the agreement of both counterparties. As with other instruments with binding contracts, FRA positions can be closed using off-setting contracts.

Terms Used

There are a number of terms you need to know if you are to understand how FRAs work and are used. The table below indicates the terms and their meanings.

Term	Which means...
Contract Currency and Amount	The currency and amount of the notional loan/deposit
Trade Date	The date the deal is actually made
Fixing Date	This is **two business days before** the start of the FRA. It is the date when the LIBOR, or other, reference rate is **fixed**. The settlement amount is calculated using this rate. For domestic currency FRAs the fixing date is usually the **same** as the settlement date.
Settlement Date	This is the date when the contract period **starts** and cash compensation is paid
Maturity Date	The date the contract ends
Contract Period	This is the term of the notional loan/deposit – the period from settlement to maturity in days
Contract Rate	The agreed forward interest rate for the contract period – the price of the FRA in % per annum

Valuing Forward Rate Agreements

FRAs are typically quoted as a two-way price with bid-offer rates, in the same way as money market deposit rates.

Prices are often quoted in standard terms, such as whole months and round numbers for notional size, although terms can be tailored to precise dates and non-standard sizes.

Standard terms are detailed in the table below:

3-month series			6-month series		
	Starts forward	**Ends forward**		**Starts forward**	**Ends forward**
1 x 4	1 month	4 months	**1 x 7**	1 month	7 months
2 x 5	2 months	5 months	**2 x 8**	2 months	8 months
3 x 6	3 months	6months	**3 x 9**	3 months	9 months
6 x 9	6 months	9 months	**6 x 12**	6 months	12 months

The value of a forward rate agreement is derived from the current interest rate and the future interest rate covering the tenor of the FRA, as implied from longer-dated money market instruments or debt instruments. These interest rates can be derived using similar calculations to those used for valuing **Commercial Paper** in the previous section of this book.

There are three main instruments used to derive the prices of FRAs:
- Treasury Bills
- Interest Rate Futures
- Zero coupon bonds (similar to commercial paper but with a longer maturity)

Before we examine how to value a forward rate agreement, it is worth comparing FRAs with interest rate futures as these contracts share many features in common. For example, they are both used to fix the interest rate payable or receivable over some specific period in the future. The precise requirements of the user determine whether an FRA or interest rate future is the more appropriate contract for hedging.

Comparing FRAs with Interest Rate Futures Contracts

As interest rate futures contracts could easily be used in place of
FRAs, it is useful to compare the following aspects of the instruments:

	Forward Rate Agreement...	Interest Rate Futures Contract...
Trading	It is an OTC contract between counterparties. In some cases the deal may be made via a broker.	Contracts are traded in pits or electronically on an Exchange.
Contract Terms	Amount, period and settlement procedures are negotiated between the counterparties.	Amounts, expiry dates and settlement periods are fixed and standardised by the Exchange.
Confidentiality	There are no obligations placed on the counterparties to divulge the terms of the contract. Different market-makers may well quote different bid/offer prices.	Deals are transacted open out cry or using electronic systems. Orders and trades are immediately visible and transparent to all market players. On an Exchange there is only one market price at any one time.
Margin Payments	No margin payments are required. However, dealers will often require some form of collateral to be posted with them in order to mitigate against credit risk (see below). Settlement is in cash, and is the difference between the "forward rate" when the deal is executed and the actual rate at maturity.	Initial margin is paid as a % of the trade amount – marked-to-market. The margin payments are held by the clearing house. Variation margin is also paid to the clearing house on a daily basis depending on the market price movement.
Credit Risk	Each side is exposed to the credit risk of the counterparty, only if they are in a profitable position on the deal. This is because the contract is settled in cash with the net difference between the forward rate and actual rate at maturity being paid from one counterparty to the other. At the outset of the deal, it is not known which way the payment will be made, so both sides are taking on **potential future credit risk**.	The trading counterparty for a futures contract is the exchange clearing house. Therefore when trading interest rate futures, the credit risk is simply the credit risk of the clearing house, which is usually a very high quality counterparty.
Right of Offset	An FRA contract is binding and cannot be cancelled or assigned to a third party without the agreement of both sides.	Interest rate futures contracts can be off-set.

FRAs in the Market Place

FRA Settlement Payments

The settlement rate is usually determined two business days **before** the period of the notional loan/deposit for the specified reference rate, for example, LIBOR. It is important to note that the settlement payment is made at the **beginning** of the loan period rather than at maturity – the usual procedure for money market deposits. Therefore the settlement payment has to be discounted to its present value at the current market interest rate.

You will need to know two equations in order to calculate settlement payments – both equations are very similar. One caters for the situation where the settlement rate is **greater** than the contract rate so the FRA buyer compensates the seller. The other equation is for the opposite situation where the settlement rate is **less** than the contract rate so the FRA seller compensates the buyer.

Settlement rate **greater** than contract rate

$$\text{Settlement payment} \quad = \quad \frac{(L - R) \times D \times A}{(B \times 100) + (L \times D)} \qquad ...Equation\ 13a$$

Settlement rate **less** than contract rate

$$\text{Settlement payment} \quad = \quad \frac{(R - L) \times D \times A}{(B \times 100) + (L \times D)} \qquad ...Equation\ 13b$$

L = Settlement rate as a number **not** %
R = Contract rate as a number **not** %
B = Day basis – 360 or 365
D = Contract period in days
A = Contract amount

Example 1
It is the 10th April 1997 and the XYZ corporate treasurer foresees a forward funding requirement for 3 months (92 days) from 16th June to 15th September 1997. The treasurer thinks that there is a possible rise in interest rates and therefore wants to hedge against any interest rate rise. The treasurer buys a 2 x 5 FRA on the 10th April from OkiBank with the following terms:

FRA contract amt.	$10,000,000
Fixing date:	12th June 1997
Settlement date:	16th June 1997
Maturity date:	15th Sept. 1997
Contract rate:	6.75% pa
Year basis:	360 days

What is the settlement due if the LIBOR 3-month fixing rate is 7.25% the fixing date 10th June, and who receives payment?

Even though XYZ have bought an FRA contract they still have to raise the funds they require for 16th June to 15th September in the money markets at the increased rate of 7.25%. However, as the interest rates have risen, OkiBank have to compensate XYZ a cash sum. The settlement amount is therefore calculated using Equation 13a.

$$\text{Settlement payment} \quad = \quad \frac{(7.25 - 6.75) \times 92 \times 10,000,000}{(360 \times 100) + (7.25 \times 92)}$$

$$= \quad \frac{460,000,000}{36667}$$

$$= \quad \mathbf{\$12,545.34}$$

At this point the FRA contract ceases to exist and the XYZ corporate treasurer can now either reinvest the FRA settlement payment in the money markets or arrange a loan for $10,000,000 – 12,545.34.

In either case the XYZ loan will be based on the current LIBOR. The FRA payment acts as a subsidy bringing down the net cost of borrowing.

But what would have happened if the treasurer's fears of an interest rate rise were unfounded and on fixing LIBOR was 6.50%? This time XYZ have to compensate OkiBank. The settlement amount can be calculated using Equation 13b.

$$\text{Settlement payment} \quad = \quad \frac{(6.75 - 6.50) \times 92 \times 10,000,000}{(360 \times 100) + (6.50 \times 92)}$$

$$= \quad \frac{230,000,000}{36598}$$

$$= \quad \mathbf{\$6,284.50}$$

Other Risks Involved in FRAs

Apart from interest rate risk, which affects the price a final settlement value of an FRA, and credit risk, which affects the counterparties' ability to deliver the cash settlement at maturity of the FRA, there is another important risk to consider.

Basis risk is the risk that the London Interbank Offered Rate (LIBOR) which applies to the settlement value of the FRA moves away from the actual interest rate on the underlying loan that is being hedged, leaving the holder with an imperfect hedge.

The interest rates on money market instruments are all closely linked to LIBOR. However, sometimes there can be market events which can cause certain instruments to deviate from LIBOR.

In this situation, a borrower who hedges using a LIBOR-linked FRA is bound to pay the forward interest rate on the underlying loan at the FRA's maturity. If the interest rate on the underlying loan rises by more than the LIBOR rate used for settling the FRA, the borrowers profit on the FRA will be less than the loss on the underlying loan. Hence the FRA provides an imperfect hedge if the interest rate on the underlying loan is different to the interest rate to which the FRA is linked.

This risk of residual loss due to imperfect hedging is called **basis risk**.

Forward/Forward Rates

In many cases FRA **strips** of contracts are used to hedge against longer term interest rate rises. A strip is simply a number of consecutive contracts. For example, a strip of four FRA contracts, 1 x 3, 3 x 6, 6 x 9, 9 x 12 could be used to hedge for a 12 month period. However, if a strip of FRAs are used what is the effective rate over the whole period as different contract rates are used for each FRA?

Suppose the following strip of two FRAs spans the two periods 0 to n and 0 to N. The rate of return for the time period n to N can be calculated using an equation based on the interest rates due for the time periods.

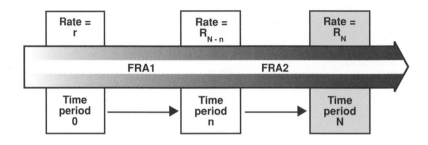

$$\text{Interest due for time period, } \mathbf{N} = \left(\text{Interest due for time period, } \mathbf{n} \right) \times \left(\text{Interest due for time period, } \mathbf{N-n} \right)$$

Therefore:

$$\left[1 + \left(\frac{R_N \times N}{B \times 100} \right) \right] = \left[1 + \left(\frac{r \times n}{B \times 100} \right) \right] \times \left[1 + \left(\frac{R_{N-n} \times N - n}{B \times 100} \right) \right]$$

$$R_{N-n} = \frac{\left[1 + \left(\frac{R_N \times N}{B \times 100} \right) \right]}{\left[1 + \left(\frac{r \times n}{B \times 100} \right) \right]} - 1 \times \frac{360 \times 100}{N}$$

...Equation 14

If you need to calculate the effective annual interest rate for a strip of FRAs the following equation can be used which is based on Equation 14.

Effective annual rate, R =

$$\left[\left[1+\left(\frac{L_{0\times3}}{4}\right)\right]\times\left[1+\left(\frac{F_{3\times6}}{4}\right)\right]\times\left[1+\left(\frac{F_{6\times9}}{4}\right)\right]\times\left[1+\left(\frac{F_{9\times12}}{4}\right)\right]\right]-1$$

$L_{0\times3}$ = Current LIBOR or reference rate

$F_{3\times6}, F_{6\times9}, F_{9\times12}$ = FRA rates for periods 3 x 6, 6 x 9 and 9 x 12 respectively

...Equation 15

Example 2

XYZ Corporation now needs to protect interest rates for a six month period beginning in 6 months time – a 6 x 12 forward position. The XYZ corporate treasurer could use a 6 x 12 FRA. However, a strip of two 3-month FRAs, 6 x 9 and 9 x 12, offers the treasurer the flexibility of reversing the hedge at the 9 month period if necessary. The strip also provides a market limit for a 6 x 12 FRA quote.

XYZ need to borrow $5,000,000 in 6 months time for a loan period of 6 months, but the treasurer thinks interest rates will rise in this time. The treasurer investigates quotes from a number of banks offering FRAs indexed on a 3-month LIBOR basis.

FRA	Bank A	Bank B
6 x 9 (91d)	6.21 – 6.15	6.23 – 6.18
9 x 12 (92d)	6.28 – 6.22	6.30 – 6.25

The treasurer accepts the bid FRA prices from Bank A as the cheaper and buys a strip of two FRAs – 6 x 9 plus 9 x 12. This effectively locks in the interest rates for the 6-month borrowing period.

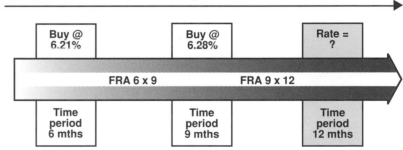

Money Market Derivatives

What is the effective FRA rate?

The effective FRA rate for the strip is calculated using Equation 15.

$$\left[1 + \left(\frac{R_{6 \times 12} \times N}{B \times 100}\right)\right] = \left[1 + \left(\frac{R_{6 \times 9} \times n}{B \times 100}\right)\right] \times \left[1 + \left(\frac{R_{9 \times 12} \times N - n}{B \times 100}\right)\right]$$

$$= \left[1 + \left(\frac{6.21 \times 91}{360 \times 100}\right)\right] \times \left[1 + \left(\frac{6.28 \times 92}{360 \times 100}\right)\right]$$

$$= 1.0157 \times 1.01605$$

$$= 1.03200$$

Therefore $R_{6 \times 12}$ = $(1.03200 - 1) \times \dfrac{360 \times 100}{183}$

$$= 6.2955 \text{ or } 6.30\% \text{ rounded up}$$

The screen below shows the Forward Rate Agreement Speed Guide.

```
FORWARD RATE AGREEMENTS - REUTERS SPEED GUIDE                        FRA/1
Detailed below are retrieval codes for key FORWARD RATE AGREEMENT displays.

=MAJOR CURRENCY FRAs==================   =FRAs by CURRENCY Cont================
Major Currency FRAs............<TOPFRA>   BRITISH POUND.................<GBPFRA>
Garvin Guy Butler..........<TOPFRA=GGB>   Garvin Guy Butler..........<GBPFRA=GGB>
Harlow Butler Asia........<TOPFRA=HBAA>   Harlow Butler Asia........<GBPFRA=HBAA>
Harlow Butler Europe......<TOPFRA=HBEL>   Harlow Butler Europe......<GBPFRA=HBEL>
The TOKYO FOREX...........<TOPFRA=TKFX>   Tradition UK..............<GBPFRA=TRDL>
Tradition UK FRAs.........<TOPFRA=TRDL>   Tullett & Tokyo...........<GBPFRA=TTKL>
Tullett & Tokyo...........<TOPFRA=TTKL>   CANADIAN DOLLAR...............<CADFRA>
                                          Harlow Butler Europe......<CADFRA=HBEL>
=FRAs by CURRENCY=====================    Tullett & Tokyo...........<CADFRA=TTKL>
AUSTRALIAN DOLLAR..............<AUDFRA>   CZECH KORUNA Tullets......<CZKFRA=TTKL>
AUSTRALIAN DOLLAR..............<AUFRA>    DANISH KRONE..................<DKKFRA>
Harlow Butler Asia........<AUDFRA=HBAA>
Harlow Butler Europe......<AUDFRA=HBEL>   More currencies on pages <FRA/2>-3
Tullett & Tokyo...........<AUDFRA=TTKL>
AUSTRIAN SCHILLING.............<ATSFRA>   =NEWS and ANALYSIS====================
BELGIAN FRANC.................<BEFFRA>    All Reuters Money News....<MONEY/NEWS1>
Harlow Butler Europe......<BEFFRA=HBEL>   Daily Diary..................[M-DIARY]
Questions/Comments: contact your local Help Desk - see <PHONE/HELP> for details
==============================================================================
Main Index<REUTERS>          Money Index<MONEY>              Next Page<FRA/2>
    LOST? Selective Access?..<USER/HELP>        Reuters Support..<PHONE/HELP>
```

The screen below displays the Major Currency FRAs.

TOPFRA		FRAs - Majors			LINKED DISPLAYS		MONEY
	USD	FRAs	DEM	FRAs	JPY	FRAs	GBP
1X4	5.80	5.84	16:06 3.13	3.16	14:19 0.63	0.66	15:44 6.96
2X5	5.84	5.88	16:07 3.15	3.18	14:19 0.63	0.66	15:44 7.03
3X6	5.92	5.96	15:49 3.15	3.18	14:19 0.66	0.69	15:44 7.10
4X7	5.99	6.03	16:05 3.22	3.25	15:37 0.72	0.75	15:44 7.16
5X8	6.05	6.09	16:05 3.25	3.28	15:37 0.77	0.80	15:44 7.21
6X9	6.05	6.09	16:02 3.29	3.32	15:37 0.86	0.89	15:44 7.28
7X10	6.11	6.15	16:05 3.32	3.35	15:37 0.92	0.95	15:44 7.30
8X11	6.15	6.19	15:50 3.34	3.37	14:12 0.99	1.02	15:44 7.34
9X12	6.20	6.24	15:50 3.40	3.42	15:33 1.06	1.09	15:44 7.36
12X15	6.31	6.35	15:52 3.56	3.59	15:26 1.26	1.29	15:44 7.34
15X18	6.47	6.50	15:43 3.74	3.77	15:26 1.49	1.52	06:33 7.31
18X21	6.56	6.59	15:42 4.05	4.06	15:52 1.46	1.47	12:09 7.04
21X24	6.58	6.61	16:08 4.42	4.45	21:57 1.46	1.46	21:56 7.45
1X7	5.96	5.98	16:07 3.18	3.22	14:46 0.70	0.74	09:49 7.14
2X8	5.99	6.03	16:07 3.21	3.24	14:14 0.72	0.75	15:44 7.19
3X9	6.04	6.08	16:07 3.24	3.27	15:37 0.76	0.79	15:44 7.26
4X10	6.10	6.14	16:07 3.28	3.31	14:14 0.84	0.87	15:44 7.29
5X11	6.15	6.19	16:05 3.31	3.34	14:13 0.90	0.93	15:44 7.34
6X12	6.17	6.21	15:51 3.35	3.38	14:13 0.98	1.01	15:44 7.38

REUTERS

Using the screen below can be useful as you can display Bid and Ask prices for a number of currencies from different contributors simultaneously. For example, you decide to look at 3 x 6 rates for DEM FRAs from 3 different contributors in order to select the best rates for you for buying and selling. You look at the rates and decide that those from HBEL are best. You now decide to check these rates and calculate the forward/forward bid and ask prices from deposit rates displayed in the lower screen.

Exercise

From the 3-month and 6-month Bid and Ask deposit rates shown opposite calculate the forward/forward Bid and Ask rates. Assume 3-months is 90 days and 6-months is 180 days.

a) Forward/forward Bid rate

b) Forward/forward Ask rate

You can check your answers over the page.

	FRMW

Currency	DEM	Currency	DEM	Currency	DEM
Contributor	HBEL	Contributor	TTKL	Contributor	TRDL
Term	All 3m FRAs	Term	All 3m FRAs	Term	All 3m FRAs

FRA	Bid	Ask	Source	FRA	Bid	Ask	Source	FRA	Bid	Ask	Source
1X4	3.13	3.16	HBEL	1X4	3.16	3.16	TTKL	1X4	3.14	3.16	TRDL
2X5	3.15	3.18	HBEL	2X5	3.15	3.18	TTKL	2X5	3.16	3.18	TRDL
3X6	3.15	3.18	HBEL	3X6	3.18	3.21	TTKL	3X6	3.19	3.21	TRDL
4X7	3.22	3.25	HBEL	4X7	3.22	3.25	TTKL	4X7	3.23	3.25	TRDL
5X8	3.25	3.28	HBEL	5X8	3.26	3.3	TTKL	5X8	3.26	3.28	TRDL
6X9	3.29	3.32	HBEL	6X9	3.29	3.32	TTKL	6X9	3.3	3.32	TRDL
7X10	3.32	3.35	HBEL	7X10	3.33	3.36	TTKL	7X10	3.33	3.35	TRDL
8X11	3.34	3.37	HBEL	8X11	3.3	3.33	TTKL	8X11	3.35	3.37	TRDL
9X12	3.39	3.42	HBEL	9X12	3.39	3.42	TTKL	9X12	3.4	3.42	TRDL
12X15	3.56	3.59	HBEL					12X15	3.56	3.58	TRDL
15X18	3.74	3.77	HBEL					15X18	n/v	n/v	TRDL
3F1	3.16	3.19	HBEL					18X21	4.04	4.05	TRDL
3F2	3.25	3.28	HBEL					21X24	n/v	n/v	TRDL

	DEM	DEM	DEM	DEM
	HBEL	HBEL	TTKL	TTKL
Period	Bid	Ask	Bid	Ask
2M	3	3.125	3	3.125
3M	3	3.125	3	3.125
6M	3.0625	3.1875	3.0625	3.1875
9M	3.125	3.25	3.125	3.25
1Y	3.125	3.25	3.1875	3.3125

Answers to Exercise

a) Forward/forward bid rate = 2.976%
    Use Equation 2 – for Bid use Far depo Bid and Near depo Ask

$$\text{Interest} = \frac{(3.0625 \times 180) - (3.125 \times 90)}{(180 - 90) \times \left[1 + \left(\dfrac{3.125 \times 90}{360 \times 100}\right)\right]}$$

$$= \frac{270.00}{90.703125}$$

b) Forward/forward bid rate = 3.349%
    Use Equation 2 – for Ask use Far depo Ask and Near depo Bid

$$\text{Interest} = \frac{(3.1875 \times 180) - (3.00 \times 90)}{(180 - 90) \times \left[1 + \left(\dfrac{3.00 \times 90}{360 \times 100}\right)\right]}$$

$$= \frac{303.75}{90.6750}$$

Your notes

Interest Rate Futures

 Interest Rate Futures are exchange-traded forward rate agreements with standard contract sizes and maturity dates which are cash-settled on a daily basis throughout the life of the contract.

The underlying reference interest rate for short-term interest rate futures is typically the three-month Eurocurrency deposit rate. For example, the three-month Eurodollar future, traded on the Chicago Mercantile Exchange (CME), uses the interest rate on US dollar deposits outside the US for its settlement rate. Similarly, the Euromark futures contract, traded on the London International Financial Futures and Options Exchange (LIFFE), uses three-month Eurodeutschmark deposit for its reference rate.

The main features of interest rate futures are:

- Standard contract specifications (size, maturity date, quotation, minimum price movement)

- Offset transactions (a long and short position in similar futures contracts can be 'cancelled out'. Only a small proportion of futures contracts ever reach maturity)

- Public market (prices are freely available and widely published)

- Trade counterparty is the clearing house (low credit risk)

Exchange Contracts

Short- and long-term interest rate futures contracts are traded on exchanges worldwide. Some of the more important contracts are summarised in the charts below.

LIFFE			
Short-term Cash settled based on LIBOR		**Unit of trading**	
Three month Sterling (Short Sterling)		GBP 500,000	
Three month Eurodeutschmark (Euromark)		DEM 1,000,000	
Three month Eurolira		ITL 1,000,000,000	
Three month Euroswiss Franc (Euroswiss)		CHF 1,000,000	
Three month ECU		ECU 1,000,000	
Three month Eurodollar		USD 1,000,000	

Long-term Government Bonds	Nominal value	Maturity range years	Notional coupon, %
Long Gilt (UK)	GBP 50,000	10 - 15	9
Bund (German)	DEM 250,000	8.5 - 10	6
JGB (Japanese)	JPY 100,000,000	7 - 11	6
BTP (Italian)	ITL 200,000,000	8 - 10.5	12

Money Market Derivatives

Chicago Mercantile Exchange (CME)

Short-term Cash settled based on interbank rates	Unit of trading
Three month Eurodollar	USD 1,000,000
One month LIBOR	USD 3,000,000
One year T-bills	USD 500,000
Three month Euromark	DEM 1,000,000
Three month Euroyen	JPY 100,000,000
13-week US T-bills	USD 1,000,000
(This contract is for physical delivery)	

Chicago Board of Trade (CBOT)

Long-term Government Bonds	Nominal value	Maturity range years	Notional coupon, %
US T-bonds	USD 100,000	At least 15	8
10 year US T-notes	USD 100,000	6.5 - 10	8

Typical Contract Specifications

Short-term

Futures contracts specifications vary from type to type and from exchange to exchange. Have a look at the following 3-month LIFFE 'Short Sterling' contract details below.

LIFFE 3-month Sterling Interest Rate Future		
Unit of Trading	£500,000	This is the standard contract size
Delivery Months	Mar, Jun Sept, Dec	This is the trading cycle of contract months
Delivery Day	First business day after the last trading day	This is the day contract is settled
Last Trading Day	11.00 Third Wednesday of delivery month	This is the last day and time on which trading can take place
Quotation	100 minus rate of interest	The futures price is quoted according to the type of future
Minimum Price Movement (Tick size and value)	0.01 (£12.50)	This is the smallest amount a contract can change value and the 'tick' size
Trading Hours	07.15 – 16.02 London time	Exchange trading hours – open outcry
APT Trading Hours	16.27 – 17.57	Computer-based trading system hours

But What Does It All Mean?

This interest rate futures contract is for a **notional** amount of £500,000 – unit of trading – which is placed on a 3-month deposit commencing on the delivery day (maturity) of the contract, at an interest rate which is implied in the futures price agreed at the time of the trade.

Typically for financial futures there are 4 delivery months per year – March, June, September and December. It is also possible to have maturity dates out to several years but 'far month' contracts are much less liquid than the 'near months'. This means that it is not always possible to get prices for 'far months'.

Short-term futures are not quoted as an interest rate percentage. Instead they are quoted as:

> **100 minus the implied forward interest rate**

Example

A forward implied interest rate for a $1 million deposit is 5.55%.

The futures contract price would therefore be 100 – 5.55 = 94.45.

This convention for pricing short-term futures is based on the way T-bills are quoted – at a discount from the face value of the bill.

The price movement of a futures contract is measured in **ticks**. The **minimum price movement** for a contract is determined by the Exchange. Depending on the contract, its value is expressed in terms of basis points – a **basis point** is one hundredth of one percent, 0.01%. So one tick equals one basis point.

This means that a tick has a specific value determined using the following equation:

$$\text{Tick} = \frac{\text{Unit of}}{\text{trading}} \times \frac{\text{Basis points}}{100} \times \frac{\text{Proportion of year over}}{\text{which contract runs}}$$

Example

The tick value for the 3-month LIFFE Short Sterling contract is:

$$= £500,000 \times \frac{0.01}{100} \times \frac{1}{4}$$

$$= £12.50$$

On the last day of trading, if a futures position is still open, most short-term interest rate futures are cash settled against the Exchange Delivery Settlement Price (EDSP). The exception is the 13-week US T-bills contract which involves physical delivery of the instruments.

The EDSP depends on the exchange but typically involves a calculation of interest rates for the Eurocurrency deposit in question. For example, LIFFE use the British Banking Association Interest Settlement Rate (BBAISR) and the CME uses an average of a survey of rates of the London interbank rates for Eurodollars, LIBOR and Euromark.

On the last day of trading the futures contract ceases to exist and the underlying cash market instrument and futures prices are the same. It is the difference in contract and settlement prices that is paid in cash – as the principal of these contracts is notional no delivery can take place on expiry.

Long-term Interest Rate Futures

The contract specifications for these interest rate futures are very similar to those for short-term instruments. The major difference is that settlement is by physical delivery of bonds or notes with coupon rates and maturity dates stipulated by the exchange.

Although some long-term futures for bonds have prices and minimum price movements quoted as hundredths of a basis point, UK Gilts and US T-bonds are quoted as thirty-seconds of a percentage point.

Example

A UK Long Gilt futures quoted at 111-23 means a price of 111 23/32. However there are indications that the market convention for UK Gilts and US T-bonds may be changed in the near future to that of using basis points.

Tick values are easy to calculate for long-term futures:

Tick = Unit of trading x Minimum price movement

The contract details for CBOT T-bonds are shown opposite.

Chicago Board of Trade US Treasury Bond Futures		
Unit of Trading	T-Bond with face value $100,000	This is the standard contract size
Delivery Months	Mar, Jun Sept, Dec	This is the trading cycle of contract months
Delivery Day	Last business day of delivery month	This is the day contract is settled
Last Trading Day	7th business day preceding last business day of month	This is the last day and time on which trading can take place
Quotation	Points and 32nds of point	The futures price is quoted according to the type of future
Minimum Price Movement (Tick size and value)	1/32 of a point ($31.25)	This is the smallest amount a contract can change value and the 'tick' size
Trading Hours	07.20 – 14.00 Chicago time	Exchange trading hours – open outcry
Project A Trading Hours	14.30 – 16.60 22.30 – 06.00	Computer-based trading system hours

Profit and Loss on a Futures Contract

This is easy to calculate using the following method:

1. Determine the number of ticks the price has moved up or down. The number of ticks is the number of one-hundredths of the quotation price.

2. Multiply the number of ticks by the tick value and the number of contracts.

Profit/ loss = Number of ticks x Tick value x Number of contracts

Example

Two 3-month CBOT US T-bonds contracts are bought when the interest rate is 6.25%. The contracts are therefore priced at $100 - 6.25 = 93.75$.

At the delivery date the 3-month LIBOR stands at 6.10% which represents a price of $100 - 6.10 = 93.90$.

The contract has therefore gained in value and the number of ticks equals $93.90 - 93.75 = 15$.

$$
\begin{aligned}
\text{The profit on the contract} \quad &= \quad 15 \ \times \ \$31.25 \ \times \ 2 \\
&= \quad \$937.50
\end{aligned}
$$

Hedging Revisited

In the previous three sections we have encountered the concept of hedging, and considered the detailed specifications of two popular hedging instruments, namely forward rate agreements (FRAs) and interest rate futures.

So far, we have a vague idea of how FRAs and Interest Rate Futures can be used to hedge underlying positions in the cash markets, by taking an offsetting position in a derivative instrument. However, in order to be a useful hedge, the offsetting position in the derivative instrument must generate profits and losses which very closely match those of the underlying cash market instrument.

This task of generating similar cash flows is not trivial, but is the key to successful hedging. It is easy to see that the more closely the cash flows of the cash market and derivatives instruments mirror each other, the better the hedge. The question is, how many futures contracts, or FRAs, must be traded to offset the cash flows of a loan of a particular principal value?

The number of contracts required, known as the **hedge ratio**, is calculated from the following equation:

Number of contracts required =

$$
\frac{\text{Sum to be hedged}}{\text{Unit of trading}} \times \frac{\text{Actual number of days}}{\text{Day basis} \times \text{No. contracts/year}} \times \frac{\text{Number of futures}}{\text{contracts per year}}
$$

For most short-term interest rate futures this equation reduces to:

$$
\text{Number of contracts required} = \frac{\text{Sum to be hedged}}{\text{Unit of trading}}
$$

In the examples that follow the sums to be hedged have been selected to match the unit of trading amounts to simplify the calculations.

Short Hedge – Selling Futures

A short hedge can be used by an investor needing to hedge against price falls resulting from rising interest rates. This type of hedge can also be used to hedge a future loan to prevent higher borrowing costs.

Example

It is 12th June and a corporate treasurer has just borrowed £1 million for a 3-month period at an interest rate of 6.0%. In 3-months time the loan will roll-over and the treasurer is worried that interest rates will rise by then. The treasurer decides to hedge his position by selling 3-month LIFFE Short Sterling futures at 93.50. But how many?

$$\text{Number of contracts required} = \frac{£1,000,000}{£500,000} = 2$$

It is 11th September and the loan is rolled over and interest rates have risen to 6.75%. What is the result of the treasurer's hedge?

Money markets	Futures market
12th June	
Fears that interest rate will rise from 6%	Sell 2 x Sept contracts at 93.50 (implied interest rate of 6.5%)
30th April	
Roll over loan at 6.75%	Buy 2 x Sept contracts for 92.75 (implied interest rate of 7.25%) to close position

Extra cost	Gain
0.75% on £1m for 3 months = £1875	75 ticks x £12.50 x 2 = £1875

This perfect hedge is unlikely in practice. For example, the futures gain is not paid as a single instalment but as daily margin payments which are described later. Also the extra roll over loan interest would not be payable until the maturity of the loan in 3 months time.

So by selling the futures contracts the corporate treasurer has hedged the expected rise in interest rates. He has to borrow at a more expensive rate in the money markets but this is compensated by the gain in buying the futures for less than they were sold at originally.

The hedge would also have worked if rates had fallen. The corporate treasurer would have borrowed at a lower rate in the money markets thus making a gain which would have been offset by a loss on the futures because they would have risen in price from the original sale price.

Long Hedge – Buying Futures

A long hedge is typically used by lenders of cash market funds who need to fix an interest rate for a future date and are worried that interest rates might fall.

Example

It is 12th June and a corporate treasurer has USD funds to lend in July. The treasurer is worried that rates may fall during June thus affecting the interest he is likely to receive.

The corporate treasurer will have $50 million to lend and decides to hedge his position using CBOT 30-Day Fed Funds futures. The unit of trading is $5 million and the tick size is $41.67 per basis point.

$$\text{Number of contracts required} = \frac{50,000,000}{5,000,000} \times \frac{31}{30 \times 12} \times 12 = 10.33$$

This means that the treasurer has to buy 10 contracts – a perfect hedge is not possible – and hold the futures until maturity or close out prior to expiration.

Suppose the following:

	1st July	31st July
30-Day Fed Funds futures price	94.56	95.16
Implied 30-Day interest rate	5.44%	4.84%

On 1st July the rates have fallen, as expected by the treasurer to 4.80%. What is the result of the treasurer's hedge?

Money markets	Futures market
1st July	
Deposits $50 million at 4.80%	Buy 10 futures at 94.56
31st July	
Receive back $50 million plus interest at 4.80% for 1 month.	Sell 10 futures at 95.16
Interest = $206,666.66	Gain on long position = 60 ticks x $41.67 x 10 = $25,002.00

Net gain on position = 206,666.66 + 25,002.00 = $231,668.66

Net % return $= \dfrac{231,668.66}{50,000,000} \times \dfrac{360}{31}$

$= 0.0538$

$= 5.38\%$

The perfect hedge requires a 5.44% return, but as only 10 contracts could be bought, this compares well with a cash market return on unhedged funds at 4.80%.

Speculation

Speculators attempt to exploit price movements in the markets and thus provide additional liquidity for hedging activities. Speculators do not necessarily have a position and use their market knowledge to profit.

Derivative instruments, such as FRAs and interest rate futures, are attractive instruments for speculators because, unlike investments in the cash market, they do not require the exchange of principal. However, they still produce profits and losses equivalent to an investment in the cash market. This phenomenon, where cash market returns can be generated by deploying only a small fraction of the capital that would be needed to invest in the cash market, is known as **leverage**.

Example

A trader is expecting that the June balance of trade figures will be better than expected causing short-term interest rates to fall and therefore futures prices to rise. Based on this view the trader buys one 3-month June LIFFE Short Sterling contract at 93.55. This implies a 3-month GBP interest rate of 6.45%.

The next day the trader views the news and is proven correct – interest rates have fallen by 0.5%. The trader therefore sells his contract at the new market price of 94.05 and gains 50 ticks.

His profit is 50 x £12.50 x 1 = £625.00.

Suppose, however, that the trade figures had been worse than expected and interest rates had risen by 0.5%? The trader would have closed out the contract at 93.05 and made a loss of 50 ticks which is £625.00.

Money Market Derivatives

Relationship with OTC forward contracts

An interest rate future contract is in effect an exchange traded 3-month Forward Rate Agreement (FRA). It is the equivalent of a FRA with daily margins.

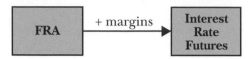

The two instruments are compared in the table below.

FRA	Interest Rate Future
• Flexible	• Standard contract terms
• OTC market	
• No margin required	• Exchange traded
	• Margin required
• Credit risk between counterparties	• No credit risk as clearing house stands as counterparty
• No right of offset	
• Terms of contract are confidential	

The chart below compares the relative ways in which the two instruments are used to hedge interest rate price movements.

To hedge an interest rate ..	Fall	Rise
Futures	**Buy**	**Sell**
FRAs	**Sell**	**Buy**

Trading Strategies for Interest Rate Futures

There are a number of strategies that traders adopt in order to hedge positions which do not have 'perfect' matches in the futures markets. The simplest strategies used are:

- Futures strips

- Stacking futures

- Spread trading

Futures Strips

These are used to hedge interest rate exposures which span several futures expiry dates, or span dates which do not exactly match futures expiry dates.

The buyer of a September LIFFE Short Sterling future at 94.29 effectively commits him or herself to lending a notional £500,000 for 3 months commencing on the contract expiry rate of 5.71%. The seller of the same contract commits him or herself to borrowing the notional amount.

Example
It is early June and a corporate treasurer calls a bank to ask for the price of a one year deposit loan for £5 million starting in September – a 3 x 15 forward price. The treasurer is worried that rates will rise in the next three months and wishes to hedge the current loan interest rates. The period required for the hedge spans four consecutive futures expiry dates and the treasurer can sell a **strip** of four futures. The number of contracts required to sell (borrow effectively) is 10 per contract – the unit of trading for the contract is £500,000.

	Sept	Dec	Mar	June	Sept
Exposure					
Futures strip	Sell 10	Sell 10	Sell 10	Sell 10	

REUTERS

Have a look at the prevailing futures prices that the treasurer sells the contracts:

> Sell 10 Sept contracts at 94.29   Implied rate 5.71%
> Sell 10 Dec contracts at 94.27   Implied rate 5.73%
> Sell 10 Mar contracts at 93.95   Implied rate 6.05%
> Sell 10 Jun contracts at 93.56   Implied rate 6.44%

Using a strip of futures has effectively locked in the interest rate for the forward 12 month period but what is the rate? The average of the four interest rates is 5.98% but unfortunately the calculation is not that simple!

The general equation to calculate a forward-forward rate is given below:

$$F_{a\,x\,b} = \frac{(L_a \times d_a) \times (L_b \times d_b)}{\left[1 + \left(\left(L_b \times \dfrac{d_b}{360 \text{ or } 365}\right)\right)\right]} \times \frac{1}{(d_b - d_a)}$$

$F_{a\,x\,b}$ = Forward starting in **a** days and ending in **b** days

L_a = Long period interest rate as a decimal

L_b = Short period interest rate as a decimal

d_a = Long period in days

d_b = Short period in days

The rate is in fact a compound of the notional quarterly interest rate payments given by the following equation:

$$F = 1 - \left[\left(1 + \frac{R_1}{4}\right) \times \left(1 + \frac{R_2}{4}\right) \times \ldots \left(1 + \frac{R_n}{4}\right) \right]$$

> F = Forward compound rate
> R_n = Rate for period n
> n = Number of contracts in strip

In this example the rate is 6.12%.

Suppose in September, the one year LIBOR is 6.75%. If the treasurer had accepted a quote of 6.12% then the loss covering the cash loan would have been 5,000,000 x 0.0063 = £31,500.

However, if the treasurer closes out 10 contracts for each period by buying, then the gains are as follows. For each contract subtract the buy from the previous sell price and to calculate the profit multiply the number of ticks by £12.50 and by 10 for the number of contracts.

> Buy 10 Sept contracts at 93.55   +74 ticks profit = £9,250
> Buy 10 Dec contracts at 93.45   +82 ticks profit = £10,250
> Buy 10 Mar contracts at 93.35   +60 ticks profit = £7,500
> Buy 10 June contracts at 93.26   +30 ticks profit = £3,750
> Total gains = £30,750

The net loss to the treasurer is therefore 31,500 − 30,750 = £750.

The hedge is not perfect but a large loss which could have resulted from not hedging the deposit has been averted.

The use of strips is restricted to prices for the far months required, but what happens if this is not the case?

Stacking Futures

Suppose in the previous example that the September futures contract was the only one available. There is still a risk that interest rate will rise over the next year but the treasurer has only one contract available.

In such a situation a **stack** of futures are used. In this case 40 contracts are used – 4 x 10 contracts for the four periods. Using the same futures prices for selling and buying 40 September futures with a gain of 74 ticks results in a profit of 74 x £12.50 x 40 = £37,000.

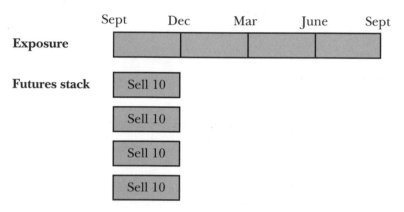

The effectiveness of using a stack of futures depends on the yield curve of interest rates. If the yield curve retains its shape then the hedge using a stack is as effective as using a strip of futures. If the yield curve is positive and steepens, then the stack produces poorer results. However, even though the stack may not be as effective as desired it produces better results than no hedge at all!

```
┌──────────────────────────────────────────────────────────────┐
│EXCHANGE TRADED INTEREST RATE FUTURES - REUTERS SPEED GUIDE  FUT/IR1│
│Detailed below are the retrieval codes for Exchange traded Interest rate Futures│
│                                                                │
│=INTEREST RATE FUTURES=============    =INTEREST RATE FUTURES Cont============│
│AFFM Guilder Bond Future.......<O#EBB:>  CME (IMM) 1-month LIBOR........<O#EM:>│
│BDP 10Yr Portuguese Govt.Bond<O#BDPOT:>  CME (IMM) 3-month Eurodollar...<O#ED:>│
│BDP Mkt Overview (Porto)........<BDP1>   CME (IMM) 90-day US T-Bill.....<O#TB:>│
│BDP Calculated Spreads..........<BDP2>   CME (IMM) 1Yr US T-Bill........<O#YR:>│
│BDP 3Mth Lisbor................<O#LBO:>  CME (IMM) Euromark.............<O#EK:>│
│BFOE BEF BIBOR 3nth Future.....<O#BIB:>  CME (IMM) Euroyen.............<O#EY:>│
│BFOE National Govt Bond........<O#BGB:>  CME (IMM) Fed Funds...........<O#FT:>│
│BMF Brazilian C Bond..........<O#BCB:>   CME Brady Bonds - Argentine FRB.<O#AT:>│
│BMF Brazilian EI Bond.........<O#BEI:>   CME Brady Bonds - Mexican Par...<O#MN:>│
│CBOT 30 day IR Future..........<O#FF:>   CME Brady Bonds - Brazilian C...<O#BE:>│
│CBOT 2-year US T-Note..........<O#TU:>   CME Brady Bonds - Brazilian EI..<O#BE:>│
│CBOT 5-year US T-Note..........<O#FV:>   CPSE 3nth CIBOR................<O#RDK:>│
│CBOT 10-year US T-Note.........<O#TY:>   CPSE Danish Govt 8% 2001.....<O#DK01T:>│
│CBOT 30-year US T-Bond.........<O#US:>   CPSE Danish Govt 8% 2006.....<O#DK06T:>│
│CBOT Long-Term Municipal Bd.....<O#MB:>  CPSE Realkredit Mtg 6% 2026....<O#RKE:>│
│CBOT Treasury US Spread.....<O#TY-US:>   DTB German Govt Bond...........<O#BDL:>│
│CBOT German Govt Bond..........<O#BU:>   DTB Medium Term Notional Bond..<O#BDM:>│
│Cheapest to Deliver Pages...<RTRTSYB>-9  DTB German LIBOR Future.......<O#LIB1:>│
└──────────────────────────────────────────────────────────────┘
```

```
┌──────────────────────────────────────────────────────────────┐
│EXCHANGE TRADED INTEREST RATE FUTURES - REUTERS SPEED GUIDE  FUT/IR2│
│Detailed below are the retrieval codes for Exchange Traded Interest Rate Futures│
│                                                                │
│=INTEREST RATE FUTURES Cont============    =INTEREST RATE FUTURES Cont============│
│DTB Schatz Short term future..<O#SH2Z:>  LIFFE US T-Bond...............<O#FUS:>│
│FINEX Emerging Mkt Debt.........<O#LX:>  Manila Intl Futures Exch Index<MIQAA>-Z│
│Finnish Govt Benchmark Bond....<O#FBF=>  MACE Euro USD Future...........<O#UD:>│
│Finnish OM HELIBOR.............<O#HEI:>  MACE T-Bill 90 day Future......<O#XT:>│
│Finnish OM ROF 2001 Bond.....<O#FI01T:>  MACE 5-year US T-Note..........<O#XV:>│
│Finnish OM ROF 2006 Bond.....<O#FI06T:>  MACE 10yr T-Note Future........<O#XN:>│
│HFKE HKD HIBOR Future..........<O#HIR:>  MACE 30-year US T-Bond.........<O#XB:>│
│LIFFE 3-month ECU IR...........<O#FCU:>  MATIF Market Overview..........<MATIF>│
│LIFFE Euro DMK 1nth............<O#FEM:>  MATIF 3-month PIBOR...........<O#PIB:>│
│LIFFE Euro DMK 3nth............<O#FED:>  MATIF ECU Bond................<O#PEC:>│
│LIFFE Euro CHF 3nth............<O#FES:>  MATIF Notional Bond...........<O#PTB:>│
│LIFFE Euro ITL 3nth............<O#FEL:>  MATIF CAC 40 Index............<O#FCH:>│
│LIFFE Euro YEN 3nth............<O#FEY:>  MATIF BOBL....................<O#FBO:>│
│LIFFE German Govt Bond........<O#FDB:>   MATIF calculated spreads.......<MATIF1>│
│LIFFE Italian Govt Bond.......<O#FIB:>   MATIF OAT DEM Bund............<O#FGL:>│
│LIFFE Japanese Govt Bond......<O#FYB:>   MATIF BTP DEM Bund............<O#IGL:>│
│LIFFE Long Gilt...............<O#FLG:>   MATIF Bono DEM Bund...........<O#SGL:>│
│LIFFE Short Sterling..........<O#FSS:>   MATIF T-Note DEM Bund.........<O#UGL:>│
│==========================================================│
│Futures Guide <FUTURES>      Previous Page <FUT/IR1>    Continued on <FUT/IR3>│
│  LOST? Selective Access?..<USER/HELP>   Reuters Phone Support..<PHONE/HELP>│
└──────────────────────────────────────────────────────────────┘
```

The above screens are taken from the Exchange Traded Interest Rate Futures Speed Guide and list all the contracts and easy access to chains of prices.

The screen below compares prices of Euroyen contracts from LIFFE and SIMEX.

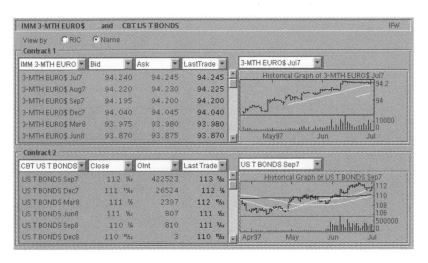

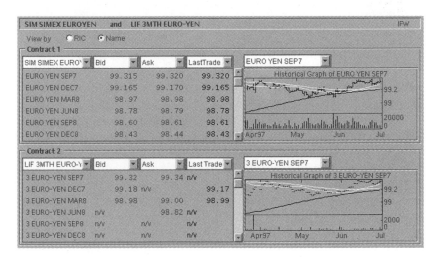

The above screen shows details for the IMM 3-month Eurodollar contracts and the long-term CBOT US T-Bonds contracts.

Interest Rate Swaps (IRS)

An **Interest Rate Swap (IRS)** is an agreement between two counterparties to exchange the interest payments, based on the same underlying notional principal amount, on fixed dates over the life of the contract.

Interest rate swaps are traded over-the-counter (OTC) and are one of the most widely traded money market instruments in the world.

In its most common form, the **fixed-floating swap**, one counterparty pays a fixed rate of interest and the other pays a floating rate based on a reference rate, such as LIBOR. There is no exchange of principal and the interest rate payments are made on a notional amount.

An interest rate Swap is the 'derivative equivalent' of two counterparties both borrowing the same amount — each using a different interest rate basis — and then exchanging the interest payments.

As there is no exchange of principal, the credit risk is limited to the interest payments receivable from the counterparty. Most commonly, the interest payments between the two counterparties are netted so that the credit risk is limited to the net cash flow between the counterparties.

Example

The point of interest rate swaps is that they allow borrowers to separate the basis on which they pay interest from the underlying money market instrument they use to actually borrow money.

For example, a borrower who wishes to pay the fixed one-year rate of interest on borrowings it needs in place for one year, but who can only gain funding using short-term 3-month Commercial Paper, can use an interest rate swap where it **receives** the 3-month LIBOR rate and **pays** the one year fixed rate. Each time the 3-month CP matures, it is simply rolled into the next month.

Thus the borrower pays interest at the 3-month LIBOR rate on its borrowings, receives the 3-month LIBOR rate from the swap and pays the one-year fixed rate on the swap, creating a net interest rate payable of the one-year fixed rate.

Such a simple fixed-floating swap is called **a plain vanilla Interest Rate Swap**

Floating-floating swaps are also available, known as **Basis Swaps** or **Diff Swaps**.

Terms and Specifications

The terms that need to be agreed for an Interest Rate Swap transaction include:

- Effective date
  This is the date when interest starts to accrue on both 'legs' of the swap. For plain vanilla swaps, this is taken as spot and LIBOR is foxed on the trade date. These are the same conventions as used in money market deposits.

- Termination date
  This is the end of the contract, otherwise known as expiry or maturity, when the final interest payments are calculated ad valued.

- Notional amount
  The amount used for calculating interest payments on both sides

- Fixed rate payer/receiver
  As most swaps involve both a fixed leg and a floating leg, it can be misleading to refer to 'buyers' and 'sellers' when referring to counterparties. For clarity, one counterparty is usually known as the **fixed rate payer** and the other counterparty is known as the **fixed rate receiver**.

- Interest Rate Basis
  This includes all details relating to the calculation of interest payments, including:
  — Reference interest rate, for example LIBOR
  — Payment periods and dates
  — Day count conventions

- Arrangement fees

Market Activity in IRSs

Interest rate swaps are the most widely traded derivatives contracts and form an important part of the world's capital markets.

According to the International Swaps and Derivatives Association (ISDA), the industry body made up of swap dealers which conducts a market survey every six months, the volume of outstanding IRS contracts outstanding at 30th June 1997 June totalled $22.115 trillion in notional principal. To show the rate at which this market is expanding, this total is double the figure ISDA recorded 18 months earlier at the year end of 1995.

ISDA figures show that the USD is still the most popular for IRS transactions.

Currency	%Total	USD equivalent (in billions)
USD	29.2	6,449
JPY	22.4	4,944
DEM	12.9	2,864
FRF	9.4	2,068
GBP	7.6	1,678
Other	18.6	4,112
Total =	100	22,115

Hedging with Interest Rate Swaps

In the previous example, we saw how using an interest rate swap allowed a borrower to pay a one-year fixed rate even though it could only access the three-month money market for funding.

It is this access to different markets, together with the high liquidity of the swaps market, that makes interest rate swaps such an attractive funding tool for borrowers.

The underlying principle of interest rate swaps is that they allow borrowers to hedge the rate of interest they will pay on their borrowings for a known period into the future. Whereas a forward rate agreement will allow a borrower to fix an interest rate for maybe three months in three months' time, an IRS can allow a borrower to fix the interest rate payable for up to 30 years from today.

This allows borrowers who would not normally be able to borrow in the long-term debt markets, for example if their credit rating is not sufficiently high, to raise funds in the short-term money markets and swap them into long-term interest rates. This gives borrowers an extra degree of certainty about their funding for long-term projects, and allows many projects to go ahead that might otherwise be considered too risky due to the risk of interest rates rising.

Note - Remember in Chapter 1 we discussed how interest rates are used as a tool by governments and central banks to dampen or stimulate economic activity. Business projects which are funded at fixed rates of interest, by using interest rate swaps, are immune from rising interest rates. The flip side of this is that if borrowing is swapped into long-term fixed rates, the borrower does not benefit from any falls in interest rates.

It is not only borrowers that use interest rate swaps. Speculators also find IRSs attractive instruments, as the absence of any exchange of principal means speculators can gain **leverage** through using them.

Example

XYZ Corporation borrows USD 10 million from Bank A, paying floating rate three-month LIBOR plus 200 basis points. XYZ Corporation then transacts a five-year interest rate swap with Bank B, receiving three-month LIBOR and paying a five-year fixed rate. XYZ Corporation is effectively borrowing as if it had issued a five-year bond, even though it is unable to access the long-term debt market. XYZ Corporation must roll its loan from Bank A every three months for five years.

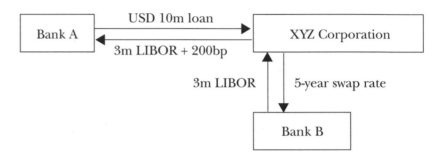

Interest Rate Swaps — Market-Makers

Most IRS contracts involve a market-maker who constantly quotes bid and offer prices for swaps. In this case, the bank is acting as an **intermediary** between counterparties who wish to pay fixed rates and counterparties who wish to receive fixed rates. Banks who act as market-makers for IRS transactions need to have a high credit rating, as counterparties are exposed to the bank's credit risk over the whole life of the swap contract, which could last for 30 years.

The bid and offer quotes from the market-maker are presented as **swap rates** - the fixed rates at which the market-maker is prepared to execute a receive fixed or pay fixed position in a swap. The swap rate is quoted as a spread over the government Treasury Bill/Note/Bond with the same maturity. This spread is known as the **swap spread**.

For example, a market-maker may quote "**70/75 over**" for a swap based on a five-year Treasury Note which has a yield of 7.00%. This means the market-maker pays fixed at a rate of 7.70% for a five year swap or receives fixed at a rate of 7.75%.

Example – a Double Swap
Consider the following situation:
ABC is a corporation that can either borrow at a fixed rate of 10% or issue a Floating Rate Note (FRN) with an interest rate of LIBOR + 1%. ABC would prefer fixed rate interest payments for their loan as it wishes to fund the building of a new factory.

XYZ is a money market fund which has invested in floating rate assets yielding LIBOR + 0.2%. XYZ would prefer to receive fixed interest rates as it knows it could beat its yearly targets if it locks in its interest rate now.

PQR Bank is a USD Interest Rate Swap market-maker, quoting a fixed rate of 70/75 over for a five-year IRS against a floating rate of LIBOR flat (ie, no spread). The five-year Treasury is yielding 8.00%.

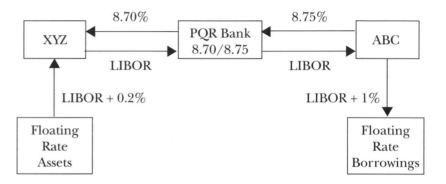

Summary:

Cash flow	XYZ	ABC
Pays	LIBOR	LIBOR + 1% + 8.75%
Receives	LIBOR + 0.2% + 8.70%	LIBOR
Net Payment	8.90%	9.75%
Without swap	–	10.00%
Saving	–	0.25%
Loan basis	Fixed	Fixed

Valuing Interest Rate Swaps

At the outset of an interest rate swap transaction, the instrument has no value to either party. What this means is that the present value of the future cash flows for each 'leg' of the swap are the same — ie, the net present value is zero. This is because the fixed rate leg of the swap is valued as the average interest rate that, over time, equals the expected future value of the floating rate payments.

The present value of the floating rate payments is calculated by determining the forward rates for each payment period over the life of the swap and then discounting each payment by the appropriate discount factor.

The interest rate swap will only show a profit or loss for the counterparties if interest rates deviate from the forward rates. That is, a swap counterparty can only profit from an IRS if the future does not occur in the way the forward markets predict. **If interest rates rise or fall in line with the predictions of the forward market over the life of the contract, neither counterparty will profit or lose on the transaction**.

Swap Curves

We have previously considered the yield curve, which is a plot of interest rates against maturity for money market and debt market instruments. The same activity — plotting interest rates against maturity — can be carried out for swaps.

 A **swap curve** is a plot of the fixed rate available on an interest rate swap against the available maturities.

For the purposes of valuing an IRS, the transaction can be thought of as a series of coupon payments from an imaginary **synthetic fixed rate bond** on the fixed leg netted against a series of interest payments from an imaginary **synthetic Floating Rate Note (FRN)** on the floating leg.

The swap curve can be thought of as the yield curve for these synthetic fixed rate bonds.

Example – Fixed side – Straight bond: Floating side – FRN
Suppose a plain vanilla swap has been arranged between XYZ Corporation and ABC Bank for a $100 millions notional principal amount for a 3 year period. On the fixed side the payments are 9.30% on an annual basis; on the floating side the payments are 12 months LIBOR.

The cash flows over the 3 year period would look something like those shown in the chart below.

Payments equivalent to coupons from a straight bond

Fixed	9.30%	9.30%	9.30%
Payment 1	Payment 1	Payment 2	Payment 3
Floating	LIBOR?	LIBOR?	LIBOR?

Payments equivalent to those from a Floating Rate Note

A plain vanilla swap can therefore be valued as follows:

Notional straight bond present value	–	Notional floating instrument present value

XYZ and ABC enter into the swap on the stated conditions. On the spot date LIBOR is fixed at 7.50% for the first payment. As has been mentioned the swap has no value at the start of the agreement. On the first payment date the 3 year swap rate is now quoted at 9.00% on the fixed side and 12 months LIBOR is fixed at 7.79%. What is the value of the swap now? Is the swap an asset or a liability to the receiver of the fixed side?

What is the value now of the swap that matures in the future? The present value of the fixed side can be calculated using the general straight bond valuation equation. For a bond with an annual coupon this is Equation 1.

$$\text{Present Value (PV)} = \frac{C}{1 + R} + \frac{C}{(1 + R)^2} + ... + \frac{(C + 100)}{(1 + R)^n}$$

Where: C = Coupon rate
R = Discount or swap rate as a decimal
n = Number of years to maturity

...Equation 1

In this example then: C = 9.30%; R = 0.090; n = 3

$$PV = \frac{9.30}{1.09} + \frac{9.30}{(1.09)^2} + \frac{109.30}{(1.09)^3}$$

$$= \ \$100.7594 \text{ million}$$

The present value for the floating side can be calculated using the more direct relationship between the present and future value of an instrument, Equation 2.

$$PV = \frac{\text{Future Value}}{(1 + R)}$$

$$= \frac{\text{Principal} + \text{Interest due}}{(1 + R)}$$

Where: R =   Discount or LIBOR rate
as a decimal

...*Equation 2*

In this example then: Principal = 100 millions; Interest = 7.50; $R = 0.0779$. Because the floating rate is based on Actual/360 the values used need to be adjusted to a 365 day year.

$$PV = \frac{\left[100 + \left(7.50 \ \times \ \dfrac{365}{360} \right) \right]}{1 + \left(0.0779 \ \times \ \dfrac{365}{360} \right)}$$

$$= \ \$99.7257 \text{ millions}$$

The net value of the swap is therefore $1.03 millions in favour of the fixed side. This is because the swap rate quoted by the bank at the end of the first payment is less than the coupon rate of 9.30% on the position. The floating side has lost value because LIBOR has increased.

Treating the value of a swap as the difference between a straight bond and a floating rate instrument gives rise to market-makers hedging or **warehousing** a swap position by temporarily buying or selling the underlying bond.

The payer of the fixed side **buys** the underlying which can then be sold to offset the position if the swap rates fall.

The receiver of the fixed side **sells** the underlying to offset any losses if swap rates rise.

The calculations here are quite complicated and time consuming to perform. In practice, traders will often use a graphical representation to assess the relationship of the swap with a benchmark instrument of the same maturity. The graphical representation used is the **spot curve** or **Zero Coupon yield curve**.

Pricing from the Spot Curve

The Yield To Maturity (YTM) curve is simply a graph of YTM values of bonds against maturity period. Unfortunately this is a simplistic view of yields and it is better to use a graph of **spot rate** against maturity period. The spot rate is a measure of the YTM on an instrument at any moment in time which takes into account a variety of market factors. A graph of spot rate against maturity is known as a spot curve. It is also known as a Zero Coupon yield curve because the spot rate for an instrument is equivalent to the yield on an instrument which has no coupon repayment – zero coupon. This means that spot rates for a series of instruments with zero coupons for a range of maturity periods can be compared directly.

The curves represent the perceived relationship between the return on an instrument and its maturity – usually measured in years. Depending on the shape of the curve it is described as either:

❑ Positive

❑ Negative or inverse

Positive yield curve

In this case the shorter term interest rates are **lower** than the longer term rates. This is usually the case – the longer the period of the investment the higher the yield paid. If an interest rate rise is expected, then investors will move their assets into long term instruments which produces a fall in short term rates and an increase in long term rates.

Negative or inverse curve

When short term rates fall investors move their investments into longer term instruments to lock in a higher rate of return. This increase in supply of long term funds causes the long term rates to fall.

The shapes of 'theoretical' yield curves are shown below – in practice they may not appear so clear!

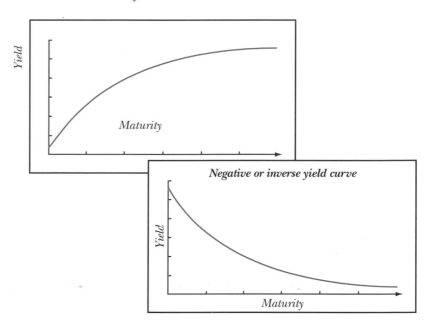

Positive yield curve

Negative or inverse yield curve

Yield curves are used to identify anomalies between instruments of similar credit standing, for example, an IRS and a T-bond of similar maturity.

The following chart may help in assessing the value of an instrument when compared to its spot curve.

Instrument curve	Instrument value
Above spot	Cheap
Below spot	Expensive

How does the spot curve help in pricing a swap? A more accurate way of considering an IRS is to consider the instrument as a series of fixed cash flows on one side combined with a series of notional floating cash flows on the other which are considered as a **strip of FRAs or futures contracts**.

In other words the spot curve rates are used to calculate, in advance, the net settlement amount of each future interest payment date.

The swap rate is effectively an average rate for a strip of FRAs or futures contracts.

The calculations are quite complex and in the previous example if the swap were valued using this more accurate method, then the net value in favour of the fixed side is $1.043 millions.

Fixed/floating terms

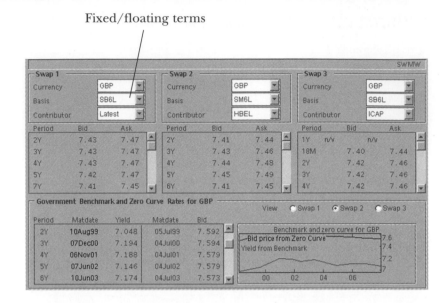

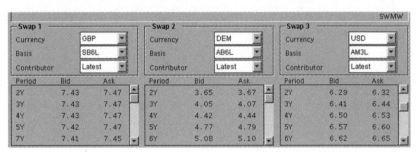

The screens above display three different contributor quotes for the same currency. Different contributors may use different swap terms so you may need to check this in the Basis fields.

Options on Interest Rate Futures

An **Option on an Interest Rate Future** is an agreement by which the buyer of the option pays the seller a **premium** for the right, but not the obligation, to buy or sell a specified amount of interest rate futures on or before an agreed date at an agreed price.

An option to buy is a **call option**.

An option to sell is a **put option**.

The specified amount is the contract amount, or notional value.

The agreed date is the **expiry** of the option. A **European style option** allows the holder to buy or sell the underlying futures **only on the expiry date**. An **American style option** allows the holder to buy or sell the underlying futures **on or any time before the expiry date**.

The relationship between the rights and obligations for the different types of options is summarised in the following diagram – you may find it useful to refer to when considering some of the examples which follow.

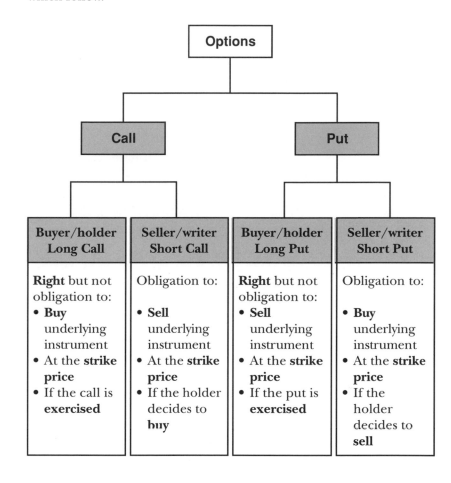

Interest Rate options are financial derivatives first introduced in the 1980s to hedge interest rate exposure.

If the option is exchange traded, then it is settled using the same conditions as for the underlying futures contracts. There are two types of exchange traded options on futures contracts:

- Options on **short-term** interest rate futures contracts which are **cash settled** if the option expires

- Options on **long-term** interest rate futures contracts which are settled on **government bonds** if the option expires

OTC interest rate options are used to control maximum and minimum levels of borrowing and lending money and are in effect options on forward rate agreements (FRAs). These options are described in greater detail in the section *Options on FRAs – Interest Rate Guarantees*.

The diagram below indicates the availability of interest rate options.

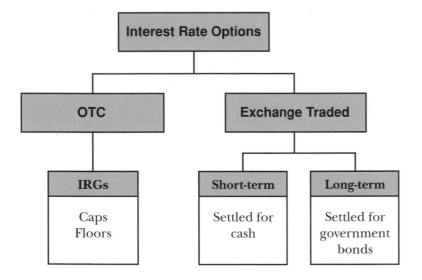

Exchange Traded Interest Rate Options

The underlying instrument for interest rate options on an exchange can either be for cash or for government bonds. Exchange traded options are standardised in terms of :

- Underlying instrument and its trading amount

- Strike prices – in general exchanges try to have a range of in-the-money, at-the-money and out-of-the-money strike prices

- Expiry dates

- Style – most exchange options are American

- Premium quotations – these are percentage rates expressed in decimal points for short-term contracts and as fractions for long-term contracts

- Margin payments are required to be paid to the clearing house

In effect interest rate options on futures give the buyer or the seller of the instrument the right to lend or borrow money. The following chart indicates these rights from the buyer's perspective – sellers would have the opposite views.

Option	Buyer	Used to Hedge
Call	Gives right to **lend** money at a predetermined rate	**Falling** interest rates
Put	Gives right to **borrow** money at a predetermined rate	**Rising** interest rates

Typical Contract Specifications

Options contracts details vary from type to type and from exchange to exchange but the following examples taken from a LIFFE contract and a CBOT contract are typical specifications.

Option on 3-month Sterling Interest Rate Future	
Underlying contract	One 3-month Sterling futures contract – GBP500,000
Premium quotations	Multiples of 0.01 (0.01%)
Minimum Price Fluctuation (Tick)	0.01 (£12.50)
Contract expiry	March, June, September, December
Exercise procedure	American

This is the standard contract size.

Quotes as either decimals or fractions of rate

This is the smallest amount a contract can change value and the 'tick' size.

Option contracts are referred to by the trading cycle of the futures contract months.

This means that contract can be exercised on or before expiry date – American

Options on US Treasury Bond Futures	
Underlying contract	One US Treasury Bond futures contract – $100,000
Premium quotations	Multiples of 1/64th of a point
Minimum Price Fluctuation (Tick)	1/64 ($15.625)
Contract expiry	March, June, September, December
Exercise procedure	American

Options on Interest Rate Futures in the Market Place

This section deals with typical contract quotations and how options are traded and premiums are calculated for interest rate options which are derived from exchange traded futures contracts based on:

- Short-term interest rate instruments

- Long-term interest rate instruments

Typical Exchange Contract Quotations

Interest rate option quotations are available from the financial press such as the *Financial Times* and *The Wall Street Journal* and from products such as Reuters Money 3000. The information appears in a similar style to that in the following examples.

Financial press – Option on short-term Interest Rate futures contract

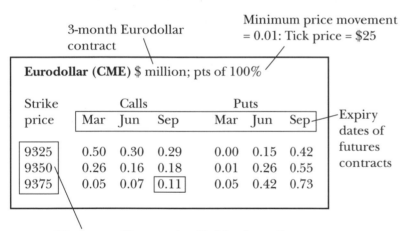

3-month Eurodollar contract

Minimum price movement = 0.01: Tick price = $25

Eurodollar (CME) $ million; pts of 100%

Strike price	Calls			Puts		
	Mar	Jun	Sep	Mar	Jun	Sep
9325	0.50	0.30	0.29	0.00	0.15	0.42
9350	0.26	0.16	0.18	0.01	0.26	0.55
9375	0.05	0.07	0.11	0.05	0.42	0.73

Expiry dates of futures contracts

The rates of interest implied in the strike prices are calculated by deducting the quoted strike price from 100.

A March 9350 strike represents a forward rate interest of 100 – 93.50 = 6.50%

The information in the chart allows you to calculate the premium cost of any option which is quoted.

Example
Suppose you need to hedge a 6.25% interest rate on a 3-month Eurodollar investment starting at the end of September. To hedge the return on this investment you decide to use an option. You will need to buy a Sep call option but what strike price should you use?

The strike price for 6.25% is simply determined by subtracting 6.25 from 100. So the strike price is 100 – 6.25 = 93.75. Buying a Sep call option gives you the right, but not obligation, to buy a 3-month Eurodollars futures contract on or before the September expiry date at an interest rate of 6.25%. But how much will you have to pay the seller for this right?

Contract premium price
This is calculated using the following simple equation:

$$\text{Premium cost} = \text{Number of ticks} \times \text{Tick size}$$

From the chart opposite the premium for a **Sep9375 call** is 0.11. So the premium cost is therefore:

$$= \frac{0.11 \text{ (quote)}}{0.01 \text{ (tick size)}} \times \$25 \text{ (tick size)}$$

$$= 11 \times \$25 = \$275.00$$

Example

A buyer of a **LIFFE** Short Sterling Jun9300 call allows the option to expire. This gives the buyer the right to receive interest at a rate of 7.00% on the underlying futures contract. At the time of expiry the EDSP is 9375 – an interest rate of 6.25%. Therefore the buyer receives a cash settlement:

$$= \ (9375 \ - \ 9300) \ \times \ £12.50$$

$$= \ 75 \ \times \ £12.50 = \ £937.50$$

The option premium was 0.30. This means that the premium cost was:

$$= \ 30 \ \times \ £12.50 = \ £375.00$$

The net profit on the option is therefore £937.50 − 375.00 = £562.50.

A simpler way of calculating the option profit is to use the following equation:

Profit = (EDSP − Strike price − Premium in ticks) × Tick value

So in this case the profit is calculated as:

$$= \ (9375 \ - \ 9300 \ - \ 30) \ \times \ £12.50$$

$$= \ 45 \ \times \ £12.50 = \ £562.50$$

Trading Strategies for Options

There are many strategies available in the options markets – some are quite complex and have colourful names.

The various strategies are usually represented diagrammatically as **break-even graphs** which show the potential for making a profit. The diagrams use the break-even point as the basis for the diagram where

Break-even point   =   Strike price ± premium

The most basic buy /sell strategies for puts and calls are illustrated using profit/loss charts in the following examples. You may find it useful to refer to option strategies in general by referring to the *An Introduction to Derivatives* ISBN 0-471-83176-X.

Depending on whether the market player is a buyer or seller of a call or put, gains or losses either have ceiling values or are limitless.

Money Market Derivatives

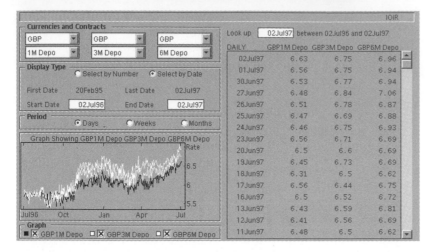

The screen above is taken from the Interest Rate History page. IOIR, which displays the deposit rates you select for up to three currencies simultaneously – you can choose any combination of currencies and deposit periods as required from the drop down menus. Here, the interest rate history for GBP is shown.

The screens below can be useful if you need to know the option delta values and whether an option premium is In-The-Money, At-The-Money or Out-Of-The-Money.

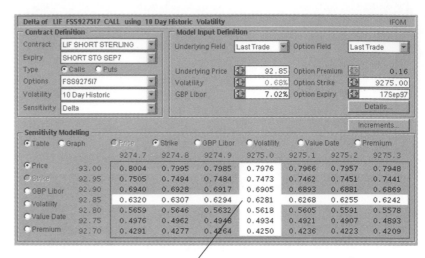

Here you can see that the Call for this 9275 strike for the September contract which has an underlying value of 92.85 has a delta value of 0.6281 which means it is ITM

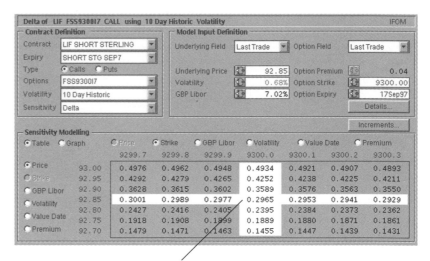

Here you can see that the Call for this 9300 strike for the September contract which has an underlying value of 92.85 has a delta value of 0.2965 which means it is OTM

Options on FRAs (Caps and Floors)

An **Interest Rate Guarantee** is an agreement which can be considered an option on a series of forward rate agreements.

An **Interest Rate Cap** is an agreement between counterparties in which the seller agrees to make payments to the buyer if the underlying **floating interest rate exceeds** an agreed strike rate.

An **Interest Rate Floor** is an agreement between counterparties in which the seller agrees to make payments to the buyer if the underlying **floating interest rate falls below** an agreed strike rate.

Caps and floors are OTC options which in effect 'guarantee' buyers a hedge against rising and falling interest rates, respectively. Hence these options are sometimes called **interest rate guarantees**.

The underlying floating interest rate for caps and floors is typically LIBOR, although these instruments can be, and often are, traded with other underlying floating interest rates, such as prime rates and commercial paper rates.

The following chart summarises some of the differences between buyers of caps and floors. Sellers of the instruments have the opposite positions to those indicated here for buyers.

Buyers of a ...	
Cap	**Floor**
• **Pay** the seller a **premium**	• **Pay** the seller a **premium**
• Hedge against a **rise** in interest rates above an agreed level for an agreed period	• Hedge against a **fall** in interest rates below an agreed level for an agreed period
• Are **borrowers** of money	• Are **lenders** of money

Some of the advantages offered by these OTC options include:

- Flexibility covering a wide range of maturity periods, amounts and strike prices

- The one-off cost of the option premium is known at the beginning of the transaction

- A single agreement may cover a maturity period of several years and is therefore less costly in fees

Money Market Derivatives

Caps

A cap is a series of options that gives the buyer the right, but not the obligation, to pay the lower of the market rate or strike rate.

In using a cap the buyer sets a maximum limit on the interest expense and can also benefit from a stable or declining interest rate.

A cap is a lid on a series of FRAs which coincide with the roll-over dates on a loan which.

The cost to the buyer is limited to the premium which is paid to the seller – the buyer has no further obligations.

Most caps are based on LIBOR and the following example illustrates how a cap works.

Example

A corporate treasurer has borrowed $10 million on a floating rate basis for 15 months using 3-month LIBOR roll-over dates. The treasurer believes that interest rates will rise and wants to cap the loan at 6.00%. The treasurer buys a cap option and pays a premium to the seller.

The treasurer's loan can therefore be considered to be a series of FRAs starting in 3 months from the first loan period – 3 x 6, 6 x 9, 9 x 12, 12 x 15.

If on any roll over date LIBOR exceeds the cap rate agreed, the seller of the option has to pay the treasurer the difference between LIBOR and the cap rate as a cash settlement.

The chart opposite indicates the LIBOR fluctuations over 15 months and the various payments made to the buyer of the cap.

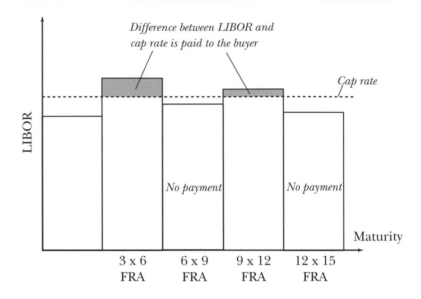

If LIBOR is above the cap rate then the corporate treasurer can take out a loan at LIBOR knowing that the extra cost above the agreed cap rate is guaranteed by the option. In other words the corporate treasurer's interest payments have been limited to the cap level set.

If LIBOR is below the cap rate, then the seller makes no payments to the buyer. However, the corporate treasurer now pays interest at a lower rate than the cap level which is within the interest rate maximum set.

The overall effect is that the corporate treasurer protects his interest rate payments from rises above a cap level while simultaneously taking advantage of any falls in interest rates.

REUTERS

Floors

These are the opposite type of options to caps in as much as they provide the buyer with a guaranteed **minimum** interest rate. They can be considered to be a series of put options on FRAs all with the same strike price.

A buyer of a floor is hedging against falling interest rates and is seeking to maintain a minimum rate of return whilst being able to benefit from any interest rates rises.

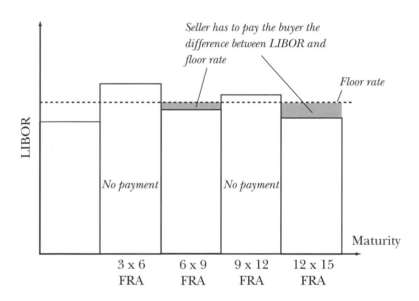

Seller has to pay the buyer the difference between LIBOR and floor rate

Floor rate

LIBOR

No payment   *No payment*

Maturity

3 x 6 FRA   6 x 9 FRA   9 x 12 FRA   12 x 15 FRA

If the floor is above LIBOR, then the seller or writer of the option has to pay the buyer the difference between the rates.

Collars

The collar is the natural combination of a cap and a floor where a market player wants to restrict interest rates between guaranteed maximum and minimum limits and reduce overall premium costs.

This can be achieved by **buying a cap** to place a maximum interest rate limit whilst simultaneously **selling a floor** to earn premium income **or vice versa**.

Summary	
Caps	**Floors**
• Protect buyers from **rising** interest rates above an agreed level whilst allowing the opportunity to benefit from any fall in rates	• Protect buyers from **falling** interest rates below an agreed level whilst allowing the opportunity to benefit from any rise in rates
• Establish a **maximum borrowing cost** for buyers over the maturity period of the option	• Establish a **minimum rate of return** for buyers over the maturity period of the option
• Do not affect the underlying loan	• Do not affect the underlying deposit or investment
• Provide a flexible alternative to fixed rate **borrowing**	• Provide a flexible alternative to fixed rate **lending**
• Are a series of **call options** on FRAs all with the same strike price	• Are a series of **put options** on FRAs all with the same strike price

Collar – Buyer of a Cap/Seller of a Floor

A **collar** is the simultaneous purchase of an out-of-the-money cap and the sale of an out-of-the-money floor.

If a counterparty is paying interest on a loan they can *buy* a cap and *sell* a floor to create a maximum and a minimum interest rate they will have to pay. If a counterparty is receiving interest they can *sell* a cap and *buy* a floor to create a maximum and a minimum interest rate they will receive.

Note that the converse of these two actions will not work, ie, buying a cap and selling a floor if you are receiving interest.

Example
A corporate treasurer borrowing money decides to limit borrowing costs to 6.0% because the current interest rates are only slightly higher than this. This is therefore the treasurer's cap. At the same time the treasurer sells a floor at 4.0% thus placing a collar on interest rate payments and earns premium income. The collar is indicated in the chart below.

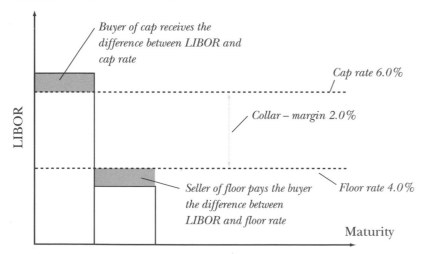

The option guarantees that if LIBOR rises above 6.0%, then the treasurer receives payment from the seller. If LIBOR falls below 4.0%, then the treasurer will have to make a payment to the floor buyer.

Collar – Buyer of a Floor/Seller of a Cap
Example
In a similar way to the previous example a corporate treasurer wishes to hedge an investment by setting the minimum rate of return he expects. This is therefore the treasurer's floor. At the same time the treasurer sells a cap which will earn premium income. If the floor is bought at 5.0% and the cap sold at 7.0%, then the collar is indicated in the chart below.

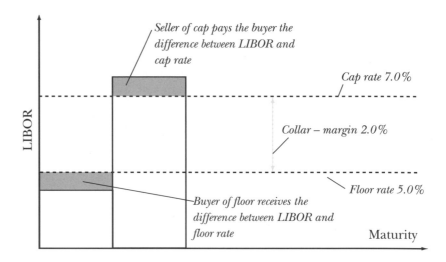

If LIBOR falls below 5.0%, then the treasurer receives a payment from the floor option. If LIBOR rises above 7.0% then the treasurer will have to make a payment to the cap buyer. However, the treasurer's view is that interest rates will not rise and that the cap option will not be exercised.

For collars in general, because the option involves a simultaneous purchase and sale, the premium charges involved are partially or fully eliminated. One premium is received whilst the other is paid.

IRGs in the Market Place

This section deals with typical OTC caps and floors quotations and the importance of implied volatilities in pricing these quotations.

Typical OTC Contract Quotations

Interbank quotations for IRGs are not made using basis points. Instead professional options market-makers use complex analytical models to calculate option prices based on the following factors.

1. The prevailing LIBOR rate

2. Strike price

3. Time to expiry

4. The term structure of interest rates

5. Price volatility of the prevailing LIBOR rate

Of the factors, **price volatility** is the only one for which the market-maker does not have a precise value. So what is this price volatility?

Price volatility is the degree of movement of interest rates. The primary focus in pricing options is to be able to calculate accurately a forecast or expectation of volatility over the life of an option. Obviously the more accurate the calculations the more chance the market-maker has of making a profit. However, recent bank losses involving options trading have shown how easy it is to get things wrong!

So how are the price volatility values used for the calculations derived? The volatility used for pricing an option is calculated using statistical standard deviations of historic underlying price movements over a given period, expressed as an annualised percentage.

Example

A market-maker might quote 11.50 – 13.50 % volatility for a 3 month LIBOR GBP at-the-money cap.

This two-way Bid/Ask price quotation means:

On **Bid** side   The market-maker will **buy** puts or calls at 11.50% per annum

On **Ask** side   The market-maker will **sell** puts or calls at 13.50% per annum

This Bid/Ask spread in volatility translates into a corresponding spread in the option premium.

The prices are for at-the-money options – the strike price is at the current underlying forward rate.

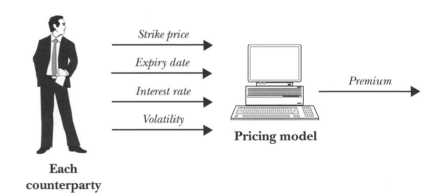

The screen below displays the Implied Volatilities Speed Guide. If the <IRGS/1> field is double-clicked, the top right screen, which shows caps and floors options for various currencies and from various contributors, will become available. Double-clicking on the <GBPCA=ICAP> option will bring up another screen displaying At-The-Money volatilities for GBP from Intercapital Brokers Ltd.

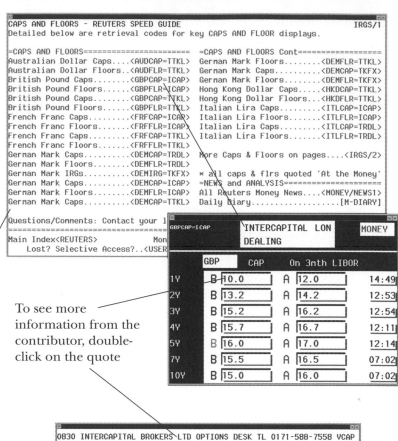

```
CAPS AND FLOORS - REUTERS SPEED GUIDE                          IRGS/1
Detailed below are retrieval codes for key CAPS AND FLOOR displays.

=CAPS AND FLOORS======================   =CAPS AND FLOORS Cont==================
Australian Dollar Caps....<AUDCAP=TTKL>  German Mark Floors........<DEMFLR=TTKL>
Australian Dollar Floors..<AUDFLR=TTKL>  German Mark Caps..........<DEMCAP=TKFX>
British Pound Caps........<GBPCAP=ICAP>  German Mark Floors........<DEMFLR=TKFX>
British Pound Floors......<GBPFLR=ICAP>  Hong Kong Dollar Caps.....<HKDCAP=TTKL>
British Pound Caps........<GBPCAP=TTKL>  Hong Kong Dollar Floors...<HKDFLR=TTKL>
British Pound Floors......<GBPFLR=TTKL>  Italian Lira Caps........<ITLCAP=ICAP>
French Franc Caps.........<FRFCAP=ICAP>  Italian Lira Floors......<ITLFLR=ICAP>
French Franc Floors.......<FRFFLR=ICAP>  Italian Lira Caps........<ITLCAP=TRDL>
French Franc Caps.........<FRFCAP=TTKL>  Italian Lira Floors......<ITLFLR=TRDL>
French Franc Floors.......<FRFFLR=TTKL>
German Mark Caps..........<DEMCAP=TRDL>  More Caps & Floors on pages....<IRGS/2>
German Mark Floors........<DEMFLR=TRDL>
German Mark IRGs..........<DEMIRG=TKFX>  * all caps & flrs quoted 'At the Money'
German Mark Caps..........<DEMCAP=ICAP>  =NEWS and ANALYSIS====================
German Mark Floors........<DEMFLR=ICAP>  All Reuters Money News....<MONEY/NEWS1>
German Mark Caps..........<DEMCAP=TTKL>  Daily Diary.................[M-DIARY]

Questions/Comments: Contact your l
====================================
Main Index<REUTERS>              Mon
     Lost? Selective Access?..<USER
```

```
GBPCAP=ICAP      INTERCAPITAL LON    MONEY
                 DEALING

         GBP      CAP    On 3nth LIBOR
  1Y   B 10.0   A 12.0            14:49
  2Y   B 13.2   A 14.2            12:53
  3Y   B 15.2   A 16.2            12:54
  4Y   B 15.7   A 16.7            12:11
  5Y   B 16.0   A 17.0            12:14
  7Y   B 15.5   A 16.5            07:02
 10Y   B 15.0   A 16.0            07:02
```

```
IMPLIED OPTION VOLATILITIES - REUTERS SPEED GUIDE                VOL/1
All data represents implied volatilities.  To access information please
double-click on the code in <> or [].

=FOREIGN EXCHANGE VOLATILITIES=========================================
Contributed OTC FX Option Volatilities...............................<OPS/FX1>
Guide to Contributed FX Option Volatilities..........................<OPS/FX3>
Implied Volatility of Currency Options traded on Philadelphia Exchange....<PHVM>
Implied Volatility of ATM Currency Options Traded on MATIF.........<MAT/OPTEX3>
News on Currency Options..............................................[FX/OPT]

=INTEREST RATE VOLATILITIES============================================
Caps and Floors......................................................<IRGS/1>
Swaptions.........................................................<SWAPTION/1>
Implied Volatility of ATM PIBOR Options Traded on MATIF..............<O#.PIB+>

=COMMODITY VOLATILITIES================================================
Contributed OTC Gold and Silver Volatilities...............<SGCC> <MANG>
Implied Volatility of ATM White Sugar Options Traded on MATIF.........<O#.OSU+>


Questions/Comments: Contact your local Help Desk - see <PHONE/HELP> for details
================================================================================
Main Index<REUTERS>  Money Index<MONEY>  Commod Index<COMMOD>  Next page<VOL/2>
     Lost? Selective Access?..<USER/HELP>     Reuters Phone Support..<PHONE/HELP>
```

To see more information from the contributor, double-click on the quote

```
0830 INTERCAPITAL BROKERS LTD OPTIONS DESK TL 0171-588-7558 VCAP
         IMPLIED VOLATILITIES: AT THE MONEY CAPS & FLOORS


    DEM LIBOR V6M          GBP LIBOR V3M
    CAPS      FLOORS       CAPS      FLOORS
 1Y 13.0-16.0 13.0-16.0  1Y 10.0-12.0 10.0-12.0
 2Y 17.0-19.0 17.0-19.0  2Y 13.2-14.2 13.2-14.2
 3Y 19.0-20.0 19.0-20.0  3Y 15.2-16.2 15.2-16.2
 4Y 18.5-19.5 18.5-19.5  4Y 15.7-16.7 15.7-16.7
 5Y 17.7-18.7 17.7-18.7  5Y 16.0-17.0 16.0-17.0
 7Y 16.3-17.5 16.3-17.5  7Y 15.5-16.5 15.5-16.5
10Y 14.3-15.3 14.3-15.3 10Y 15.0-16.0 15.0-16.0


    X-PAGE UPDATING-X
```

Swaptions

What is a Swaption?

A **Swaption** is a financial derivative which grants the right, but not the obligation, to buy or sell an interest rate swap (IRS) on agreed terms of interest rate, maturity, fixed or floating rate payer, on or by an agreed date. In return for this right the buyer of a swaption pays the seller a premium.

If you need an overview of options and swaps derivatives or you need to remind yourself about the types of derivatives available, then you may find it useful to refer to the *An Introduction to Derivatives* ISBN 0-471-83176-X at this stage.

Swaptions are OTC contracts used by market players who seek the advantages of an IRS but who also would like to benefit from any favourable interest rate movements.

Swaptions, in common with other options, use the terms call and put. However, their meanings are not quite as obvious as before. The meanings and uses of swaptions calls and puts are described in the chart below.

Call Swaption	Put Swaption
• Also called a **payer** or **right-to-pay** swaption	• Also called a **receiver** or **right-to-receive** swaption
• The buyer has the right to **pay the fixed side to** and receive the floating side from the holder of the underlying IRS	• The buyer has the right to **receive the fixed side from** and pay the floating side to the holder of the underlying IRS
• The buyer is hedging against **falling** interest rates	• The buyer is hedging against **rising** interest rates

Who uses Swaptions?

Banks and Corporations

Swaptions are used by the same market participants who use IRSs – banks and multinational corporations.

Swaptions are used increasingly by these market players for two main reasons:

- To hedge exposure on interest rates

- To speculate in the swaps markets in order to make a profit from offsetting fixed/floating rate transactions

Swaptions offer similar benefits to corporations and banks as IRSs:

- Counterparties are able to convert underlying interest rates from fixed to floating and vice versa over a long term period

- Usually there are cost savings to both sides

- IRSs provide access to markets not normally available to the market players, for example, for reasons relating to credit rating

Swaptions in the Market Place

This section deals with examples of how call and put swaptions work in the market place.

Call Swaptions

Example

XYZ Corporation decides to hedge against falling interest rates using a **1 plus 4 call swaption**. This means they **buy** an instrument which grants the right to exercise the option in one year for an underlying 4 year receive fixed/pay floating swap for a swap rate of 6.5%.

This means that if XYZ, the swaption holder, exercises its right in a year, it will receive a fixed rate of 6.5% and pay floating rate LIBOR.

To justify exercising the swaption, the interest rates of the underlying instrument must be **less** than the swap strike rate.

At expiration the current rate for a 4 year receive fixed/pay floating swap is 6.0% (ie, the swap rate is 6.0%). IRS is 6.0%/LIBOR. XYZ exercises its right on the swaption and makes a net gain of 0.5% in interest rate payments, so hedging against falling interest rates.

The process is illustrated in the chart opposite.

Payments	XYZ receive	XYZ pay	Net % position
Fixed	6.50%	6.00%	+ 0.50
Floating	LIBOR	LIBOR	Cancel out

The screen on top right is the **Speed Guide** for Swaptions. As with other OTC option prices the Bid and Ask quotes from the various contributors are as volatilities. If you double-click in the **<USDSTN=TXFX>** field you will see Swaption volatilities for the USD from the **Tokyo Forex Co Ltd**. If you double-click in the **<DEMSWPTNS=TTKL>** field you will see the volatilities from **Tullets** on DEM – these are mid-quotes.

```
SWAPTIONS - REUTERS SPEED GUIDE                                 SWAPTION/1
Detailed below are retrieval codes for key SWAPTION displays.

=SWAPTIONS=============================  =SWAPTIONS Cont===================
Australian Dollar......<AUDSWPTNS=TTKL>  US Dollar.............<USDSWPTNS=TTKL>
British Pound............<GBPSTN=ICAP>   US Dollar.............<USDSTN=TKFX>
British Pound...........<GBPSTN1=ICAP>   US Dollar.............<USDSTN1=TKFX>
French Franc...........<FRFSWPTNS=TTKL>
French Franc............<FRFSTN=ICAP>
French Franc...........<FRFSTN1=ICAP>
German Mark.............<DEMSTN=ICAP>    =RELATED GUIDES==================
German Mark............<DEMSTN1=ICAP>    Broker Index...............<BROKER>
German Mark..........<DEMSWPTNS=TTKL>    Specialist Data Guide........<SPECIAL>
Hong Kong Dollar.....<HKDSWPTNS=TTKL>    Cross Market Package......<CROSS/MKT1>
Italian Lira............<ITLSTN=ICAP>
Italian Lira...........<ITLSTN1=ICAP>
Japanese Yen............<JPYSTN=TKFX>    =NEWS and ANALYSIS==============
Japanese Yen...........<JPYSTN1=TKFX>    All Reuters Money News....<MONEY/NEWS1>
Japanese Yen.........<JPYSWPTNS=TTKL>    Daily Diary...............[M-DIARY]
Spanish Peseta..........<ESPSTN=ICAP>    Broker Index...............<BROKER>
Spanish Peseta.........<ESPSTN1=ICAP>
Questions/Comments: Contact your local Help Desk - see <PHONE/HELP> for details
=============================================================================
Main Index..<REUTERS>                                    Money Index..<MONEY>
    LOST? Selective Access?..<USER/HELP>        Reuters Support..<PHONE/HELP>
```

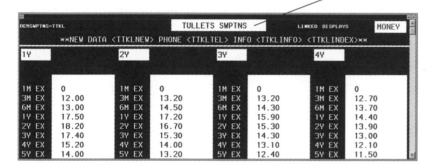

TULLETS SWPTNS LINKED DISPLAYS MONEY

DEMSWPTNS=TTKL
NEW DATA <TTKLNEW> PHONE <TTKLTEL> INFO <TTKLINFO> <TTKLINDEX>

	1Y		2Y		3Y		4Y
1M EX	0	1M EX	0	1M EX	0	1M EX	0
3M EX	12.00	3M EX	13.20	3M EX	13.20	3M EX	12.70
6M EX	13.00	6M EX	14.50	6M EX	14.30	6M EX	13.70
1Y EX	17.50	1Y EX	17.20	1Y EX	15.90	1Y EX	14.40
2Y EX	18.20	2Y EX	16.70	2Y EX	15.30	2Y EX	13.90
3Y EX	17.40	3Y EX	15.30	3Y EX	14.30	3Y EX	13.00
4Y EX	15.20	4Y EX	14.00	4Y EX	13.10	4Y EX	12.10
5Y EX	14.00	5Y EX	13.20	5Y EX	12.40	5Y EX	11.50

TKFX - SWAPTION LINKED DISPLAYS

USDSTN=TKFX
THE TOKYO FOREX CO.,LTD.   Full Index on page <TKFXINDEX>

	USD	STN		USD	STN		USD	STN	
	1Y			2Y			3Y		
1M EX	10.5	12.5	00:04	12.1	14.1	00:04	12.0	14.0	00:04
3M EX	11.0	13.0	00:04	12.4	14.4	00:04	12.3	14.3	00:04
6M EX	12.0	14.0	00:04	13.2	15.2	00:04	13.1	15.1	00:04
9M EX	13.6	15.6	00:04	14.0	16.0	00:04	14.0	16.0	00:04
1Y EX	13.6	15.6	00:04	14.0	16.0	00:04	14.0	16.0	00:04
2Y EX	14.9	16.9	00:04	14.6	16.6	00:04	14.5	16.5	00:04
3Y EX	14.8	16.8	00:04	14.5	16.5	00:04	14.3	16.3	00:04
4Y EX	14.6	16.6	00:04	14.4	16.4	00:04	14.2	16.2	00:04
5Y EX	14.4	16.4	00:04	14.2	16.2	00:04	14.0	16.0	00:04
7Y EX	13.6	15.6	00:04	13.4	15.4	00:04	13.2	15.2	00:04
10Y EX	12.7	14.7	00:04	12.4	14.4	00:04	12.2	14.2	00:04

Summary

You have now finished this section and you should have a clear understanding of the following Derivative Instruments:

As a check on your understanding you should try the Quick Quiz Questions on the next page. You may also find the section Overview useful as a revision aid.

- Forward Rate Agreement (FRA)

- Interest Rate Futures

- Interest Rate Swap (IRS)

- Options on Interest Rate Futures

- Options on FRAs – Interest Rate Guarantees (IRGs)

- Options on IRSs – Swaptions

Your notes

Quick Quiz Questions

1. If you as a customer buy a FRA you are:

   ❑ a) Protecting against a rise in interest rates
   ❑ b) Protecting against a fall in interest rates
   ❑ c) Taking a cash delivery of principal from the counterparty
   ❑ d) Making a cash delivery of principal to the counterparty

2. Today is the fixing date for a 1x4 FRA which you sold for 5.67%. LIBOR has been fixed at 6.00%. Which of the following statements is true?

   ❑ a) You pay the counterparty
   ❑ b) The counterparty pays you
   ❑ c) No payment takes place until later

3. Which of the following statements best describes why corporations may prefer to use FRAs rather than Interest Rate futures contracts to hedge?

   ❑ a) FRAs are more liquid
   ❑ b) FRA prices are less volatile
   ❑ c) FRAs are priced more competitively
   ❑ d) FRAs are OTC and can be tailored

4. A Forward/forward rate is the direct result of:

   ❑ a) Market expectations of future interest rates
   ❑ b) Prices quoted for exchange traded Interest Rate futures
   ❑ c) Values derived from existing deposit rates
   ❑ d) None of the above

5. Bank A sells Bank B a 3 x 6 USD FRA at a contract rate of 5.86%. On the settlement the LIBOR 3-month fixing rate is 5.75%. The FRA contract details are as follows:

FRA contract amt.:	$50,000,000
Contract period:	90 days
Contract rate:	5.86% pa
Year basis:	360 days

   a) What is the cash settlement amount involved?
   b) Who receives payment?

   Answer a)

   Answer b)

6. Which of the following interest rates is implied for a LIFFE 3-month Short sterling futures contract with a price of 93.18?

   ❑ a) 5.82%
   ❑ b) 6.72%
   ❑ c) 6.82%
   ❑ d) 7.82%

Quick Quiz Questions

7. If you place an order for a futures contract, when will you be required to pay initial margin?

    ❑ a) At expiry of the contract
    ❑ b) Only if you buy a contract
    ❑ c) At the time of trading the contract
    ❑ d) Only if you sell a contract

8. Consider the following CME Eurodollar futures prices.
    Mar 9378 Jun 9374 Sep 9370 Dec 9366

    Which one of the following statements is true?

    ❑ a) The USD yield curve is inverted
    ❑ b) The USD yield curve is positive
    ❑ c) A weak USD on foreign exchanges is expected
    ❑ d) None of the above

9. A trader at XYZ Bank thinks that trade figures will be better than expected resulting in a short-term interest rate fall. He buys 5 June LIFFE 3-month Short sterling contracts at 93.72. The contract's minimum price movement is 0.01 and the tick value is £12.50.

    a) What is the implied interest rate for the contract?
    b) If the trader is correct and interest rates fall and he sells the contract at 93.17, how much profit does the dealer make?
    c) If the trader is wrong and he has to close the contract at 94.03, what is his loss?

    Answer a)

    Answer b)

Answer c)

10. In an IRS, the principal amounts involved are usually:

    ❑ a) Exchanged at the end date
    ❑ b) Exchanged at the start date
    ❑ c) Not exchanged
    ❑ d) Exchanged at an interim date

11. In an IRS, interest payments are exchanged:

    ❑ a) On a net basis at the end of each interest period
    ❑ b) On a gross basis at the end of each interest period
    ❑ c) At the start of each interest period, as with a FRA
    ❑ d) On a cumulative basis at maturity

12. A client asks you to quote for a 2 year GBP IRS. You quote 7.43 – 7.39. The client deals at 7.39. What have you done?

    ❑ a) Agreed to receive fixed/pay floating
    ❑ b) Transacted a basis swap
    ❑ c) Agreed to pay fixed/receive floating
    ❑ d) Transacted a fixed/fixed swap

13. A borrower pays LIBOR + $\frac{5}{8}$% for floating USD. He decides to fix his interest repayments using an IRS. He receives a quote of 6.75 – 80 using the same interest basis and decides to fix. What will be the net cost of his borrowing?

    ❑ a) 6.750%
    ❑ b) 6.800%
    ❑ c) 7.375%
    ❑ d) 7.425%

Quick Quiz Questions

14. Using the chart of premium prices for options on Eurodollars answer the following:

Eurodollar (CME) $ million; pts of 100%

Strike price	Calls Mar	Jun	Sep	Puts Mar	Jun	Sep
9325	0.50	0.30	0.29	0.00	0.15	0.42
9350	0.26	0.16	0.18	0.01	0.26	0.55
9375	0.05	0.07	0.11	0.05	0.42	0.73

Tick size for this contract is 0.01 and the tick value is $25

a) Why are the Calls with higher strikes cheaper than those with lower strikes, and why are the Puts with higher strikes more expensive than those with lower strikes?

Answer:

b) At what price would the buyer of a 9325 Jun Put break even at expiry?

Answer:

c) What is the maximum interest rate that the buyer of a 9375 Sept Put is guaranteed on a future loan?

Answer:

d) What is the premium cost for a 9350 Jun Call?

Answer:

15. Your company obtained a 3-year rollover credit for $10 million on the basis of 6-month LIBOR from XYZ Bank one year ago. As Treasurer you are of the opinion that interest rates are likely to rise in the future. Therefore you want to hedge against an interest rise of 0.25% above the prevailing interest level of 5.00%.

a) Do you buy a Cap or Floor?
   Answer:

b) Note the terms of the contract here:

Underlying index	
Term	
Reset period	
Strike	
Notional amount	

Quick Quiz Questions

c) If the premium costs 120 basis points, how much does the option cost you?

Answer:

d) At the first settlement date 6-month LIBOR is at 6.00%. Do you exercise the option? Calculate any settlement amount involved.

Answer:

e) At the third settlement date the rate is 5.00%. Do you exercise this option?

Answer:

16. Your organisation wishes to speculate by placing $10 million in FRNs for 2 years based on 6-month LIBOR. Although you are convinced that interest rates will rise from their current rate of 5.00% and you would like to benefit from any rise, you would still like to protect yourself against an adverse movement of 1% in interest rates.

a) Do you buy a Cap or Floor?

Answer:

b) Note the terms of the contract here:

Underlying index	
Term	
Reset period	
Strike	
Notional amount	

c) If the premium costs 50 basis points, how much does the option cost you?

Answer:

d) At the first settlement date 6-month LIBOR is at 3.50%. Do you exercise the option? Calculate any settlement amount involved.

Answer:

e) At the third settlement date the rate is 6.00%. Do you exercise this option?

Answer:

You can check your answers on page 232.

Overview

Money Market Derivatives

Key Concepts:

- **Basic Risk**
  Basis risk is the risk that the London Interbank Offered Rate (LIBOR) which applies to the settlement value of the FRA moves away from the actual interest rate on the underlying loan that is being hedged, leaving the holder with an imperfect hedge.

- **Hedging**
  The underlying principle of hedging is that as price movements in the cash market move one way, the move is offset by an equal and opposite move in the price of **the hedging instrument** (almost always a **derivative instrument**).

- **Leverage**
  This phenomenon, where cash market returns can be generated by deploying only a small fraction of the capital that would be needed to invest in the cash market is known as **leverage**.

Definition

A **Derivative Instrument** is one whose value changes with changes in one or more underlying market variables, such as interest rates or foreign exchange rates. A Derivative Instrument is essentially an agreement between two counterparties in which they agree to transfer an asset or amount of money on or before a specified future date at a specified price.

Main Types

- **Forward Rate Agreements (FRAs)**

A **Forward Rate Agreement** is an agreement between two counterparties which fixes the rate of interest that will apply to a specified notional future loan or deposit commencing and maturing on specified future dates.

- **Interest Rate Futures**

Interest Rate Futures are exchange-traded forward rate agreements with standard contract sizes and maturity dates which are cash-settled on a daily basis throughout the life of the contract.

- **Interest Rate Swaps (IRS)**

An **Interest Rate Swap (IRS)** is an agreement between two counterparties to exchange the interest payments, based on the same underlying notional principal amount, on fixed dates over the life of the contract.

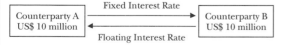

Fixed Interest Rate

| Counterparty A US$ 10 million | ⟷ | Counterparty B US$ 10 million |

Floating Interest Rate

- **Options on Interest Rate Futures**

An **Option on an Interest Rate Future** is an agreement by which the buyer of the option pays the seller a **premium** for the right, but not the obligation, to buy or sell a specified amount of interest rate futures on or before an agreed date at an agreed price.

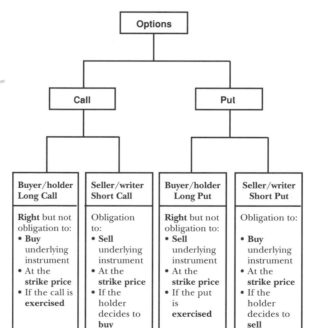

Buyer/holder Long Call	Seller/writer Short Call	Buyer/holder Long Put	Seller/writer Short Put
Right but not obligation to: • **Buy** underlying instrument • At the **strike price** • If the call is **exercised**	Obligation to: • **Sell** underlying instrument • At the **strike price** • If the holder decides to **buy**	**Right** but not obligation to: • **Sell** underlying instrument • At the **strike price** • If the put is **exercised**	Obligation to: • **Buy** underlying instrument • At the **strike price** • If the holder decides to **sell**

- **Interest rate Cap**

An **Interest Rate Cap** is an agreement between counterparties in which the seller agrees to make payments to the buyer if the underlying **floating interest rate exceeds** an agreed strike rate.

- **Interest Rate Floor**

An **Interest Rate Floor** is an agreement between counterparties in which the seller agrees to make payments to the buyer if the underlying **floating interest rate falls below** an agreed strike rate.

- **Swaptions**

A **Swaption** is a financial derivative which grants the right, but not the obligation, to buy or sell an interest rate swap (IRS) on agreed terms of interest rate, maturity, fixed or floating rate payer, on or by an agreed date. In return for this right the buyer of a swaption pays the seller a premium.

Quick Quiz Answers

	✔ or ✘
1. a)	❑
2. a)	❑
3. d)	❑
4. c)	❑

5. a) $13,555.14   ❑

Use Equation 1b.

$$\text{Settlement} = \frac{(5.86 - 5.75) \times 90 \times 50,000,000}{(360 \times 100) + (5.75 \times 90)}$$

$$= \frac{0.11 \times 90 \times 50,000,000}{36000 + (517.5)}$$

b) Bank B pays Bank A   ❑

6. c)   ❑

7. c)   ❑

8. b)   ❑

9. a) 6.28%   ❑
Implied interest rate = 100 − 93.72
= 6.28

b) £3437.50   ❑
Contract moves   93.72 − 93.17 = 0.55 = 55 ticks
Therefore profit = 55 × £12.50 × 5 = £3437.50

c) £1937.50   ❑
Contract moves   94.03 − 93.72 = 0.55 = 31 ticks
Therefore profit = 31 × £12.50 × 5 = £1937.50

	✔ or ✘
10. c)	❑
11. a)	❑
12. c)	❑
13. d)	❑

14. a) The higher the strike the lower the Call prices because they are further Out-of-The -Money. The higher the Put prices because they are further In-The-Money.   ❑

b) Put break even = Strike − Premium   ❑
= 93.25 − 0.15
= 93.10

c) Maximum interest rate locked in by the potential borrower is given by
100 − (Strike − Premium)   ❑

= 100 − (93.75 − 0.73)
= 100 − 93.02
= 6.98%

d) Premium is 0.16, the tick size for this contract is 0.01 and the tick value is $25   ❑

Premium cost = 0.16/0.01 × $25
= 16 × 25
= $400

Quick Quiz Answers

✔ or ✖

15. a) Buy a Cap ☐

b) ☐

Underlying index	6 month LIBOR
Term	2 years
Reset period	Every 6 months
Strike	5.00 + 0.25 = 5.25
Notional amount	$10,000,000

c) 1.20% of $10,000,000 = $120,000 ☐

d) You exercise the option because you have to borrow at 6.00%. ☐

You receive compensation

$$= \frac{10,000,000 \times 0.75 \times 180}{100 \times 360}$$ ☐

$$= \$37,500$$ ☐

e) You do not exercise the option because you can borrow in the market at 5.00%

✔ or ✖

16. a) Buy a Floor ☐

b) ☐

Underlying index	6 month LIBOR
Term	2 years
Reset period	Every 6 months
Strike	5.00 – 1.00 = 4.00
Notional amount	$10,000,000

c) 0.50% of $10,000,000 = $50,000 ☐

d) You exercise the option because you have to lend at 3.50%.
You receive compensation

$$= \frac{10,000,000 \times 0.50 \times 180}{100 \times 360}$$

$$= \$25,000$$ ☐

e) You do not exercise the option because you can lend in the market at 6.00% ☐

How well did you score? You should have managed to get most of these questions correct. If you didn't you may need to revise some of the materials.

Further Resources

Books

The Dictionary of Financial Risk Management
Gary Gastineau and Mark P Kritzman, Irwin Professional Publishing, 1996
ISBN   1 883 24914 7

Options, Futures, and Other Derivatives
John C. Hull, Prentice Hall Press, 1997
ISBN   0 138 87498 0

Swap & Derivative Financing: The Global Reference to Products, Pricing, Applications and Markets
Satyajit Das, Probus Pub Co. 1994
ISBN   1 557 38542 4

Option Pricing Mathematical Models & Computation
Paul Wilmott, Jeff DeWynne and Sam Bowison, American
Educational Systems, 1997
ISBN   0 952 20820 2

McMillan on Options
Lawrence G. McMillan, John Wiley & Sons Inc., 1996
ISBN   0 471 11960 1

Understanding Options
Robert W. Kolb, John Wiley & Sons Inc., 1995
ISBN   0 471 08554 5

Understanding Swaps
John F. Marshall, John Wiley & Sons Inc., 1993
ISBN   0 471 30827 7

A Complete Guide to the Futures Markets: Fundamental Analysis, Technical Analysis, Trading, Spreads, and Options
Jack Schwager, John Wiley & Sons Inc., 1994
ISBN   0 471 89376 5

The Penguin International Dictionary of Finance
Graham Bannock & William Manser, Penguin, 2nd Edition 1995
ISBN   0 140 51279 9

Investments
William F. Sharpe, Gordon J. Alexander & Jeffrey V. Bailey, Prentice Hall, 5th Edition 1995
ISBN   0 131 83344 8

A–Z of International Finance
Stephen Mahony, FT/Pitman Publishing, 1997
ISBN   0 273 62552 7

Financial Derivatives
David Winstone, Chapman & Hall, 1st Edition 1995
ISBN   0 412 62770 1

Booklets

Chicago Mercantile Exchange
*   An Introduction to Futures and Options: Currency

Swiss Bank Corporation
*   Financial Futures and Options
*   Options: The fundamentals
    ISBN   0 964 11120 9

Chicago Board of Trade
*   Financial Instruments Guide
*   An Introduction to Options on Financial Futures
*   Trading in Futures

London International Financial Futures and Options Exchange
*   An Introduction
*   Options: a guide to trading strategies

Reuters Money 3000 – Training Programme

Further Resources (continued)

Internet Web sites
RFT Website
*   **http://www.wiley-rft.reuters.com**
This is the series' companion website where additional quiz
questions, updated screens and other information may be found.

Your notes

Your notes

Introduction

Earlier in the book, we took an overview of the money markets and foreign exchange market, examining the relationships between these markets. In addition, we briefly considered the instruments commonly used in the money markets and foreign exchange markets.

We have also examined money market instruments more closely.

Now, we will take a more detailed look at foreign exchange instruments. In particular, we will examine the parameters which must be defined in order to place a value on these instruments, together with basic valuation techniques.

This chapter is split into two sections, reflecting the characteristics of groups of foreign exchange instruments. The sections are: transaction and fx derivatives.

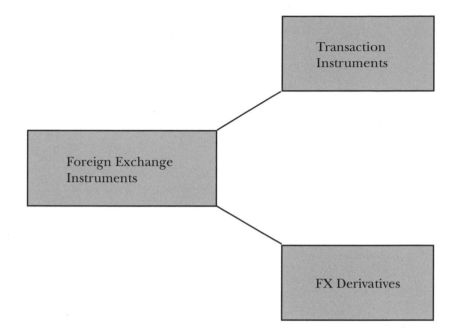

This section should take about one hour of study time. You may not take as long as this or it may take a little longer – remember your learning is individual to you.

Fixed exchange rates are a little bit like coiled spring. Compression makes the volatility greater.
– Lawrence Summers, U.S. Deputy Treasury Secretary, quoted in the *Financial Times*, September 9, 1997.

Spot Transactions

Currencies versus USD

An **FX Spot Transaction** is a deal in which two counterparties exchange two different currencies at an agreed exchange rate for settlement in two business days time.

The term 'spot' originates from when deals were done 'on the spot' but delivery took place two business days later.

Two days after the deal

Two days after the deal

Even though technology has advanced since then, making almost instantaneous communications systems available, the majority of spot deals are still for delivery two business days after the trade date.

FX transactions are normally quoted by market-makers who display two-way bid-offer quotes to buy and sell the currency in question. These quotes are for buying and selling currency against a **base currency**, usually USD. For example, USD/JPY = 131.700 – 780. The currency being quoted against the base currency is called the **counter currency**.

In order for quotes to be unambiguous, they follow the following convention:

1. Establish which is the **base currency**
2. The customer **buys** the counter currency (ie, sells the base currency) at the rate shown on the left side of the quote, and **sells** the counter currency (ie, buys the base currency) at the rate shown on the right side of the quote.

In the USD/JPY example above, the customer can buy JPY for USD at a rate of 131.700 JPY per USD, and sell JPY for USD at a rate of 131.780 JPY per USD. This bid-offer spread always favours the market-maker and is how they generate much of their revenue.

In the **bid-offer spread**, the market-maker is **bidding to buy** the base currency at the rate on the left, and **offering to sell** the base currency at the rate on the right.

Terms and Specifications: Foreign Exchange

The tables that follow explain spot FX market terms in more detail.

The Big Figure	This part of the price is not quoted by dealers. The big figure is only mentioned when it is necessary to confirm the trade or in extremely volatile markets. In the example on the previous page the Big figure is 1, although traders may also say the big figure is 71, or 1.71.
Pips	The smallest increment a price moves. Spot traders quote the last two digits of the price. Pips are also known as **points**.
The Spread	This is the variable unit difference between the Bid and Offer prices – in this case 10 pips. You will appreciate why FX deals involve large amounts and why the spreads will vary from the following examples: 1 pip on 1 million base currency results in a profit/loss effect of 100 in the counter currency for quotes to 4 decimal places, for example, USD/DEM 1.7110 and 1.7111: USD 1,000,000 x 1.7110 = DEM 1,711,000 USD 1,000,000 x 1.7111 = DEM 1,711,100 = DEM 100 1 pip on 1 million base currency results in a profit/loss effect of 10,000 in the counter currency for quotes to 2 decimal places, for example, USD/JPY 107.10 and 107.11: USD 1,000,000 x 107.10 = JPY 107,100,000 USD 1,000,000 x 107.11 = JPY 107,110,000 = JPY 10,000 Spreads will also vary depending on the liquidity of the market.

Bid	This is the price at which the market-maker is prepared to buy the base currency. In the example on the previous page the market-maker will buy $1 for JPY 131.700. The market-maker **buys** dollars; **sells** Yen.
Offer	This is the price at which the market-maker is prepared to sell the base currency. In the example on the previous page the market-maker will sell $1 for JPY 131.780. The market-maker **sells** dollars; **buys** Yen.
The Figure	Traders use this term when quoting a rate which **ends in 00**. For example, if the rate is USD/DEM = 1.7095/1.7100, then it will be quoted as **'ninety five - the figure'**. If USD/DEM = 1.7100/05 the rate will be quoted as **'figure - five'**. Similarly for a rate USD/JPY = 107.00/10, the price will be quoted as **'figure - ten'**. It is important to remember that even if a quote in USD/DEM is 1.7100 it is never rounded to 1.71 and likewise for other currencies.
Choice	This term is used when a trader is willing to buy or sell the base currency at the **same rate**. For example, if a trader is willing to either buy or sell at a rate USD/DEM = 1.7105, the rate will be quoted as **'5 choice'**.

Yours and Mine/ Given and Paid	A trader quotes the following:
	USD/DEM = 1.7105/1.7110
	
	In this case the market-maker is willing to buy USD at 1.7105. If another trader – the market-taker – likes this **bid** price and agrees to **sell** USD he will receive 1.7105 Deutschmarks for each $1 sold. To indicate his intentions he may use the term **yours**. This means the market-taker is **'hitting the bid'**. Once the trade is made the market-maker may say **'given at 05'** to report the market activity.
	
	This terminology indicates the trend. If the term 'given' is heard several times it could indicate selling activity is high.
	
	If the market-taker is willing to **buy** USD at the market-maker's **offer** price, then he will use the term **mine** and pay 1.7110 Deutschmarks for each $1. Mine means **'taking the offer'**. Traders may also refer to this as a 'lifting the offer'. Once the trade is made the market-maker may say **'10 paid'** to report the market activity.
	
	This terminology also indicates the trend. If the term 'paid' is heard several times it could indicate buying activity is high.
	
	To conclude:
	
	    Yours/Mine = trade done
	
	    Given/Paid = reports activity

Long	This is when a currency is being bought. For example, if you buy USD against DEM you are long USD and short DEM. Traders who go long USD (and short DEM) are **'bullish'** on the USD – they believe the USD will appreciate in value.
Short	This is when a currency is sold with a view to buying it back at a cheaper rate in the future. For example, if you sell USD against DEM you are short USD and long DEM. Traders who go short USD (and long DEM) are **'bearish'** on the USD – they believe the USD will depreciate in value.
Flat or square	No position exists.
Liquidity	This is the depth of the market and its ability to absorb sudden shifts in supply and demand. For example, an illiquid market exists when buyers and sellers become scarce, and relatively small trades cause significant moves in market prices.

Some currency pairs have their own terms –

    GBP/USD is known as **Cable.** This term came about because GBP/USD was the first currency pair to be targeted by traders in London and New York who used a single **cable** telegraph link running under the Atlantic Ocean.

    USD/CHF is known as **Dollar-Swissy**

    USD/FRF is known as **Dollar-Paris**

Brokers

Brokers act as intermediaries between counterparties, matching buy
and sell orders. Counterparties remain anonymous to each other
until completion of the deal, and this rule is strictly enforced by
regulators. Brokers exist to find the best prices for their clients and
therefore know which dealer has the highest bid and lowest offer.
They earn their income from commission on deals. They do not
trade currencies on their own account.

Although voice brokers – who are often pictured in the media
holding three telephones or more at once – are widely used in the FX
market, an ever-increasing proportion of the FX market is traded
through electronic order matching systems or electronic order
routing systems.

The result is that bid-offer spreads are gradually narrowing, making it
harder for traditional brokers to earn the same amount of
commission.

Your notes

Working Out a Net Position

Whenever market participants hold open positions in currencies – that is, they hold unhedged positions in currencies which are not their domestic accounting currency – it is necessary for them to work out their aggregate position across all the various deals they have done.

Average Rates

When only a few spot deals are transacted daily, profit and loss positions can be calculated quite easily. However on a busy FX desk the situation is a little different. In this case the average rate on the position is calculated and compared with the current market rate in order to determine whether or not the dealer's position is in profit.

Example
Suppose you are a USD/DEM dealer and after a hectic period of trading you need to know your position – are you long or short in USD? You also need to know the average rate at which the position was created. How do you calculate the average rate? To calculate the average rate:

1. Determine your total net DEM balance
2. Divide amount from 1. by net USD balance

Suppose   DEM balance = 12,737,000 and USD balance = 9,000,000

Then   Average rate $= \dfrac{12,737,000}{9,000,000} = 1.4152$

Effectively you are 'long 9 USD at 1.4152'. One deal buying 9,000,000 USD at 1.4152 would result in the same position.

Suppose the market is now 1.4160/70. To square your position you would need to sell 9,000,000 USD at 1.4160. So your profit since the start of the day would be:

Profit = – (9,000,000 x 1.4152) DEM + (9,000,000 x 1.4160) DEM
       = – 12,736,800 + 12,744,000
       = DEM 7200

A quicker way to calculate the profit is as follows:
Profit =   9,000,000 x (1.4160 – 1.4152)
       =   9,000,000 x 0.0008
       =   DEM 7200

The dealer will perform this profit calculation many times during the day. Dealing managers need to know positions at the end of each day – whether or not they have been squared. This does **not** mean that to determine profit and loss, the dealer actually has to square his position. All that is happening is that the net position is **marked-to-market** at the current rates of exchange.

The maximum size of a dealer's open position is controlled by limits set by the risk manager. This limit is set according to the bank's appetite for risk, the trader's track record of profitability and the relative risk/reward performance of the trader.

Obviously a trader who makes more profit while taking less risk is given larger limits than a trader who makes less profit while taking larger risks. The analysis and decision process involved in setting limits is complex, and is constantly evolving as new techniques are developed for measuring and managing risk.

Market-making: Using the spread

The spread is a device which allows dealers to manage their positions and adjust their market quotes to take account of market conditions, such as liquidity – the ease with which buyers and sellers can be found – and volatility – the size and speed of market moves. The wider the spread the more defensive the price and the greater the room for manoeuvre. The market-maker's spread contains an assessment of the likely cost of recovering an unwanted position.

The spread is therefore the dealers' first line of defence in reversing an unwanted position. Such reversals carry a degree of risk as rates may move against dealers or sufficient liquidity may not be available to absorb a large deal.

Calculating Profit and Loss

Once a market participant knows his/her net position, it is possible to calculate the net profit or loss on the position.

Example
Consider this case where the result is a loss.

10.00 am	**11.00 am**
Buy USD 5 million from Bank A at DEM 1.7145	USD has weakened and sell USD 5 million to Bank B at DEM 1.7112

The net loss is calculated as follows:

$$= -(5,000,000 \times 1.7145)\,DEM \;+\; (5,000,000 \times 1.7112)\,DEM$$
$$\qquad\quad \text{To Bank A} \qquad\qquad\qquad \text{From Bank B}$$

$$= -8,572,500 \;+\; 8,556,000 \;DEM$$

$$= -DEM \; 16,500 \text{ net loss}$$

This means that the net loss is 'locked in' in accounting terms as it is recorded today. The actual cash transaction takes place on the value date when your nostro account **decreases** by DEM 16,500.

If the profit/loss account is expressed in USD, then the profit for DEM is divided by the current spot rate – 1.7112 in this case.

> *The profit or loss on a spot position is the net cash balance remaining after the deal has been settled*

Spot transactions in the market place

Most transactions in the market place do not involve complicated calculations – just the ability to multiply or divide. However, you do have to know which side of the quote you are on – bid or offer!

Example 1
You have USD 1,000,000 and the quote rate is on-screen. At what price should you sell USD and buy DEM? How many DEM do you receive?

> **USD/DEM**
> **1.7123/1.7133**

You are selling USD and buying DEM so you sell at the rate the market-maker is prepared to buy USD – the **Bid** price of 1.7123.

At this rate you will receive 1,000,000 x 1.7123 = DEM 1,712,300.

Example 2
You have 1,000,000 DEM and the quote rate is on-screen. At what price should you sell DEM and buy USD? How many USD do you receive?

> **USD/DEM**
> **1.7123/1.7133**

You are selling DEM and buying USD so you buy at the rate the market-maker is prepared to sell USD – the **Ask/Offer** price of 1.7133.

At this rate you will receive 1,000,000 ÷ 1.7133 = USD 583,668.94.

Example 3
You have USD 1,000,000 and the quote rate is on-screen. At what price should you sell USD and buy GBP? How many GBP do you receive?

> **GBP/USD**
> **1.6210/1.6215**

This time the quote is indirect and the base currency is GBP. You are selling USD and buying GBP so you buy GBP at the rate the market-maker is prepared to sell GBP – the **Ask/Offer** price of 1.6215.

At this rate you will receive 1,000,000 ÷ 1.6215 = GBP 616,712.92.

The screen below shows spot rates from three different contributors for USD/DEM.

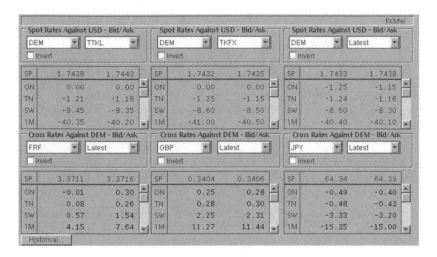

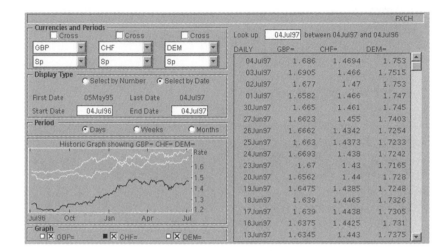

The screen above shows spot rates for GBP/USD, USD/CHF and USD/DEM for 1997, both graphically and as a table.

Cross Rate Transactions

Definitions
A **Cross rate** is a currency pair in which **neither** currency involved in the exchange is the US dollar, (USD).

Cross rates are quoted in the financial press such as the *Financial Times* and *The Wall Street Journal*.

Currency Crossrates

	Dollar	Pound	SF	Yen	DM	FF
France	5.5625	9.1308	3.8984	.04499	3.3789	–
Germany	1.6463	2.7023	1.1538	.01331	–	.29596
Japan	123.65	202.97	86.659	–	75.110	22.229
Switzerland	1.4269	2.3422	–	.01154	.86673	.25651
UK	0.6920	–	.42695	.00493	.37005	.10952
US	–	1.6415	.70084	.00809	.60744	.17978

```
WX=                      Cross - Majors
RIC         Bid      Ask      Srce Time   RIC         Bid      Ask      Srce Time
DEM=        1.7453   1.7463   SEBH 07:04   JPY=        112.33   112.43   DRE1 07:04
DEMGBP=R    0.3385   0.3388        07:04   JPYDEM=R    1.5529   1.5545        07:04
DEMJPY=R    64.33    64.36         07:04   JPYGBP=R    0.5257   0.5265        07:04
DEMCHF=R    0.8373   0.8376        07:04   JPYCHF=R    1.2999   1.3020        07:04
DEMFRF=R    3.3736   3.3741        07:04   JPYFRF=R    5.2332   5.2388        07:04
GBP=        1.6916   1.6928   DDBL 07:04   CHF=        1.4615   1.4625   DRE1 07:04
GBPDEM=R    2.9524   2.9534        07:04   CHFDEM=R    119.42   119.50        07:04
GBPJPY=R    190.02   190.14        07:04   CHFGBP=R    0.4042   0.4045        07:04
GBPCHF=R    2.4708   2.4740        07:04   CHFJPY=R    76.82    76.87         07:04
GBPFRF=R    9.9585   9.9678        07:04   CHFFRF=R    4.0271   4.0299        07:04
FRF=        5.8837   5.8847   SOGE 07:04   FRF=        5.8837   5.8847   SOGE 07:04
FRFDEM=R    0.29629  0.29648       07:04   FRFJPY=R    19.05    19.10         07:04
FRFCHF=R    24.8027  24.8281       07:04   FRFGBP=R    0.1003   0.1004        07:04
```

Cross rates are derived from USD quotes and although they are widely available it is useful to know how they are derived.

Suppose you are in France on your way to Germany and need to convert French francs into Deutschmarks. You need to use the exchange rate for DEM/FRF. In theory you would need to do two things:

1. **Buy** USD with your FRF at the market-maker's **offer** price – the price the bank sells you dollars for francs.

2. **Buy** DEM with your USD at the market-maker's **bid** price – the price the bank buys dollars for Deutschmarks.

The result is:

	You buy	You sell
1.	~~USD~~	FRF
2.	DEM	~~USD~~
=	DEM	/ FRF

Cross rates are denoted using the usual SWIFT codes for the currency pair. For example, GBP/CHF denotes Sterling against Swiss Francs and is called Sterling-Swissy. In this cross rate GBP is the base currency and CHF the counter currency.

Calculating Cross Rates

Direct or Dollar Cross Rates

You are a dealer quoting a DEM/CHF price. A client wishes to sell DEM and buy CHF. In this case the client would hit the bid of your DEM/CHF price because the client is selling the base currency.

But how did you calculate the cross rate you are quoting?

For **direct rates**, bid and ask cross rates for currency pairs may be calculated using the chart below, where for currencies 1 and 2 the bid and ask rates are B1 and A1, B2 and A2 respectively.

Currency pairs	Bid	Ask
USD/Currency 1 USD/Currency 2	B1 B2	A1 A2

Cross rates	Bid	Ask
Currency 1/Currency 2	$\dfrac{B2}{A1}$	$\dfrac{A2}{B1}$
Currency 2/Currency 1	$\dfrac{B1}{A2}$	$\dfrac{A1}{B2}$

Suppose the spot rates are as follows:

$$USD/DEM = 1.7000/10$$
$$USD/CHF = 1.5100/10$$

Therefore, using the convention in the chart Currency 1 = DEM, and Currency 2 = CHF.

Using the chart the **Bid** DEM/CHF rate

$$= \frac{B2}{A1} = \frac{1.5100}{1.7010} = 0.8877$$

Using the chart the **Ask** DEM/CHF rate

$$= \frac{A2}{B1} = \frac{1.5110}{1.7000} = 0.8888$$

Your two way cross rate for DEM/CHF is therefore 0.8877/0.8888. In practice the rate is quoted to 100 DEM so the rate is 88.77/88.88.

If you need to calculate the CHF/DEM cross rate then repeat the process using the chart details.

Using the chart the **Bid** CHF/DEM rate

$$= \frac{B1}{A2} = \frac{1.7000}{1.5110} = 1.1251$$

Using the chart the **Ask** CHF/DEM rate

$$= \frac{A1}{B2} = \frac{1.7010}{1.5100} = 1.1265$$

Your two way cross rate for CHF/DEM is therefore 1.1251/1.1265. In practice the rate is quoted to 100 CHF so the rate is 112.51/112.65.

The calculations so far have involved currencies which are both quoted directly against the USD. What if one of the currencies is quoted indirectly against the USD?

In the screen shown below there are three different DEM Bid/Ask spot rates from different contributors and three different latest cross rates against DEM for FRF, GBP and JPY. It doesn't matter if the cross rates are direct or indirect.

The screens below show rates for a variety of cross currencies for the past year, both graphically and as tables. When there are no contributor prices then Reuters prices are used.

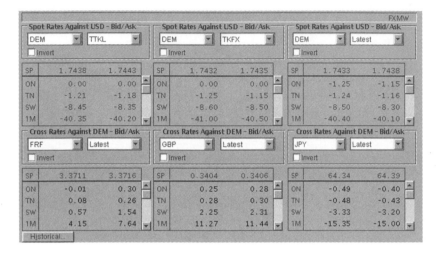

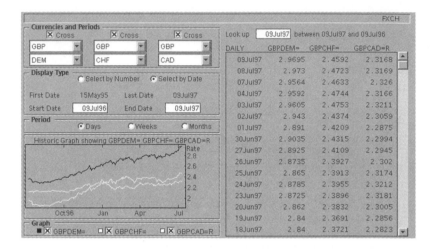

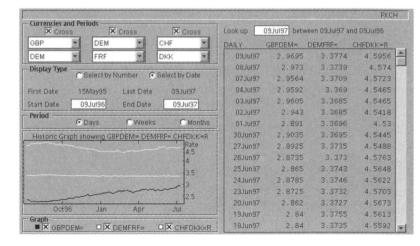

Forward Outright Transactions

 A **Forward Outright Transaction** is an agreement between two counterparties to exchange two different currencies at a rate which is agreed today, for delivery on an agreed future date.

What makes a forward outright different from a spot transaction? Have a look at the following example.

Example

It is 14th July 1997 and a bank's corporate customer based in Frankfurt needs to buy USD against DEM in 3 months time. Although the customer has DEM, he does not have USD and has bought spare machine parts in the US which will be invoiced in USD. What can the customer do? Have a look at the following possible scenarios.

- *Scenario 1*: The customer can wait and do nothing hoping that the US dollar remains at the same level or goes down

- *Scenario 2*: Buy USD spot today and deposit them for 3 months in the money markets.

- *Scenario 3*: Deal a forward outright and buy USD today for a 3 month delivery date.

But how does the corporate customer know what to do? Have a look at the various outcomes to the scenarios.

Scenario 1 – outcome
In this case the customer would probably not be prepared to wait for 3 months and then deal in the spot market. What if the US dollar appreciates against the Deutschmark? The customer would need more DEM to buy USD.

Scenario 2 – outcome
This scenario involves two trades:

> **Spot** – buy USD and sell DEM, and
> **Deposit** – invest USD for 3 months.

If the customer did not hold DEM he would need to borrow DEM to honour the spot deal of DEM sold against USD. He would then have to pay interest on the DEM borrowing.

Scenario 3 – outcome
This involves only one trade and no capital is required upfront. The corporate client is quoted a 3 month USD/DEM forward outright rate in forward points. This rate is derived by adding/subtracting the forward points to/from the prevailing spot rate.

The chart below follows the course of events in the forward outright transaction:

Corporate customer

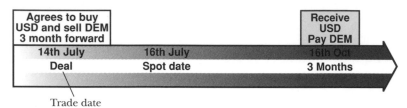

Trade date

The chart shows that the deal takes place on the 14th July 1998. Spot is 16th July and delivery is 3 months after the spot date – 16th October 1998.

At settlement, value date 16th October 1998, whatever the exchange rate is for spot USD/DEM, the currency amounts will be exchanged at the original agreed outright price. The transaction is non-negotiable.

But how are the forward value dates and forward outright rates determined?

Forward Points

Forward points are used to quote from the spot FX quote. These forward points represent the interest rate differential between the two currencies involved in the transaction.

Forward points are added or subtracted from the spot rate in order to calculate the absolute forward exchange rate. If forward points are added to the spot rate, the forward rate is said to be at a **premium** to the spot rate. If forward points are subtracted, the forward rate is at a **discount** to spot.

Discount or Premium?

If the interest rate of the base currency is **higher** than the counter currency, forward points are subtracted and the **base currency is said to trade at a discount** in the forward market. Alternatively, this can be expressed as the **counter currency trading at a premium** in the forward market.

If the interest rate of the base currency is **lower** than the counter currency (which is more common in recent years), forward points are added and the **base currency is said to trade at a premium** in the forward market. Alternatively, this can be expressed as the **counter currency trading at a discount** in the forward market.

Example

You are interested in the 3-month USD/DEM forward exchange rate. The 3-month money market deposit rates for USD and DEM are 5.5% and 3.5% respectively. The spot mid-rate is 1.5350 – this is used here to simplify the calculations. What should the forward points be? The following procedure illustrates the process. Assume you have $1000 to deposit...

① If you deposit the $1000 for 3 months at 5.5%, then at maturity you would receive interest equal to:

$$1000 \times \frac{5.5}{100} \times \frac{90}{360} = \$13.75$$

So, after 3 months you would have your principal plus the interest, a sum of $1013.75.

② If you exchange the $1000 for DEM, then you sell USD for DEM at the spot rate of 1.5350. So you now have DEM 1535.

③ Now you deposit the DEM 1535 for 3 months at 3.5%. At maturity you would receive interest equal to:

$$1535 \times \frac{3.5}{100} \times \frac{90}{360} = DEM\ 13.43$$

So, after 3 months you would have your principal plus the interest, a sum of DEM 1548.43.

If the spot rate equalled the forward rate, then the DEM could be converted back to USD. This would produce:

$$\frac{1548.43}{1.5350} = \$1008.75$$

However, in step 1 the interest was $1013.75. So if nothing were to happen if you had changed USD into DEM, deposited the DEM for 3 months and then changed the DEM back to USD, you would lose $5.00.

To prevent such a loss and the potential for arbitrage, the forward rate is fixed such that the interest from selling DEM back to USD is the same as the USD interest.

④ The forward rate calculated by dividing the DEM interest by the USD interest:

$$\frac{1548.43}{1013.75} = 1.5274$$

This rate is called the **arbitrage-free forward rate**.

The process is illustrated in the diagram below.

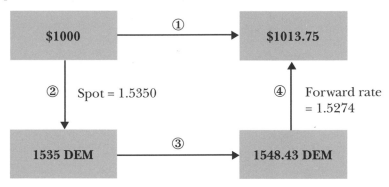

The difference between the forward and spot rates is 1.5274 – 1.5350 = – 0.0076. This difference is expressed as – **76 forward points**. In this case the base currency rates are higher than the counter currency so the points are **negative** so the forward points have to be **deducted** from the spot rate. If the base currency rates were lower than the counter currency, then the points are **positive** and have to be **added** to the spot rate.

Forward points are determined by interest rate differentials which dictate whether the prices are at a discount or premium.

Traders quote in points and do not tend to indicate positive or negative values. In these cases the chart below will help you determine whether to add or deduct the points.

Forward points	Base currency trading	Quote currency trading	Forward rate =
From left to right – points descend	at a **discount**	at a **premium**	Spot **minus** forward points
From left to right – points ascend	at a **premium**	at a **discount**	Spot **plus** forward points

The following may help to remember what to do:

points **D**escend – **D**educt points

points **A**scend – **A**dd points

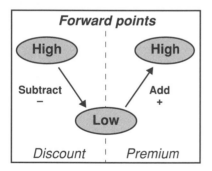

Around Par

Sometimes you will see the situation where the forward points are at a discount and a premium in the same two-way price. This situation arises when there is a very slight interest rate differential.

For example, you may see –1.0/+1.0 on a screen. In this case a trader would say 'one around par' – **par being zero**. If the points were –3/+3 it would be expressed as 'three around par'.

Example
If the USD/DEM points were around par as follows

	Spot	3 mths
USD/DEM	1.7100/10	–1/+1

the forward points would be deducted if traded at –1 and added if traded at +1.

Forward Outright Transactions in the Market Place

Forward Rates

Now that you have seen how forward points are quoted, you must be able to **read the points** correctly in order to determine the correct forward rates. There are a few simple rules for reading the points which will ensure you calculate forward rates correctly.

The first rule deals with 4 decimal place rates.

Rule: 4 Decimal Place Rate
1. Remove the decimal point from the spot rate and move it **4 places to the right – you may find it convenient to add a zero after the point**.
2. Write down the forward points, **including any decimal point**.
3. Perform any addition or subtraction of the points as necessary.
4. Move the decimal back **4 places to the left** in the new, calculated forward rate.

Example 1

Given a spot of 1.7150 and USD/DEM 3-month forward points 59/58, you trade at 58 points. What forward rate would the deal ticket show?

1. Move point 4 places right   =   17150.
2. Deduct forward points   =   58
                           =   17092.
3. Move point 4 places left   =   1.7092

The deal ticket will show:

Spot	1.7150
Fwd	1.7092

The second rule deals with 2 decimal place rates.

Rule: 2 Decimal Place Rate
1. Remove the decimal point from the spot rate and move it **2 places to the right – you may find it convenient to add a zero after the point**.
2. Write down the forward points, **including any decimal point**.
3. Perform any addition or subtraction of the points as necessary.
4. Move the decimal back **2 places to the left** in the new, calculated forward rate.

Example 2

Given a spot of 102.90 and USD/JPY 3-month forward points 112/110, you trade at 112 points. What forward rate would the deal ticket show?

1. Move point 2 places right   =   10290.
2. Deduct forward points   =   112
                           =   10178.
3. Move point 2 places left   =   101.78

The deal ticket will show:

Spot	102.90
Fwd	101.78

Forward Pricing

Traders will use the following formulae to calculate the forward points. Formula 1 gives a more precise calculation.

Formula 1 (ACI)

$$\text{Forward points} = \frac{(B - A) \times (S \times T)}{(A \times T) + (100 \times DB)}$$

A = Base currency interest rate
B = Counter currency interest rate
S = Spot rate
T = Time in days
DB = Day basis for the year

Example

Using the example where the 3-month deposit rates for USD and DEM are 5.5% and 3.5% respectively and the spot mid-point rate is 1.5350.

$$\text{Forward points} = \frac{(3.5 - 5.5) \times (1.5350 \times 90)}{(5.5 \times 90) + (100 \times 360)}$$

$$= \frac{-2 \times 1.5350 \times 90}{495 + 36000}$$

$$= -0.007571$$

= This would be quoted as
– 76 points

Formula 2 gives a much more approximate figure but is quick and easy to use.

Formula 2

$$\text{Forward points} = \frac{\text{Spot} \times \text{Interest rate differential} \times \text{Time in days}}{100 \times \text{Day basis}}$$

Example

Using the example where the 3-month deposit rates for USD and DEM are 5.5% and 3.5% respectively and the spot mid-point rate is 1.5350.

$$\text{Forward points} = \frac{1.5350 \times -2 \times 90}{36000}$$

$$= -0.007675$$

This would be quoted as
– 77 points

Notes

When using these formulae it is important to remember the following:

1. If USD rates were lower than DEM rates then the calculation would produce a positive figure which would indicate a USD premium.

2. By looking at interest rates for both currencies you will be able to determine whether the forward points are at a discount or premium. In other words is the base currency interest rate higher or lower? Once you have determined whether the points are at a discount or premium you will still need to use one of the formulae to calculate the number of points.

3. For GBP/USD rates remember that the day basis is 365 because Sterling (base currency) deposits use A/365.

4. Any forward points can be calculated given the interest rates for the two currencies involved. The formulae can be used for any currency pair including cross rates.

The screen below displays the spot rate and forward points for **fixed periods** for any selected currency. There is also a **FX Calculator** which displays the forward points and rates for broken dates when the **Maturity Dates** in the **Results fields** are keyed in.

The screen below shows forward points for fixed periods and broken dates for three USD/DEM contributors.

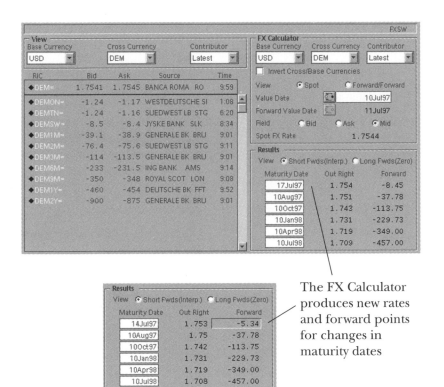

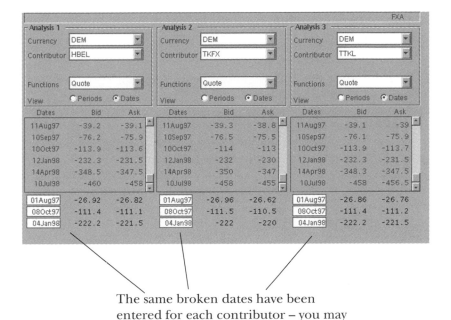

The FX Calculator produces new rates and forward points for changes in maturity dates

The same broken dates have been entered for each contributor – you may need to compare the quotations

FX Swaps

 An **FX swap** is a pair of currency transactions, one purchase, one sale, for two different value dates, one of which is spot.

FX swaps are one of the most widely traded instruments in the foreign exchange market, accounting for significantly more volume than spot FX or forward outright transactions.

FX swaps are executed as a single transaction with an individual counterparty. However, for profit and loss calculation purposes, the deal is booked as two distinct, but linked, deals with one deal corresponding to each leg of the swap.

It is important to understand that FX swaps are **not** the same as currency swaps or interest rate swaps (IRSs).

Currency swaps involve an exchange of the principal amounts, followed by exchange of interest payments over the life of the deal. FX swaps involve full exchange of principal at both dates and no interest payments.

Interest rates swaps involve only one currency whereas FX and currency swaps always involve two currencies.

Three types of swap are commonly used.

- **Spot against forward**
  In this case the first exchange – **first leg** – takes place on the spot date, two business days following the transaction, and the reverse of that exchange – **second leg** – takes place on the future date, for example, 1 month from the spot date.

- **Forward against forward**
  In this case the first exchange takes place on a forward date – **first leg** – and the transaction is reversed on a later forward date – **second leg**. For example, a forward against forward swap may begin in 3 months time from spot – first leg – and end in 6 months time from spot – second leg. This is known as a **3 x 6 forward/forward swap**.

- **Short dates**
  These are swaps which run for less than a month. For example, the first leg could be today, and the second leg tomorrow (O/N – overnight).

In an FX swap transaction, the base currency defines the amount of counter currency at the delivery date. The forward delivery quote is quoted in forward points which, in this case, are call **swap points**.

Example

On 10th July Bank A agrees a $10 million USD/DEM 3 month FX swap transaction. The amount of base currency in each leg of the deal is the same. Bank A needs to buy USD spot and sell USD forward against DEM.

The chart below indicates the course of events over time:

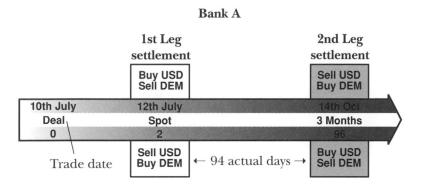

You might like to compare this chart with the one for the forward outright example described previously where nothing happens at spot.

Forward Value Dates

The forward value dates for FX swaps are determined in exactly the same way as for forward outright transactions for fixed, short and broken dates. There are a four main types of value dates which are important to understand for FX swaps

Fixed Periods

FX swaps have a maturity or tenor structure which coincides with interbank deposits in the money markets. The fixed period maturities are indicated in the chart below.

Fixed periods	Months				
Period or tenor	1	2	3	6	12

For FX swaps transacted for a fixed period the **first leg** involves **spot** and the **second leg** one of the **forward** value dates calculated from spot – these are known as spot runs. A **run** is 1,2,3,6 and 12 months from spot and a **complete run** includes all the remaining months, that is, 4,5,7,8,9,10 and 11. Fixed periods are also known as **straight-dates**.

Short Dates

Short dates are used for FX swaps which run for less then a month. The most active short dates are shown in the chart below.

Short Dates	1st Leg Value Date	2nd Leg Value Date
O/N Overnight	Today	First business day after today
T/N Tomorrow-next 'Tom-next'	First business day after today	Second business day after today **= spot**
S/N Spot-next	Spot	First business day after spot
S/W Spot-one week	Spot	1 week after spot **= 7 actual days**

Broken Dates

In practice many customers need FX swaps for periods intermediate between fixed dates. These intermediate periods are known as **broken**, **cock** or **odd** dates.

Example

Today is 9th July 1997, spot 11th July. A broken date would be spot first leg, second leg 25th September. This falls between the 2 and 3 month run value dates of 11th September and 13th October respectively.

This is an OTC market so banks will quote for virtually any broken date required – Money 3000 can be used for the calculations involved. A process of linear interpolation may be used to calculate broken dates. For example, to calculate a two and a half month price, a trader could use 2 and 3 month prices.

Example

Spot – September IMM (1997)

1st Leg   Spot – as usual

2nd Leg   Value dates which coincide with the expiration date of one of the currency derivative contracts traded on the **International Monetary Market (IMM)**, which is a division of the **Chicago Mercantile Exchange (CME)**. These dates are the **third Wednesday** of the months **March, June, September** and **December**. So in this example the date is 17th September 1997. If you wish to use IMM value dates then you will need to know the dates of the third Wednesdays of the months March, June, September and December.

Forward/Forward Dates

All the fixed period examples dealt with so far have used spot as the first leg value date for FX swap transactions. However, forward/forward contracts are also possible. The chart below shows the events for a 2 x 5 forward/forward swap using the 3rd July as spot – both forward dates are calculated from spot.

Market-maker

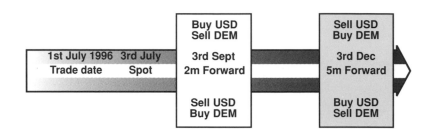

Market-taker

The procedure for determining the value date for each leg is exactly the same as for fixed periods except that the first leg is also a forward date.

Swap Market Conventions and Terminology

Bid/Offer – Offer/Bid

As you know the convention for spot is to quote the **bid** or buying price and the **offer** or selling price.

For example, if USD/DEM spot price is quoted at 1.4100/05 this means a market-maker is:

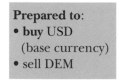

Prepared to:		Bid	Offer		Prepared to:
• **buy** USD (base currency) • sell DEM		**1.4100**	/	**1.4105**	• **sell** USD (base currency) • buy DEM

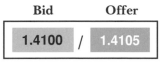

For FX swaps the focus is on the **forward leg**.

For example if the USD/DEM swap points are quoted at 59/58 this means a market-maker is:

Swap points

Prepared to:		59	/	58		Prepared to:
buy USD (base currency) and sell DEM (quote currency) **on 2nd leg**						sell USD (base currency) and buy DEM (quote currency) **on 2nd leg**

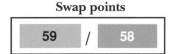

The forward trader outside London is focussing on the base currency. In the above example where the quote is 59/58 the trader refers to 59 as the **bid** and 58 as the **offer**. This is because at 59 he is **buying USD** forward and at 58 he is **selling USD** forward.

The forward trader in London focusses on the counter currency in just the same way as was mentioned for discount and premium forward points. In the above example where the quote is 59/58 the London trader refers to 59 as the **offer** and 58 as the **bid**. This is because at 59 he is **selling DEM** forward and at 58 he is **buying DEM** forward.

The swap quotation remains the same for both traders – 59/58 – and the points are still deducted from spot to calculate the forward rate. The difference arises only in the terminology used.

Sell/Buy – Buy/Sell

In spot trades you buy or sell one currency for another. In FX swaps involving two legs for the transaction you can **sell spot and buy forward (S/B)** or you can **buy spot and sell forward (B/S)**.

New York

Outside London, for example, in the US, the market-maker looks at the swap points quotes as follows:

Swap points 59/58

Trade: 2nd leg	Bid/Offer	Swap side
Buys USD and Sells DEM	Bid	Left
Sells USD and Buys DEM	Offer	Right

London

In London the market-maker looks at the swap points quotes as follows:

Swap points 59/58

Trade: 2nd leg	Offer/Bid	Swap side
Buys USD and **Sells** DEM	Offer	Left
Sells USD and **Buys** DEM	Bid	Right

Confused?

When trading on a price quoted a market-taker may say 'yours' or 'mine'. But what does this mean?

Outside London the market-taker will say:

Yours =	**Buy and Sell base currency**	=	**Hitting the Bid**
Mine =	**Sell and Buy base currency**	=	**Taking the Offer**

In London the market-maker will say:

Yours =	**Buy and Sell counter currency**	=	**Hitting the Bid**
Mine =	**Sell and Buy counter currency**	=	**Taking the Offer**

To avoid misunderstandings traders may prefer to say 'On the left' or 'On the right' or they may say 'At 59' or 'At 58'.

The FX Swap Deal Ticket

A FX swap trade will generate one deal ticket. The details recorded on a deal ticket will include the following information:

- Trade date
- Type of deal – swap
- Counterparty
- Direction of deal – Buy + Sell, Sell + Buy
- Amounts
- Currencies
- Exchange rates and forward points
- Value dates
- Payment instructions
- Via – Broker, direct

This is a deal ticket from *Deal Manager*, a Reuters position-keeping and risk management product for FX and money market dealers.

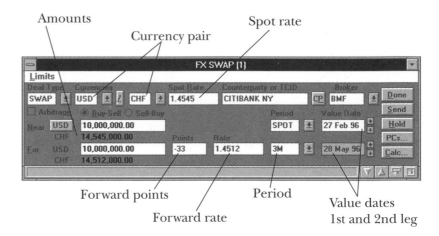

Amounts · Currency pair · Spot rate · Forward points · Forward rate · Period · Value dates 1st and 2nd leg

Who uses FX Swaps?

Banks

FX swaps are arranged as a single transaction with a single counterparty. Because the bank usually contracts to purchase and sell the same amount of currency at specified rates there is no FX open risk. Swaps are mainly used by forward traders for the following reasons:

- **Speculation** on interest rate differentials

- **Managing cash flows** within dealing rooms

- **Providing a service** to their internal and external clients

- **Carrying out arbitrage** to take advantage of price discrepancies between two instruments

Speculation

Just as a spot trader speculates on exchange rates, a forward trader speculates on interest rate differentials.

Example

A forward trader believes that over the next 3 months US interest rates will remain stable. However, he also believes that DEM rates will rise due to inflation in the German economy. This means he feels that the interest rate differential between USD and DEM will narrow.

The forward trader would like to take a position on this information. At the time the market looks like this:

3 month USD/DEM Swap	73/72
1 week USD/DEM Swap	5.5/5
3 month depo DEM	3.22/3.25
3 month depo USD	5.21/5.25

There are two things the forward trader could do:

1. Borrow DEM 3 months and run the position day-to-day, hoping the rise will come quickly so he can lend them out at the higher rates he expects to see shortly.

2. Use an FX swap – buy and sell DEM (sell and buy USD) and run the day-to-day position.

The forward trader buys and sells the DEM at 72 points in his favour. If the Bundesbank does raise rates at the next council meeting, then the forward points are likely to move to the right. In fact they move to 53/52. The forward trader would then be able to unwind his position at 53 points against him by selling and buying DEM producing a straight profit of 19 points. However, if he ran the position for the week, he would incur the cost of running the position – each day he would need to sell and buy DEM to square the position. This cost for the week is 5.5 points against him – so his net profit is approximately 13.5 points, although the forward date is now one week nearer, which will affect the swap points.

Cash management

The forward trader manages the **short-term** cash flows in the dealing room. This is carried out, for example, for the spot and money market desks as well as the forward desk, by transacting short dated swaps.

Example 1

Today is Monday, 6th January 1998 and all business is dealt value spot 8th January. All open positions from the various traders will have a value date of 8th January which, when trading begins the next day, 7th January, does not correspond to the new value date of 9th January.

To adjust the value date, swaps are dealt in the Tom Next or T/N market. A T/N swap has first leg value tomorrow, and second leg value the next day. T/N business is a pure cash management operation and will be carried out in the morning. There is little or no speculation in T/N. Large amounts are traded in T/N as open positions are adjusted or 'rolled-over'.

T/N transaction

Original spot value date 'rolled-over'

	6th January	7th January	8th January	9th January
Spot	Deal		+USD -DEM	
Tomorrow/ Next		Deal	-USD +DEM	+USD -DEM

FX Swap

The chart above shows that the long USD position with value date 8th January has been rolled-over to match the new value date of 9th January.

Example 2

A corporate client trades a forward outright to buy USD against DEM at a fixed rate for a 3-month delivery date. The corporate customer has covered his exchange rate risk but the bank has to take on the risk to deliver USD against DEM at a set price in 3 months. If the dollar strengthens, then the bank will have have to pay more to purchase the USD to deliver to the client in 3 months time.

In order to cover this risk the bank could do the following:

1. Borrow DEM for 3 months
2. Use these DEM to **buy USD** spot
3. Place the USD on deposit for 3 months.

The bank has already purchased the dollars it has agreed to sell to the client in 3 months' time.

By covering this forward outright, the bank is entering into money market operations – borrowing DEM and lending USD. The bank may choose not to deal extensively in the deposit market due to balance-sheet constraints, since each customer forward deal would increase the bank's balance-sheet by the size of the deal, both for the borrowing and the lending.

A much cheaper alternative is to cover the forward outright by a **FX swap**, which keeps the whole operation off balance-sheet.

The first thing the bank would do is cover the spot risk. Having sold USD forward to the client, it should buy USD spot. Now the bank is long USD spot but short USD 3 months forward.

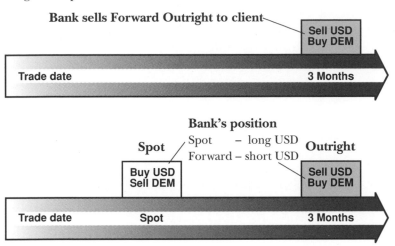

Bank sells Forward Outright to client

Sell USD
Buy DEM

Trade date — 3 Months

Bank's position

Spot — long USD
Forward – short USD

Spot — Buy USD / Sell DEM

Outright — Sell USD / Buy DEM

Trade date — Spot — 3 Months

To bridge the time gap between the two cash flows a swap can be executed:

- Sell USD/Buy DEM — Spot
- Buy USD/Sell DEM — 3-months forward

The first leg of the swap funds the spot transaction. The second leg produces the funds for the client's forward outright deal. This example illustrates how a bank can manage a position created by an outright, using an FX swap.

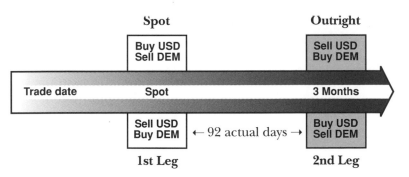

Spot — Buy USD / Sell DEM

Outright — Sell USD / Buy DEM

Trade date — Spot — 3 Months

1st Leg — Sell USD / Buy DEM ← 92 actual days → Buy USD / Sell DEM — 2nd Leg

Internal and external clients

Within the dealing room the forward trader may be requested by the corporate dealer to provide a swap price for a corporate client. But why would a corporate client need to deal an FX swap?

Example

Suppose a German corporate client needs to buy spare machine parts in the US which will be invoiced in USD. The corporate client could trade a forward outright transaction and agree to buy USD against DEM at a forward 3 month date. Imagine now that the date is approaching when the client will receive the USD bought and settle the DEM sold.

The corporate client now receives news that there has been a delay in producing and shipping the spare parts which will now be a month late. The USD are no longer required to pay the invoice on the original date but will be required a month later. What can the corporate client do in this case? The client can use an FX swap to postpone or 'rollover' the maturity date for the extra month.

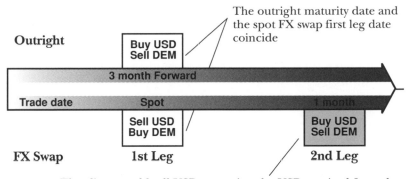

The outright maturity date and the spot FX swap first leg date coincide

Outright — Buy USD / Sell DEM

3 month Forward

Trade date — Spot — 1 month

FX Swap — Sell USD / Buy DEM (1st Leg) — Buy USD / Sell DEM (2nd Leg)

The client would sell USD spot using the USD received from the delivery of the outright and buy USD forward. The client is now long USD for the new value date. The client's USD requirement has been rolled over for a month.

You can now see that the corporate client used the outright deal to initiate a position and the FX swap to move a position.

Arbitrage

Arbitrage occurs when market take advantage of price discrepancies that appear in the same or related instruments at the same time. **Arbitrageurs**, as these market players are often called, are constantly on the look out for those instances where one segment of a related market has either moved ahead, or not caught up to a related market. This is regarded as a kind of 'easy money', in that if it is done properly, there is no risk – other than credit risk, and a profit is assured.

For example, the DEM/CHF cross is derived from USD/DEM and USD/CHF quotes. DEM/CHF has its own quotations that are based on the respective USD/DEM and USD/CHF quotes. However, there are occasions in which one or both of the components of the cross may move before the cross can adjust itself. An arbitrageur, in this case a cross trader, tries to take advantage of these occurrences by simultaneously executing appropriate trades in the DEM/CHF, USD/DEM, and USD/CHF markets.

The same types of arbitrage opportunities exist in the forward FX markets. FX forwards are priced based on the interest rate differentials that exist between two currencies. Usually, the forward prices are adjusted whenever the components move but there are times when the formulated alignment between components and prices are out of line. The good traders always try to take advantage of easy money.

Valuing FX Swaps

Forward Rates

Now that you have seen how forward points are quoted, you must be able to **read the points** correctly in order to determine the correct forward rates. There are a few simple rules for reading the points which will ensure you calculate forward rates correctly.

The first rule deals with 4 decimal place rates.

Rule:	4 decimal place rate

1. Remove the decimal point from the spot rate and move it **4 places to the right – you may find it convenient to add a zero after the point**.

2. Write down the forward points, **including any decimal point**.

3. Perform any addition or subtraction of the points as necessary.

4. Move the decimal back **4 places to the left** in the new, calculated forward rate.

Example 1

Given a spot of 1.7150 and USD/DEM 3 month forward points 59/58, you trade at 58 points. What forward rate would the deal ticket show?

1. Move point 4 places right   =   17150.
2. Deduct forward points   =   <u>58</u>
                            =   <u>17092.</u>
3. Move point 4 places left   =   1.7092

The deal ticket will show:

Spot	1.7150
Fwd	1.7092

Example 2

Given a spot of 1.7150 and USD/DEM T/N forward points 0.9/0.8, you trade at 0.9 points. What forward rate would the deal ticket show?

1.	Move point 4 places right	=	17150.0
2.	Deduct forward points	=	0.9
		=	17149.1
3.	Move point 4 places left	=	1.71491

The deal ticket will show:

1st leg	1.7150
2nd leg	1.71491

In this example the spot has been applied to the 1st leg. Traders may also apply the spot to the second leg which facilitates the calculation since the points are deducted.

1st leg	1.71509
2nd leg	1.7150

The same applies to O/N swaps. The spot rate can be applied to the 1st or 2nd leg even though neither value date is spot.

The second rule deals with 2 decimal place rates.

Rule:	**2 decimal place rate**

1. Remove the decimal point from the spot rate and move it **2 places to the right – you may find it convenient to add a zero after the point**.

2. Write down the forward points, **including any decimal point**.

3. Perform any addition or subtraction of the points as necessary.

4. Move the decimal back **2 places to the left** in the new, calculated forward rate.

Example 3

Given a spot of 102.90 and USD/JPY 3 month forward points 112/110, you trade at 112 points. What forward rate would the deal ticket show?

1.	Move point 2 places right	=	10290.
2.	Deduct forward points	=	112
		=	10178.
3.	Move point 2 places left	=	101.78

The deal ticket will show:

Spot	102.90
Fwd	101.78

Example 4

Given a spot of 102.90 and USD/JPY T/N forward points 1.4/1.2, you trade at 1.4 points. What forward rate would the deal ticket show?

1.	Move point 2 places right	=	10290.0
2.	Deduct forward points	=	1.4
		=	10288.6
3.	Move point 2 places left	=	102.886

The deal ticket will show:

1st leg	102.90
2nd leg	102.886

In Example 4 the spot has been applied to the 1st leg, although to facilitate the calculation the spot could have been applied to the 2nd leg:

1st leg	102.914
2nd leg	102.90

Forward pricing

Traders will use the following formulae to calculate the forward points. Formula 1 gives a more precise calculation.

Formula 1 (ACI)

$$\text{Forward points} = \frac{(B - A) \ \times \ (S \times T)}{(A \times T) \ + \ (100 \times DB)}$$

A = Base currency interest rate
B = Counter currency interest rate
S = Spot rate
T = Time in days
DB = Day basis for the year

Example

Using the example where the 3-month deposit rates for USD and DEM are 5.5% and 3.5% respectively and the spot mid-point rate is 1.5350.

$$\text{Forward points} = \frac{(3.5 - 5.5) \ \times \ (1.5350 \times 90)}{(5.5 \times 90) \ + \ (100 \times 360)}$$

$$= \frac{-2 \ \times \ 1.5350 \times 90}{495 \ + \ 36000}$$

$$= \ -0.007571$$

= This would be quoted as
– 76 points

Formula 2 gives a much more approximate figure but is quick and easy to use.

Formula 2

$$\text{Forward points} = \frac{\text{Spot x Interest rate differential x Time in days}}{100 \ \times \ \text{Day basis}}$$

Example

Using the example where the 3-month deposit rates for USD and DEM are 5.5% and 3.5% respectively and the spot mid-point rate is 1.5350.

$$\text{Forward points} = \frac{1.5350 \ \times \ -2 \ \times 90}{36000}$$

$$= \ -0.007675$$

= This would be quoted as
– 77 points

Notes

When using these formulae it is important to remember the following:

1. If USD rates were lower than DEM rates then the calculation would produce a positive figure which would indicate a USD premium.

2. By looking at interest rates for both currencies you will be able to determine whether the forward points are at a discount or premium. In other words is the base currency interest rate higher or lower? Once you have determined whether the points are at a discount or premium you will still need to use one of the formulae to calculate the number of points.

3. For GBP/USD rates remember that the day basis is 365 because Sterling (base currency) deposits use A/365.

4. Any forward points can be calculated given the interest rates for the two currencies involved. The formulae can be used for any currency pair including cross rates.

Example

The example below shows how to find the 3 x 6 forward points for a USD/DEM FX swap. Today is the 8th July, so the value date is 10th July. In the FX calculator the forward value date for 3 months has been entered – 10th October. In the results field you can find the forward points for the second leg at 6 months – 10th January.

Forward 3 month date entered here

Forward 6 month points here

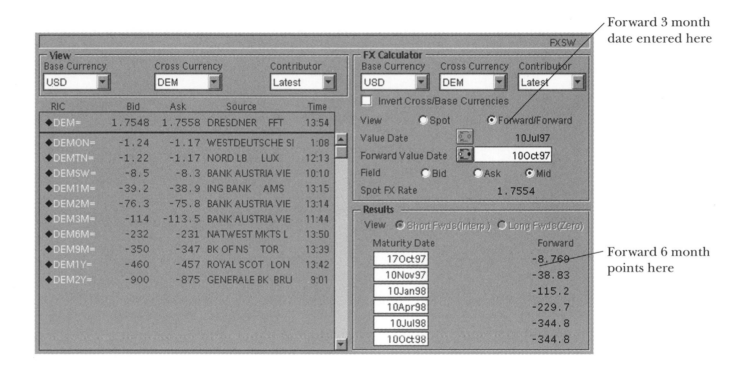

Summary

You have now finished this section and you should have a clear understanding of the following Transaction Instruments:

- Spot Transactions – Currencies versus USD

- Spot Transactions – Cross Rates

- Forward Outright Transactions

- FX Swaps

As a check on your understanding you should try the Quick Quiz Questions on the next page. You may also find the section Overview useful as a revision aid.

Your notes

Quick Quiz Questions

The following dialogue is a conversation between two FX dealers. Read it through and then answer the questions opposite.

Hello mate, Citibank NY here. What's Cable in 5?

Dealer A

Figure Five.

Dealer B

Mine.

Dealer A

Done. Val 12th. Big figure 1.67. Dollars to my NYC.

Dealer B

Cheers. Pounds to Barclays LDN.

Dealer A

1. a) Which dealer is the market-maker and which the market-taker?

   b) What currency pair is being traded?

   c) Is this an American or European quotation?

   d) What is the base currency?

   e) What is the quoted exchange rate?

   f) What is the spread?

   g) What does **mine** mean?

   h) What has the market-taker bought and sold?

   i) Calculate how much quote currency is being traded.

   j) If the market-taker had said **yours** – at what rate would he trade?

Quick Quiz Questions

2. You have quoted a bank a spot rate for USD/CHF as 1.4270/80. They say 'I take 5'. What do they mean?

☐ a) They need a short break to consider
☐ b) They buy USD 5 million at 1.4270
☐ c) They buy CHF 5 million at 1.4270
☐ d) They buy USD 5 million at 1.4280

3. When a broker says 'Pay 5 for 10, offer 15 at 20', which of the following describes his meaning?

☐ a) You can sell $10 million at 5 and buy $15 million at 20
☐ b) The market is 5/15 and there are $10 million behind the bid and $20 million on the offer
☐ c) You can pay 10 for $5 million and take 20 for $15 million
☐ d) You can buy $5 million for the price of $10 million, and sell $15 million for the price of $20 million

4. When is your delivery risk greatest on an FX deal done today for value spot?

☐ a) Today
☐ b) Tomorrow
☐ c) Settlement day
☐ d) The same today, tomorrow and on settlement day

5. You are made four GBP/USD prices

i) 1.6865/75 ii) 1.6868/78 iii) 1. 6874/79 iv) 1.6866/76

You wish to sell your GBP. Which is the best price?

☐ a) 1.6865
☐ b) 1.6879
☐ c) 1.6874
☐ d) 1.6866

6. You have been asked to quote a spot USD/JPY price to a customer. You think he wants to buy JPY. Which of the following quotes is the most profitable for you?

☐ a) 102.25/35
☐ b) 102.40/50
☐ c) 102.45/55
☐ d) 102.60/70

7. On the screen you see that MegaBank is displaying the following spot rates against the USD

USD/DEM	1.6400/10
USD/CHF	1.4220/30
GBP/USD	1.6880/90
USD/JPY	123.40/50

☐ a) A customer wishes to buy DEM. What is the rate and is this the bank's bid or offer price?

☐ b) What is the spread on the Swiss Franc?

☐ c) At what rate will MegaBank buy GBP?

☐ d) At what rate does MegaBank pay to buy ¥5 million?

8. In order to sell Swiss Francs for French Francs, which must you do first?

   □ a) Sell Swiss francs for US dollars at the bank's bid rate for US dollars
   □ b) Sell Swiss francs to buy French francs at the bank's selling rate for French francs
   □ c) Sell Swiss francs to buy US dollars at the bank's selling rate for US dollars against Swiss francs
   □ d) None of the above

9. MegaBank quotes the following spot rates against the USD.

USD/DEM	1.6400/10
USD/CHF	1.4220/30
GBP/USD	1.6880/90

   a) What is the cross rate in Deutschmarks for buying one Swiss franc?

   b) What is the cross rate in Swiss francs for selling one British pound?

10. The following banks are quoting rates for GBP/USD and USD/DEM. You wish to sell GBP to buy DEM.

Bank	GBP/USD	USD/DEM
A	1.6853/63	1.6458/68
B	1.6855/65	1.6459/69
C	1.6852/64	1.6460/70
D	1.6856/66	1.6457/67
E	1.6854/68	1.6456/66

a) Which bank would you sell GBP to and buy USD from?

b) Which bank would you sell USD to and buy DEM from?

c) What is the cross rate for GBP/DEM using the best rates for you?

11. The following banks are quoting rates for USD/CHF and USD/JPY. You wish to sell CHF to buy JPY.

Bank	USD/CHF	USD/JPY
A	1.4247/57	123.74/98
B	1.4246/58	123.74/95
C	1.4245/56	123.70/90
D	1.4248/59	123.73/95
E	1.4249/60	123.75/85

a) Which bank would you sell CHF to and buy USD from?

b) Which bank would you sell USD to and buy JPY from?

c) What is the cross rate for CHF/JPY using the best rate for you?

12. Which of the following best describes what forward points represent?

   ❑ a) The amount of money by which you change the value of a currency against another
   ❑ b) The interest rate differential over a specified period between two currencies
   ❑ c) The relative strength of one currency against another
   ❑ d) The future value of a currency

13. You have quoted a customer spot GBP/ITL 2704/2714, with 3-month forward points 16/19. Your customer sells you £2 million 3-months forward. How much ITL do you have to pay your customer?

   ❑ a) 54,400,000
   ❑ b) 5,466,000
   ❑ c) 5,460,000
   ❑ d) 5,446,000

14. A customer calls asking for a 3-month forward outright quote in USD/DEM. Spot is 1.6463/68. The forward points are 114/112. What price do you quote?

   ❑ a) 1.6351/54
   ❑ b) 1.6349/56
   ❑ c) 1.6577/80
   ❑ d) 1.6575/82

15. Listed below are banks' spot and forward rates for USD/JPY.

	Bank A	Bank B	Bank C
Spot	122.00/50	122.00/25	121.90/15
3 mths	36/33	37/34	38/36

   a) Which bank would you purchase JPY forward from for the best rate?

   b) What is the spot rate?

   c) What are the forward points?

   d) What is the outright rate?

16. Listed below are banks' spot and forward rates for GBP/USD.

	Bank A	Bank B	Bank C
Spot	1.6330/40	1.6831/39	1.6832/42
3 mths	39/36	42/38	39/36

   a) Which bank would you purchase GBP forward from for the best rate?

   b) What is the spot rate?

   c) What are the forward points?

   d) What is the outright rate?

17. Which of the following statements does **not** apply to FX swaps?

    ❏ a) Consists of a pair of transactions, usually one for spot and the other for a forward date
    ❏ b) Can replace two market transactions
    ❏ c) Eliminates credit risk with the counterparty
    ❏ d) Can be used to exploit arbitrage opportunities

18. Indicate whether the following statements are True or False concerning an FX swap. FX Sswaps can be used to:

    a) Obtain cheaper funds ❏ True ❏ False

    b) Invest in the currency of your choice ❏ True ❏ False

    b) Arbitrage between deposits and forward points
    ❏ True ❏ False

19. What is the basic difference between a forward outright transaction and an FX swap?

20. When would you typically use an FX swap?

21. The one-month (30 days) swap points for a currency are quoted as 120/100 and the 2-month (60 days) points at 160/140. What rate should you quote for a 45 day swap, assuming no special factors prevail?

    ❏ a) 130/110
    ❏ b) 135/125
    ❏ c) 140/120
    ❏ d) 280/240

You can check your answers on page 277.

Overview

```
┌──────────────────────────┐
│  Transaction Instruments │
└──────────────────────────┘
```

Main Types

- **Spot Transactions**

  An **FX Spot Transaction** is a deal in which two counterparties exchange two different currencies at an agreed exchange rate for settlement in two business days time.

- **Forward Outright Transactions**

  A **Forward Outright Transaction** is an agreement between two counterparties to exchange two different currencies at a rate which is agreed today, for delivery on an agreed future date.

- **FX Swaps**

  An **FX swap** is a pair of currency transactions, one purchase, one sale, for two different value dates, one of which is spot.

Key Concepts:

- **Calculating Cross Rates**

Currency pairs	Bid	Ask
USD/Currency 1	B1	A1
USD/Currency 2	B2	A2

Cross rates	Bid	Ask
Currency 1/Currency 2	$\dfrac{B2}{A1}$	$\dfrac{A2}{B1}$
Currency 2/Currency 1	$\dfrac{B1}{A2}$	$\dfrac{A1}{B2}$

- **Forward points**

Forward points	Base currency trading	Quote currency trading	Forward rate =
From left to right – points descend	at a **discount**	at a **premium**	Spot **minus** forward points
From left to right – points ascend	at a **premium**	at a **discount**	Spot **plus** forward points

- **Broken Dates**

  In practice many customers need FX swaps for periods intermediate between fixed dates. These intermediate periods are known as **broken**, **cock** or **odd** dates.

- **Arbitrage**

  Arbitrage occurs when market take advantage of price discrepancies that appear in the same or related instruments at the same time. **Arbitrageurs**, as these market players are often called, are constantly on the look out for those instances where one segment of a related market has either moved ahead, or not caught up to a related market. This is regarded as a kind of 'easy money', in that if it is done properly, there is no risk – other than credit risk, and a profit is assured.

Quick Quiz Answers

		✔ or ✘
1. a)	**Dealer A is the market-taker** **Dealer B is the market-maker**	❑
b)	Sterling/US Dollars, GBP/USD – cable	❑
c)	American quotation – **GBP**/USD	❑
d)	Sterling	❑
e)	1.6700/05	❑
f)	5 pips or points	❑
g)	Dealer A buys Sterling – takes the offer	❑
h)	Dealer A has bought Sterling and sold US Dollars	❑
i)	Quote currency is USD Amount traded = £5,000,000 x 1.6705 = **$8,352,500**	❑
j)	The figure – 1.6700	❑

		✔ or ✘
2.	d)	❑
3.	a)	❑
4.	c)	❑
5.	c)	❑
6.	a)	❑
7.	a) 1.6400. The bank's bid price for buying USD/selling DEM	❑ ❑
	b) 10 pips	❑
	c) 1.6880	❑
	a) 123.50 – the bank is buying	❑
8.	c)	❑
9.	a) 1.6410 ÷ 1.4220 = 1.1540 CHF/DEM	❑
	b) 1.6880 x 1.4220 = 2.4000 GBP/CHF	❑
10.	a) Bank D at 1.6856	❑
	b) Bank C at 1.6460	❑
	c) 1.6856 x 1.6460 = 2.7745 GBP/DEM	❑

✔ or ✘

11. a) Bank C at 1.4256 ☐

b) Bank E at 123.75 ☐

c) 123.75 ÷ 1.4256 = 86.806 CHF/JPY ☐

12. b) ☐

13. a) ☐

14. b) ☐

15. a) Bank A ☐

b) 122.00 ☐

c) − 0.36 ☐

d) 121.64 ☐

16. a) Bank B ☐

b) 1.6839 ☐

c) − 0.0038 ☐

d) 1.6801 ☐

17. c) ☐

18. a) True ☐

b) True ☐

c) True ☐

✔ or ✘

19. A forward outright transaction involves one exchange of funds whereas an FX swap involves two exchanges ☐

20. Typically FX swaps are used to:
- Manage short-term cash flows and rollover value dates ☐
- Hedge currency risk forward ☐
- Speculate on interest rate differentials ☐
- Carry out arbitrage ☐

21. c) ☐

How well did you score? You should have managed to get most of these questions correct. If you didn't you may need to revise some of the materials.

Further Resources

Books
The Foreign Exchange and Money Markets Guide
Julian Walmsley, John Wiley & Sons, Inc., 1992
ISBN   0 471 53104 9

New Financial Instruments, 2nd Ed.
Julian Walmsley, John Wiley & Sons, Inc., 1998
ISBN   0 471 12136 3

The Penguin International Dictionary of Finance
Graham Bannock & William Manser, Penguin, 2nd Edition 1995
ISBN   0 14 051279 9

Investments
William F. Sharpe, Gordon J. Alexander & Jeffrey V. Bailey, Prentice
Hall, 5th Edition 1995
ISBN   0 131 83344 8

A-Z of International Finance
Stephen Mahony, FT/Pitman Publishing 1997
ISBN   0 273 62552 7

Booklets
Chicago Board of Trade
Financial Instruments Guide

Internet
RFT Website
* **http://www.wiley-rft.reuters.com**
This is the series' companion website where additional quiz
questions, updated screens and other information may be found.

ACI – the Financial Markets Association
* **http://www.aciforex.com**
This is one of the largest fx associations with over 24,000 members in
79 countries of which 59 have affiliated national associations.

Your notes

Your notes

This section should take about one hour of study time. You may not take as long as this or it may take a little longer – remember your learning is individual to you.

The new finance is like a highway. It's more efficient. It gets you to where you are going better. But the accidents are worse.
– Lawrence H. Summers, Deputy U.S. Treasury Secretary, on newly deregulated banking markets around the world, quoted in the *Wall Street Journal*, May 7, 1997.

Synthetic Agreements for Foreign Exchange (SAFEs)

Synthetic Agreements for Foreign Exchange (SAFEs) encompass foreign exchange agreements (FXAs), which are otherwise known as non-deliverable forwards (NDFs), and exchange rate agreements (ERAs).

A **foreign exchange agreement**, or **non-deliverable forward**, is a notional forward transaction in which the counter currency is not delivered at maturity, but the deal is instead cash-settled in the base currency. This is equivalent to an FX forward outright together with a reverse spot FX deal on the settlement date.

An **exchange rate agreement** is a notional forward/ forward swap transaction in which the counter currency is not delivered on the settlement date, but the deal is instead cash-settled in the base currency. This is equivalent to a "forward" foreign exchange agreement (ie, spot becomes forward, and forward becomes forward forward).

The purpose of SAFEs is to hedge against fluctuations in swap points and to lock in forward FX differentials. They are also widely used for trading currencies which are not freely convertible, where delivery of the counter currency may infringe local regulations.

Uses of SAFEs

Banks and Corporations

The main market players using SAFEs are banks and international finance companies for the following two main reasons:

- Buying SAFEs provides a hedge against rising FX swap points

- Selling SAFEs provides a hedge against falling FX swap points

As for FRAs the settlement rates most commonly used are those issued by the **British Bankers Association (BBA)**.

The screen below shows the BBA settlement forward spread rates against the USD.

```
BBA SETTLEMENT FORWARD SPREAD RATES - DOLLAR                        SAFE1

          B                       See <SAFE2> for fixings against GBP
       ---------                  ------------------------------------
          DEM        GBP        FRF        ECU        ITL        JPY
       --------   --------   --------   --------   --------   --------
Spot    1.7538     1.6930     5.9141     1.1223    1708.11     112.63
1M      -.00388    -.00170    -.01206                          -.507
2M      -.00759    -.00336    -.02360                          -.982
3M      -.01134    -.00523    -.03514                         -1.519

6M      -.02310    -.01085    -.07131                         -2.945
9M      -.03474    -.01651    -.10750                         -4.298
12M     -.04594    -.02188    -.14236                         -5.651
Source  <UFSA>-C   <UFSD>-F   <UFSM>-O   <UFSP>-R   <UFSU>-W   <UFSG>-I


Example SAFE Ric <DEM1MSFSR=>      See <BBALIBORS> for BBA LIBOR Index
```

FX Derivatives

SAFEs in the Market Place

The following example provides an indication of the way a market player may use an ERA.

Example
A German bank buys US Treasury securities maturing in 6 months for the equivalent value of DEM 10 million. The bank decides to hedge the exchange risk for the first 3 months using a spot 3-month FX swap, buying USD spot and selling them in 3 months.

This hedges the first 3 months exposure but what can the bank do to protect itself for the last 3 month period?

There are a number of strategies to cover the exposure which the bank can consider, including the following:

Strategy 1
Wait until the end of the first 3 month period and then trade another spot 3-month FX swap. If the bank does this there is an element of risk that rates could move against them for the final 3 month period.

Strategy 2
Trade a forward/forward FX swap for the period – a 3 x 6 month swap, buying USD in 3 months and selling them in 6 months.

Strategy 3
Trade a 3-month 3 x 6 ERA to hedge against any unfavourable swap points movement combined with the spot 3-month FX swap.

The bank decides to use *Strategy 3* as the ERA will hedge the swap points on the second spot 3-month FX swap. The process is indicated in the chart opposite.

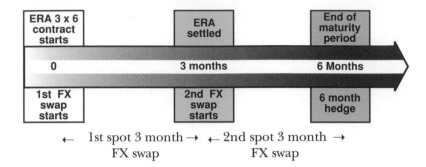

The settlement amount due for the ERA is paid on maturity of the first spot 3-month FX swap. In other words at the beginning of the notional swap period. As this amount relates to a maturity in 6 months time it is discounted back to the settlement date.

The settlement amount can be calculated from the following equation:

$$\text{Settlement} = \frac{\left(\begin{array}{cc} \text{Swap points} & - & \text{Swap points} \\ \text{for trade} & & \text{for settlement} \end{array} \right) \times \text{Contract amount}}{1 + \left(\text{Interest rate} \times \dfrac{\text{Swap period in days}}{360\ (365)} \right)}$$

Where interest rate is LIBOR for the foreign currency swap period

REUTERS

Currency Futures

A **Currency Future** is an exchange-traded deliverable* FX forward with standard contract size and maturity date.

Currency futures are used to hedge currency risk in a similar way to FX forwards. There are two basic types:
- Currency futures against the USD
- Currency futures for cross rates — ie, two non-USD currencies

Currency futures were introduced by the International Money Market (IMM) division of CME in 1972. Although the IMM still holds a significant market share of contracts traded, exchanges such as SIMEX, MidAmerica Commodity Exchange (MAC) and FINEX, the financial division of the New York Cotton Exchange, all offer currency futures contracts. As the different exchanges have different contract specifications and use different conventions you should be careful when comparing details.

IMM and SIMEX operate a mutual offset system (MOS) such that when the IMM is closed trades executed on SIMEX can be transferred back to IMM as new or closing out trades when it re-opens and vice versa.

* *Note:* Only a small percentage (less than 3%) of currency futures are delivered. The majority are closed out before maturity – rather like commodity futures.

An exchange-traded currency futures contract has the following characteristics:

- A **standardised specification** in terms of unit of trading, trading cycle of contract months, delivery days, quotation, minimum price movement etc.

- The **opportunity to trade** the instrument and offset the original contract with an equal and opposite trade. Very few contracts, less than 2%, are delivered.

- A **public market** in that prices for contracts are freely available. Trading takes place open outcry on an exchange floor and prices are published on exchange indicator boards, in the financial press and by providers such as Reuters.

- Once a trade has been made a **clearing house** acts as the counterparty to both sides of the trade. The contract is not directly between buyer and seller. The clearing house takes on the credit risk should a counterparty default. This is important because it means anyone can have access to the markets provided they have the required creditworthiness by the clearing house – in this way large organisations have no advantage over smaller organisations or investors.

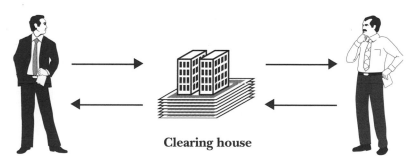

Clearing house

If a currency futures contract expires then the delivery involves one side of the contract receiving/paying one currency whilst the other party receives/pays the other currency.

Exchange Contracts

The first exchange-traded currency futures were established in 1972 on the International Monetary Market (IMM) – now part of the CME. Currency futures contracts are now traded on other exchanges worldwide. Some of the more important IMM contracts are summarised in the chart below.

IMM	
Futures against the USD	**Unit of trading**
Pound Sterling	GBP 62,500
Deutschmark	DEM 125,000
Japanese Yen	JPY 12,500,000
Swiss Franc	CHF 125,000
French Franc	FRF 500,000
Australian Dollar	AUD 100,000
Mexican Peso	MXN 500,000
Cross Currency	
Deutschmark/Yen	DEM 125,000

It is important to note that currency futures are not as liquid as interest rate futures. Have a look at the following table which indicates the volumes of various contracts traded on IMM/CME for 1995/96.

Futures Contract	Type	Volume of Contracts
DEM	Currency	5,976,716
JPY	Currency	5,025,723
GBP	Currency	2,890,584
3-month Eurodollar	Interest rate	**89,987,368**

Source: CFTC Annual Report 1996

Typical contract specifications

Futures contracts details vary from type to type and from exchange to exchange but the following example taken from an IMM contract is typical.

This is the standard contract size.

IMM Deutschmark Futures	
Trading Unit	DM 125,000
Price Quote	US $ per Deutschmark
Minimum Price Fluctuation (Tick)	0.0001 pt ($12.50/pt = $12.50)
Daily Price Limit	200 points
Contract Months	Mar, Jun, Sep, Dec
Trading Hours (Chicago Time)	7.20 am – 2.00 pm Last day 7.20 am – 9.16 am
Last Day of Trading	Two business days before the third Wednesday of the contract month
Delivery Date	Third Wednesday of the contract month

This is the smallest amount a contract can change value and the 'tick' size.

This is the trading cycle of contract months.

This is the last day and time on which trading can take place.

This is the day contracts are settled.

Most exchanges such as IMM quote currency futures prices in **American terms** or as indirect quotes. This means that a variable amount of USD is quoted against one unit of foreign currency. For example, in the DEM quote opposite, for March the settlement price means:

$$1 \text{ DEM} = \$0.6819$$

This convention is opposite to that used in the spot FX markets where **European terms** or direct quotes are used for quotes against the USD. The equivalent forward price quoted conventionally – indirectly – is $1 \div 0.6819 = 1.4665$ USD/DEM. Using this exchange pricing system means that when **spot prices move up**, then **futures prices move down**. It is worth remembering that as spot prices for GBP/USD are conventionally quoted indirectly, currency futures prices also appear indirectly. You will need to be careful about the exchange pricing system being used, for example, FINEX quote their futures contracts in European terms.

For cross rate quotations the convention is to use one unit of base currency against a variable amount of the cross currency. For example, a DEM/JPY cross currency future quote means:

$$1 \text{ DEM} = \text{the quoted amount of JPY}$$

Currency Futures in the Market Place

This section deals with a number of important matters concerning how currency futures are priced and used which you will need to understand:

How are Currency Futures Prices Determined?

Currency futures prices are closely related to the spot FX market rates but the difference between the futures and spot prices is due to the difference in delivery dates. This difference is known as the **swap** and is determined from the following equation:

$$\textbf{Swap} = \textbf{Futures price} - \textbf{Spot price}$$

The swap reflects the cost of carrying one currency against another between trade and delivery dates and is derived from the interest rate differential between the two currencies. As the futures contract approaches its delivery date the swap converges to zero. Ultimately, at the delivery date, the futures price equals the spot price. The swap over the duration of a futures contract is illustrated below.

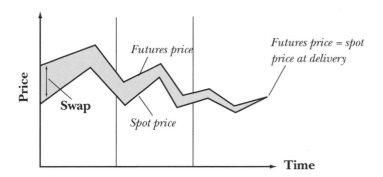

The value of the swap can be calculated for currencies against the USD using the following equation:

$$\text{Swap} = \text{Spot rate} \times \left(\begin{array}{c} \text{USD} \\ \text{interest} \\ \text{rate} \end{array} - \begin{array}{c} \text{Other} \\ \text{currency} \\ \text{interest rate} \end{array} \right) \times \frac{\text{days to delivery}}{360 \text{ (365 for GBP)}}$$

How a Currency Futures Contract Works

Currency futures are traded on an exchange, which acts as the counterparty for both the buyer and seller of every contract. Buyers and sellers are required to deposit a **margin** with the exchange's clearing House which is calculated to cover the counterparties' potential losses arising from changes in the value of the futures contract.

The **initial margin** is a small percentage of the contract value and it is recalculated on a daily basis. This means counterparties may have to deposit more margin — or receive some margin from the exchange clearing house — on a daily basis. This extra margin is called **variation margin**. This system of maintaining margin means the credit risk for both parties — both the trader and the exchange — is limited to the daily variation in value, rather than the potential variation over the whole tenor of the contract.

Dealing on margin is an example of **gearing** or **leverage**. Gearing allows investors to trade large notional amounts while only needing to deposit a small proportion of the contract value. This means the profits (and losses!) can be very large compared with the actual amount of money invested. For example, a 31,000 margin payment can fund a position in the FX market equivalent to a 310,000 forward position.

In volatile markets, this leverage can result in traders not having enough capital to cover their margin payments, resulting in bankruptcy.

The process is illustrated as follows:

On the Contract Date
The seller sells contract to the buyer and both deposit initial margin with the clearing house

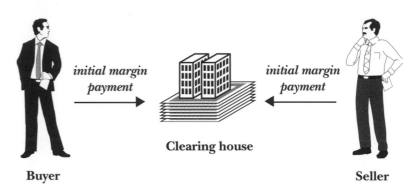

During the Contract
The seller's and the buyer's profit and loss account is adjusted daily

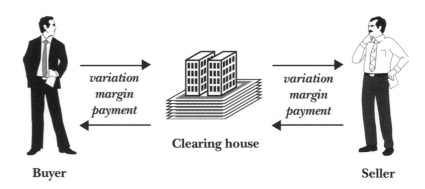

On the Delivery Date or Contract Closure

The seller's and the buyer's profit and loss account is settled for the last time

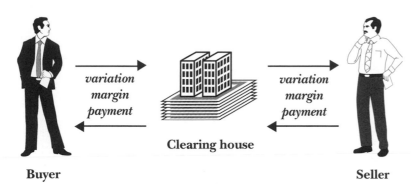

Buyer   **Clearing house**   **Seller**

Profit and Loss on a Futures Contract

This is easy to calculate using the following method:

1. Determine the number of ticks the price has moved up or down. The number of ticks is the number of one-hundredths of the quotation price.

2. Multiply the number of ticks by the tick value and the number of contracts.

> Profit/ loss = Number of ticks x Tick value x Number of contracts

Example

On 20th December, a dealer at MegaBank has a view that GBP will appreciate over the next three months and so purchases 10 GBP March contracts at 1.5720 and deposits USD10,000 in the margin account. Remember that the notional contract size is GBP 62,500, so his position is equivalent to a GBP 625,000 forward position. During the tenor of the contract, the margin account is adjusted daily according to the futures' price changes.

The dealer's view is correct and by early February he decides to sell his position and take the profit. He sells the March contracts at 1.5944.

For GBP the minimum price = 0.0002 points

$$\text{Tick size} = \$12.50$$

So the profit = Number of ticks x tick size x number of contracts

The number of ticks in this case $= \dfrac{(1.5944 - 1.5720)}{2} \text{ x } 10000$

$$= 112$$

Therefore profit $= 112 \text{ x } \$12.50 \text{ x } 10$

$$= \$14,000$$

The screens on this page can compare up to two contracts and display various information on the contracts selected.

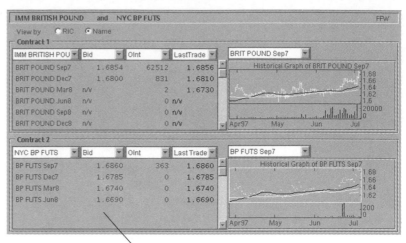

GBP futures prices and spot FX are both in American terms

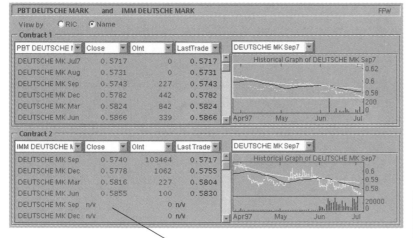

Most exchanges quote prices in American terms as here. However, NYC (FINEX) quote their DEM prices in European terms – as in the spot market

The size of the Open Interest in contracts gives some indication of the importance of the IMM as a futures exchange

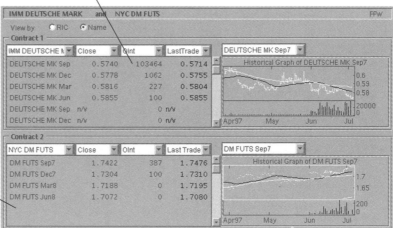

Currency Swaps

A **Currency Swap** involves the exchange of interest payments in one currency for those in another.

Currency swaps typically require an **exchange of principal**. Usually the notional principal is exchanged at inception at the prevailing spot rate. Interest rate payments are then passed back on a fixed, floating or zero-coupon basis. The principal is then re-exchanged at maturity at the initial spot rate.

In effect, a currency swap allows a borrower or lender to swap a loan in one currency for a loan in another currency without incurring currency risk. (Important note — currency risk is not incurred **only if the swap is held until maturity.**)

A currency swap is essentially a **simultaneous spot transaction followed by a series of FX forward transactions**.

Currency swaps usually have maturities of at least one year.

❶ Spot exchange of principal
The exchange of principal takes place at the start of the agreement, usually at an agreed exchange rate of **spot**.

❷ Exchange of interest rate payments
During the agreement period a series of interest payments are exchanged at agreed forward dates. In the case of a fixed-to-fixed swap, both sides swap fixed interest rates based on the principal amounts and at fixed rates agreed for the contract.

❸ Re-exchange of principal
On maturity of the agreement, the principal amounts are re-exchanged at the original spot rate. Even though years may have passed and the spot rate changed dramatically, the principal amounts involved have not changed so the original spot rate is used as neither side is disadvantaged.

Comparing FX Swaps and Currency Swaps

In an FX swap the interest rate differential between the two currencies is taken into account in the forward points for the forward delivery date. For a currency swap the interest rate differential is paid during the life of the swap at each payment date. This means that the principal amounts can be swapped at the original spot rate at both the beginning and end of the OTC agreement.

Within the global markets currency swaps are second in importance to IRSs in terms of the face value of OTC contracts outstanding in terms of both notional outstanding values and average daily turnover.

Data from the *ISDA Summary of Market Survey Statistics: 1997 Year End* confirm the dominance of the IRS markets as the chart below shows.

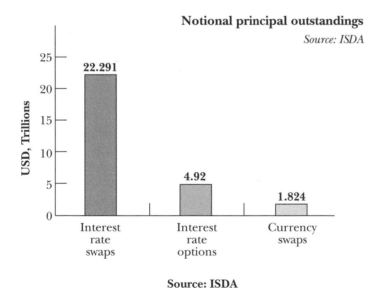

Notional principal outstandings

Source: ISDA

Source: ISDA

Uses of Currency Swaps

Example

XYZ is a Japanese multinational which needs to borrow US$100 million for 5 years to fund development of an overseas factory in the US. XYZ can borrow JPY in the domestic market at a fixed 5-year rate of 1.5% but USD would cost LIBOR + 0.25%. The current spot rate is USD/JPY 130.00.

XYZ issues a 5-year Euroyen bond to raise ¥13 billion, which pays a coupon of 1.5%. At the prevailing spot rate, the notional value of the Euroyen bond is equivalent to US$100 million principal. XYZ needs dollars to fund the factory's development.

ABC, a US bank, requires $100million worth of yen for 5 years to fund expansion. ABC would prefer fixed rate borrowing so that it knows its future cash flow requirements. ABC can borrow dollars in the domestic US market at LIBOR flat, but borrowing yen for 5 years on a fixed rate basis would cost 3.5%.

XYZ and ABC agree to a currency swap to take advantage of each counterparty's favourable borrowing rates in their own markets. Assuming the credit ratings of the two counterparties are equal, the savings will be split approximately equally between the parties.

In general terms, could you explain to a colleague what will happen in the currency swap?

The chart below summarises both organisation's positions.

Rates	XYZ can borrow	ABC can borrow
Fixed JPY @	3.25%	3.50%
Floating USD @	LIBOR + 0.25%	LIBOR
Required basis	**Fixed**	**Floating**

In order to obtain the type of loan both organisations require they enter into a swap agreement. Both organisations need to assess the risks involved if the other side defaults on payments – if this does happen then the party who does not receive an interest payment still has to pay the interest due on the underlying loan.

This is how the currency swap works...

❶ Exchange of principal

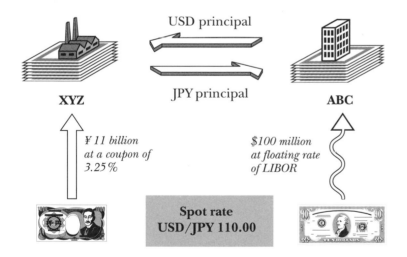

❷ Exchange of interest payments
Every six months there is an exchange of interest payments.
- XYZ make **floating rate** payments of US LIBOR to ABC
- ABC make **fixed rate** payments of JPY 3.25% to XYZ

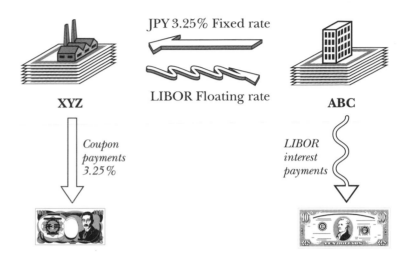

The chart below shows how both sides benefit from the swap.

	XYZ	ABC
Pays out	LIBOR + 3.25%	3.25% + LIBOR
Receives in	3.25%	LIBOR
Payments =	LIBOR	3.25%
Without swap	LIBOR + 0.25%	3.50%
Savings	**0.25%**	**0.25%**

Both XYZ and ABC make the same savings as both are of equal credit ratings. If there had been a difference in ratings then the proportions of total savings would have been biased to the organisation with the better credit rating as in the case of IRSs.

❸ Re-exchange of principal – 5 years later

Because the principal loans are repaid at the same amounts borrowed 5 years previously, the original spot rate is used for the re-exchange of principal amounts.

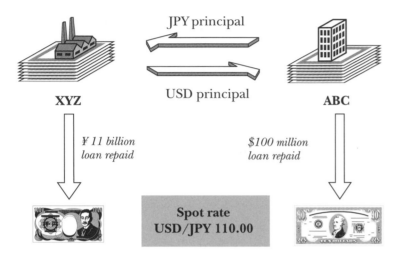

Market-makers

As with IRSs a currency swap does not have to take place directly between two end-users. Most currency swap agreements now involve a market-maker and two separate clients who wish to enter a swap, but not necessarily with each other. For example, it may be that the perceived credit risks involved in a direct swap agreement are not acceptable to one or both parties. By acting as a two-way market-maker a bank acts as an intermediary creating a double swap in which both parties are effectively guaranteed interest payments will take place.

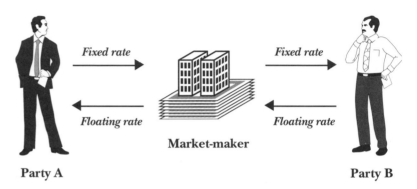

Of course, the market-maker does not enter into these swaps for no reward. The intermediary is paid a fee which is either based on the principal notional amount involved, a spread between the two-way prices quoted for swap repayments – the **swap rate**, or both.

It is unlikely that the market-maker has the underlying assets to match the exchange of principal amounts. As a result the bank usually matches a currency swap with an offsetting contract with another counterparty to manage the interest rate and FX exposures.

If the offsetting contract conditions match those of the original contract exactly, then the risks have been removed. However, there are still credit risks to be considered for both counterparties in the offsetting contracts.

Banks quote swap rates at the current spot rates against USD 6-month LIBOR. You will see prices quoted as **Bid** and **Ask** for a range of currencies. For example, you may see bank quotes similar to those for GBP shown in the chart below.

Maturity	Bid	Ask
2Y	6.71	6.75
3Y	7.17	7.21
4Y	7.48	7.52
5Y	7.68	7.72
7Y	7.96	8.00
10Y	8.26	8.30

But what do these rates mean? For example, for a 4-year period the bank is willing to enter into a swap at the current spot rate on the following terms:

- The bank **receives** the fixed **Ask** price of 7.52% on GBP and **pays** a floating 6-month LIBOR on USD

- The bank **pays** the fixed **Bid** price of 7.48% on GBP and **receives** a floating 6-month LIBOR on USD

By matching two offsetting currency swaps, the market-maker effectively is at the centre of a **double swap**.

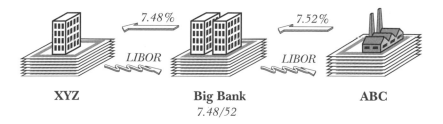

| XYZ | **Big Bank** 7.48/52 | ABC |

In the US and to a lesser extent in the UK, swap rates are quoted over the yield on a Treasury note with comparable maturity.

For example, a market-maker may quote '**70/75 over**' for a swap based on a 5-year T-bond which has a yield of 8.00%. This means the market-maker pays at a rate of 8.70% and receives at a rate of 8.75%

When comparing currency swaps, it is important to evaluate each instrument on a consistent basis, so that market participants are comparing like-with-like.

Are currency swaps as simple as has been described? Well, in principle the answer is yes, but in practice there are a number of issues to be reconciled if you are trying to compare swap rates. In other words are you comparing like-with-like?

Differences between swap rates can arise based on the following:

- Quotation terms for fixed and floating rates

- The underlying instruments used to calculate swap rates

- The frequency of interest rate payments

- Day count bases used to calculate interest rate payments

These issues are all discussed in the next section.

If you were asked to explain the mechanics of a currency swap to a colleague would be able to do it?

Currency Swaps in the Market Place

This section deals with a number of important matters concerning currency swaps which you will need to understand:

- Differences between swaps

- Swap spreads

- Swap valuations

Differences between swaps

The four main types of difference between swaps mentioned at the end of the last section, will now be explained more fully.

Quotation terms

Within the US markets in particular there are a number of different ways interest payments can be calculated for fixed and floating rates together with a number of different ways payment schedules can be stipulated. Different swaps may use a combination of any of the following terms

Terms	Fixed rate	Floating rate
Rate quotation	• Absolute level • Spread over Treasury instrument	• Any LIBOR • Prime rate • CD, CP or T-bill
Payment schedule	• Quarterly • Semi-annually • Annually	• Periodic • Irregular
Basis	• Eurobond • T-bond • Money market instrument	• Bond • Money market Instrument

Underlying instruments

The instruments used to calculate swap rates for different currencies vary. For example, USD swaps are usually quoted as a spread over the appropriate Treasury instrument which have semi-annual coupons; DEM swaps are quoted on an annual Eurobond basis.

The chart below indicates the various instruments used for the major currencies together with the day count method used for the interest payment calculations.

Currency	Quoted as...	Coupon	Day count
USD	Spread over T-bond	Semi-annual	Actl /Actl
DEM	Fixed Eurobond	Annual	30 /360
CHF	Fixed Eurobond	Annual	30 /360
FRF	Fixed Eurobond	Annual	30 /360
GBP	Spread over Gilt	Semi-annual	Actl /365
JPY	Fixed Government bond	Semi-annual	Actl /365

Frequency of interest payments

In order to compare swap rates fairly you may need to convert annual payments into semi-annual or vice versa.

The chart below indicates the equations to use to convert yields or swap rates as appropriate.

From ➡	To ➡	Use ➡
Semi-annual	Annual	$R_A = \left[\left(1 + \dfrac{R_S}{2} \right)^2 \right] - 1$
Annual	Semi-annual	$R_S = 2 \times \left[\sqrt{(1 + R_A)} - 1 \right]$ R_A = Annual rate % ÷ 100 R_S = Semi-annual rate % ÷ 100

Day count bases

You may also need to convert swap rates depending on the day count basis used to calculate interest payments in order to compare like-with-like or value swaps.

The chart below gives the various methods of converting different day counts.

From ➡	To ➡	Use ➡
30/360 or Actual/365	Actual/360	Yield x $\dfrac{360}{365}$
Actual/360	30/360 or Actual/365	Yield x $\dfrac{365}{360}$
Actual/365	30/360	No adjustment
30/360	Actual/365	No adjustment

Swap Spreads

Interest rate trends cause variations in swap spreads over the yield curves for government benchmark instruments.

When interest rates are expected to **fall** there are many fixed rate issuers wanting to swap into paying **floating** and receiving **fixed**, so spreads **narrow**.

When interest rates are expected to **rise** there are plenty of borrowers wanting to swap into **fixed** but not many willing to receive it, so spreads **widen**.

Another factor affecting swap spreads is credit risk. In a swap the market player and the market-maker take on each other's risk. If either party fails to honour payment commitments, then the other party has an unwanted interest rate exposure.

For currency swaps fixed and floating payments are made, so the risk of loss has to take into account an estimate of the **volatility** of the future floating rate basis, for example, LIBOR.

Swap pricing

Swap rates are essentially an indicator of the present value of forward interest rates. The fixed swap rate is the average of the floating rates over the tenor of the contract, as predicted by the FRAs.

Consider a fixed-for-floating currency swap in which XYZ Corporation and ABC Bank enter into a 5-year agreement to swap $100 million for DEM 170 millions at a spot rate of USD/DEM = 1.7000. Every 6 months XYZ pay ABC a fixed rate of 6.00% DEM and in return ABC pays US LIBOR on the floating side to XYZ.

XYZ   6.00% DEM Fixed   **ABC**

US LIBOR Floating

Both payments are
made every 6 months

The spot rate for the transaction is 1st June so the first payment is due on 1st December. The amount of interest due on the 1st December is already known on the 1st June. How can this be the case? The answer is that LIBOR for the first payment is fixed on the 1st June as the floating rate **to be paid in 6 months time**. In a similar manner the 1st December LIBOR fixing determines the rate to be paid for the second payment on the following 1st June and so on until the final payment in 5 years.

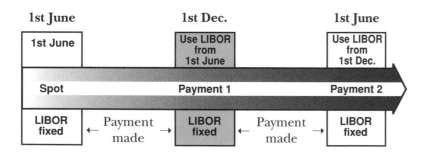

In terms of pricing this fixed-for-floating swap the transaction can be thought of as a series of **coupon payments** from an imaginary **straight bond** on the **fixed side** against a series of payments from an imaginary or **synthetic floating rate note (FRN)** on the **floating side**.

Payments equivalent to coupons from a straight bond

Fixed	6.00% DEM	6.00% DEM	6.00% DEM
Payment 1	Payment 1	Payment 2	Payment 3
Floating	US LIBOR	US LIBOR	US LIBOR

Payments equivalent to those from a floating rate note

The present value of the fixed side can be calculated using the general straight bond valuation equation. For a bond with a face value of $100 and with an annual coupon this is Equation 1.

$$\text{Present Value (PV)} = \frac{C}{1 + R} + \frac{C}{(1 + R)^2} + \dots + \frac{(C + 100)}{(1 + R)^n}$$

Where: C = Coupon rate
R = Discount or swap rate as a decimal
n = Number of years to maturity

...Equation 1

The present value for the floating side can be calculated using the more direct relationship between the present and future value of an instrument, Equation 2.

$$PV = \frac{\text{Future Value}}{(1 + R)}$$

$$= \frac{\text{Principal} + \text{Interest due}}{(1 + R)}$$

Where: R =   Discount or LIBOR rate
as a decimal

...Equation 2

Pricing from the spot curve

The yield to maturity (YTM) curve is simply a graph of YTM values of bonds against maturity. Unfortunately this is a simplistic view of yields and it is better to use a graph of **spot rate** against maturity period. The spot rate is a measure of the YTM on an instrument at any moment in time which takes into account a variety of market factors. A graph of spot rate against maturity is known as a spot curve or zero coupon yield curve, because the spot rate for an instrument is equivalent to the yield on an instrument which has no coupon repayment – zero coupon. This means that spot rates for a series of instruments with zero coupons for a range of maturity periods can be compared directly.

A zero coupon can be thought of as a discount curve for longer maturities.

The curves represent the perceived relationship between the return on an instrument and its maturity – usually measured in years. Depending on the shape of the curve it is described as either:

- Positive

- Negative or inverse

Positive yield curve
In this case the shorter term interest rates are **lower** than the longer term rates. This is usually the case – the longer the period of the investment the higher the yield paid.

Negative or inverse curve
When short term rates fall investors move their investments into longer term instruments to lock in a higher rate of return. This increase in supply of long term funds causes the long term rates to fall.

The shapes of 'theoretical' yield curves are shown below – in practice they may not appear so clear!

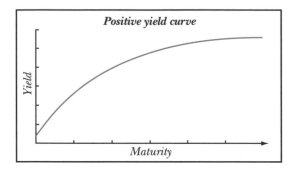

Yield curves are used to identify anomalies between instruments of different credit standing, for example, an IRS and a T-bond of similar maturity.

Traders can compare the spreads of different instruments over the spot curve to see if they are relatively cheap or expensive. For two instruments of identical credit standing and the same maturity the one with the larger spread is cheaper.

So how are swap prices determined? The following example is simple and outlines the process for a currency swap for a one year maturity.

Example – Fixed-for-floating currency swap rates

ABC is a bank deciding on the rates for a one-year currency swap in which it will pay fixed and receive 6-month LIBOR. The floating rates are already known from the LIBOR curve but how much should the bank charge on the fixed side?

The profitability of the swap is zero if the net present value of the two 6-month floating rate payments equals the interest payments on the fixed side.

At the start of the swap the first LIBOR is known and is equal to 9.00%. The second 6-month LIBOR can be implied from the LIBOR yield curve.

LIBOR yield curve		
6 month	12 month	18 month
9.00%	9.50%	10.00%

The return on investing $1 at LIBOR 9.00% for 6 months is $0.045. So after 6 months the $1 invested is worth $1.045. 12-month LIBOR is 9.50%. What rate of interest is therefore required for the second 6 month LIBOR payment to turn $1.045 into $1.095?

This can be calculated using Equation 2.

$$PV = \frac{\text{Future Value}}{(1 + R)}$$

$$1.045 = \frac{1.095}{(1 + R)}$$

$$R = \left(\frac{1.095}{1.045}\right) - 1$$

$$= 0.04785$$

So the rate for the 6 month period is 2 x 0.04785 = 9.57%. This rate is the expected 6-month rate in 6 months time implied from the yield curve. In other words $1.045 invested at 9.57% for 6 months would yield $1.095.

So the two **floating rates** for the two payments are 9.00% and 9.57%.

These floating rates can now be used to calculate the fixed rate by equating them with a break-even value.

To do this the interest flows are discounted to the present value. Suppose the notional principal of the swap is $100. Using Equation 1 the present value of the first floating payment can be calculated using the 6 month LIBOR yield curve.

$$PV = \frac{C}{1 + R}$$

For first payment:

$$PV = \frac{4.50}{1 + 0.090/2}$$

$$= \$4.3062$$

For second payment:

$$PV = \frac{4.785}{1 + 0.095}$$

$$= \$4.3699$$

Therefore total interest = 4.3062 + 4.3699 = $8.6761

Equation 1 can be used again to calculate the fixed rate for the present value cash flow which has just been calculated. If C is the fixed rate, then ...

$$PV = \frac{C/2}{1 + R} + \frac{C/2}{1 + R}$$

First 6 month payment   *Second 6 month payment*

$$8.6761 = \frac{C/2}{1 + 0.09/2} + \frac{C/2}{1 + 0.095}$$

$$8.6761 = \frac{C}{2}\left(\frac{1}{1 + 0.09/2} + \frac{1}{1 + 0.095} \right)$$

$$8.6761 = \frac{C}{2}\left(0.9569 + 0.9132 \right)$$

$$C = 2 \times \left(\frac{8.6761}{1.8701} \right)$$

$$C = 9.28\%$$

This means that a fixed rate of 9.28% equals the return on the floating rates of 9.00% and 9.57% for the two 6 month periods.

The value calculated is the swap rate. In order to ensure profitability the bank's offered swap rate would be **lower** than this.

Using this method to price the swap depends on the rate that is discounted to calculate cash flows. This example used the spot rate for zero coupon yields but a forward rate could have been used for forward/forward rates for the period between the first and second fixed coupon dates.

The screens below display the DEM and GBP rates from Tullets.

The screen below is taken from the Currency and Interest Rate Swaps Speed Guide.

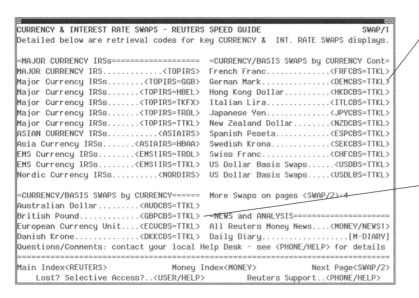

```
CURRENCY & INTEREST RATE SWAPS - REUTERS SPEED GUIDE          SWAP/1
Detailed below are retrieval codes for key CURRENCY &  INT. RATE SWAPS displays.

=MAJOR CURRENCY IRSs==================  =CURRENCY/BASIS SWAPS by CURRENCY Cont=
MAJOR CURRENCY IRS.............<TOPIRS>  French Franc.............<FRFCBS=TTKL>
Major Currency IRSs........<TOPIRS=GGB>  German Mark..............<DEMCBS=TTKL>
Major Currency IRSs.......<TOPIRS=HBEL>  Hong Kong Dollar.........<HKDCBS=TTKL>
Major Currency IRSs.......<TOPIRS=TKFX>  Italian Lira.............<ITLCBS=TTKL>
Major Currency IRSs.......<TOPIRS=TRDL>  Japanese Yen.............<JPYCBS=TTKL>
Major Currency IRSs.......<TOPIRS=TTKL>  New Zealand Dollar.......<NZDCBS=TTKL>
ASIAN CURRENCY IRSs...........<ASIAIRS>  Spanish Peseta...........<ESPCBS=TTKL>
Asia Currency IRSs.......<ASIAIRS=HBAA>  Swedish Krona............<SEKCBS=TTKL>
EMS Currency IRSs........<EMS1IRS=TRDL>  Swiss Franc..............<CHFCBS=TTKL>
EMS Currency IRSs.......<EMS1IRS=TTKL>   US Dollar Basis Swaps......<USDBS=TTKL>
Nordic Currency IRSs..........<NORDIRS>  US Dollar Basis Swaps.....<USDLBS=TTKL>

=CURRENCY/BASIS SWAPS by CURRENCY======  More Swaps on pages <SWAP/2>-4
Australian Dollar........<AUDCBS=TTKL>
British Pound............<GBPCBS=TTKL>  =NEWS and ANALYSIS=====================
European Currency Unit....<ECUCBS=TTKL> All Reuters Money News....<MONEY/NEWS1>
Danish Krone.............<DKKCBS=TTKL>  Daily Diary..................[M-DIARY]
Questions/Comments: contact your local Help Desk - see <PHONE/HELP> for details
===============================================================================
Main Index<REUTERS>          Money Index<MONEY>            Next Page<SWAP/2>
   Lost? Selective Access?..<USER/HELP>      Reuters Support..<PHONE/HELP>
```

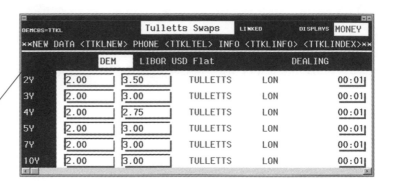

```
DEMCBS=TTKL                    Tulletts Swaps   LINKED      DISPLAYS MONEY
**NEW DATA <TTKLNEW> PHONE <TTKLTEL> INFO <TTKLINFO> <TTKLINDEX>**
                    DEM    LIBOR USD Flat              DEALING
2Y     2.00     3.50        TULLETTS      LON          00:01
3Y     2.00     3.00        TULLETTS      LON          00:01
4Y     2.00     2.75        TULLETTS      LON          00:01
5Y     2.00     3.00        TULLETTS      LON          00:01
7Y     2.00     3.00        TULLETTS      LON          00:01
10Y    2.00     3.00        TULLETTS      LON          00:01
```

```
GBPCBS=TTKL                    Tulletts Swaps   LINKED      DISPLAYS MONEY
**NEW DATA <TTKLNEW> PHONE <TTKLTEL> INFO <TTKLINFO> <TTKLINDEX>**
                    GBP    LIBOR USD Flat              DEALING
2Y    -0.50     1.50        TULLETTS      LON          00:04
3Y    -0.50     1.50        TULLETTS      LON          00:04
4Y    -0.50     1.50        TULLETTS      LON          00:04
5Y    -0.50     1.50        TULLETTS      LON          00:05
7Y    -0.50     1.50        TULLETTS      LON          00:05
10Y   -0.50     1.00        TULLETTS      LON          00:05
```

Currency Options – on Cash & on Futures

A **currency option** is an agreement between two counterparties in which the option buyer pays the seller a premium for the right, but not the obligation, to buy or sell a specified quantity of a specified underlying instrument on or before an agreed date (the **expiry** or **maturity date**) at an agreed exchange rate, called the **strike price**.

A **call option** is an option to **buy** the underlying instrument.
A **put option** is an option to **sell** the underlying instrument.
When the underlying instrument is bought or sold, it is called **exercising the option**.

An **American style** option can be exercised **on or before the expiry date**.
A **European style** option can be exercised **only on the expiry date**.

Usually, a currency option has spot FX as its underlying instrument.

The relationship between the rights and obligations for the different types of options is summarised in the following diagram – you may find it useful to refer to when considering some of the examples which follow.

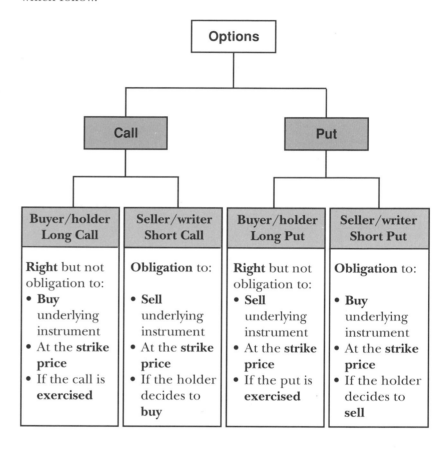

Currency Options Trading

Currency options are financial derivatives which are used to hedge exchange rate risk. They are particularly useful for organisations involved in the international import/export trade.

Currency options are available on both cash and currency futures contracts and are traded OTC and on exchanges worldwide. The following diagram indicates the availability of currency options.

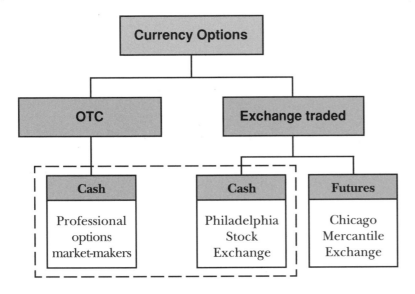

Currency options were first traded on exchanges in the 1980s. A number of exchanges list currency options but the two most important exchanges in terms of volume of turnover are:

- Philadelphia Stock Exchange (PHLX) for options on cash

- Chicago Mercantile Exchange's division – the Index and Option Market (IOM) for options on IMM currency futures contracts

Although exchange trading is far more colourful and exciting in practice the OTC daily turnover in currency options is far greater than for exchange-traded options – OTC currency options account for about 90% of the market.

OTC Currency Options Trading

OTC currency options are available from many professional options market-makers. The options can be tailored to meet a wide variety of customer needs in terms of amounts, currency pair, strike price and expiry dates. Characteristically OTC transactions:

- Take place directly between counterparties or via an options broker

- Are completely flexible, for example, any expiry date can be traded – most OTC currency options expire under 6 months. Although there is some standardisation in the busiest markets, the precise details between the counterparties are freely negotiated.

- Require no margin payments

- Are quoted for good sized contracts

- Are usually European style – exercise can only take place on the expiry date

Exchange-traded Currency Options

The underlying instrument for currency options on an exchange can either be a fixed amount of spot currency or an equivalent currency futures contract. Exchange-traded options are standardised in terms of :

- Underlying instrument and its trading amount

- Strike prices – in general exchanges try to have a range of in-the-money, at-the-money and out-of-the-money strike prices

- Expiry dates

- Style – most exchange options are American

- Premium quotations – most currency options are quoted in American terms or indirect quotations which is the opposite to quotations in the spot FX markets

- Margin payments are required to be paid to the Clearing house

If a currency option is exercised what is actually delivered? The charts opposite summarise the situations for both options on cash and options on futures contracts.

Although the options on cash and futures contracts are different, in practice, they are closely related. Options on futures contracts are American style and they are referred to by the month in which the underlying futures contract matures not by the expiration month of the option. An option on a futures contract taken to expiry results in a similar settlement transaction as that for an option on cash – on expiry a futures contract price is equal to the spot price.

This example is for a foreign currency versus the USD:

Option on cash	Buyer/holder has right to:	Seller/writer has obligation to:
Call	**Buy** Foreign currency **Sell** USD	**Sell** Foreign currency **Buy** USD
Put	**Sell** Foreign currency **Buy** USD	**Buy** Foreign currency **Sell** USD

Option on futures contract	Buyer/holder has right to:	Seller/writer has obligation to:
Call	**Buy** a futures contract – **Go long**	**Sell** a futures contract – **Go short**
Put	**Sell** a futures contract – **Go short**	**Buy** a futures contract – **Go long**

OTC v Exchange Trading

There are obvious advantages to customers using OTC transactions which are tailored to their specific needs. However, there are also several disadvantages, particularly those associated with credit risk.

Contracts traded on exchanges are open outcry and premium prices are freely available and published. In the OTC markets there is some degree of price uniformity now but the main difference between the two markets concerns credit. The margin system associated with exchange trading virtually eliminates credit risk, whereas OTC transactions are still subject to the credit status of the counterparties.

Exchange traded	OTC
• Prices readily available	• Prices less visible
• Trading in an open outcry, competitive arena with many traders	• Players trade using the phone or options brokers
• Contracts are standardised and published	• Contract conditions are negotiated
• Positions are easily traded out	• Positions are not easily offset or transferred
• Few contracts result in physical delivery or expiry	• Majority of trades result in delivery or expiry
• Clearing house guarantees all contracts	• Counterparty risk
• Market players are not known to each other	• Counterparties are known
• Exchange trading hours and rules	• 24-hour markets which are less well regulated

Exchange contracts

Options on cash are mainly traded on the Philadelphia Stock Exchange. Most of the options are traded against the USD but some cross-currency options are traded. Options on futures contracts are mainly on the Chicago Mercantile Exchange's division – the Index and Option Market (IOM) for IMM currency futures. The charts below indicate a range of currency options available.

Philadelphia Stock Exchange	
Options on cash against the USD	**Unit of trading**
Pound Sterling	GBP 31,250
Deutschmark	DEM 62,500
Japanese Yen	JPY 6,250,000
Swiss Franc	CHF 62,500
French Franc	FRF 250,000
Australian Dollar	AUD 50,000
Canadian Dollar	CAD 50,000
Cross currency	
Deutschmark/Yen	DEM 62,500

Chicago Mercantile Exchange – IOM	
Options on IMM currency futures contracts	**Unit of trading**
Pound Sterling	GBP 62,500
Deutschmark	DEM 125,000
Japanese Yen	JPY 12,500,000
Swiss Franc	CHF 125,000
French Franc	FRF 500,000
Australian Dollar	AUD 100,000
Cross currency	
Deutschmark/Yen	DEM 125,000

Typical contract specifications

Options contracts detail varies from type to type and from exchange
to exchange but the following examples taken from an IMM contract
and a Philadelphia Stock Exchange contract are typical specifications.

Options on IMM British Pound Futures	
Underlying contract	One GBP future contract – GBP 62,500
Strike price	$0.01 intervals
Premium quotations	US cents per GBP
Minimum Price Fluctuation (Tick)	0.0002 ($12.50)
Contract expiry	Option expiry each and every week of the year
Exercise procedure	American

This is the standard contract size.

Strike prices are published differing by this interval

These are in American terms or indirect quotes

This is the smallest amount a contract can change value and the 'tick' size.

Option contracts are referred to by the trading cycle of the futures contract months.

This means that contract can be exercised on or before expiry date – American or on the expiry date – European

Options on cash	
Underlying contract	GBP 31,250
Strike price	$0.01 intervals
Premium quotations	US cents per GBP
Minimum Price Fluctuation (Tick)	$0.01
Contract expiry	Variety of expiry dates mid-month, month end & long
Exercise procedure	American or European

Who uses Currency Options?

Banks and Corporate Customers

A forward FX contract can be used to fix a definite exchange rate price to buy or sell currency today for a future date. A currency option offers the same opportunity but it allows buyers of calls/puts to take advantage of any favourable currency exchange rate movements which may occur during the contract period.

The right of a buyer to exercise an option is paid for by the premium charged by the seller of the option. The cost of this premium which is paid upfront (value spot) has to be considered by the buyer when deciding whether or not to use a currency option or forward FX transaction.

In their basic form OTC currency options are purchased from a bank for a premium and settled by exercise or effectively selling the option back to the bank.

In the professional options markets, traders use a wide range of combinations of options to hedge positions or to speculate.

Importers/Exporters

Currency options are particularly useful for organisations tendering for overseas contracts where payments for goods or services would be received in a foreign currency if the tender is successful. If there is a long delay between tendering and receiving news of success or not, FX exchange rate movements could have a significant impact on the trader's profitability. A currency option can be used to hedge the FX risk involved in such a tender.

Example

A UK exporter has tendered for a contract overseas for services to be paid in USD and it will be 6 months before the outcome of the tender is known. To hedge the tender, the exporter buys a GBP call contract from XYZ Bank. This gives the exporter the right to **buy GBP** from and **sell USD** to the bank on expiry.

The exporter pays XYZ a premium for this option – the strike price agreed is 1.6000 so the option for £31,250 has a contract value of $50,000 (1.6000 x £31,250). In 6 months time there are a number of outcomes depending on the success or not of the tender and the prevailing FX spot rate. These outcomes are summarised below:

Tender outcome	GBP/USD value	Result
Successful	GBP rise/USD fall Spot = 1.7000	Option is **exercised** to buy GBP at 1.6000 because £31,250 is now worth $53,125 in the spot market
Successful	GBP fall/USD rise Spot = 1.5000	Option is allowed to **expire** because £31,250 is now worth $46,875 in the spot market
Unsuccessful	GBP rise/USD fall Spot = 1.7000	Even though there is no need to buy GBP the option is exercised to buy at 1.6000, then sold in the market at 1.7000 at a profit
Unsuccessful	GBP fall/USD rise Spot = 1.5000	Option is allowed to expire – the only cost is that of premium

Currency Options in the Market Place

This section deals with typical contract quotations and how option premiums are calculated for currency options that are:

- Exchange-traded

- OTC

Typical Exchange Contract Quotations

Currency option quotations are available from the financial press such as the *Financial Times* and *The Wall Street Journal* and from products such as Reuters Money 3000. The information appears in a similar style to those in the following examples.

Financial press – Option on cash

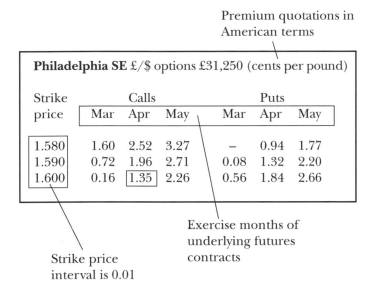

Premium quotations in American terms

Philadelphia SE £/$ options £31,250 (cents per pound)

Strike price	Calls			Puts		
	Mar	Apr	May	Mar	Apr	May
1.580	1.60	2.52	3.27	–	0.94	1.77
1.590	0.72	1.96	2.71	0.08	1.32	2.20
1.600	0.16	1.35	2.26	0.56	1.84	2.66

Exercise months of underlying futures contracts

Strike price interval is 0.01

The information in the chart allows you to calculate the contract amount of USD and the premium cost of any option which is quoted.

Contract amount of USD
This is calculated using the following simple equation:

> **Amount USD = Strike price x Unit of trading**

Example
A USD denominated option for a GBP put with a strike price of 1.6000 would entitle the holder of the contract to **sell** the underlying GBP for 1.6000 x 31,250 = $50,000.

Contract premium price
This is calculated using the following simple equation:

> **Premium cost = Premium quote in USD x Unit of trading**

Example
How much will the premium be for a USD denominated **Apr1.6000 GBP call** be? In other words how much does it cost for the right to **buy** GBP 31,250 at a strike of 1.6000. From the chart the premium is quoted at 1.35 US cents per GBP. So the premium cost

$$= \$0.0135 \text{ x } 31,250$$

$$= \$421.88$$

Typical OTC Contract Quotations

The price of a currency option is determined by a number of factors listed here:

1. The spot price of the underlying currency pair

2. Strike price

3. Time to expiry

4. Risk free interest rates in both currencies being traded

5. Price volatility of the currency pair

Professional options market-makers use a pricing model such as the Garman-Kohlhagen version of the Black-Scholes option pricing model to calculate option prices based on these five factors.

Of the factors, **price volatility** is the only one for which the market-maker does not have a precise value. So what is this price volatility?

Price volatility is the degree of price movement of one currency against another. The primary focus in pricing options is to be able to calculate accurately a forecast or expectation of spot volatility over the life of an option. Obviously the more accurate the predictions the more chance the market-maker has of making a profit and the less chance of making a loss. However, recent bank losses involving options trading have shown how easy it is to get things wrong!

So how are the volatilities used for the calculations derived? The volatilities used in calculating an option price are calculated using statistical standard deviations of historic underlying price movements over a given period, expressed as a percentage per annum.

The volatilities implied by option prices can be viewed as the markets' forecasts of the proportional percentage range, up or down, within which the underlying currency price is expected to finish at the expiry date of the option.

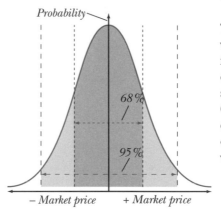

The confidence level of the volatility forecast being correct for one standard deviation either side of the mean in a statistical normal distribution is 68%. For two standard deviations the confidence level of forecasting the correct volatility range is 95%.

Example

USD/DEM has a one year forward market value of 1.6500 and the one year volatility is forecast at 10%. So the standard deviation is ±0.0165 and two standard deviations is ±0.0330.

The price ranges for the two confidence levels are shown in the table below:

Confidence level	USD/DEM price range
68%	1.6335 to 1.6665 (1.6500 ± 0.0165)
95%	1.6170 to 1.6830 (1.6500 ± 0.0330)

So one year volatility at 10% means that the spot rate will lie somewhere between 1.6335 and 1.6665. The volatility does not indicate a direction – the rate could be higher or lower than 1.6500.

Valuing Currency Options

OTC option quotations are different from exchange traded quotations in that professional options market-makers use **volatility** to quote the price of an option. This is because, for a given maturity, strike price, interest rate and spot rate, there is a one-to-one correspondence between the actual price of an option and its volatility.

In other words, a quote in volatility terms corresponds to a unique option price, and vice versa.

Example

A market-maker might quote 9.45 – 9.65 % volatility for a 3-month USD/DEM option

This two-way Bid/Ask price quotation means:

On **Bid** side   The market-maker will **buy** puts or calls at 9.45% per annum

On **Ask** side   The market-maker will **sell** puts or calls at 9.65% per annum

The market-makers are therefore trading volatility.

The prices are for at-the-money forward options – the strike price is at the current underlying forward rate.

Once the counterparties want to trade, all the factors, including the volatilities, are entered into each side's pricing models to calculate the premium to be paid. If both sides agree then the transaction proceeds – for currency options the Garman-Kohlhagen version of the Black-Scholes option pricing model is almost universally used.

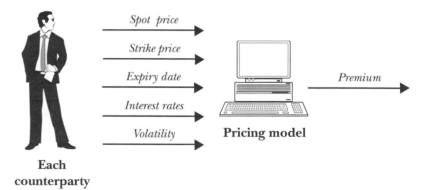

The following chart is a summary of the movement in premium levels for options based on the movement of four of the pricing factors. You may find it useful in looking at historic option prices.

Increase in...	Price of **Call**	Price of **Put**
Strike price	↓	↑
Forward price	↑	↓
Expiry date	↑	↑
Volatility	↑	↑

Options are quoted and traded in volatility terms only interbank. If a corporate client asks a bank for an option price, then the bank quotes directly in premium terms.

```
1253 SBC WARBURG      BASEL  061-2889118 GENEVE 022-3764240 SBZO
     OPTIONS USD/CHF  LUGANO 091-296555  ZURICH 01-2394150
   STRIKE  SPOT LEVEL  1.4620         VALUE        11-JUL-97
           15-SEP-97   15-DEC-97      16-MAR-98    15-JUN-98
 C  1.425  3.80- 4.10  4.40- 4.70    4.70- 5.00   4.85- 5.15
 C  1.450  2.40- 2.70  3.20- 3.50    3.60- 3.90   3.85- 4.15
 C  1.475  1.35- 1.65  2.25- 2.55    2.75- 3.05   3.05- 3.35
 C  1.500  0.65- 0.95  1.50- 1.80    2.00- 2.30   2.35- 2.65
 P  1.425  1.25- 1.55  3.35- 3.65    5.15- 5.45   6.75- 7.05
 P  1.450  2.30- 2.60  4.65- 4.95    6.55- 6.85   8.25- 8.55
 P  1.475  3.75- 4.05  6.15- 6.45    8.15- 8.45   9.90-10.20
 P  1.500  5.55- 5.85  7.90- 8.20    9.90-10.20  11.65-11.95
```

OTC Dealing Conventions

As you can imagine because of the complex nature of options there is considerable scope for confusion when trading unless some standard conventions and terminology are used. In 1985, the British Bankers Association in conjunction with the major market-makers introduced a set of market conventions known as LICOM Terms – London Interbank Currency Options Market recommended standard terms and conditions. These LICOM Terms were intended to encourage good market practice and reduce the need for legal documentation. Shortly after the introduction of LICOM Terms, similar terms were established in the US, and by 1990 these were known as USICOM Terms. Following the involvement of other international markets, such as those in Canada and Japan, the **International Currency Options Market (ICOM) Master Agreement** was first published in 1992 and subsequently revised in 1997.

Counterparties using ICOM Terms typically confirm the following when trading a currency option:

- **Trade date**
- **Buyer and Seller**
- **Option style – American or European**
- **Option type – Put or Call**
- **Call currency denomination and amount**
- **Put currency denomination and amount**
- **Strike price**
- **Expiry date**
- **Expiry time**
- **Expiry settlement date**
- **Premium**
- **Price**
- **Premium payment date**
- **Premium payment instructions**

Trading Strategies for Options

There are many strategies available in the options markets – some are quite complex and have colourful names.

The various strategies are usually represented diagrammatically as **break-even graphs** which show the potential for making a profit. The diagrams use the break-even point as the basis for the diagram where

> **Break-even point = Strike price ± premium**

The most basic buy/sell strategies for puts and calls are illustrated using profit/loss charts in the following examples. You may find it useful to refer to option strategies in general by referring to the *An Introduction to Derivatives* (ISBN 0-471-83176-X) in the *Reuters Financial Training* series.

Depending on whether the market player is a buyer or seller of a call or put, gains or losses either have ceiling values or are limitless.

Your notes

Buying a call option

In this case a bank buys a 1.6000GBP call with a premium of 2.0 cents per pound. The break-even graph looks like this:

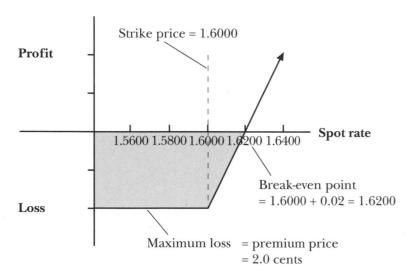

Selling a call option

In this case a bank sells a 1.6000GBP Call with a premium of 2.0 cents per pound. The break-even graph looks like this:

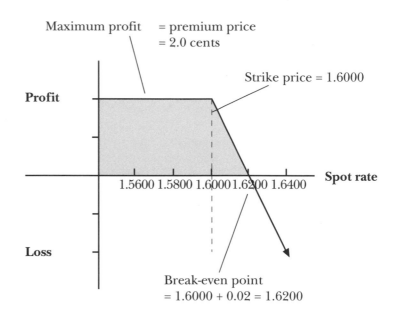

Spot rate	Outcome
> 1.6200	Profit increases and is unlimited as spot rate rises
1.6200	Break-even point
1.6000 – 1.6200	Loss which decreases as spot increases
< 1.6000	Loss is limited to a maximum of the premium price

Spot rate	Outcome
> 1.6200	Loss increases as spot increases and is unlimited
1.6200	Break-even point
1.6200 – 1.6000	Profit increases as spot decreases
< 1.6000	Maximum profit is equal to the premium

Buying a put option
In this case a bank buys a 1.6000GBP put with a premium of 2.0 cents per pound. The break-even graph looks like this:

Selling a put option
In this case a bank sells a 1.6000GBP put with a premium of 2.0 cents per pound. The break-even graph looks like this:

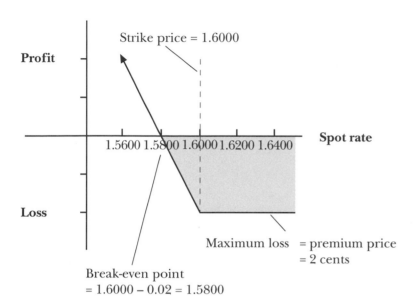

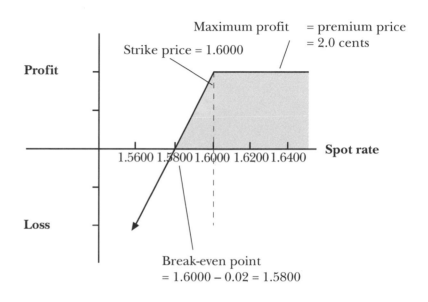

Spot rate	Outcome
> 1.6000	Maximum loss is equal to the premium
1.6000 – 1.5800	Loss decreases as spot increases
1.5800	Break-even point
< 1.5800	Profit increases as spot decreases and is unlimited

Spot rate	Outcome
> 1.6000	Maximum profit is equal to the premium
1.6000 – 1.5800	Profit increases as spot increases
1.5800	Break-even point
< 1.5800	Loss increases as spot decreases and is unlimited

The screens here display information for GBP Currency options with American and European terms on the Philadelphia Stock Exchange.

```
EXCHANGE TRADED CASH CURRENCY OPTIONS - REUTERS SPEED GUIDE          OPT/FX1
Detailed below are Retrieval codes for key Exchange Traded Currency Options.

=CURRENCY OPTIONS=====================  =CURRENCY OPTIONS Cont================
BELFOX USD/BEF...............<O#UBO*.b>  PHLX CAD (Amer)..............<O#XCD*.X>
EOE Dollar/Guilder...........<O#EUG*.E>  PHLX CAD (Eur)...............<O#CCD*.X>
EOE Dollar/Guilder Jumbo.....<O#EUH*.E>  PHLX CAD (Amer) Month-end....<O#CDW*.X>
MATIF USD/DEM................<O#DDM*.n>  PHLX CAD (Eur) Month-end.....<O#ECD*.X>
MATIF USD/FRF................<O#DFF*.n>  PHLX DEM (Amer)..............<O#XDM*.X>
MATIF GBP/DEM................<O#SDM*.n>  PHLX DEM (Eur)...............<O#CDM*.X>
MATIF DEM/FRF................<O#MFF*.n>  PHLX DEM (Amer) Month-end....<O#DMW*.X>
MATIF DEM/ITL................<O#MLI*.n>  PHLX DEM (Eur) Month-end.....<O#EDM*.X>
PHLX FCO Volatilities.........<PHVM>-V   PHLX DEM LTOs (Eur)..........<O#YDM*.X>
PHLX AUD (Amer)..............<O#XAD*.X>  PHLX DEM 3-D (3rd Week Exp)..<O#XDC*.X>
PHLX AUD (Eur)...............<O#CAD*.X>
PHLX AUD (Amer) Month-end....<O#ADW*.X>
PHLX AUD (Eur) Month-end.....<O#EDA*.X>
PHLX GBP (Amer)..............<O#XBP*.X>  More Opts on pages <OPT/FX2>-3
PHLX GBP (Eur)...............<O#CBP*.X>
PHLX GBP (Amer) Month-end....<O#BPW*.X>  =NEWS AND ANALYSIS===================
PHLX GBP (Eur) Month-end.....<O#EPO*.X>  All Reuters Money News....<MONEY/NEWS1>
PHLX GBP LTSs (Eur)..........<O#YPX*.X>  Daily Diary..................<M-DIARY>
```

```
BRITISH POUND    PHO/    USD      .XBP PHO/    LT↑1.6890    15:50 H1.6952 L1.6832
Strike Mth   Calls Bid    Ask    Volume Time  Puts  Bid    Ask    Volume Time
161    JUL7                               :                              12:46
162    JUL7                             09:21               0.13         09:00
163    JUL7                               :                 0.13         13:32
164    JUL7 ↓4.91  4.73   4.98    20 14:22                  0.13         15:03
165    JUL7        3.73   3.98       09:02                  0.14           :
166    JUL7        2.75   3.00       09:01         0.02     0.17         13:52
167    JUL7        1.87   2.02         :           0.10     0.25           :
168    JUL7        1.07   1.22    13:31↓0.30       0.29     0.44     19 14:34
169    JUL7        0.47   0.62         :           0.65     0.80           :
170    JUL7        0.21   0.36         :           1.34     1.49           :
171    JUL7        0.06   0.21         :                                   :
172    JUL7        0.01   0.16         :                                   :
173    JUL7               0.14         :                                   :
174    JUL7               0.13         :                                   :
175    JUL7                             :                                   :
```

```
BRIT POUND       PHO/    USD      .CBP PHO/    LT↑1.6890    15:50 H1.6952 L1.6832
Strike Mth   Calls Bid    Ask    Volume Time  Puts  Bid    Ask    Volume Time
161    JUL7                               :                              08:25
162    JUL7                               :                              12:12
163    JUL7                               :                 0.13         16:49
164    JUL7        4.70   4.95          :                   0.13           :
165    JUL7                               :                 0.14           :
166    JUL7                            07:50         0.02   0.17         11:46
167    JUL7        1.87   2.02       16:52          0.10    0.25         14:29
168    JUL7        1.06   1.21       16:23          0.29    0.44           :
169    JUL7        0.46   0.61          :           0.64    0.79           :
170    JUL7        0.21   0.36          :           1.33    1.48           :
171    JUL7        0.06   0.21          :                                  :
172    JUL7        0.01   0.16          :                                  :
173    JUL7               0.14          :                                  :
174    JUL7               0.13          :                                  :
175    JUL7                              :                                  :
```

Summary

You have now finished this section and you should have a clear understanding of the following fx derivatives:

- Synthetic Agreements for Foreign Exchange (SAFEs)

- Currency Futures

- Currency Swap

- Currency Options – on Cash and on Futures

As a check on your understanding you should try the Quick Quiz Questions on the next page. You may also find the section Overview useful as a revision aid.

Your notes

Quick Quiz Questions

1. The Deutschmark futures contract size on the IMM is DEM 125,000. It is February and a US importer is expecting a payment of DEM 500,000 in five months time. What action can the importer take to lock in the US dollar value of his anticipated future payment?

   ❏ a) Sell DEM 500,000 five months forward
   ❏ b) Buy 5 June DEM futures contracts
   ❏ c) Sell 4 June DEM futures contracts
   ❏ d) Buy 4 June DEM futures contracts

2. An IMM Swiss Franc currency futures Bid price is quoted at 0.7000. What is this quote in spot FX terms?

   ❏ a) 1.4285
   ❏ b) 1.4286
   ❏ c) 1.4288
   ❏ d) 1.4289

3. The IMM Deutschmark currency futures contract has a trading unit of DEM 125,000. If the current quote is 0.6058, how many USD will the buyer pay for 5 contracts?

   ❏ a) $378.63
   ❏ b) $3,786.25
   ❏ c) $37,862.50
   ❏ d) $378,625.00

4. MegaBank's traders believe that the Japanese Yen is likely to appreciate against the British pound. What action can the traders take?

   ❏ a) Buy British pound/Yen futures
   ❏ b) Sell British pound/Yen futures
   ❏ c) Buy British pound futures and sell Yen futures
   ❏ d) Buy Yen futures and sell British pound futures

5. In February, MegaBank buys a GBP 1.6800 March Put option on the IMM at a cost of 1.5¢. The contract trading unit is £62,500. Which of the following statements is/are true?

   ❏ a) The strike price of the option is 1.5
   ❏ b) MegaBank has the right to buy GBP and sell USD at $1.6800
   ❏ c) MegaBank has the right to sell GBP and buy USD at $1.6800
   ❏ d) The expiry date of the option will be sometime in June

6. Using the information in Question 5, it is now the second week in March and the GBP/USD exchange rate is 1.6600. Which of the following is/are appropriate actions for MegaBank?

   ❏ a) Exercise the option
   ❏ b) Allow the option to expire
   ❏ c) Sell the option

7. You see details of a European style option. Which of the following statements describes this type of option correctly?

   ❑ a) The option can only be traded in Europe
   ❑ b) The option can only be exercised on its expiry date
   ❑ c) The option can be exercised at any time prior to and including its expiry date
   ❑ d) The option is subject to EU tax laws

8. The GBP 1.6800 September Put on PHLX is trading at 3.10. The trading unit for the contract is £31,250.

   a) How much premium should the buyer of 15 contracts pay?

   b) Where should GBP be trading at the expiry of this contract for the buyer to exercise the option?

   c) Where should GBP be trading at the expiry of this contract for the buyer to realise a net profit?

9. Which of the following statements concerning the seller of a Call option on currency is correct? The seller has:

   ❑ a) An obligation to deliver USD and receive currency
   ❑ b) An obligation to deliver currency and receive USD
   ❑ c) A right to deliver USD and receive currency
   ❑ d) A right to deliver currency and receive USD

10. Which of the following statements concerning the buyer of a USD Call/DEM Put option on currency is correct? The buyer has:

   ❑ a) An obligation to deliver USD and receive DEM
   ❑ b) An obligation to deliver DEM and receive USD
   ❑ c) A right to deliver USD and receive DEM
   ❑ d) A right to deliver DEM and receive USD

You can check your answers on page 321.

Overview

```
┌─────────────────────────┐
│     FX Derivatives      │
└─────────────────────────┘
```

Main Types

- **Synthetic Agreements for Foreign Exchange (SAFEs)**

Synthetic Agreements for Foreign Exchange (SAFEs) encompass foreign exchange agreements (FXAs), which are otherwise known as non-deliverable forwards (NDFs), and exchange rate agreements (ERAs).

A **foreign exchange agreement**, or **non-deliverable forward**, is a notional forward transaction in which the counter currency is not delivered at maturity, but the deal is instead cash-settled in the base currency. This is equivalent to an FX forward outright together with a reverse spot FX deal on the settlement date.

An **exchange rate agreement** is a notional forward/forward swap transaction in which the counter currency is not delivered on the settlement date, but the deal is instead cash-settled in the base currency. This is equivalent to a "forward" foreign exchange agreement (ie, spot becomes forward, and forward becomes forward forward).

Currency Futures

A **Currency Future** is an exchange-traded deliverable* FX forward with standard contract size and maturity date.

Currency futures are used to hedge currency risk in a similar way to FX forwards. There are two basic types:
- Currency futures against the USD
- Currency futures for cross rates — ie, two non-USD currencies

Currency Swaps

A **Currency Swap** involves the exchange of interest payments in one currency for those in another.

A currency swap is essentially a **simultaneous spot transaction followed by a series of FX forward transactions**.

Currency Options – on Cash & on Futures

A **currency option** is an agreement between two counterparties in which the option buyer pays the seller a premium for the right, but not the obligation, to buy or sell a specified quantity of a specified underlying instrument on or before an agreed date (the **expiry** or **maturity date**) at an agreed exchange rate, called the **strike price**.

Key Concepts:

- **Clearing House**

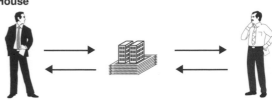

- **Options**

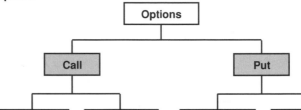

```
                    ┌──────────┐
                    │ Options  │
                    └──────────┘
              ┌───────────┴───────────┐
          ┌────────┐              ┌────────┐
          │  Call  │              │  Put   │
          └────────┘              └────────┘
```

Buyer/holder Long Call	Seller/writer Short Call	Buyer/holder Long Put	Seller/writer Short Put
Right but not obligation to: • **Buy** underlying instrument • At the **strike price** • If the call is **exercised**	**Obligation** to: • **Sell** underlying instrument • At the **strike price** • If the holder decides to **buy**	**Right** but not obligation to: • **Sell** underlying instrument • At the **strike price** • If the put is **exercised**	**Obligation** to: • **Buy** underlying instrument • At the **strike price** • If the holder decides to **sell**

- **Options – Trading Strategies**

Spot rate	Outcome
> 1.6200	Profit increases and is unlimited as spot rate rises
1.6200	Break-even point
1.6000 – 1.6200	Loss which decreases as spot increases
< 1.6000	Loss is limited to a maximum of the premium price

Spot rate	Outcome
> 1.6200	Loss increases as spot increases and is unlimited
1.6200	Break-even point
1.6200 – 1.6000	Profit increases as spot decreases
< 1.6000	Maximum profit is equal to the premium

Spot rate	Outcome
> 1.6000	Maximum loss is equal to the premium
1.6000 – 1.5800	Loss decreases as spot increases
1.5800	Break-even point
< 1.5800	Profit increases as spot decreases and is unlimited

Spot rate	Outcome
> 1.6000	Maximum profit is equal to the premium
1.6000 – 1.5800	Profit increases as spot increases
1.5800	Break-even point
< 1.5800	Loss increases as spot decreases and is unlimited

Quick Quiz Answers

Your notes

	✔ or ✘
1. c)	❏
2. b)	❏
3. d)	❏
4. d)	❏
5. c)	❏
6. a) and c)	❏
7. b)	❏
8. a) 31,250 x 15 x 0.031 = USD 14,531.25	❏
b) If price of spot falls below 1.6800	❏

8. c) Breakeven $\quad=\quad$ Strike – Premium   ❏
    $\quad\quad\quad\quad\quad=\quad$ 1.6800 – 0.031
    $\quad\quad\quad\quad\quad=\quad$ 1.6490

    To profit, spot needs to be below 1.6490   ❏

9. a)	❏
10. d)	❏

How well did you score? You should have managed to get most of these questions correct. If you didn't you may need to revise some of the materials.

Further Resources

Books

The Dictionary of Financial Risk Management
Gary Gastineau and Mark P Kritzman, Irwin Professional Publishing, 1996
ISBN   1 883 24914 7

Options, Futures, and Other Derivatives
John C. Hull, Prentice Hall Press, 1997
ISBN   0 138 87498 0

Swap & Derivative Financing: The Global Reference to Products, Pricing, Applications and Markets
Satyajit Das, Probus Pub Co. 1994
ISBN   1 557 38542 4

Option Pricing Mathematical Models & Computation
Paul Wilmott, Jeff DeWynne and Sam Bowison, American Educational Systems, 1997
ISBN   0 952 20820 2

McMillan on Options
Lawrence G. McMillan, John Wiley & Sons Inc., 1996
ISBN   0 471 11960 1

Understanding Options
Robert W. Kolb, John Wiley & Sons Inc., 1995
ISBN   0 471 08554 5

Understanding Swaps
John F. Marshall, John Wiley & Sons Inc., 1993
ISBN   0 471 30827 7

A Complete Guide to the Futures Markets: Fundamental Analysis, Technical Analysis, Trading, Spreads, and Options
Jack Schwager, John Wiley & Sons Inc., 1994
ISBN   0 471 89376 5

The Penguin International Dictionary of Finance
Graham Bannock & William Manser, Penguin, 2nd Edition, 1995
ISBN   0 140 51279 9

Investments
William F. Sharpe, Gordon J. Alexander & Jeffrey V. Bailey, Prentice Hall, 5th Edition, 1995
ISBN   0 131 83344 8

A–Z of International Finance
Stephen Mahony, FT/Pitman Publishing, 1997
ISBN   0 273 62552 7

Financial Derivatives
David Winstone, Chapman & Hall, 1st Edition, 1995
ISBN   0 412 62770 1

Booklets
Chicago Mercantile Exchange
• An Introduction to Futures and Options: Currency

Swiss Bank Corporation
• Financial Futures and Options
• Options: The fundamentals
  ISBN   0 964 11120 9

Chicago Board of Trade
• Financial Instruments Guide
• An Introduction to Options on Financial Futures
• Trading in Futures

London International Financial Futures and Options Exchange
• An Introduction
• Options: a guide to trading strategiesInternet Web sites

Internet Web sites
RFT Website
• **http://www.wiley-rft.reuters.com**
This is the series' companion website where additional quiz questions, updated screens and other information may be found.

Glossary Of Foreign Banking Terms

courtesy of Charles J. Kaplan, President of Equity Analytics, Ltd

This is a slightly edited version of the Equity Analytics Glossary of Foreign Banking Terms. The full version can be found on the internet at the URL address, http://www.e-analytics.com/glossary/glossar6.htm. The Publisher will not be responsible for any inaccuracies found in the glossary below. Queries should not be addressed to Equity Analytics, Ltd. At glossaries@equityanalytics.com.

A

B

Bank For International Settlements (BIS)
The BIS, located in Basle, Switzerland, was established in 1930 to administer the post-World War I reparations agreements. Since the 1960s, the BIS has evolved into an important international monetary institution, and has provided a forum in which central bankers meet and consult on a monthly basis. As an independent financial organization, the BIS performs a variety of banking, trustee, and agent functions, primarily with central banks. At present the BIS has 29 members, 28 of which are central banks. The Federal Reserve is represented at BIS meetings, but is not a member. The BIS is the only international financial institution in which most Eastern European countries are members. The Soviet Union, East Germany, and Albania, however, are not members.

C

Current Account Balance
The difference between the nation's total exports of goods, services, and transfers and its total imports of them. It excludes transactions in financial assets and liabilities.

D

E

Eurodollars
Deposits denominated in U.S. dollars at banks and other financial institutions outside the United States. Although this name originated because of the large amounts of such deposits held at banks in Western Europe, similar deposits in other parts of the world are also called Eurodollars.

F

Foreign Exchange Desk
The foreign exchange trading desk at the New York Federal Reserve Bank. The desk undertakes operations in the exchange markets for the account of the Federal Open Market Committee, and as agent for the U.S. Treasury and for foreign central banks.

Foreign Exchange Transactions
Purchase or sale of the currency of one nation with that of another. Foreign exchange rates refer to the number of units of one currency needed to purchase one unit of another, or the value of one currency in terms of another.

Glossary Of Foreign Banking Terms

G, H

I

International Banking Facility (IBF)
In general, these facilities can accept time deposits from foreign customers free of reserve requirements and interest rate limitations, and can lend to foreigners if the funds are for the conduct of foreign business outside of the U.S. Net borrowing from these facilities by domestic banking offices is subject to reserve requirements.

International Monetary Fund (IMF)
An international organization with 146 members, including the United States. The main functions of the International Monetary Fund are to lend funds to member nations to finance temporary balance of payments problems, to facilitate the expansion and balanced growth of international trade, and to promote international monetary cooperation among nations. The IMF also creates special drawing rights (SDR's), which provide member nations with a source of additional reserves. Member nations are required to subscribe to a Fund quota, paid mainly in their own currency. The IMF grew out of the Bretton Woods Conference of 1944.

J, K, L, M, N, O, P, Q, R

S

Special Drawing Rights (SDR's)
A type of international money created by the IMF and allocated to its member nations. SDRs are an international reserve asset, although they are only accounting entries (not actual coin or paper, and not backed by precious metal). Subject to certain conditions of the IMF, a nation that has a balance of payments deficit can use SDRs to settle debts to another nation or to the IMF.

Swap Arrangements
Short-term reciprocal lines of credit between the Federal Reserve and 14 foreign central banks as well as the Bank for International Settlements. Through a swap transaction, the Federal Reserve can, in effect, borrow foreign currency in order to purchase dollars in the foreign exchange market. In doing so, the demand for dollars is increased and the dollar's foreign exchange value is increased. Similarly, the Federal Reserve can temporarily provide dollars to foreign central banks through swap arrangements.

T

Trade Deficit
Refers to the amount by which merchandise imports exceed merchandise exports.

Directory of Futures & Options Exchanges

courtesy of Numa Financial Systems Ltd

The following directory is taken from the **Numa Directory of Futures & Options Exchanges** which can be found on the internet at the URL address, *http://www.numa.com/ref/exchange.htm*. The Publisher will not be responsible for any inaccuracies found in the listing below. Kindly address any queries Numa Financial Systems Ltd via their home page at *http//www.numa.com*.

Argentina

Buenos Aires Stock Exchange
(Bolsa de Comercio de Buenos Aires)
Sarmiento 299, Buenos Aires
Tel: +54 1 313 3334
Fax: +54 1 312 9332
Email : cau@sba.com.ar
URL: http://www.merval.sba.com.ar

Merfox
(Mercados de Futuros y Opciones SA)
Samiento 299, 4/460, Buenos Aires
Tel: +54 1 313 4522
Fax: +54 1 313 4472

Buenos Aires Cereal Exchange
(Bolsa de Cereales de Buenos Aires)
Avenida Corrientes 127, Buenos Aires
Tel: +54 1 311 9540
Fax: +54 1 311 9540
Email : bolcerc@datamarkets.com.ar

Buenos Aires Futures Market
(Mercado a Termino de Buenos Aires SA)
Bouchard 454, 5to Piso, Buenos Aires
Tel: +54 1 311 47 16
Fax: +54 1 312 47 16

Rosario Futures Exchange
(Mercado a Termino de Rosario)
Cordoba 1402, Pcia Santa Fe, Rosario
Tel: +54 41 21 50 93
Fax: +54 41 21 50 97
Email : termino@bcr.com.ar

Rosario Stock Exchange
(Mercado de Valores de Rosario SA)
Cordoba Esquina Corrientes, Pcia Santa Fe, Rosario
Tel: +54 41 21 34 70
Fax: +54 41 24 10 19
Email : titulos@bcr.com.ar

Rosario Board of Trade
(Bolsa de Comercio de Rosario)
Cordoba 1402, Pcia Santa Fe, Rosario
Tel: +54 41 21 50 93
Fax: +54 41 21 50 97
Email : titulos@bcr.com.ar

La Plata Stock Exchange
(Bolsa de Comercio de La Plata)
Calle 48, No. 515, 1900 La Plata, Buenos Aires
Tel: +54 21 21 47 73
Fax: +54 21 25 50 33

Mendoza Stock Exchange
(Bolsa de Comercio de Mendoza)
Paseo Sarmiento 199, Mendoza
Tel: +54 61 20 23 59
Fax: +54 61 20 40 50

Cordoba Stock Exchange
(Bolsa de Comercio de Cordoba)
Rosario de Santa Fe 231, 1 Piso, Cordoba
Tel: +54 51 22 4230
Fax: +54 51 22 6550
Email : bolsacba@nt.com.ar

Mercado Abierto Electronico SA
(Mercado Abierto Electronico SA)
25 de Mayo 565, 4 Piso, Buenos Aires
Tel: +54 1 312 8060
Fax: +54 1 313 1445

Armenia

Yerevan Stock Exchange
22 Sarian Street, Yerevan Centre
Tel: +374 2 525 801
Fax: +374 2 151 548

Australia

Australian Stock Exchange
Exchange Centre, 20 Bond Street, Sydney
Tel: +61 29 227 0000
Fax: +61 29 235 0056
Email : info@asx.com.au
URL: http://www.asx.com.au

Sydney Futures Exchange
SFE
30-32 Grosvenor Street, Sydney
Tel: +61 29 256 0555
Fax: +61 29 256 0666
Email : sfe@hutch.com.au
URL: http://www.sfe.com.au

Austria

Austrian Futures & Options Exchange
(Osterreichische Termin Und Optionenborse)
OTOB
Strauchgasse 1-3, PO Box 192, Vienna
Tel: +43 1 531 65 0
Fax: +43 1 532 97 40
Email : contactperson@otob.ada.at
URL: http://www.wtab.at

Vienna Stock Exchange
(Wiener Borse)
Wipplingerstrasse 34, Vienna
Tel: +43 1 53 499
Fax: +43 1 535 68 57
Email : communications@vienna-stock-exchange.at
URL: http://www.wtab.at

Bahrain

Bahrain Stock Exchange
P.O. Box 3203, Manama
Tel: +973 261260
Fax: +973 256362
Email : bse@bahrainstock.com
URL: http://www.bahrainstock.com

Bangladesh

Dhaka Stock Exchange
Stock Exchange Building, 9E & 9F, Motijheel C/A, Dhaka
Tel: +880 2 956 4601
Fax: +880 2 956 4727
Email : info@dse.bdnet.net

Barbados

Securities Exchange of Barbados
5th Floor, Central Bank Building, Church Village, St Michael
Tel: +1809/1246 246 436 9871
Fax: +1809/1246 246 429 8942
Email : sebd@caribf.com

Belgium

Brussels Stock Exchange
(Societe de la Bourse de Valeurs Mobilieres de Bruxelles)
Palais de la Bourse, Brussels
Tel: +32 2 509 12 11
Fax: +32 2 509 12 12
Email : dan.maerten@pophost.eunet.be
URL: http://www.stockexchange.be

European Association of Securities Dealers Automated Quotation
EASDAQ
Rue des Colonies, 56 box 15, 1000 Brussels
Tel: +32 2 227 6520
Fax: +32 2 227 6567
Email : easdaq@tornado.be
URL: http://www.easdaq.be/

Belgian Futures & Options Exchange
BELFOX
Palais dc la Bourse, Rue Henri Mausstraat, 2,, Brussels
Tel: +32 2 512 80 40
Fax: +32 2 513 83 42
Email : marketing@belfox.be
URL: http://www.belfox.be

Antwerp Stock Exchange
(Effectenbeurs van Antwerpen)
Korte Klarenstraat 1, Antwerp
Tel: +32 3 233 80 16
Fax: +32 3 232 57 37

Bermuda

Bermuda Stock Exchange
BSE
Email : info@bse.com
URL: http://www.bsx.com

Bolivia

Bolivian Stock Exchange
(Bolsa Boliviana de Valores SA)
Av. 16 de Julio No 1525, Edif Mutual La Paz, 3er Piso, Casillia 12521,
La Paz
Tel: +591 2 39 29 11
Fax: +591 2 35 23 08
Email : bbvsalp@wara.bolnet.bo
URL: http://bolsa-valores-bolivia.com

Botswana

Botswana Stock Exchange
5th Floor, Barclays House, Khama Crescent, Gaborone
Tel: +267 357900
Fax: +267 357901
Email : bse@info.bw

Brazil

Far-South Stock Exchange
(Bolsa de Valores do Extremo Sul)
Rua dos Andradas, 1234-8 Andar, Porte Alegre
Tel: +55 51 224 3600
Fax: +55 51 227 4359

Santos Stock Exchange
(Bolsa de Valores de Santos)
Rua XV de Novembro, 111, Santos
Tel: +55 132 191 5119
Fax: +55 132 19 1800

Regional Stock Exchange
(Bolsa de Valores regional)
Avenida Dom Manuel, 1020, Fortaleza
Tel: +55 85 231 6466
Fax: +55 85 231 6888

Parana Stock Exchange
(Bolsa de Valores do Parana)
Rua Marechal Deodoro, 344-6 Andar, Curitiba
Tel: +55 41 222 5191
Fax: +55 41 223 6203

Minas, Espirito Santo, Brasilia Stock Exchange
(Blsa de Valores Minas, Espirito Santo, Brasilia)
Rua dos Carijos, 126-3 Andar, Belo Horizonte
Tel: +55 31 219 9000
Fax: +55 21 273 1202

Rio de Janeiro Stock Exchange
(Bolsa de Valores de Rio de Janeiro)
Praca XV de Novembro No 20, Rio de Janeiro
Tel: +55 21 271 1001
Fax: +55 21 221 2151
Email : info@bvrj.com.br
URL: http://www.bvrj.com.br

Sao Paolo Stock Exchange
(Bolsa de Valores de Sao Paolo)
Rua XV de Novembro 275, Sao Paolo
Tel: +55 11 233 2000
Fax: +55 11 233 2099
Email : bovespa@bovespa.com.br
URL: http://www.bovespa.com.br

Bahia, Sergipe, Alagoas Stock Exchange
(Bolsa de Valores Bahia, Sergipe, Alagoas)
Rua Conselheiro Dantas, 29-Comercio, Salvador
Tel: +55 71 242 3844
Fax: +55 71 242 5753

Brazilian Futures Exchange
(Bolsa Brasileira de Futuros)
Praca XV de Novembro, 20, 5th Floor, Rio de Janeiro
Tel: +55 21 271 1086
Fax: +55 21 224 5718
Email : bbf@bbf.com.br

The Commodities & Futures Exchange
(Bolsa de Mercadoris & Futuros)
BM&F
Praca Antonio Prado, 48, Sao Paulo
Tel: +55 11 232 5454
Fax: +55 11 239 3531
Email : webmaster@bmf.com.br
URL: http://www.bmf.com.br

Pernambuco and Paraiba Stock Exchange
(Bolsa de Valores de Pernambuco e Paraiba)
Avenida Alfredo Lisboa, 505, Recife
Tel: +55 81 224 8277
Fax: +55 81 224 8412

Bulgaria

Bulgarian Stock Exchange
1 Macedonia Square, Sofia
Tel: +359 2 81 57 11
Fax: +359 2 87 55 66
Email : bse@bg400.bg
URL: http://www.online.bg/bse

Canada

Montreal Exchange
(Bourse de Montreal)
ME
The Stock Exchange Tower, 800 Square Victoria, C.P. 61, Montreal
Tel: +1 514 871 2424
Fax: +1 514 871 3531
Email : info@me.org
URL: http://www.me.org

Vancouver Stock Exchange
VSE
Stock Exchange Tower, 609 Granville Street, Vancouver
Tel: +1 604 689 3334
Fax: +1 604 688 6051
Email : information@vse.ca
URL: http://www.vse.ca

Winnipeg Stock Exchange
620 - One Lombard Place, Winnipeg
Tel: +1 204 987 7070
Fax: +1 204 987 7079
Email : vcatalan@io.uwinnipef.ca

Alberta Stock Exchange
21st Floor, 300 Fifth Avenue SW, Calgary
Tel: +1 403 974 7400
Fax: +1 403 237 0450

Toronto Stock Exchange
TSE
The Exchange Tower, 2 First Canadian Place, Toronto
Tel: +1 416 947 4700
Fax: +1 416 947 4662
Email : skee@tse.com
URL: http://www.tse.com

Winnipeg Commodity Exchange
WCE
500 Commodity Exchange Tower, 360 Main St., Winnipeg
Tel: +1 204 925 5000
Fax: +1 204 943 5448
Email : wce@wce.mb.ca
URL: http://www.wce.mb.ca

Toronto Futures Exchange
TFE
The Exchange Tower, 2 First Canadian Place, Toronto
Tel: +1 416 947 4487
Fax: +1 416 947 4272

Cayman Islands

Cayman Islands Stock Exchange
CSX
4th Floor, Elizabethan Square, P.O Box 2408 G.T., Grand Cayman
Tel: +1345 945 6060
Fax: +1345 945 6061
Email : CSX@CSX.COM.KY
URL: http://www.csx.com.ky/

Chile

Santiago Stock Exchange
(Bolsa de Comercio de Santiago)
La Bolsa 64, Casilla 123-D, Santiago
Tel: +56 2 698 2001
Fax: +56 2 672 8046
Email : ahucke@comercio.bolsantiago.cl
URL: http://www.bolsantiago.cl

Bolsa Electronica de Chile
Huerfanos 770, Piso 14, Santiago
Tel: +56 2 639 4699
Fax: +56 2 639 9015
Email : info@bolchile.cl
URL: http://www.bolchile.cl

China

Wuhan Securities Exchange Centre
WSEC
2nd Floor, Jianghchen Hotel, Wuhan
Tel: +86 27 588 4115
Fax: +86 27 588 6038

China Zhengzhou Commodity Exchange
CZCE
20 Huanyuan Road, Zhengzhou
Tel: +86 371 594 44 54
Fax: +86 371 554 54 24

Shanghai Cereals and Oils Exchange
199 Shangcheng Road, Pudong New District, Shanghai
Tel: +86 21 5831 1111
Fax: +86 21 5831 9308
Email : liangzhu@public.sta.net.cn

China -Commodity Futures Exchange, Inc of Hainan
CCFE
Huaneng Building, 36 Datong Road, Haikou, Hainan Province
Tel: +86 898 670 01 07
Fax: +86 898 670 00 99
Email : ccfehn@public.hk.hq.cn

Guandong United Futures Exchange
JingXing Hotel, 91 LinHe West Road, Guangzhou
Tel: +86 20 8755 2109
Fax: +86 20 8755 1654

Shenzhen Mercantile Exchange
1/F Bock B, Zhongjian Overseas Decoration , Hua Fu Road, Shenzhen
Tel: +86 755 3343 502
Fax: +86 755 3343 505

Shanghai Stock Exchange
15 Huang Pu Road, Shanghai
Tel: +86 216 306 8888
Fax: +86 216 306 3076

Beijing Commodity Exchange
BCE
311 Chenyun Building, No. 8 Beichen East Road, Chaoyang District, Beijing
Tel: +86 1 492 4956
Fax: +86 1 499 3365
Email : sunli@intra.cnfm.co.cn

Shenzhen Stock Exchange
203 Shangbu Industrial Area, Shenzhen
Tel: +86 755 320 3431
Fax: +86 755 320 3505

Colombia

Bogota Stock Exchange
BSE
Carrera 8, No. 13-82 Pisos 4-9, Apartado Aereo 3584, Santafe de Bogota
Tel: +57 243 6501
Fax: +57 281 3170
Email : bolbogot@bolsabogota.com.co
URL: http://www.bolsabogota.com.co

Medellin Stock Exchange
(Bolsa de Medellin SA)
Apartado Aereo 3535, Medellin
Tel: +57 4 260 3000
Fax: +57 4 251 1981
Email : 104551.1310@compuserve.com

Occidente Stock Exchange
(Bolsa de Occidente SA)
Calle 10, No. 4-40 Piso 13, Cali
Tel: +57 28 817 022
Fax: +57 28 816 720
Email : bolsaocc@cali.cetcol.net.co
URL: http://www.bolsadeoccidente.com.co

Costa Rica

National Stock Exchange
(Bolsa Nacional de Valores, SA)
BNV
Calle Central, Avenida 1, San Jose
Tel: +506 256 1180
Fax: +506 255 0131

Cote D'Ivoire (Ivory Coast)

Abidjan Stock Exchange
(Bourse des Valeurs d'Abidjan)
Avenue Marchand, BP 1878 01, Abidjan 01
Tel: +225 21 57 83
Fax: +225 22 16 57

Croatia (Hrvatska)

Zagreb Stock Exchange
(Zagrebacka Burza)
Ksaver 208, Zagreb
Tel: +385 1 428 455
Fax: +385 1 420 293
Email : zeljko.kardum@zse.hr
URL: http://www.zse.hr

Cyprus

Cyprus Stock Exchange
CSE
54 Griva Dhigeni Avenue, Silvex House, Nicosia
Tel: +357 2 368 782
Fax: +357 2 368 790
Email : cyse@zenon.logos.cy.net

Czech Republic

Prague Stock Exchange
PSE
Rybna 14, Prague 1
Tel: +42 2 2183 2116
Fax: +42 2 2183 3040
Email : marketing@psc.vol.cz
URL: http://www.pse.cz

Denmark

Copenhagen Stock Exchange & FUTOP
(Kobenhavns Fondsbors)
Nikolaj Plads 6, PO Box 1040, Copenhagen K
Tel: +45 33 93 33 66
Fax: +45 33 12 86 13
Email : kfpost@xcse.dk
URL: http://www.xcse.dk

Ecuador

Quito Stock Exchange
(Bolsa de Valores de Quito CC)
Av Amazonas 540 y Carrion, 8vo Piso
Tel: +593 2 526 805
Fax: +593 2 500 942
Email : bovalqui@ecnet.ec
URL: http://www.ccbvq.com

Guayaquil Stock Exchange
(Bolsa de Valores de Guayaquil, CC)
Av. 9 de Octubre, 110 y Pinchina, Guayaquil
Tel: +593 4 561 519
Fax: +593 4 561 871
Email : bvg@bvg.fin.ec
URL: http://www.bvg.fin.ec

Egypt

Alexandria Stock Exchange
11 Talaat Harp Street, Alexandria
Tel: +20 3 483 7966
Fax: +20 3 482 3039

Cairo Stock Exchange
4(A) El Cherifeen Street, Cairo
Tel: +20 2 392 1402
Fax: +20 2 392 8526

El Salvador

El Salvador Stock Exchange
(Mercado de Valores de El Salvador, SA de CV)
6 Piso, Edificio La Centroamericana, Alameda Roosevelt No 3107,
San Salvador
Tel: +503 298 4244
Fax: +503 223 2898
Email : ggbolsa@gbm.net

Estonia

Tallinn Stock Exchange
Ravala 6, Tallinn
Tel: +372 64 08 840
Fax: +372 64 08 801
Email : tse@depo.ee
URL: http://www.tse.ee

Finland

Helsinki Stock Exchange
HSE
Fabianinkatu 14, Helsinki
Tel: +358 9 173 301
Fax: +358 9 173 30399
Email : mika.bjorklund@hex.fi
URL: http://www.hse.fi

Finnish Options Exchange
(Suomen Optioporssi Oy)
FOEX
Erottajankatu 11, Helsinki
Tel: +358 9 680 3410
Fax: +358 9 604 442
Email : info@foex.fi
URL: http://www.foex.fi

Finnish Options Market
SOM
Keskuskatu 7, Helsinki
Tel: +358 9 13 1211
Fax: +358 9 13 121211
Email : webmaster@hex.fi
URL: http://www.som.fi

France

Paris Stock Exchange
(Bourse de Paris)
39 rue Cambon, Paris
Tel: +33 1 49 27 10 00
Fax: +33 1 49 27 13 71
Email : 100432.201@compuserve.com

MONEP
(Marche des Options Negociables de Paris)
MONEP
39, rue Cambon, Paris
Tel: +33 1 49 27 18 00
Fax: +33 1 9 27 18 23
URL: http://www.monep.fr

MATIF
(Marche a Terme International de France)
MATIF
176 rue Montmartre, Paris
Tel: +33 33 1 40 28 82 82
Fax: +33 33 1 40 28 80 01
Email : larrede@matif.fr
URL: http://www.matif.fr

Germany

Stuttgart Stock Exchange
(Baden-Wurttembergische Wertpapierborse zu Stuttgart)
Konigstrasse 28, Stuttgart
Tel: +49 7 11 29 01 83
Fax: +49 7 11 22 68 11 9

Hanover Stock Exchange
(Niedersachsische Borse zu Hanover)
Rathenaustrasse 2, Hanover
Tel: +49 5 11 32 76 61
Fax: +49 5 11 32 49 15

Dusseldorf Stock Exchange
(Rheinisch-Westfalische Borse zu Dusseldorf)
Ernst-Schneider-Platz 1, Dusseldorf
Tel: +49 2 11 13 89 0
Fax: +49 2 11 13 32 87

Berlin Stock Exchange
(Berliner Wertpapierborse)
Fasanenstrasse 85, Berlin
Tel: +49 30 31 10 91 0
Fax: +49 30 31 10 91 79

German Stock Exchange
(Deutsche Borse AG)
FWB
Borsenplatz 4, Frankfurt-am-Main
Tel: +49 69 21 01 0
Fax: +49 69 21 01 2005
URL: http://www.exchange.de

Hamburg Stock Exchange
(Hanseatische Wertpapierborse Hamburg)
Schauenburgerstrasse 49, Hamburg
Tel: +49 40 36 13 02 0
Fax: +49 40 36 13 02 23
Email : wertpapierboerse.hamburg@t-online.de

Deutsche Terminborse
DTB
Boersenplatz 4, Frankfurt-am-Main
Tel: +49 69 21 01 0
Fax: +49 69 21 01 2005
URL: http://www.exchange.de

Bavarian Stock Exchange
(Bayerische Borse)
Lenbachplatz 2(A), Munich
Tel: +49 89 54 90 45 0
Fax: +49 89 54 90 45 32
Email : bayboerse@t-online.de
URL: http://www.bayerischeboerse.de

Bremen Stock Exchange
(Bremer Wertpapierborse)
Obernstrasse 2-12, Bremen
Tel: +49 4 21 32 12 82
Fax: +49 4 21 32 31 23

Ghana

Ghana Stock Exchange
5th Floor, Cedi House, Liberia Road, PO Box 1849, Accra
Tel: +233 21 669 908
Fax: +233 21 669 913
Email : stockex@ncs.com.gh
URL: http://ourworld.compuserve.com/homepages/khaganu/
stockex.htm

Greece

Athens Stock Exchange
ASE
10 Sophocleous Street, Athens
Tel: +30 1 32 10 424
Fax: +30 1 32 13 938
Email : mailto:aik@hol.gr
URL: http://www.ase.gr

Honduras

Honduran Stock Exchange
(Bolsa Hondurena de Valores, SA)
1er Piso Edificio Martinez Val, 3a Ave 2a Calle SO, San Pedro Sula
Tel: +504 53 44 10
Fax: +504 53 44 80
Email : bhvsps@simon.intertel.hn

Hong Kong

Hong Kong Futures Exchange Ltd
HKFE
5/F, Asia Pacific Finance Tower, Citibank Plaza, 3 Garden Road
Tel: +852 2842 9333
Fax: +852 2810 5089
Email : prm@hfke.com
URL: http://www.hkfe.com

Hong Kong Stock Exchange
SEHK
1st Floor, One and Two Exchange Square, Central
Tel: +852 2522 1122
Fax: +852 2810 4475
Email : info@sehk.com.hk
URL: http://www.sehk.com.hk

Chinese Gold and Silver Exchange Society
Gold and Silver Commercial Bui, 12-18 Mercer Street
Tel: +852 544 1945
Fax: +852 854 0869

Hungary

Budapest Stock Exchange
Deak Ferenc utca 5, Budapest
Tel: +36 1 117 5226
Fax: +36 1 118 1737
URL: http://www.fornax.hu/fmon

Budapest Commodity Exchange
BCE
POB 495, Budapest
Tel: +36 1 269 8571
Fax: +36 1 269 8575
Email : bce@bce-bat.com
URL: http://www.bce-bat.com

Iceland

Iceland Stock Exchange
Kalkofnsvegur 1, Reykjavik
Tel: +354 569 9775
Fax: +354 569 9777
Email : gw@vi.is

India

Cochin Stock Exchange
38/1431 Kaloor Road Extension, PO Box 3529, Emakulam, Cochin
Tel: +91 484 369 020
Fax: +91 484 370 471

Bangalore Stock Exchange
Stock Exchange Towers, 51, 1st Cross, JC Road, Bangalore
Tel: +91 80 299 5234
Fax: +91 80 22 55 48

The OTC Exchange of India
OTCEI
92 Maker Towers F, Cuffe Parade, Bombay
Tel: +91 22 21 88 164
Fax: +91 22 21 88 012
Email : otc.otcindia@gems.vsnl.net.in

Jaipur Stock Exchange
Rajasthan Chamber Bhawan, MI Road, Jaipur
Tel: +91 141 56 49 62
Fax: +91 141 56 35 17

The Stock Exchange ñ Ahmedabad
Kamdhenu Complex, Ambawadi, Ahmedabad
Tel: +91 79 644 67 33
Fax: +91 79 21 40 117
Email : supvsr@08asxe

Delhi Stock Exchange
3&4/4B Asaf Ali Road, New Delhi
Tel: +91 11 327 90 00
Fax: +91 11 327 13 02

Madhya Pradesh Stock Exchange
3rd Floor, Rajani Bhawan, Opp High Court, MG Road, Indore
Tel: +91 731 432 841
Fax: +91 731 432 849

Magadh Stock Exchange
Industry House, Suinha Library Road,
Patna
Tel: +91 612 223 644

Pune Stock Exchange
Shivleela Chambers, 752 Sadashiv Peth, Kumethekar Road, Pune
Tel: +91 212 441 679

The Stock Exchange, Mumbai
Phiroze Jeejeebhoy Towers, Dalal Street, Bombay
Tel: +91 22 265 5860
Fax: +91 22 265 8121
URL: http://www.nseindia.com

Uttar Pradesh Stock Exchange
Padam Towers, 14/113 Civil Lines, Kanpur
Tel: +91 512 293 115
Fax: +91 512 293 175

Bhubaneswar Stock Exchange Association
A-22 Falcon House, Jharapara, Cuttack Road, Bhubaneswar
Tel: +91 674 482 340
Fax: +91 674 482 283

Calcutta Stock Exchange
7 Lyons Range, Calcutta
Tel: +91 33 209 366

Coimbatore Stock Exchange
Chamber Towers, 8/732 Avanashi Road, Coimbatore
Tel: +91 422 215 100
Fax: +91 422 213 947

Madras Stock Exchange
Exchange Building, PO Box 183, 11 Second Line Beach, Madras
Tel: +91 44 510 845
Fax: +91 44 524 4897

Ludhiana Stock Exchange
Lajpat Rai Market, Near Clock Tower, Ludhiana
Tel: +91 161 39318

Kanara Stock Exchange
4th Floor, Ranbhavan Complex, Koialbail, Mangalore
Tel: +91 824 32606

Hyderabad Stock Exchange
3-6-275 Himayatnagar, Hyderabad
Tel: +91 842 23 1985

Gauhati Stock Exchange
Saraf Building, Annex, AT Road, Gauhati
Tel: +91 361 336 67
Fax: +91 361 543 272

Indonesia

Jakarta Stock Exchange
(PT Bursa Efek Jakarta)
Jakarta Stock Exchange Building, 13th Floor, JI Jenderal Sudiman,
Kav 52-53, Jakarta
Tel: +62 21 515 0515
Fax: +62 21 515 0330
Email : webmaster@jsx.co.id
URL: http://www.jsx.co.id

Surabaya Stock Exchange
(PT Bursa Efek Surabaya)
5th Floor, Gedung Madan Pemuda, 27-31 Jalan Pemuda, Surabaya
Tel: +62 21 526 6210
Fax: +62 21 526 6219
Email : heslpdesk@bes.co.id
URL: http://www.bes.co.id

Indonesian Commodity Exchange Board
(Badan Pelaksana Bursa Komoditi)
Gedung Bursa, Jalan Medan Merdeka Selatan 14, 4th Floor, Jakarta Pusat
Tel: +62 21 344 1921
Fax: +62 21 3480 4426

Capital Market Supervisory Agency
(Baden Pelaksana Pasar Modal)
BAPEPAM
Jakarta Stock Exchange Building, 13th Floor, JI Jenderal Sudiman, Kav 52-53, Jakarta
Tel: +62 21 515 1288
Fax: +62 21 515 1283
Email : bapepam@indoexchange.com
URL: http://www.indoexchange.com/bapepam

Iran

Tehran Stock Exchange
228 Hafez Avenue, Tehran
Tel: +98 21 670 309
Fax: +98 21 672 524
Email : stock@neda.net
URL: http://www.neda.net/tse

Ireland

Irish Stock Exchange
28 Anglesea Street, Dublin 2
Tel: +353 1 677 8808
Fax: +353 1 677 6045

Irish Futures & Options Exchange
IFOX
Segrave House, Earlsfort Terrace, Dublin 2
Tel: +353 1 676 7413
Fax: +353 1 661 4645

Israel

Tel Aviv Stock Exchange Ltd
TASE
54 Ahad Haam Street, Tel Aviv
Tel: +972 3 567 7411
Fax: +972 3 510 5379
Email : etti@tase.co.il
URL: http://www.tase.co.il

Italy

Italian Financial Futures Market
(Mercato Italiano Futures)
MIF
Piazza del Gesu' 49, Rome
Tel: +39 6 676 7514
Fax: +39 6 676 7250

Italian Stock Exchange
(Consiglio de Borsa)
Piazza degli Affari, 6, Milan
Tel: +39 2 724 261
Fax: +39 2 864 64 323
Email : postoffice@borsaitalia.it
URL: http://www.borsaitalia.it

Italian Derivatives Market
IDEM
Piazza Affari 6, Milan
Tel: +39 2 72 42 61
Fax: +39 2 72 00 43 33
Email : postoffice@borsaitalia.it
URL: http://www.borsaitalia.it

Jamaica

Jamaica Stock Exchange
40 Harbour Street, PO Box 1084, Kingston
Tel: +1809 809 922 0806
Fax: +1809 809 922 6966
Email : jse@infochan.com
URL: http://www.jamstockex.com

Japan

Tokyo Commodity Exchange
(Tokyo Kogyoin Torihikijo)
TOCOM
10-8 Nihonbashi, Horidome-cho, Chuo-ku, 1-chome, Tokyo
Tel: +81 3 3661 9191
Fax: +81 3 3661 7568

Japan Securities Dealing Association
(Nihon Shokengyo Kyokai)
Tojyo Shoken Building, 5-8 Kayaba-cho, 1-chome, Nihonbashi, Tokyo
Tel: +81 3 3667 8451
Fax: +81 3 3666 8009

Osaka Textile Exchange
(Osaka Seni Torihikijo)
2-5-28 Kyutaro-machi, Chuo-ku, Osaka
Tel: +81 6 253 0031
Fax: +81 6 253 0034

Tokyo Stock Exchange
(Tokyo Shoken Torihikijo)
TSE
2-1 Nihombashi-Kabuto-Cho, Chuo-ku, Tokyo
Tel: +81 3 3666 0141
Fax: +81 3 3663 0625
URL: http://www.tse.or.jp

Kobe Raw Silk Exchange
(Kobe Kiito Torihiksho)
KSE
126 Higashimachi, Chuo-ku, Kobe
Tel: +81 78 331 7141
Fax: +81 78 331 7145

Kobe Rubber Exchange
(Kobe Gomu Torihiksho)
KRE
49 Harima-cho, Chuo-ku, Kobe
Tel: +81 78 331 4211
Fax: +81 78 332 1622

Nagoya Stock Exchange
(Nagoya Shoken Torihikijo)
NSE
3-17 Sakae, 3-chome, Naka-ku, Nagoya
Tel: +81 81 52 262 3172
Fax: +81 81 52 241 1527
Email : nse@po.iijnet.or.jp
URL: http://www.iijnet.or.jp/nse-jp/

Nagoya Textile Exchange
2-15 Nishiki 3 Chome, Naka-ku, Naka-ku, Nagoya
Tel: +81 52 951 2171
Fax: +81 52 961 6407

Osaka Securities Exchange
(Osaka Shoken Torihikijo)
OSE
8-l6, Kitahama, 1-chome, Chuo-ku, Osaka
Tel: +81 6 229 8643
Fax: +81 6 231 2639
Email : osakaexc@po.iijnet.or.jp
URL: http://www.ose.or.jp

Tokyo Grain Exchange
(Tokyo Kokumotsu Shohin Torihikijo)
TGE
1-12-5 Nihonbashi, Kakigara-cho, 1-Chome, Chuo-ku, Tokyo
Tel: +81 3 3668 9321
Fax: +81 3 3661 4564
Email : webmas@tge.or.jp
URL: http://www.tge.or.jp

Tokyo International Financial Futures Exchange
TIFFE
1-3-1 Marunouchi, Chiyoda-ku, Tokyo
Tel: +81 3 5223 2400
Fax: +81 3 5223 2450
URL: http://www.tiffe.or.jp

Hiroshima Stock Exchange
KANEX
14-18 Kanayama-cho, Naka-ku, Hiroshima
Tel: +81 82 541 1121
Fax: +81 82 541 1128

Fukuoka Stock Exchange
KANEX
2-14-2 Tenjin, Chuo-ku, Fukuoka
Tel: +81 92 741 8231
Fax: +81 92 713 1540

Niigata Securities Exchange
(Niigata Shoken Torihikijo)
1245 Hachiban-cho, Kamiokawame-don, Niigata
Tel: +81 25 222 4181
Fax: +81 25 222 4551

Sapporo Securities Exchange
(Sapporo Shoken Torihikijo)
5-14-1 Nishi-minami, I-jo, Chuo-ku, Sapporo
Tel: +81 11 241 6171
Fax: +81 11 251 0840

Kammon Commodity Exchange
(Kammon Shohin Torihikijo)
1-5 Nabe-cho, Shimonoseki
Tel: +81 832 31 1313
Fax: +81 832 23 1947

Kyoto Stock Exchange
KANEX
66 Tachiurinishi-machi, Higashinotoin-higashiiru, Shijo-dori, Shimogyo-ku, Kyoto
Tel: +81 75 221 1171
Fax: +81 75 221 8356

Maebashi Dried Cocoa Exchange
(Maebashi Kanken Torihikijo)
1-49-1 Furuichi-machi, Maebashi
Tel: +81 272 52 1401
Fax: +81 272 51 8270

Cubu Commodity Exchange
3-2-15 Nishiki, Naka-ku, Nagoya
Tel: +81 52 951 2170
Fax: +81 52 961 1044

Yokohama Raw Silk Exchange
(Yokohama Kiito Torihikijo)
Silk Centre, 1 Yamashita-cho, Naka-ku, Yokohama
Tel: +81 45 641 1341
Fax: +81 45 641 1346

Kansai Agricultural Commodities Exchange
KANEX
1-10-14 Awaza, Nishi-ku, Osaka
Tel: +81 6 531 7931
Fax: +81 6 541 9343
Email : kex-1@kanex.or.jp
URL: http://www.kanex.or.jp

Jordan

Amman Financial Market
PO Box 8802, Ammam
Tel: +962 6 607171
Fax: +962 6 686830
Email : afm@go.com.jo
URL: http://accessme.com/AFM/

Kenya

Nairobi Stock Exchange
PO Box 43633, Nairobi
Tel: +254 2 230692
Fax: +254 2 224200
Email : nse@acc.or.ke

Korea (South)

Korea Stock Exchange
KSE
33 Yoido-dong, Youngdeungpo-gu, Seoul
Tel: +82 2 3774 9000
Fax: +82 2 786 0263
Email : world@www.kse.or.kr
URL: http://www.kse.or.kr

Kuwait

Kuwait Stock Exchange
PO Box 22235, Safat, Kuwait
Tel: +965 242 3130
Fax: +965 242 0779

Latvia

Riga Stock Exchange
Doma Iaukums 6, Riga
Tel: + 7 212 431
Fax: + 7 229 411
Email : rfb@mail.bkc.lv
URL: http://www.rfb.lv

Lithuania

National Stock Exchange of Lithuania
Ukmerges St 41, Vilnius
Tel: +370 2 72 14 07
Fax: +370 2 742 894
Email : office@nse.lt
URL: http://www.nse.lt

Luxembourg

Luxembourg Stock Exchange
(Societe Anonyme de la Bourse de Luxembourg)
11 Avenue de la Porte-Neuve
Tel: +352 47 79 36-1
Fax: +352 47 32 98
Email : info@bourse.lu
URL: http://www.bourse.lu

Macedonia

Macedonia Stock Exchange
MSE
Tel: +389 91 122 055
Fax: +389 91 122 069
Email : mse@unet.com.mk
URL: http://www.mse.org.mk

Malaysia

Kuala Lumpur Commodity Exchange
KLCE
4th Floor, Citypoint, Komplex Dayabumi, Jalan Sulta Hishamuddin,
Kuala Lumpur
Tel: +60 3 293 6822
Fax: +60 3 274 2215
Email : klce@po.jaring.my
URL: http://www.klce.com.my

Kuala Lumpur Stock Exchange
KLSE
4th Floor, Exchange Square, Off Jalan Semantan, Damansara
Heights, Kuala Lumpur
Tel: +60 3 254 64 33
Fax: +60 3 255 74 63
Email : webmaster@klse.com.my
URL: http://www.klse.com.my

The Kuala Lumpur Options & Financial Futures Exchange
KLOFFE
10th Floor, Wisma Chase Perdana, Damansara Heights, Jalan
Semantan, Kuala Lumpur
Tel: +60 3 253 8199
Fax: +60 3 255 3207
Email : kloffe@kloffe.com.my
URL: http://www.kloffe.com.my

Malaysia Monetary Exchange BHD
4th Floor, City Point, PO Box 11260, Dayabumi Complex, Jalan
Sultan Hishmuddin, Kuala Lumpur
Email : mme@po.jaring.my
URL: http://www.jaring.my/mme

Malta

Malta Stock Exchange
27 Pietro Floriani Street, Floriana, Valletta 14
Tel: +356 244 0515
Fax: +356 244 071
Email : borza@maltanet.omnes.net

Mauritius

Mauritius Stock Exchange
Stock Exchange Commission, 9th Floor, SICOM Building, Sir
Celicourt Anselme Street, Port Louis
Tel: +230 208 8735
Fax: +230 208 8676
Email : svtradha@intnet.mu
URL: http://lynx.intnet.mu/sem/

Mexico

Mexican Stock Exchange
(Bolsa Mexicana de Valores, SA de CV)
Paseo de la Reforma 255, Colonia Cuauhtemoc, Mexico DF
Tel: +52 5 726 66 00
Fax: +52 5 705 47 98
Email : cinform@bmv.com.mx
URL: http://www.bmv.com.mx

Morocco

Casablanca Stock Exchange
(Societe de la Bourse des Valeurs de Casablanca)
98 Boulevard Mohammed V, Casablanca
Tel: +212 2 27 93 54
Fax: +212 2 20 03 65

Namibia

Namibian Stock Exchange
Kaiserkrone Centre 11, O Box 2401, Windhoek
Tel: +264 61 227 647
Fax: +264 61 248 531
Email : tminney@nse.com.na
URL: http://www.nse.com.na

Netherlands

Financiele Termijnmarkt Amsterdam NV
FTA
Nes 49, Amsterdam
Tel: +31 20 550 4555
Fax: +31 20 624 54l6

AEX-Stock Exchange
AEX
Beursplein 5, PO Box 19163, Amsterdam
Tel: +31 20 550 4444
Fax: +31 20 550 4950
URL: http://www.aex.nl/

AEX-Agricultural Futures Exchange
Beursplein 5, PO Box 19163, Amsterdam
Tel: +31 20 550 4444
Fax: +31 20 623 9949

AEX-Options Exchange
AEX
Beursplein 5, PO Box 19163, Amsterdam
Tel: +31 20 550 4444
Fax: +31 20 550 4950
URL: http://www.aex-optiebeurs.ase.nl

New Zealand

New Zealand Futures & Options Exchange Ltd
NZFOE
10th Level, Stock Exchange Cen, 191 Queen Street, Auckland 1
Tel: +64 9 309 8308
Fax: +64 9 309 8817
Email : info@nzfoe.co.nz
URL: http://www.nzfoe.co.nz

New Zealand Stock Exchange
NZSE
8th Floor Caltex Tower, 286-292 Lambton Quay, Wellington
Tel: +64 4 4727 599
Fax: +64 4 4731 470
Email : info@nzse.org.nz
URL: http://www.nzse.co.nz

Nicaragua

Nicaraguan Stock Exchange
(BOLSA DE VALORES DE NICARAGUA, S.A.)
Centro Financiero Banic, 1er Piso, Km. 5 1/2 Carretera Masaya
Email : info@bolsanic.com
URL: http://bolsanic.com/

Nigeria

Nigerian Stock Exchange
Stock Exchange House, 8th & 9th Floors, 2/4 Customs Street, Lagos
Tel: +234 1 266 0287
Fax: +234 1 266 8724
Email : alile@nse.ngra.com

Norway

Oslo Stock Exchange
(Oslo Bors)
OSLO
P.O. Box 460, Sentrum, Oslo
Tel: +47 22 34 17 00
Fax: +47 22 41 65 90
Email : informasjonsavdelingen@ose.telemax.no
URL: http://www.ose.no

Oman

Muscat Securities Market
Po Box 3265, Ruwi
Tel: +968 702 665
Fax: +968 702 691

Pakistan

Islamabad Stock Exchange
Stock Exchange Building, 101-E Fazal-ul-Haq Road, Blue Area, Islamabad
Tel: +92 51 27 50 45
Fax: +92 51 27 50 44
Email : ise@paknet1.ptc.pk

Karachi Stock Exchange
Stock Exchange Building, Stock Exchange Road, Karachi
Tel: +92 21 2425502
Fax: +92 21 241 0825
URL: http://www.kse.org

Lahore Stock Exchange Po Box 1315, 19 Khayaban e Aiwan e Iqbal, Lahore
Tel: +92 42 636 8000
Fax: +92 42 636 8484

Panama

Panama Stock Exchange
(Bolsa de Valores de Panama, SA)
Calle Elvira Mendex y Calle 52, Edif Valarino, Planta Baja
Tel: +507 2 69 1966
Fax: +507 2 69 2457
URL: http://www.urraca.com/bvp/

Paraguay

Ascuncon Stock Exchange
(Bolsa de Valores y Productos de Ascuncion)
Estrella 540, Ascuncion
Tel: +595 21 442 445
Fax: +595 21 442 446
Email : bolsapya@pla.net.py
URL: http://www.pla.net.py/bvpasa

Peru

Lima Stock Exchange
(La Bolsa de Valores de Lima)
Pasaje Acuna 191, Lima
Tel: +51 1 426 79 39
Fax: +51 1 426 76 50
Email : web_team@bvl.com.pe
URL: http://www.bvl.com.pe

Philippines

Philippine Stock Exchange
Philippine Stock Exchange Cent, Tektite Road, Ortigas Centre, Pasig
Tel: +63 2 636 01 22
Fax: +63 2 634 51 13
Email : pse@mnl.sequel.net
URL: http://www.pse.com.ph

Manila International Futures Exchange
MIFE
7/F Producer's Bank Centre, Paseo de Roxas, Makati
Tel: +63 2 818 5496
Fax: +63 2 818 5529

Poland

Warsaw Stock Exchange
Gielda papierow, Wartosciowych w Warszawie SA, Ul Nowy Swiat 6/
12, Warsaw
Tel: +48 22 628 32 32
Fax: +48 22 628 17 54
Email : gielda@kp.atm.com.pl

Portugal

Oporto Derivatives Exchange
(Bolsa de Derivados do Oporto)
BDP
Av. da Boavista 3433, Oporto
Tel: +351 2 618 58 58
Fax: +351 2 618 56 66

Lisbon Stock Exchange
(Bolsa de Valores de Lisboa)
BVL
Edificio da Bolsa, Rua Soeiro Pereira Gomes, Lisbon
Tel: +351 1 790 99 04
Fax: +351 1 795 20 21
Email : webmaster@bvl.pt
URL: http://www.bvl.pt

Romania

Bucharest Stock Exchange
BSE
Doamnei no. 8, Bucharest
Email : bse@delos.ro
URL: http://www.delos.ro/bse/

Romanian Commodities Exchange
(Bursa Romana de Marfuri SA)
Piata Presei nr 1, Sector 1, Bucharest
Tel: +40 223 21 69
Fax: +40 223 21 67

Russian Federation

Moscow Interbank Currency Exchange
MICEX
21/1, Sadovaya-Spasskay, Moscow
Tel: +7 095 705 9627
Fax: +7 095 705 9622
Email : inmicex@micex.com
URL: http://www.micex.com/

Russian Exchange
RCRME
Myasnitskaya ul 26, Moscow
Tel: +7 095 262 06 53
Fax: +7 095 262 57 57
Email : assa@vc-rtsb.msk.ru
URL: http://www.re.ru

Moscow Commodity Exchange
Pavilion No. 4, Russian Exhibition Centre, Moscow
Tel: +7 095 187 83 07
Fax: +7 095 187 9982

St Petersburg Futures Exchange
SPBFE
274 Ligovski av., St Petersburg
Tel: +7 812 294 15 12
Fax: +7 812 327 93 88
Email : seva@spbfe.futures.ru

Siberian Stock Exchange
PO box 233, Frunze St 5, Novosibirsk
Tel: +7 38 32 21 06 90
Fax: +7 38 32 21 06 90
Email : sibex@sse.nsk.su

Moscow Central Stock Exchange
9(B) Bolshaya Maryinskaya Stre, Moscow
Tel: +7 095 229 88 82
Fax: +7 0995 202 06 67

Moscow International Stock Exchange
MISE
Slavyanskaya Pl 4, Bld 2, Moscow
Tel: +7 095 923 33 39
Fax: +7 095 923 33 39

National Association of Securities Market Participants
(NAUF)
Floor 2, Building 5, Chayanova Street 15, Moscow
Tel: +7 095 705 90
Fax: +7 095 976 42 36
Email : naufor@rtsnet.ru
URL: http://www.rtsnet.ru

Vladivostock Stock Exchange
VSE
21 Zhertv Revolyutsii Str, Vladivostock
Tel: +7 4232 22 78 87
Fax: +7 4232 22 80 09

St Petersburg Stock Exchange
SPSE
274 Ligovsky pr, St Petersburg
Tel: +7 812 296 10 80
Fax: +7 812 296 10 80
Email : root@lse.spb.su

Saudi Arabia

Saudi Arabian Monetary Authority
SAMA
PO Box 2992, Riyadh
Tel: +966 1 466 2300
Fax: +966 1 466 3223

Singapore

Singapore Commodity Exchange Ltd
SICOM
111 North Bridge Road, #23-04/, Peninsula Plaza
Tel: +65 338 5600
Fax: +65 338 9116
Email : sicom@pacific.net.sg

Stock Exchange of Singapore
No. 26-01/08, 20 Cecil Street, The Exchange
Tel: +65 535 3788
Fax: +65 535 6994
Email : webmaster@ses.com.sg
URL: http://www.ses.com.sg

Singapore International Monetary Exchange Ltd
SIMEX
1 Raffles Place, No. 07-00, OUB Centre
Tel: +65 535 7382
Fax: +65 535 7282
Email : simex@pacific.net.sg
URL: http://www.simex.com.sg

Slovak Republic

Bratislava Stock Exchange
(Burza cenny ch papierov v Bratislave)
BSSE
Vysoka 17, Bratislava
Tel: +42 7 5036 102
Fax: +42 7 5036 103
Email : kunikova@bsse.sk
URL: http://www.bsse.sk

Slovenia

Commodity Exchange of Ljubljana
Smartinskal 52, PO Box 85, Ljubljana
Tel: +386 61 18 55 100
Fax: +386 61 18 55 101
Email : infos@bb-lj.si
URL: http://www.eunet.si/commercial/bbl/bbl-ein.html

Ljubljana Stock Exchange, Inc
LJSE
Sovenska cesta 56, Lbujljana
Tel: +386 61 171 02 11
Fax: +386 61 171 02 13
Email : info@jse.si
URL: http://www.ljse.si

South Africa

Johannesburg Stock Exchange
JSE
17 Diagonal Street, Johannesburg
Tel: +27 11 377 2200
Fax: +27 11 834 3937
Email : r&d@jse.co.za
URL: http://www.jse.co.za

South African Futures Exchange
SAFEX
105 Central Street, Houghton Estate 2198, Johannesburg
Tel: +27 11 728 5960
Fax: +27 11 728 5970
Email : jani@icon.co.za
URL: http://www.safex.co.za

Spain

Citrus Fruit and Commodity Market of Valencia
(Futuros de Citricos y Mercaderias de Valencia)
2, 4 Libreros, Valencia
Tel: +34 6 387 01 88
Fax: +34 6 394 36 30
Email : futuros@super.medusa.es

Spanish Options Exchange
(MEFF Renta Variable)
MEFF RV
Torre Picasso, Planta 26, Madrid
Tel: +34 1 585 0800
Fax: +34 1 571 9542
Email : mefrv@meffrv.es
URL: http://www.meffrv.es

Spanish Financial Futures Market
(MEFF Renta Fija)
MEFF RF
Via Laietana, 58, Barcelona
Tel: +34 3 412 1128
Fax: +34 3 268 4769
Email : marketing@meff.es
URL: http://www.meff.es

Madrid Stock Exchange
(Bolsa de Madrid)
Plaza de la Lealtad 1, Madrid
Tel: +34 1 589 26 00
Fax: +34 1 531 22 90
Email : internacional@bolsamadrid.es
URL: http://www.bolsamadrid.es

Barcelona Stock Exchange
Paseo Isabel II No 1, Barcelona
Tel: +34 3 401 35 55
Fax: +34 3 401 38 59
Email : agiralt@borsabcn.es
URL: http://www.borsabcn.es

Bilbao Stock Exchange
(Sociedad Rectora de la Bolsa de Valoes de Bilbao)
Jose Maria Olabarri 1, Bilbao
Tel: +34 4 423 74 00
Fax: +34 4 424 46 20
Email : bolsabilbao@sarenet.es
URL: http://www.bolsabilbao.es

Valencia Stock Exchange
(Sociedad Rectora de la Bolsa de Valoes de Valencia)
Libreros 2 y 4, Valencia
Tel: +34 6 387 01 00
Fax: +34 6 387 01 14

Sri Lanka

Colombo Stock Exchange
CSE
04-01 West Bloc, World Trade Centre, Echelon Square, Colombo 1
Tel: +94 1 44 65 81
Fax: +94 1 44 52 79
Email : cse@sri.lanka.net
URL: http://www.lanka.net/cse/

Swaziland

Swaziland Stock Market
Swaziland Stockbrokers Ltd, 2nd Floor Dlan'ubeka House, Walker St, Mbabane
Tel: +268 46163
Fax: +268 44132
URL: http://mbendi.co.za/exsw.htm

Sweden

The Swedish Futures and Options Market
(OM Stockholm AB)
OMS
Box 16305, Brunkebergstorg 2, Stockholm
Tel: +46 8 700 0600
Fax: +46 8 723 1092
URL: http://www.omgroup.com

Stockholm Stock Exchange Ltd
(Stockholm Fondbors AB)
Kallargrand 2, Stockholm
Tel: +46 8 613 88 00
Fax: +46 8 10 81 10
Email : info@xsse.se
URL: http://www.xsse.se

Switzerland

Swiss Options & Financial Futures Exchange AG
SOFFEX
Selnaustrasse 32, Zurich
Tel: +41 1 229 2111
Fax: +41 1 229 2233
Email : webmaster@swx.ch
URL: http://www.bourse.ch

Swiss Exchange
SWX
Selnaustrasse 32, Zurich
Tel: +41 1 229 21 11
Fax: +41 1 229 22 33
URL: http://www.bourse.ch

Taiwan

Taiwan Stock Exchange
Floors 2-10, City Building, 85 Yen Ping Road South, Taipei
Tel: +886 2 311 4020
Fax: +886 2 375 3669
Email : intl-aff@tse.com.tw
URL: http://www.tse.com.tw

Thailand

The Stock Exchange of Thailand
SET
2nd Floor, Tower 1, 132 Sindhorn Building, Wireless Road, Bangkok
Tel: +66 2 254 0960
Fax: +66 2 263 2746
Email : webmaster@set.or.th
URL: http://www.set.or.th

Trinidad and Tobago

Trinidad and Tobago Stock Exchange
65 Independence Street, Port of Spain
Tel: +1809 809 625 5108
Fax: +1809 809 623 0089

Tunisia

Tunis Stock Exchange
(Bourse des Valeurs Mobilieres de Tunis)
Centre Babel - Bloc E, Rue Jean-Jacques Rousseau, Montplaisir, Tunis
Tel: +216 1 780 288
Fax: +216 1 789 189

Turkey

Istanbul Stock Exchange
(Istanbul Menkul Kiymetler Borasi)
ISE
Istinye, Istanbul
Tel: +90 212 298 21 00
Fax: +90 212 298 25 00
Email : info@ise.org
URL: http://www.ise.org

United Kingdom

The London Securities and Derivatives Exchange
OMLX
107 Cannon Street, London
Tel: +44 171 283 0678
Fax: +44 171 815 8508
Email : petter.made@omgroup.com
URL: http://www.omgroup.com/

International Petroleum Exchange of London Ltd
IPE
International House, 1 St. Katharine's Way, London
Tel: +44 171 481 0643
Fax: +44 l7l 481 8485
Email : busdev@ipe.uk.com
URL: http://www.ipe.uk.com

London International Futures & Options Exchange
LIFFE
Cannon Bridge, London
Tel: +44 171 623 0444
Fax: +44 171 588 3624
Email : exchange@liffe.com
URL: http://www.liffe.com

London Metal Exchange
LME
56 Leadenhall Street, London
Tel: +44 171 264 5555
Fax: +44 171 680 0505
Email : lsnow@lmetal.netkonect.co.uk
URL: http://www.lme.co.uk

The Baltic Exchange
Tel: +44 171 623 5501
Fax: +44 171 369 1622
Email : enquiries@balticexchange.co.uk
URL: http://www.balticexchange.co.uk

London Stock Exchange
LSE
Old Broad Street, London
Tel: +44 171 797 1000
Fax: +44 171 374 0504

Tradepoint Investment Exchange
35 King Street, London
Tel: +44 171 240 8000
Fax: +44 171 240 1900
Email : g171@dial.pipex.com
URL: http://www.tradepoint.co.uk

London Commodity Exchange
LCE
1 Commodity Quay, St. Katharine Docks, London
Tel: +44 l7l 48l 2080
Fax: +44 171 702 9923
URL: http://www.liffe.com

Directory of Futures & Options Exchanges

United States

New York Stock Exchange
NYSE
11 Wall Street, New York
Tel: +1 212 656 3000
Fax: +1 212 656 5557
URL: http://www.nyse.com

Minneapolis Grain Exchange
MGE
400 S. Fourth St., Minneapolis
Tel: +1 612 338 6216
Fax: +1 612 339 1155
Email : mgex@ix.netcom.com
URL: http://www.mgex.com

Philadelphia Stock Exchange
PHLX
1900 Market Street, Philadelphia
Tel: +1 215 496 5000
Fax: +1 215 496 5653
URL: http://www.phlx.com

Kansas City Board of Trade
KCBT
4800 Main St., Suite 303, Kansas City
Tel: +1 816 753 7500
Fax: +1 816 753 3944
Email : kcbt@kcbt.com
URL: http://www.kcbt.com

Chicago Board Options Exchange
CBOE
400 S. LaSalle Street, Chicago
Tel: +1 312 786 5600
Fax: +1 312 786 7409
Email : investor_services@cboe.com
URL: http://www.cboe.com

Chicago Board of Trade
CBOT
141 West Jackson Boulevard, Chicago
Tel: +1 312 435 3500
Fax: +1 312 341 3306
Email : comments@cbot.com
URL: http://www.cbt.com

New York Mercantile Exchange
NYMEX
4 World Trade Center, New York
Tel: +1 212 938 222
Fax: +1 212 938 2985
Email : marketing@nymex.com
URL: http://www.nymex.com

Chicago Stock Exchange
CHX
One Financial Place, 440 S. LaSalle St, Chicago
Tel: +1 312 663 222
Fax: +1 312 773 2396
Email : marketing@chiacgostockex.com
URL: http://www.chicagostockex.com

MidAmerica Commodity Exchange
MIDAM
141 W. Jackson Boulevard, Chicago
Tel: +1 313 341 3000
Fax: +1 312 341 3027
Email : comments@cbot.com
URL: http://www.midam.com

Philadelphia Board of Trade
1900 Market Street, Philadelphia
Tel: +1 215 496 5357
Fax: +1 215 496 5653

The Cincinnati Stock Exchange
400 South LaSalle Street, Chicago
Tel: +1 312 786 8803
Fax: +1 312 939 7239

REUTERS

Boston Stock Exchange, Inc
BSE
38th Floor, One Boston Place, Boston
Tel: +1 617 723 9500
Fax: +1 617 523 6603
URL: http://www.bostonstock.com

Nasdaq Stock Market
1735 K Street NW, Washington DC
Tel: +1 202 728 8000
Fax: +1 202 293 6260
Email : fedback@nasdaq.com
URL: http://www.nasdaq.com

American Stock Exchange
AMEX
86 Trinity Place, New York
Tel: +1 212 306 1000
Fax: +1 212 306 1802
Email : jstephan@amex.com
URL: http://www.amex.com

New York Cotton Exchange
NYCE
4 World Trade Center, New York
Tel: +1 212 938 2702
Fax: +1 212 488 8135
URL: http://www.nyce.com

Pacific Stock Exchange, Inc
PSE
301 Pine Street, San Francisco
Tel: +1 415 393 4000
Fax: +1 415 393 4202
URL: http://www.pacificex.com

Chicago Mercantile Exchange
CME
30 S. Wacker Drive, Chicago
Tel: +1 312 930 1000
Fax: +1 312 930 3439
Email : info@cme.com
URL: http://www.cme.com

Coffee, Sugar & Cocoa Exchange Inc.
CSCE
4 World Trade Center, New York
Tel: +1 212 938 2800
Fax: +1 212 524 9863
Email : csce@ix.netcom.com
URL: http://www.csce.com

Venezuela

Maracaibo Stock Exchange
(Bolsa de Valores de Maracaibo)
Calle 96, Esq Con Avda 5, Edificio
Banco Central de Vene, Piso 9, Maracaibo
Tel: +58 61 225 482
Fax: +58 61 227 663

Venezuela Electronic Stock Exchange
(de Venezuela)
C·mara de Comercio de Valencia, Edif. C·mara de Comercio, Av.
BolÌvar, Valencia, Edo. Carabobo, Apartado 151
Tel: +58 57.5109
Fax: +58 57.5147
Email : set@venezuelastock.com
URL: http://www.venezuelastock.com

Caracas Stock Exchange
(Bolsa de Valores de Caracas)
Edificio Atrium, Piso 1 Calle Sorocaima, Urbanizacion, El Rosal,
Caracas
Tel: +58 2 905 5511
Fax: +58 2 905 5814
Email : anafin@true.net
URL: http://www.caracasstock.com

Yugoslavia

Belgrade Stock Exchange
(Beogradska Berza)
Omladinskih 1, 3rd Floor, PO Box 214, Belgrade
Tel: +381 11 19 84 77
Fax: +381 11 13 82 42
Email : beyu@eunet.yu

Zimbabwe

Zimbabwe Stock Exchange
5th Floor, Southampton House, Union Avenue, Harare
Tel: +263 4 736 861
Fax: +263 4 791 045